A QUESTION OF IDENTITY

A Question of Identity

Edited by
ANNE J. KERSHEN

Queen Mary and Westfield College
University of London

Ashgate

Aldershot • Brookfield USA • Singapore • Sydney

Ashgate Publishing Limited
Gower House
Croft Road
Aldershot
Hants GU11 3HR
England

Ashgate Publishing Company
Old Post Road
Brookfield
Vermont 05036
USA

British Library Cataloguing in Publication Data
A question of identity. - (Studies in migration)
  1.British - Race identity 2.National characteristics
  3.Nationalism
  I.Kershen, Anne J., 1942-
  320.5'4

Library of Congress Catalog Card Number: 98-073761

ISBN 1 84014 558 7

Printed in Great Britain by The Ipswich Book Company, Suffolk

Contents

List of Figures and Tables

Contributors

Eberhard Bort is a Research Fellow at, and Associate Director of, the International Social Sciences Institute, and Lecturer at the University of Edinburgh. He has published widely on a number of diverse topics which include Irish drama and the problems of frontiers and regions. His most recent publications include: *The Irish Border: History, Politics, Culture* (1998), *Schengen and EU Enlargement: Security and Co-operation at the Eastern Frontier of European Union* (1997), and together with Malcolm Anderson (co-eds), *The Frontiers of Europe* (1998) and *Boundaries and Identities: the Eastern Frontier of the European Union* (1997).

Rod Chalmers graduated from Trinity College, Cambridge in 1996 having read Oriental Studies (Sanskrit with Indian Studies). He has worked as a Language Services Manager with the London Borough of Camden and is currently preparing to undertake a PhD on Himalayan Languages. His research interests include Indo-Aryan and Tibeto-Burman linguistics. His publications include: *Learning Sylheti* (1996), and a research paper for the European Network of Bangladesh Studies on *Sylhet: a regional language of Bangladesh* (1996).

John Eade is Reader in the Department of Sociology and Social Policy at the Roehampton Institute, London. He has published numerous articles and chapters on Bangladeshis in Britain, particularly in Tower Hamlets, and published a book, *The Politics of Community: The Bangladeshi Community in East London*. He has undertaken research in Calcutta concerning the Bengali Muslim middle class and has written about pilgrimage and tourism, co-editing with Michael Sallnow *Contesting the Sacred: The Anthropology of Christian Pilgrimage*. He has also edited *Living the Global city: Globalization a Local Process* (1997).

Katy Gardner is a lecturer in Social Anthropology at the University of Sussex. Her doctoral research was carried out in Sylhet, Bangladesh and has been published in a number of guises, including: *Songs at the Rivers Edge: Stories* *from a Bangladeshi Village* (1997); *Global Migrants, Local Lives: travel and transformation in rural Bangladesh* (1995). She has also co-authored (with David Lewis) *Anthropology, Development and the Post-Modern Challenge* (1996). Her most recent research, funded by the Leverhulme Trust, was carried out in Tower Hamlets on death and ageing among British Bengalis.

Andrew Geddes is a lecturer in Politics in the School of Politics and Communication Studies at the University of Liverpool. During the academic year 1997–98 he was a Jean Monnet European Forum Fellow at the European University Institute in Florence working on a study of EU immigration policy. He has published a number of articles and chapters: his latest book, *The Politics of Belonging: Migrants and Minorities in Contemporary Europe*, co-edited with A. Favell, will be published in 1998.

Graham Harrison is a Lecturer in Politics in the Department of Politics, Queen Mary and Westfield College, University of London. He has published work on the National Census in Mozambique in the *Review of African Political Economy* and on political corruption in Mozambique for the OECD Development Centre. He is currently researching forms of state power in rural Mozambique.

Sharman Kadish is currently Project Co-ordinator of the Survey of the Jewish Built Heritage in the UK and Ireland which is supported by the Heritage Lottery Fund. Her publications include, *Building Jerusalem: Jewish Architecture in Britain* (1996); *'A Good Jew and a Good Englishman': The Jewish Lads' and Girls' Brigade 1895–1995* (1995) and *Bolsheviks and British Jews* (1992).

Anne J. Kershen is Barnett Shine Senior Research Fellow and Director of the Centre for the Study of Migration at Queen Mary and Westfield College, University of London. She has published widely and is the author of *Uniting the Tailors* (1995); co-author of *Tradition and Change: A History of Reform Judaism in Britain 1840–1995* (1995) and editor of, and contributor to, *London the Promised Land?: The Migrant Experience in a Capital City* (1997). She is currently working on a comparative study of Jews entering the professions between 1920 and 1950 and Bangladeshis entering the professions in the 1980s and 1990s.

Chris Julios is a Public Policy postgraduate student at Queen Mary and Westfield College, University of London, currently completing a PhD on

'Implementing Bilingual Education Policy in Britain and the United States' and has carried out extensive fieldwork both in the East End of London and in New York City. She has recently published a paper on 'Bilingualism and the Construction of a New "British Identity"', in *Contemporary Political Studies*.

Philip Nanton is an Associate Fellow in the Centre of West African Studies in the University of Birmingham. He has lectured in Applied Social Policy in the Department of Local Government Studies. He has published in the field of public policy, race relations and equal opportunities and is currently researching aspects of Caribbean migration.

Wayne Parsons is Professor of Public Policy at Queen Mary and Westfield College, University of London and a graduate of the University of Wales. He was born in Cardiff and the product of a diverse Celtic background. Amongst his publications are *Keynes and the Quest for a Moral Science* (1997), *Public Policy* (1995), *The Power of the Financial Press* (1989) and *The Political Economy of British Regional Policy* (1988).

Marlena Schmool is Community Research Director of the Board of Deputies of British Jews. She has published numerous articles, chapters and surveys amongst which are: *Patterns and Trends at the End of a Century; A Profile of British Jewry* (1998); with S. Waterman, 'Literary Perspectives on Jews in Britain in the Early Twentieth Century' (1996); 'Women in the Organised British Jewish Community' (1995); 'Women in the Jewish Community: Survey Report' (1994) and 'Jewish Education and Identity among London Synagogue Members' (forthcoming).

Jo Shaw is Professor of European Law and Director of the Centre for the Study of Law in Europe at the University of Leeds. During 1998 she was a EU-Fulbright Scholar-in-Residence and Visiting Professor at Harvard Law School. She has published widely and her most recent works include *Law of the European Union* (1996) and together with S. Wheeler, *Contract Law: Cases, Materials and Commentary* (1994). She has co-edited *New Legal Dynamics of European Union* (1995) and *Collected Courses of the Academy of European* (1998). Her principal fields of research lie in EU constitution and institutions, particularly in socio-legal and interdisciplinary perspective.

Karen Trew is a Senior Lecturer in the School of Psychology at the Queen's University, Belfast. She has published a number of articles and chapters in the field of social psychology including, 'Identity and Self' (1988), 'Time for Sport? Activity Diaries of Young People', 'Complementary or Conflicting Identities?' (1996) and 'Facets of self in Northern Ireland: Explorations and Further Questions' (1995). She has co-edited, *Gender and Psychology* (1998) and *Young People's Involvement in Sport* (1997). She has recently carried out a number of large scale research projects which have included studies of social identity and the participation of young people in sport.

Preface

The Centre for the Study of Migration was established in the autumn of 1994 at Queen Mary and Westfield College, University of London, in order to provide a focal point in London for those concerned with the study of the movements of people locally, nationally and internationally. The Centre held its first conference in November 1995 and subsequently produced its first volume of essays, edited by myself, under the title, *London The Promised Land? The Migrant Experience in a Capital City*, in March 1997. The publication coincided with the Centre's second conference, one which grew directly from a discussion held at the first. 'A Question of Identity' was the title of that second conference and this volume is the outcome – a collection of the papers given at the conference together with some specially commissioned chapters which expand on the theme.

A major attribute of the Centre for the Study of Migration is its multi-disciplinary nature. This volume clearly reflects the intention of the Centre to open its doors geographically and intellectually. The chapters in this book all focus on 'questions of identity', but as is manifest from a glance at the Contributors list the authors come from a diversity of fields of study which include, anthropology, history, law, linguistics, politics, psychology and sociology. All have a common purpose, to confront one of the most challenging issues of today – identity and identification – in all its diverse forms, applications, and locations.

I should like to express my gratitude to those who have contributed to this volume and borne my repeated pleadings for adherence to deadlines and house style. I should also like to thank the members of the Centre's Steering Committee for their constant support; my colleagues in the Department of Politics; Departmental Secretary Jasmine Salucideen; the staff of QMW Library, most particularly Eilis Rafferty, and Jay, Brian and François of the Arts Faculty Computer Services Department. Special thanks to Professor Ken Young; Lord Levene, Chairman of the Centre's Advisory Board, and Advisory Board members, Lord Hattersley, Martin Paisner, Usha Prashar, Dr Richard Stone, and the late Jack Wolkind whose support was greatly valued and whose presence will be sorely missed. On a personal note I should like to thank

Martin Paisner for his continuing help and guidance, my family for their forbearance and my husband Martin for his tolerance and love at all times.

Anne J. Kershen
Director, Centre for the Study of Migration
Queen Mary and Westfield College
University of London
Summer 1998

Introduction: A Question of Identity

ANNE J. KERSHEN

As we stand on the threshold of the twenty-first century discussions and debates about issues of identity, its construction and meaning, are increasingly taking centre stage. As an ever increasing number of academics from a variety of disciplines – as evidenced by this volume – have thrown their hats eagerly and polemically into the ring there 'has been a recent explosion and critique of the concept of identity'.[1] But the discursive exercising has not been restricted to the world of academe. Around the globe individuals are attempting to understand themselves and their location by defining their identity; seeking the answers to questions which previously were only confronted when approaching ports of disembarkation:

'Who am I'   'What am I'   'Where do I belong' 'Where was I born'
(Name & gender) (Occupation) (Place of residence)   (Place of birth)

Arguably these four questions are the essential tools of identification which provide the gateway to more complex issues. The means by which we, as individuals, have the facility to *identify* ourselves in relation to others and by which others separate the 'insiders' from the 'outsiders'. Until recently it was left to government offices to analyse our *Landing Cards*, with their hastily scrawled responses to bureaucracy's questions. But recent history has persuaded, and in some instances forced, many of us to enter the complex realms of identification. The changing nature of nation-states, regional demands for political autonomy, the spread of Islam, the creation of 'fortress Europe' and the desire for acknowledgment of, and respect for, ethnic minority groups has highlighted concerns about 'who' belongs 'where'. As one commentator described the phenomenon: 'Identity comes to the fore when there are doubts about belonging.'[2] It is becoming increasingly obvious in the postmodern world that running parallel with Europeanisation, transnationalism and globalisation is a growing preoccupation with

1

regionalism, particularism and the meaning and location of 'self'.

What is most evident in the quest(ion of) for identity, is the complexity of the construct. There are two major points to bear in mind which recur throughout the chapters in this book. Firstly, that identity is in a constant state of flux and can never, nor will ever, be static and secondly that identity is multifaceted and variable; in fact many of us could, and some do, go shopping for the 'most suitable' identity as we go shopping for our seasonal wardrobes.

There is however a third point that requires consideration. The discussion so far has centred on *identity* but, bearing in mind its fluidity, what we are really considering here is what Stuart Hall calls the 'dynamic process of identification',[3] rather than the static notion of identity. Without an 'other' to identify with or differ from, self-recognition would be impossible. Only Adam, before the arrival of Eve, was without a human other to enable the identification process. But if self-recognition began in the Garden of Eden, multiple identity was not far behind. Even before the arrival of tribes, cities and the nation-state an individual could use gender and kinship to process personal belonging and separation. With the advent of modernity came the complexities of citizenship, slavery, alienation, race and religion. Once we combine these ingredients, what Robin Cohen has called, the 'Fuzzy Frontiers of Identity'[4] comes into play. As he notes in his book, and is illustrated in many of the chapters that follow, in the context of national identity the frontiers are fuzzy indeed. Yet it is not only in the geopolitical context that we find obfuscation, as I will detail below, the boundaries of identity cannot be simply and clearly drawn.

The Boundaries of Identity

1   *Geopolitical*

I have referred above to the multifaceted nature of identity, and the variety of categories through which it can be explored. One of the most prominent and widely used is that of national identity, a nation being an 'Imagined Community'[5] to be found within a cartographer's boundaries whose population has a sense of peoplehood. Linda Colley[6] has finely detailed the way in which a British identity was forged out of the separate nations (regions) of England, Ireland, Scotland and Wales. She describes how between 1707 and 1837 a sense of Britishness developed as a result of the fear of the enemy beyond, in this instance the French, and from the fusing elements of a common – Protestant

– religion. Some 150 years on, previously accepted concepts of Britishness and the construct of British identity are now in question, the constituents are deconstructing and the spectre of Europe hovers in the wings.

The crisis of British identity There is no doubting that the concept, and thus the construct, of British identity is currently in crisis. A crisis which, to gauge by the volume of recent media coverage, has spread far beyond the sanctuary of academe. No longer do we placidly accept that Britishness is synonymous with Englishness. As the sun went down on the Empire so England's supremacy began to fade. A leader which appeared in *The Times* at the end of 1997 concentrated on the current debates and referred to them as 'A battlefield for Britishness', quoting the historian Simon Schama as recently having said that, 'It is time to rediscover the meaning of being British ...'.[7] In spite of the piece's pronounced antipathy towards what it considered the 'history-with-purpose' appeal of Colley and David Cannadine, *The Times* was accurate in spotlighting the current confusion that surrounds both the origins and, as a consequence, the future direction, of Britishness. Whilst there is debate over the construct little consideration has been given to the root of the adjective, from which the confusion stems, 'British'. But then with little consensus over the fountainhead of British identity how are we expected to get the semantics right. In this volume Wayne Parsons explains that the noun 'Briton' can be traced back to *Brytaniaid* the name given to the survivors of Roman Briton and the name by which the Welsh referred to themselves until the twelfth century. Therefore, Parsons argues, the Welsh are the true Britons. He goes further, to suggest, as does *The Times*, that a 'collective British identity' dates back to the time of Henry V and the Battle of Agincourt[8] rather than to Colley's eighteenth century point of departure. However, this is not simply a two-sided debate, there are others who choose to view the construct of Britishness as an essentially nineteenth century phenomenon tied to the growth and power of Industry and Empire.[9]

Even if there is disunity over the starting point, as the contributions to this volume will confirm, there is general support for the view, that 'men and women shuffle[d] identities like cards'.[10] For example, we all identify as Britons when it comes to the Olympic Games, one of the few sporting events in which the four segments compete as a whole. When the Games were reincarnated at the beginning of the twentieth century it was automatically assumed by the nationalistic aristocratic founders that the teams would represent the best of *British* sporting prowess. Another legacy, this time of Union, is the continuing existence of the British Lions rugby team, which includes representatives from the Republic of Ireland as well as England, Scotland, Wales and Northern Ireland. In virtually all other competitive sports regional nationalism rules supreme. The nation supports the England Cricket Team, even though of recent times some names in the team list lack English, or for that matter, Scottish, Welsh or Irish resonance. Simon Gikandi suggests that, in the context of what C.L.R. James called 'Public entry into the community of nations' and the synthesis of the colonial and the colonised, cricket has played a vital role, enabling the West Indies to reign supreme in what was once 'a byword for all that is most *English* in the *British*[11] way of life'.[12] Regional separatism is evident both on and off the football field, no room for any British/English synonym here. Nationalism, in the broader and artificially constructed British context, ebbs and flows with external pressures and tensions; war, or its threat, being a major stimulus for patriotism. The enemy beyond, the French in the eighteenth century, the Russians in the mid-nineteenth century and the Boers at the beginning of the twentieth century all elicited jingoistic responses from rich and poor alike. Regional borders became invisible in the tide of (British) national emotion during these tense and testing times. The two world wars enhanced this sentiment which was at its highest point during the aptly named Festival of Britain held in 1951 to retain national pride and crank the depressed motor of British industry. Since then, with the exception of a brief period in 1982 when an 'Argentinian enemy' in the southern hemisphere resuscitated long forgotten emotions of national unity and identity, in the context of the pre-1939 concept of Britishness, it has been downhill all the way.

With positive responses from both referenda on devolution in Scotland and Wales, the 22 May 'Yes' votes bringing the prospect of peace in Northern Ireland closer and the merging of south and north within the realms of possibility, a single European currency hovering in the wings and, as John Eade points out below, the nature of British society changing as controversy over immigration continues, what 'being British' really means is becoming more and more unclear. This lack of clarity was highlighted in a survey carried out in 1994/95 to explore attitudes to British identity.[13] The survey concluded that 'national identification would weaken as a European identity took over'.[14] (The survey was carried out before the recent referenda on Scotland and Wales were held and thus could not take account of the change in regional attitudes.) And whilst 'national identification' in the context of British identity weakens, demands for separation are gaining strength. Three of the constituents of Britain are on the way to finding themselves. However, with the Empire gone and regional nationalism rapidly becoming a reality a large question mark has appeared over the notion of Englishness. And it is the meaning of Englishness that will have to be reconstructed at the dawning of the twenty-first century.

An English identity What does it mean to be English and what is Englishness? As implied above the answer to these two questions would have required little thought 100 years ago whilst requiring a great deal of consideration today. At the end of the nineteenth century, and well into the twentieth century, the stereotypical image of the Englishman, one that also served well as a role model, was either of a cricket playing, honourable, liberal, white, Christian, courageous gentleman or a hard working, plain speaking, brave, warm beer drinking, god-fearing working man prepared to give his all for his Queen (King) and country. It should be noted at this point that it was the male who featured in the national stereotypes – even though we occasionally hear of Mrs John Bull. Mackay and Thane have demonstrated that the English female had a far more universal identity.[15]

At the height of Industry and Empire, Englishness was synonymous with Britishness and to become Anglicised was to become a paid-up member of British as much as English society. In fact, until very recently to become 'Anglicised' and to become 'British' were interchangeable terms. As Sharman Kadish highlights in her chapter below on the Jewish Lads' Brigade, the ambition of most of the late nineteenth century immigrant Jews was to become 'a good Englishman', the role of the Anglo-Jewish establishment was to ensure that this happened. Neither group would have thought to question the belief that the acquisition of British citizenship in reality meant anything less than becoming an 'Englishman'. The two were inseparable.

Today, 100 years on, the immigrant successors to the Jews, the Bangladshis and the African-Caribbeans see things very differently. There is no merging of the British and English identity, as a number of my students have made clear to me. Though living in, and sometimes even born in, London they see themselves as British Bangladeshis or British African Caribbeans, Englishness does not come into the frame.[16] An analysis of this response produces two important, though not necessarily, conjoining points. A British identity denotes citizenship with its associated rights and duties but, is it possible to detect an almost imperceptible attachment to the old days of Empire? The denial of 'Englishness' appears as a rejection of the stereotypes referred to above. Here we find a clear manifestation of the variable and multiple nature of identity and the identification process which has become a feature of the post-colonial, postmodern world. In their chapters in this volume, John Eade, Rod Chalmers and Katy Gardner confirm that, in the context of the Bangladeshi community in London, Englishness is neither desired nor perceived as readily accessible. It is not just a new geopolitical identity that is being constructed by the immigrants, as we will see below in Philip Nanton's chapter on creolisation, in the 'global diaspora'[17] a migrant's identity takes on board the cultural, biological, religious and political influences from 'home' and 'away' as well as, as Gardner suggests, from a third space somewhere in between.[18]

From the above we have learnt that there are those who do not want to identify with a dominant definition of Englishness. But what is being rejected here is the old concept, that which was the mantle of the colonialist, and that which strangely enough, Gikandi tells us, is still being worn by the colonised.[19] So, as those who inhabit the territory undergo what the journalist Magnus Linklater considers to be an 'acute identity problem',[20] the hunt is on for a new 'English' identity. What is to form the basis of identification, a parliament that no longer reigns supreme, a currency that will either become marginalised or merge into Europe, a monarchy in disarray and a traditional diet – roast beef of Olde England – which is suspect? The English will have to rediscover themselves, separate their myths, roots and history from those with whom they have shared it in the past and take account of multiculturalism and religious plurality. The results will need to be well secured if the fractures that have restored the individuality of Irish, Welsh and Scottish identity do not fragment what remains.

Scottish identity When on 1 May 1997 the tired and dishevelled Tory Party was voted out of office and the fresh, brightly shining, bouncy 'New' Labour Party was elected in its place, one of the first items on the political agenda was that of devolution for Scotland and Wales. Within four months referenda were held in both regions, with positive responses in each. In Scotland 74.3 per cent voted in favour of the parliament and 63.5 per cent in favour of tax raising powers. In Wales 50.3 per cent voted 'Yes' to the more modest white paper proposals which focused on the creation of a Welsh Assembly to manage its central government budget and pass secondary legislation.[21] What had been proposed – and rejected – by the Labour government in 1978 had been approved under the next Labour government 19 years on.

Since the 1707 Act of Union with England the Scots have enjoyed legal, educational and religious devolution. Thus through their institutions the Scots maintained a notion of Scottish identity which ran parallel to their sense of Britishness. The Scottish sense of identity and means of identification can be clearly linked to an institutional history even though this was accompanied by cross-border mergers of elites through land acquisition and intermarriage,[22] a process which reinforced British identity. Throughout the eighteenth century the English attempted to weaken Scottish identity. After 1745 the wearing of the tartan was banned, the rule of the British monarch, as opposed to the Scottish chieftain, was enforced and special schools were established to enable Gaelic speaking children to be taught English.[23] However, fear of Scottish Jacobitism was soon replaced by a respect for Scottish intellect and military ability. By the nineteenth century the Scots were able, and eager, servants of the *British* Empire, as Colley tells us they 'played a leading part in making British imperialism what it was'. A tradition that continued through into the twentieth century – after all 'James Bond, Number 007, ... is also a Scot'.[24]

More recently, most particularly in the past decade, there has been a heightening of support for Scottish devolution and thus for a pronounced Scottish identity that demanded separation from the national centre. There are several theories as to why this has taken place; Vernon Bogdanor believes that 'Many Scots felt isolated and badly treated by a predominantly English [Conservative] Government between 1979 and 1997 which had relatively few MPs in Scotland'.[25] Others suggest that the reasons for change are economic rather than political. Speaking on the *Today* programme on Radio 4 in May 1998, Alan Massey put forward his view that as Scotland was now prosperous it could afford nationalism.[26] This belief stands in direct contradiction to that advanced by Cohen who suggests that separation, or nationalism, is the precursor to material benefits.[27] Recent empirical evidence demonstrates that in both Scotland and Wales the benefits appear to have preceded increased nationalism.

Welsh identity If a Scottish identity is recognisable and traceable through its institutions then a Welsh identity owes its being to its cultural heritage. It was language, literature and music, together with a respect for the history and myths of the past, that enabled the Welsh to cling to their identity. In his chapter below Parsons illustrates how, in spite of the 'Welsh Not'[28] of the nineteenth century, language became the mainstay of survival, '... the widespread availability of the Bible in Welsh from 1567 onwards meant that the place of the language in the religion and culture of the country was secured'.[29] In spite of this for almost a century Welsh identity was almost submerged beneath Britishness, combining, during the first half of the twentieth century, patriotism with, as demonstrated by some, an affinity for that which was English. It was not until 1967 that use of the Welsh language was once again legalised and 'the turning point in the story of Welsh identity' reached.

The renaissance of Welsh culture since the end of the Second World War has been accompanied by the creation of a culture-related Welsh institutional infrastructure which has enabled the development and strengthening of a sense of identity. This in spite of the diminution in the percentage of Welsh speakers – a figure which now stands at only 20 per cent of the population of Wales. In more recent times industrial expansion has run parallel to institutional growth. Southeast Wales particularly has enjoyed the benefits of commercial investment from both Europe and Asia. Has prosperity created the same form of nationalism Massey identified in Scotland? Writing in 1994, Cohen suggested that 'the prospect of material advance through separatism is notably less likely in the case of Wales'. He quotes Colin H. Williams who, 10 years earlier, argued that 'generally the advantages of cooperation, even incorporation, outweigh the disadvantages of loss of autonomy for minorities who benefit from access to wider markets, increased standards of living and unfettered participation in the central political system'.[30] Early reports of analysis of the September 1997 referendum suggest that such purely economically based views are too simplistic to explain the composition of the 'Yes' vote. There are a number of factors that have to be taken into account in the search for a (new) Welsh identity. Age, economic status and space all played their part in the decision making. Evidence suggests that: a) whereas older people still identify with a Welsh/English/Britishness which resonates with memories of Empire and the Second World War, new, younger voters are inclined to a regional patriotism; b) that the economics of identification point to a middle class affinity with Englishness; and that c) residents close to the border if not all positively 'No' are more 'undecided'. What we can say at the end of the twentieth century is that a Welsh identity is inextricably linked to the Red Dragon, the Celtic language, Welsh nationalism and a sense of Britishness which owes little to Britannia and a great deal to *Brytaniaid.*

(Northern) Irish identity[31] The other three constituencies of Great Britain have been considered in relation to their identification with Britishness. What has been awarded little space in this chapter's foregoing text is any consideration of the internal regional divisions which contribute to the complexities of both self-identity and identification by outsiders. What has been demonstrated is that in the case of England, Scotland and Wales, it is possible to discuss geopolitical identification within the context of Britishness without focusing on internal differences. The same cannot be said to be true, or indeed feasible, in any exploration of (Northern) Irish identity. The very fact that until 1922 Ireland had been 'entirely under British rule' and was then carved up – the Southern (Catholic dominated) part being granted the right to

'a Parliament having powers to make laws for the peace, order and good government of Ireland and an Executive responsible for that Parliament', whilst the residual north eastern (Protestant dominated) part remained separate with limited powers of self-government – creates a confusion in the process of identity construction. What we have here is a perfect example of a 'fuzzy frontier' – geopolitical and religious boundaries which are indivisible. Seventeenth and early eighteenth century maps provide graphic evidence of the weakening of Roman Catholicism's hold. Catholic land ownership in Ireland fell from 59 per cent in 1641 to less than 10 per cent in 1703. A country which had been colonised by Henry 11 in 1171, only began to acquire a degree of independence when the original dominant religion and its adherents became subservient to the minority ruling class which was Protestant. Whatever autonomy there was ended when fear of French invasion and the possible use of Ireland as the launching pad galvanised the British government into annexing that which it had originally colonised. English rule and Englishness took over and the Irish had to incorporate colonisation into the identity construct, to paraphrase one commentator, they had to swallow Englishness before they could absorb Irishness.[32]

In her chapter on 'The Northern Irish Identity' Karen Trew is focusing on a people who, with the prospect of peace looming,[33] 'are searching for a new way to express their identity'. A people whose 'imagined community' dates only from 1922. For many whose journey through the identity process has taken place in fear of the gun and the bomb, a real hope of peace adds a new dimension and a new item to the shopping list of possible choices which has until now included British, Irish, Catholic and Protestant; a selection which crosses the boundaries of geography, politics and religion. Significantly culture does not appear in its own right. Northern Irelanders have few universal symbols and myths upon which to draw. One commentator has suggested that 'the leaders of Irish culture wrote in English'[34] because they wished to extend their cultural horizons. The formation of the Gaelic League, Gaelic Athletes Association and the National Literary Society tells us that a desire to preserve an Irish cultural identity did exist, but that it was linked to home rule and nationalism and thus cannot be drawn upon by staunch unionists.

In her chapter, Trew explores the recognition by some of the need for an apolitical, secular 'Northern Irish' identity. One which carries with it sufficient ambiguity to allow for the inclusion of a geopolitical identity which incorporates, Britishness, Irishness and Europeaness. An identity which makes few demands. As is evidenced by the chapter, until recently the wearing of a Northern Irish identity has been dependent on the presence or not of the storm clouds of violence. Major questions now hang over any debate on (Northern) Irish Identity. What impact will the result of the 22 May 1998 referenda have on Irish identification, both self and other? Will a Northern Irish identity become acceptable to all those living in the north east of the island, irrespective of politics or religion? And, even more significantly and in the longer term, will one boundary disappear with the consequence that *all* those living on that island which lies to the west of Britain, in the geopolitical sense, once again identify themselves as simply Irish.

European identity Although the section above has concentrated on Great Britain and concepts of Britishness, the European spectre has been omnipresent, though few of those carrying a British passport, even if it is now the ubiquitous 'Eurored', will readily accept that they are 'European' in a cultural, biological or even political sense, whatever the politicians might say. For many the watery divide reinforces the notion of difference, though arguably it is the *notion* rather than the reality which predominates. The recently published *Survey on British Social Attitudes* revealed that between 1994 and 1995 the British public's attitude to the EU became less favourable. There was significant support for independence, the figure rose in one year from 53 per cent to 60 per cent. Even in Northern Ireland, where the economic benefits were more obvious, support for Europe fell from 48 per cent to 45 per cent. It remains to be seen whether the trend will continue and if, at the end of the day, the Eurosceptics will win.

The population on mainland Europe more readily identify with Europe, though many are apprehensive about singularity. So how is a European identity being constructed? Not, as Jo Shaw explains in this volume, through the age old mechanisms. As she states, 'The citizens' rights are spelt out, duties as yet are not.' To date the basis of European citizenship has been created from the top down, as such it is dominated by the economic demands and constraints that are the very soul of the EU. But, if a European identity is to be more than an economic facility in order that the Frau from Berlin, the Signora from Bologna, the Monsieur from Lyons and the Mister from Leeds might recognise their commonality, Shaw believes there has to be a social input from the bottom up. But what mechanisms are in place? In his chapter below, Andrew Geddes explains that one process of that differentiation is well under way. Who does and who does not belong in Europe is being clearly defined. The millions of immigrants within the EU have few if any rights in contrast to their European peers. The Schengen agreement heralded the pulling up of the drawbridge to Europe – though how successfully is yet to be seen – but can the intangible, the cartographer's outline on the map, really mould a sense of identity, without a sense of nationhood, one which is to run parallel to others which have their roots more firmly secured in the ethnic and national compost of history, language, culture, myth and religion. Is that identity, as is the very essence of Europe, to be economically demarcated? Writing in this volume about German identity post reunification, Eberhard Bort tells us that West German identity was 'linked to something tangible' such as the Deutschmark. Could the Euro do the same? Will Europeans accept a common identity by means of a transnational currency? Will this economically, market based policy, formulated as the outcome of political interest, really facilitate the making of an 'European' identity? Only time will tell.

2   Political Identity

The previous section has examined what this writer believes will become one of the most debated geopolitical identity issues of the early twenty-first century – the concepts and constructs of Britishness, Englishness and Europeaness and the nature of those who identify with one or more of these. So far the political focus has been tied to a geographic base, with national or regional boundaries acting as the framework within which the process of identification is, or has, taken place. Little or no space has been devoted to any discussion of 'politics' in the ideological or social context. The limitations of space do not allow for this luxury. However, this is not to say that these issues have not been addressed elsewhere in this volume. Graham Harrison, whose chapter takes us to the African continent, sees identity as a 'social construct' within which politics play a very important role. He correlates the post-colonial economic and political crisis in 'most' African states with the emergence of identity politics in urban Africa and the use of ethnic identity as a political weapon created via a social construct. Harrison demonstrates how the experience of hybridity in the context of the rural peasant undergoing urbanisation can be politicised and how, in the process, the individuals concerned adopt a new and/or additional identity, one which has been constructed and imposed from above. Within this portrait we can see the vulnerability and rawness of youth and the way in which their economic and social exploitation has enabled a construction of youth identity which can be linked to politics. It should not be assumed that the construct and adoption of youth identity is restricted to the underdog. Identity formulation is part of the life cycle and youth identity is just part of the ongoing process. Harrison also provides us with an intriguing example of the fluidity of identity in a biological-social context – the Hutu in Rwanda can adopt a Tutsi identity by means of improved economic status; we are not told whether or not the situation is reversed if good times turn to bad.

Political identity involves 'identification with' as much as being 'identified as', it is not just an internal and local constituent. It can be relayed and impacted upon the consciousness, often confusing as much as it clarifies. And it is here, in the real world of political choice, that the migrant's choice of electoral representative coincides with the process of hybridity or as Nanton's chapter in this volume suggests creolisation. Do the politically active incomers identify, and support, those from a similar, or same, ethnic background or those who seek to represent their best interests, even if not from the same cultural origins? In the context of two sets of immigrants to Britain, the eastern European Jews at the end of the nineteenth century and the Bangladehis in the 1970s and 1980s it is possible to chart the process of rapprochement and merger by charting the way in which dependence on ethnicity as a means of political identification gives way to political pragmatism. Keeping in mind that to exercise a political voice requires the status of citizenship, immigrant Jews in the late nineteenth and early twentieth centuries initially voted for co-religionists such as Samuel Montagu of the Liberal Party because he was a co-religionist and because he involved himself in their religious and political lives.[35] As acculturation and assimilation accelerated economic status and political ideology took over. Support for the Liberal Party for many gave way to association with the Labour Party; subsequently, as socioeconomic mobility entered the equation, a noticeable swing towards Conservatism is to be detected. Here is yet another example of the blurred nature of the boundaries of identity; the points at which 'class' puts pressure on political identification; class here barely distinguishable from economic status. Similarly with the Bangladeshi community, in the early 1980s – the first two Bangladeshi councillors were elected in 1982 – political life in Tower Hamlets was covertly affected by events taking place in Sylhet. As second generation Bangladeshis became more and more entrenched in local life, accompanied by the realisation that what had been intended as a sojourn was in fact becoming a permanent settlement, it was local East London politics, and the need to secure advancements in terms of housing, health and education for the third generation that took priority. Today, local government in Tower Hamlets experiences little overt input from the villages of Sylhet, local councillors and members of parliament are selected and elected because of what they can do for those living in the area, how they can improve their quality of life and improve local [race] relations.[36] In a more general context recent research has concluded that ethnic political identification is far more closely linked to socioeconomic mobility and status than to pure ethnic relationships.[37]

3   Religious and Political Identity

Until the Enlightenment Jewish identity was a religious construct which had little place in the political arena. Jews knew who and what they were and where their place was. During the first part of the nineteenth century, as Napoleon marched triumphantly through Europe, Jews in many parts of western and central Europe were forced to re-examine their identity in the light of their incorporation as citizens,[38] a condition which meant accepting obligations as well as rights. In England during the first half of the nineteenth century, even though the struggle to gain full emancipation took place at a more leisurely pace, there were those who doubted whether a member of the tribe of Israel could be both a good Jew and a loyal Englishman. These debates took on a broader and more valid dimension when Theodore Herzl began his crusade for the creation of a Jewish political state. The Jewish return to Israel as a distant religious ideal was one thing, the imminent creation of a political reality quite another. The prospect received a mixed reception from both Jews and non-Jews. A number of antisemites saw the creation of a Jewish state as a solution to the threat of Jewish political and financial power in the western world. By contrast, there were many English-born and American-born Jews who gave place of birth priority above religion, the latter being a private part of their lives. As Kadish reveals in her chapter below, for some loyalty to England was all. Men such as Louis Gluckstein, who worked fervently for a number of worthy causes, including that of British Jewry, were reluctant to accept the existence of a Jewish political state that might call into question their national loyalty. For these men the 'cricket test' presented no problems. Some anti-Zionists waited until the late 1950s before formally accepting the State of Israel.[39] It is therefore additionally ironic that, more recently, that same Jewish state, which has a 'Law of Return' for all Jews in the Diaspora built into its constitution, should now question aspects of Jewish identity – Ultra-orthodox Jews are now asking 'who is a Jew?', openly questioning the identity of certain of those who claim to be Jewish.

In confirmation of the multifaceted nature of identity and the different tools available for its recognition, Marlena Schmool, in this volume, explores the religious dimension of Jewish identity – intentionally excluding issues of Zionism and racism – setting her examination within a framework of gender. As Mackay and Thane point out in their essay on Englishwomen, and Colley in her book on the Britons, the female of the species is rarely considered under the same microscope as her male partner, a tendency which has been very obvious in the history of Jewish women in Britain whose role has been hidden and other and, as Schmool points out to us, under-researched. Semantics confirm this as the debates about Jewish citizenship have centred on the Jew as Englishman never as Englishwoman!

In keeping with the other contributors to this volume, Schmool confirms that identity, and the identification process, are dynamic, continuously evolving and informed by 'life's experiences'. She reinforces this view by illuminating her chapter with evidence that locates Jewish women's construction of religious identity through their relationship with the synagogue. In other words their expressions of religious identity and its levels are determined by the tightening or loosening of links with the synagogue, the causal factor in most cases being events in the life cycle such as marriage, child birth, *barmitzvah/ batmitzva*[40] and bereavement.

Whilst Jews in the Diaspora have, for thousands of years, been conscious of being 'a peculiar people' and thus aware of the confusions regarding their place and identity within alien societies, it is only recently, in the context of Indian migration before 1947 and that of Indian, Pakistani and Bangladeshi since the partitions, that religion has become a significant part of the discourse of subcontinental identity. Chalmers, Eade and Gardner, in their contributions to this volume, and elsewhere,[41] all explore the very recent nature of the debate about Bangladeshi identity and the confusion and creative reconstruction that surrounds it. As evidenced below, the identification process has become far more complex, with religion now an important element in the constituency. As Gardner demonstrates, the early Bangladeshi immigrants placed religious observance low on their agenda, as one of her interviewees explained, when he first arrived he was a 'broken Muslim'. Employment demands, the temptations of 'white women' for men whose wives and betrotheds were living in another continent, plus the attractions of the British way of life, meant that initially Islam played a minor role in their lives. It was something with which they rarely identified. More recently there has been a significant change, family reunification, the building of mosques, the global spread of Islam and the ageing process, has brought elders back to religion and others, as Eade explains below, determined to 'disseminate the religion of Islam particularly to young people' in order to counteract the 'melting pot of British culture'. For those, young or old, who now identify strongly with Islam, another strand has been added to the cloak of identity, one which demands of the wearer that he or she consider whether amongst other things, they are British Bangladeshi Muslim, Bangladeshi Muslim, British Muslim or simply, Muslim. Here is an example of a globalised religion which is confronting its adherents with the loyalty question, 'can you be both a good Muslim and a good …?'. It is one which, with certain strategic changes, has a very familiar ring.

It would be inappropriate to close a section on religious and political identity without a mention of Ireland, in spite of its having been referred to above in another context. Here we have perhaps the most forceful example of the [con]fusion of the boundaries of religious and political identity. The current structure of Northern Irish politics is based on religious difference enacted through political voices which vary from the stringent to the more moderate on both sides of the political spectrum. The question to be asked – writing only days after the 22 May referenda – is whether political expediency will overcome religious fervour – and identity – initially in the new Northern Irish Assembly and, subsequently, in the governing of Ireland itself, as a land united or as one divided.

4   Cultural and Physical Identity

In the context of the human experience 'culture' is the sum of numerous parts amongst which we can count language, ideas, beliefs, customs, codes, rituals, ceremonies, religion, laws and so on. A culture is something into which we are born, but at the same time, something to be learnt. It is mutable, optional and geographically transferable. In what we currently deem to be 'liberal' societies an individual is free to adopt or shed some, or all, of the parts at will. In a totalitarian society conformity may be mandatory in public though choice, as in the case of religion, language and ritual, may operate covertly. An individual may identify with one culture and yet, as a result of immigration and migration, gradually absorb elements of another. By this process cultural hybridity evolves. As Gilroy states, 'Culture does not develop along ethnically absolute lines, but in complex, dynamic patterns of syncretism'.[42]

Nanton, in his chapter in this volume, prefers to use the term creolisation to describe the process which 'forces the dominant culture into negotiation, or compromise, or the process of subversion of the dominant culture, through a "bottom up" process.' He does not restrict himself solely to African-Caribbeans in Britain in the post World War Two era. He uses the concept of creolisation to create a framework within which to compare the experience of 'conferred Identity' in the context of the Caribbean islanders as it evolved and mutated under British colonial rule in the West Indies with the way in which emigrants from those islands were initially perceived and subsequently identified in the metropolis. In both instances there has been a discernible change in the language and terms of identification used by both the subjects and the outsiders. In Britain, the designation of the Caribbean immigrant – West Indian – has metamorphosed from the language of the paternalistic, patronising coloniser to the biologically self-determined, now race related 'Black', 'Black British' and 'African-Caribbean'. According to Hall, 'Black' was the identity constructed in the early 1970s[43] by Caribbean immigrants when it became clear that the anticipated merger with the receiving society was not going to happen. For a people whose culture – in the context of language, literature, music, etc. – is only now receiving the recognition it deserves, a physical identity was perceived, at that time, to be the one which most created and embraced commonality. Its adoption might also be interpreted as an attempt to confront and embarrass the colonialists with a term which previously had been used by them as a pejorative. For many 'whites' black was a racist, not racial, descriptive. Nanton postulates that the 'conferred' Caribbean identity, one which was recognised in one form in the islands and in another in Britain, has subsequently been transformed during the passage of life in Britain. A new *creolised* Caribbean identity has emerged as a result, one which has taken on board the diverse constituents of culture from both sides of the Atlantic in order that an African-Caribbean identity should be acknowledged as diverse and dynamic, rather than that traditionally perceived as conferred by politicians and racists. Nanton's thesis is one which need not be restricted simply to the Caribbean. It could equally be applied to the eastern European immigrant experience as a means of charting the creolisation of the inhabitants of the *stetl*[44] in the promised lands of Britain and America.

One of the most valuable tools of identification is language. In his chapter Chalmers explains that he considers language to be a major force in the process of self identification undertaken by British Bangladeshis in Britain. Indeed language was a major factor in the struggle for the creation of Bangladesh. It was linguistic nationalism in the form of the protest movement against the enforced use of Urdu in place of Bengali, in what is now Bangladesh, that was a key factor in that country's creation in 1971. Chalmers illustrates how the British media has used language as a measure of the assimilation of Bangladeshis and Pakistanis, employing use of mother tongue as a stick with which to beat the immigrant community's determination to retain their ethnic identity through language. In the context of the British Bangladeshi community the issue is not simply mother tongue versus English. The majority of Bangladeshis in Britain, most particularly in East London, are from the rural and impoverished area of Sylhet. As Chalmers describes, the dominant language of this community is Sylheti, a language believed by some, incorrectly, to have no written history. It is a language with a class label, one which separates and classifies the impoverished and poorly educated rural migrant from the more affluent, urban educated Bengali speakers. In this context identification by language operates at another level, providing examples of class separation within one ethnic group so often perceived as homogeneous by outsiders. An analogy can be made here with the earlier inhabitants of the immigrant quarter of East London, the Jews from eastern Europe. They came to Britain speaking only Yiddish,[45] the language of the Pale of Settlement. As such they were immediately identified by the receiving society and their more Anglicised co-religionists as being poor – or as some would have it, pauper – and uneducated, aliens. The established Jewish community, concerned at the rising tide of anti-alienism and the creation of nationalistic organisations such as the British Brothers League, made a determined effort to discourage the use of Yiddish. The Jews' Free School in the East End, which had a student body of some 3,000 at the end of the nineteenth century, refused to allow the language to be spoken and punished those children that did. In Manchester, Jewish schoolchildren who used the *mamaluschen* (mother tongue), were made to mount a stool and stand in front of their peers as a punishment.[46] The class dimension of language has not been restricted to incomers from overseas. In the nineteenth century the Welsh language was the language of the people and the chapel, the affluent and Anglicised attended church. The significance of language to the English 'colonisers' of that period was such that, from the mid-nineteenth century, children who committed the crime of speaking Welsh in school were made to wear a sign around their necks which read 'Welsh Not' in order that their misdemeanour be recognised.

The three examples above are illustrative of the attitude of different groups towards mother tongue language at different times in history. In addition to the similarities, there are noticeable differences. As the twentieth century draws to its close the Bangladeshi community is concerned to retain its ethnic identity through language, both Sylheti and Bengali. One hundred years ago, the eastern European Jews, encouraged by their co-religionist socioeconomic superiors were compliant in shedding their foreign identity. The use of Yiddish in Britain had all but died out by the early 1950s – though it has enjoyed an academic renaissance in the past 20 years. From the nineteenth century onwards the Welsh, in some ways no different to those colonised overseas, all but lost their language. That they managed to hold onto it, until it once again became legal tender, was largely as a result of its religious currency. In each case, in the context of the British experience, for the purposes of socioeconomic advancement the English language is, and was, the one to use and with which to identify.

It has not only been in England that the role of mother tongue language has played an important part in the assimilation process. As Chris Julios demonstrates in this volume, the learning and usage of English by the Puerto Rican community of New York has played a vital part in their Americanisation and absorption into American society. However, incorporation without bias has not been straightforward. White WASPish conservatism at one end of the spectrum and peer rejection at the other end have complicated the issue. The second generation Hispanic Americans have been forced to reconstruct their identity in the light of these reactions. According to Julios their response has been to create a transnational cultural identity which accommodates prevailing social and economic needs. Whether enforced mono-lingualism[47] in schools on the West Coast of America will facilitate Anderson's theory that 'anyone can learn the language of the nation they seek to join and through the process of naturalization become a citizen and enjoy formal equality under its laws' is still debatable.[48] African-Caribbeans in Britain are only too well aware of the inadequacy of the thesis in the context of their history, which would rather confirm Enoch Powell's 1968 vision – 'The West Indian does not by being born in England become an Englishman'.[49] Even more germane are the words of a second generation Turkish immigrant in Germany who, when recently interviewed said, somewhat poignantly; 'Even if I speak German, and am German born, if I don't look like a German I am not accepted as a German'.[50]

Superficial, or surface, physical differences provide the most immediate and obvious means of 'identification with' or 'difference from'. Gender difference – though at times the external may not be the actual – skin colour, physiological characteristics and even clothes elicit the most immediate reactions of group or individual acceptance or rejection. Is there a particular significance in the choice of Gardner's *male* interviewees and Schmool's *female* subjects? The Bangladeshi elders have travelled a far more winding physical and involved route to identity than their female partners, whilst the Jewish female's means of religious identification would appear to be anchored to the biological clock and calendar. As we have seen above, a 'Black' identity was carved out of the receiving society's rejection though, as Hall so rightly suggests, this physical factor is only 'skin deep' and provides no insight into the actual mental or biological make-up of individual or group. Historically, physical characteristics have been a popular tool in the processing of group separation, one taken to its ultimate and most shocking application by the Nazis.[51] Physical and cultural identities merge once again when it comes to dress and diet. National dress and national diet act both as a means of separation and as a threshold to rapprochement. By donning the kilt, the sari and the sarong, by eating chicken masala, haggis and chicken soup with *kneidels*,[52] are outsiders acknowledging difference and, at the same time, encouraging acceptance and, perhaps, eventual merger?[53]

Conclusion

There can be no doubt that every individual has his or her own collection of identities stored in an invisible omnipresent backpack, to be made available at will in whatever combination is deemed appropriate or necessary by the wearer. Choice may not always be easy or correct. As the above has illustrated, the boundaries of identity are fuzzy and complex, part of a learning process from birth until death. As we approach the twenty-first century familiar boundaries are changing, new political, social, religious and even geographical forms are emerging demanding a constant reassessing and restructuring of personal, political, social, economic and even gender identification. Fluidity is a constant for the individual, the institution, and even the nation-state. The only surety is that we will continue to be faced with a number of questions which we can only *attempt* to answer. This volume does not set out to provide all of the questions, it seeks instead to provide an hors d'oeuvre and lay the ground for further debate. Though ultimately we may not discover our real identity we may learn from the revelations along the way. The fear is that, as with a mirage in the desert, the truth will always be just out of reach.

Notes

1   S. Hall and P. du Gay (eds), *Questions of Cultural Identity*, London, Sage, 1996, p. 1.
2   Z. Bauman, 'From Pilgrim to Tourist' in S. Hall and P. du Gay (eds), op. cit., p. 19. It should be noted that the discourse which surrounds the notion of 'belonging' is in itself complex and contentious.
3   S. Hall, *Rethinking Ethnicities*, written and presented by S. Hall on video, 1993.
4   R. Cohen, *The Fuzzy Frontiers of Identity*, London, Longman, 1994.
5   B. Anderson, *Imagined Communities: reflections on the origins and spread of nationalism*, London, Verso, 1991.
6   L. Colley, *The Britons, Forging the Nation 1707–1837*, London, Vintage, 1996.
7   *The Times*, 18 December 1997.

8   See below.

9   See D.G. Boyce, 'The Marginal British – The Irish' in R. Colls and P. Dodd (eds), *Englishness, Politics and Culture 1880–1920*, Kent, Croom Helm, 1986 and S. Gikandi, *Maps of Englishness*, New York, Columbia University Press, 1996.

10 L.Colley, op. cit., p. x.

11 Author's italics.

12 S. Gikandi, op. cit., p. 10.

13 L. Dowds and K. Young, 'National Identity' in R. Jowell, J. Curtice, A. Park, L. Brook and K. Thompson (eds), *British Social Attitudes: The 13th Report*, Aldershot, Dartmouth, 1996, p. 152.

14 Ibid., p. 142.

15 J. Mackay and P. Thane, 'The Englishwoman' in Colls and Dodd, op. cit., p. 191.

16 I am grateful to my third year undergraduate students of Bangladeshi and African-Caribbean origin for discussing their feelings about identity with me. See also, J. Eade, 'Bangladeshis in a Global City' in A.J. Kershen (ed.), *London the Promised Land?: The migrant experience in a capital city*, Aldershot, Avebury, 1997, pp. 99–103.

17 See R. Cohen, *Global Diasporas*, London, UCL Press, 1997.

18 In the postmodern world of globablisation the notion of home and away is no longer clearly defined, for many migrants where home and away are, or are perceived to be, moveable feasts.

19 S. Gikandi, op. cit., p. ix.

20 *The Times*, 19 March 1998.

21 V. Bogdanor, *Devolution to Scotland and Wales*, UK law on Line, http:/www.Leeds.ac.uk.

22 Ibid., pp. 170–3.

23 Colley, op. cit., p. 125.

24 Ibid., pp. 139 and 140. James Bond may have been a Scot in Ian Fleming's eyes but he has been portrayed on the screen by a Scotsman – Sean Connery; an Englishman – Roger Moore – whose Bond has become stereotypically English – and an Irishman – Pierce Brosnan. (I am grateful to John Eade for bringing this point to my notice.)

25 V. Bogdanor, op. cit.

26 *Today* programme, BBC Radio 4, 9 May 1998.

27 R. Cohen, *Fuzzy Frontiers*, op. cit., pp. 9–10.

28 We should not forget that the discrimination directed towards the Irish, Welsh and Scots during the nineteenth century was an early form of racism, even though not acknowledged, or even recognised, as such at the time.

29 See Parsons, chapter 2, below.

30 Quoted (and supported) in R. Cohen, *Fuzzy Frontiers*, op. cit., p. 9.

31 Parenthesis are used here as although Karen Trew's chapter in this book is on the subject of Northern Irish identity, until 1922 this is a title which did not apply.

32 R. Colls, 'Englishness and Political Culture' in Colls and Dodd, op. cit., p. 40.

33 Karen Trew completed her chapter in early 1998 and it was at the typesetters before the referendum was held in Ireland on 22 May 1998.

34 D.G. Boyce, 'The Marginal British – the Irish', op. cit., p. 238.

35 Montagu was Liberal Member of Parliament for Whitechapel 1885–1900, he was founder of the Federation of Synagogues and supporter of a nonbelligerent tailoring trade union in the 1880s. See L. Gartner, *The Jewish Immigrant in England 1870–1914*, London, George Allen and Unwin, 1960, p. 117 and A.J. Kershen, *Uniting the Tailors; Trade Unionism*

Amongst the Tailoring Workers of London and Leeds, 1872 –1939, London, Frank Cass, 1995, pp. 132–3.

36 For a study of Bangladeshis and politics in Tower Hamlets, see J. Eade, *Politics of Race and Community*, Aldershot, Avebury, 1989. John Eade confirms that the links with Sylhet, though considerably weakened over the past few years, still exist. (Author's conversation with John Eade, 4 June 1988.)

37 For the latest work in this area see S. Saggar (ed.), *Race and British Electoral Politics*, London, UCL Press, 1998.

38 See A.J. Kershen and J. Romain, *Tradition and Change: The History of Reform Judaism in Britain, 1840–1995*, Ilford, Vallentine Mitchell, 1995, pp. 24–5.

39 Ibid., pp. 115–21 and 212–16.

40 Achievement of religious majority for males and females.

41 See J. Eade, 'Bangladeshis in a Global City', op. cit. and K. Gardner, *Global Migrants, Local Lives: Travel and Transformation in Rural Bangladesh*, Oxford, Oxford University Press, 1995.

42 P. Gilroy, *There Ain't No Black in the Union Jack*, London, Hutchinson, 1987, p. 13.

43 S. Hall, op. cit.

44 Town or village in the Pale of Settlement in Russia and Russia-Poland.

45 Yiddish was and is a written language which uses Hebrew characters and is a mixture of German and Hebrew. It was acknowledged as the language of the *stetl*, though it had a literary history. For an insight into the use of Yiddish in the East End see A.J. Kershen, 'Yiddish as a Vehicle for Anglicisation' in A. Newman and S. Massel (eds), *Patterns of Migration 1850–1914*, London, Jewish Historical Society of England, 1996, pp. 59–68.

46 See R. Livshin, 'The Acculturation of the Children of Immigrant Jews in Manchester, 1890–1930' in D. Cesarani (ed.), *The Making of Modern Anglo Jewry*, Oxford, Blackwell, 1990, pp. 79–96.

47 Legislation passed in June 1998 has put an end to bilingualism in schools on the West Coast of America.

48 Quoted in Gilroy, op. cit., p. 44.

49 *The Times*, 6 November 1968.

50 Interview on the *Today* programme, BBC Radio 4, 20 January 1998.

51 There is an enormous literature on Nazi race science but for an introduction see L. Dawidowicz, *The War Against the Jews 1933–1945*, London, Weidenfeld and Nicolson, 1975, most particularly chapter 7; R. Wistrich, *Anti-Semitism The Longest Hatred*, London, Methuen, 1991 and B. Wasserstein, *Britain and the Jews of Europe 1939–1945*, London, Oxford University Press, 1988, ch. 4.

52 Dumplings made with matzo meal and chicken fat, a traditional accompaniment to chicken soup.

53 Perhaps we are nearer than we think, as spotted on a London Underground train at 8 a.m. on the morning of 9 June 1998, en route to the World Cup in France, a Sikh wearing a turban and a kilt. (I am grateful to Marlena Schmool for this sighting.)

I am grateful to John Eade for his comments on this chapter.

PART ONE
BRITISH IDENTITY

1 Being Born Lost? The Cultural and Institutional Dimensions of Welsh Identity

WAYNE PARSONS

We are exiles within
our own country; we eat our bread
at a pre-empted table. 'Show us,'
we supplicate, 'the way home',
and they laughing hiss at us:
'But you are home. Come in
and endure it,' Will nobody
explain what it is like to be born lost?
(R.S. Thomas, from 'The Lost.)[1]

I have been a multitude of shapes,
Before I assumed consistent form.
(*The Book of Taliessen*)[2]

Every day when I wake up
I Thank the Lord
I'm Welsh
(Catatonia, *International Velvet*)[3]

In the Shadow of the Dragon: Wales and the Making of Britishness

Flags are potent and visible symbols of collective identity. In war people rally to them and die for them and are buried under them – *pro patria*. Politicians, as a last refuge, can wrap themselves in the flag and call upon their people to wave and follow the primary symbol of who they are and what they share. The flag is the first thing to go up and the last thing to come down. That Wales and the Welsh can lay claim to a distinct *national* identity which has existed for many centuries may be illustrated by the fact that the ancient symbol of Wales, a dragon, is one of the oldest (if not the oldest) national flags in the

25

world. The symbol that is displayed in public buildings, uniforms, on sports shirts and elsewhere today, is a manifestation of an identity which has been possessed by the Welsh for as long as the people who occupy the country have seen themselves as a people. *Y Ddraig Goch*, the Red Dragon, was brought to Wales by the Romans over 1,800 years ago, and was adopted by the British Kings. It was, so tradition says, the flag of Arthur and Cadwallader from whom the Tudors claimed their ancestry and the right to the throne.

The English have the cross of the dragon slayer, George, and the Scots, St Andrew, but the Welsh, despite (unlike the Scots or the English) having a proper, *bone fide* indigenous saint, (*Dewi*, or David) have retained the dragon. And, of course, there is no dragon in the union flag: the crosses of saints, but no pagan red dragon. As a point of entry into understanding the complex nature of Welsh identity the red dragon is, perhaps, as good a place to start to unravel the way in which identity has been shaped in Wales as any other. For a country whose identity has for so long been virtual, rather than institutionally or politically meaningful and real, the mythical beast is a somewhat appropriate symbol to represent Wales. The dragon exists as a state of mind, rather than as an actual living, breathing creature. Both the Welsh for dragon (*ddraig*) and the English come from the Latin and Greek root 'drakon' which means serpent.[4] The dragon symbol has been used widely in both the West and the East to represent both the unity of opposites and destructive chaos. One recent authority on the subject observes, for instance, that:

> … combining characteristics of the four elements … the dragon symbolises light and dark, sun and moon, masculine and feminine and the unity underlying these opposite forces … In the East and in pre-Christian Europe, the dragon was seen as helpful and kind – indeed, the red dragon is the symbol of Wales. But Christianity, which saw the serpent as a symbol of evil, also viewed the dragon as a creature of ill-omen, representing destructiveness and inner chaos.[5]

Stories of dragons often involve battles and the quest of heroes to defeat and destroy the beast. The story popularised by Geoffrey of Monmouth is that the Welsh red dragon myth concerned the conflict between the Welsh and the Saxons. In the story there is a battle between a red dragon and a white dragon which the young Myrddin (Merlin) foretells will end with *y ddraig goch* driving out the white (Saxon) dragon.[6] In this account the dragon is both a symbol of unity and represents the triumph of a British order over Saxon chaos. Hence it is the red dragon which was to be flown at the Battle of Bosworth and it was the red dragon that became be a symbol of the Tudor state. From then on the dragon becomes a very *British* symbol indeed: it comes to represent the way in which the Britons, through a descendent of the ancient Welsh kings, have once more taken control of their country as had been foretold by the prophecies of Myrddin.

The dragon embodies much of the way in which Welsh identity was to develop. From the beginning the Welsh came to see themselves as being truly British, and that their identity as Welsh people was not undermined by being part of Britain, so much as it was underpinned by their claim to be the true Britons. The Red Dragon is the symbol of the *Brytaniaid*, the survivors of Roman Briton. Indeed, it is important to note that it was not until around the twelfth century that the Welsh refer to themselves as *Cymru*, or compatriots, rather than Britons. The term Welsh, which derives from the Saxon for stranger or foreigner, was the word that the people of the white dragon were to use to describe them, the Britons. Thus it was that the people who rallied to the dragon flag were, quite early on in their history, a *very* mixed up bunch. They had, as it were, three identities: they were *Brytaniaid* or British, the first of the ancient Celtic peoples of the Island; they were the *Cymru*, the people who had to band together to fight off the Saxons, Picts, Vikings, and Normans; and they were the *welisc* or *wealh* (the 'Welsh') , the people who were deemed to be strangers in their own land. This multiplistic sense of identity has been an enduring theme: in the 1920s, for example, Sir Alfred Zimmern saw Wales as being composed of a 'Welsh Wales', an 'English Wales' and an 'American Wales'.[7] More recently a popular idea has been that of the so called 'three Wales model' consisting a of *Y Fro Cymraeg*, (a Welsh speaking heartland), a 'Welsh Wales' and a 'British Wales'.[8] Thus in so many ways the people of Wales are still trying to grapple with and manage these layers of interweaving identity, which have evolved over hundreds of years. The dragon is an object of a continuing quest: the Welsh are still trying to find their way around what 'Wales' or *Cymru* means.

One famous dragon myth is that of uroboros who recreates himself by eating his own tail. There is much of this in the history of the land of the red dragon: for the story of the country is about a struggle not just with the outsiders, but also, and perhaps more importantly, a struggle between the Welsh themselves. The Welsh have had outbreaks of unity as other countries have had episodes of internal dissension. From the beginning the land of the dragon has been one in which much national energy has gone into consuming itself in disputes between different parts and groups of the country. Indeed, this lack of unity is one plausible reason why the Welsh originally lost their independence in the first place. Uroboros-like, out of this process of internal conflict and dispute has evolved something called a national identity. The history of this struggle is really the history of a people who, although sharing a belief in themselves as having an identity, have consistently lacked any sense of unity or consensus as to what this identity means or what the political significance of this identity may be held to be. Welsh identity has not been possessed so much as it has been processed, with the result that it has rarely, to use the words of Taliessen, been consistent in form, but invariably multiplicitous in shape. Welsh identity has, for the greater part of its history, been composed of levels and layers. Yet, despite being a small people annexed to a powerful imperial power, and having been on the verge of extinction too many times to count, Wales is still here. In an age when the problem of identity is increasingly a global phenomena, the continued existence of Wales is an experience which has, perhaps, a relevance to other peoples who, if not (as R.S. Thomas has it in his poem) born lost like the Welsh, feel that they are becoming so.

The early history of Wales is largely the story of a collection of Brythonic-Celtic tribes endeavouring to defend themselves from successive waves of invaders. The first invaders were the Romans who arrived in AD 43, and left in AD 383, bequeathing Wales improvements in agriculture and technology of all kinds as well as many Latin words which remain in modern Welsh to this day. After the departure of the Romans the Celts had to contend with numerous other invaders who pushed them further and further north and west. They called their land *Breithyn* or *Prydain*. The people who became known as the Welsh once occupied a much larger area of the island of Britain than the 8,000 square miles which now composes their homeland. They occupied the western half of Britain from what is now called Cornwall and Devon, up to Strathclyde. The extent of *British* Britain may also be seen in the many place names which are Welsh in origin such as: Cumbria (from *Cymru*), Glasgow (meaning green hollow, or *glas cou*), Melrose (*moel rhos*, meaning bare moor land), or Avon, (meaning a river). These Britons were called foreigners by the Saxons (*Wealas*) and there are a number of places outside Wales which signify that they were once British (that is foreigner) settlements: such as *Wal*lasey and *Wal*ton. By AD 655 the Saxon invaders eventually succeeded in cutting off the Western peninsula from the other Celts of Cornwall, Devon and North Britain, and from this time onwards the border between *Cymru* and *Saeson*, Wales and the English, became well defined. So much so that the boundary constructed by Offa of Mercia at around AD 784 constitutes a dividing line between the Celts and the Saxons which has lasted with remarkably little change over the successive centuries.

In the dark ages Wales was a patchwork of kingdoms which, although they forged a common identity as a result of fighting the Vikings, Saxons and Irish, were not to develop a common political and institutional structure. Periods of unity were somewhat sporadic in comparison to the position in England where, under Alfred, Edward and Athelstan, a centralised and well organised form of state was to evolve prior to the Norman conquest. But Wales from its very genesis, was a country which, although possessed of a clear and well defined sense of a common identity, lacked a political unity. It was a nation, but never a state of the kind that the English were to establish. Wales was obstinately decentralised and centred on cooperative communities rather than the rule of one authority or power. The invasion of the Normans in 1066 presented another threat to the existence of Wales; it survived and in 1267 was recognised as a separate principality under the Treaty of Montgomery. The Treaty was broken in 1282 and Wales was made a Dominion of the English King. However, for a brief time during the fifteenth century Wales once again became independent. Between 1400 and 1415 Owain Glyn Dŵr waged a long war of independence, but with the defeat of Owain, Wales was absorbed into the English state until it was finally annexed under the Act of Union in 1536.

The idea of being a separate nation state died with Owain, but in its place emerged another vision, one which had been foretold by Myrddin himself, that one day a Welshman would come and free the Britons from the yoke of the invader. That day was deemed to have arrived when, in 1485, Henry Tudor landed in Pembroke and with his fellow country men marching behind the dragon of Cadwallader, went on to defeat Richard III at Bosworth. The Welsh were no longer foreigners, they were once again Britons and their King was victorious. Well, that is what they told themselves. This myth also suited the Tudors, keen to stress their Welsh ancestry. In Shakespeare's *Henry V* we find an apt illustration of the relationship between Wales and England and the British state in the part played by Fluellen (Act IV: Scene VII).

> *K.Hen.* Then call this the field of Agincourt, Fought on the day of Crispin Crispianus.
> *Flu.* Your Grandfather of famous memory, an't please your majesty, and your great-uncle Edward the Confessor, Plack Prince of Wales, as I have read in the chronicles, fought a most prave pattle here in France.
> *K.Hen.* They did, Fluellen.
> *Flu.* Your majesty says very true: if your majesties is remembred of it, the Welshmen did good service in a garden where leeks did grow, wearing leeks in their Monmouth caps; which, your majesty know, to this hour is an honarable

badge of service; and I do believe your majesty takes no scorn to wear the leek upon Saint Tavy's day.

K.Hen. I wear it for a memorable honour; For I am Welsh, you know, good countryman.

Flu. All the water in Wye cannot wash your majesty's Welsh plood out of his pody, I can tell you that …

K.Hen. Thanks, good my countryman.

This is an interesting passage as it tells us much of how the Welsh saw their identity as being fully embodied and vindicated in the Tudors, and how this identity was also very important to the Tudors themselves. Thus it was that in the Tudor period the notion of the Welsh as the bedrock of Britishness became firmly implanted in both the minds of the Welsh and the English. In one of Shakespeare's last plays, *Cymbeline*, this theme of the contribution of Wales to the making of Britain is brought home by reference to Milford Haven (the port where Henry Tudor landed and where he gathered support to defeat Richard III) as the place where the two young princes live. Once again, it is Wales which, in Shakespeare's story, saves *Britain* – for the English.

The above quoted passage from *Henry V* also provides a sixteenth century pointer to the contemporary essence of Welsh cultural identity, language: Fluellen speaks English as a foreign language. On the one hand Welsh political identity had withered with the defeat of Owain Glyn Dŵr, but the sense of a distinct cultural identity in terms of language was to undergo something of a renaissance in the Tudor period. The hundred years which preceded the Act of Union in 1536 were, although erosive of Welsh political identity, a time of cultural renewal and awakening. In this period Welsh poetry and letters were to flower as never before. The age of the Tudors brought political stability, economic growth and access to the Court and this in turn facilitated the development of a sense of cultural difference within a British order dominated by the English state.

The relationship between Wales and England was redefined in 1536 when England finally extended its control over Wales through a series of measures that became known as the Act of Union. From henceforth Welsh ceased to be permitted as a language of law and administration: Wales would be governed from England, under English law and *in* the English language. Thus it was not simply the administrative and legal systems which were imposed on Wales in 1536, Cromwell's legislation also sought to abolish the cultural differences which could get in the way of political centralisation. Those who could not speak English would be excluded from office: no English, no job. The Act aimed to eradicate 'distinction and diversity', and this meant that, as Wales was 'annexed' and 'incorporated', there could be no toleration of a language that was not the King's English – even though he was a Welshman, of sorts.

From the Act of Union onwards the language of getting on in the world was English, and *only* English. Furthermore, from then on, cultural difference was seen by the English as dangerous and threatening. In the centuries following the Act of Union, therefore, the Welsh had to live in a British state – which they had helped to define – but on the terms set out by the English. To speak any other language but English was tolerated, but not encouraged, and was against the law in matters of the state. Inevitably, the Welsh became a subservient and insecure, if not a schizophrenic people. If you wanted to advance, you had to do so by seeing yourself as British in English terms, but to be British meant accepting the dominance of English ways, customs and culture. Despite this political dominance, the Welsh language persisted, and even grew stronger. The availability of a Welsh translation of the Bible in the sixteenth century, and the work of Welsh scholars and humanists went some way to sustain the cultural and antiquarian position of the language, but this was conducted in the framework of being British-Welsh. Being Welsh involved certain political and cultural sacrifices if the partnership – for that was how the 'annexation' was viewed – was to work. The British myth, however, was more important to the maintenance of a Welsh identity than it was ever to the English. Being British *allowed* them to be Welsh. Hence, as John Davies points out, the creation of Great Britain in 1610 met with Welsh support, for:

> Unlike the Bretons, who were incorporated into the state and nation of the French, the Welsh henceforth could feel that they were partners in a state which represented the union of three nations. It was difficult for them to consider themselves to be both Welsh and English, but to be Welsh and British was acceptable, particularly in view of the central role of the concept of Britain in the Welsh national myth. It is hardly surprising therefore that it was a Welshman – William Maurice – who advocated that James I should adopt the title of king or emperor of Great Britain.[9]

The creation of Britishness was important for the Welsh in that it enabled them to hold on to their identity whilst at the same time securing social and economic advantage in English institutions. But Britishness was important for the English for very different reasons. Britishness for the English was something which could be extended to secure the compliance and integration of a minority. Hence, in the words of the song: there would *always* be an England. England was more exclusive and more narrowly defined. Britain, on the other hand, has long been – since the annexation of Wales – a concept which was used to conquer and subdue. In the words of another song, it is *Britannia* who rules the waves. Britishness was, from 1536 onwards, the discourse of colonialism and empire. The Welsh could be British, as could the multitude of other peoples who were later to be conquered by the English. The Welsh who were so accepted into the British state would not have described themselves as English, but 'Cambro-British' or British. Fluellen and others of his kind who fought for the Tudors had claims to British nationality, but not to being English. Fluellen was British first and Welsh second, his English counterparts were English first and (perhaps) British second, if at all. And yet it was the desire to ensure that Wales was fully locked into England that resulted in a policy which proved vital to the strengthening of Welsh identity in linguistic terms: in 1563 it was decided that the Welsh should have the benefit of being able to read the Bible and *The Book of Common Prayer*. The widespread availability of the Bible in Welsh from 1567 onwards meant that the place of the language in the religious and cultural life of the country was secured. This culminated in 1588 with William Morgan's famous translation. This book was of immense importance as it 'ensured that the purity and strength of the poetic vocabulary should survive, and above all it prevented the language from degenerating into a number of dialects and perhaps from dying out completely'.[10] From then on Welsh identity and religion were to become ever more tightly knit. Welsh was the language of the Protestant religion in Wales, and religious identity and cultural identity became inextricably interlinked.

In the eighteenth century Wales experienced a great religious revival championed by the Methodist church. The success of Methodism in Wales was spectacular in both transforming the lives of the working people who had been somewhat neglected by the Anglican (and English) clergy, and transforming the cultural and political life of Wales. Later in the nineteenth century this religious radicalism was to find political expression. Alongside this religious revolution Wales was also to experience a cultural renaissance marked by the founding of the *Honourable Society of Cymmrodorion* in London in 1751. But the exciting developments in Welsh literature in this period were not reflected in any change in the political situation as Welsh politics remained dominated by anglicised gentry who had little inclination to develop a distinct Welsh political agenda. But during the eighteenth century Wales was to develop a radical politics, the most famous representative of which was Dr Richard Price whose *Observations on Civil Liberty* (1776) and *Discourse on the Love of Our Country* (1789) were to make him one of the most talked about radicals of the day. It was his ideas which prompted Edmund

Burke to write his *Reflections on the Revolution in France.*

This cultural renaissance took place, of course, in the context of the continued fabrication of a British identity aided, as Linda Colley shows in her study of British history in the period 1707–1837, by the force of a common Protestantism and the experience of war. Thus, although Wales was to emerge from the eighteenth century firmly locked into the British state, the distinctiveness of the country was still much in evidence. Britishness, argues Colley was something which was essentially 'superimposed on much older allegiances':

> By 1837, Scotland still retained many of the characteristics of a distinct nation. It was British as well as Scottish. By contrast, Wales was rather more distinct. Possessed of its own unifying language, less urbanised than Scotland and England – and – crucially – less addicted to military and imperial endeavour, it could still strike observers from outside its boundaries as being resolutely peculiar to itself. 'If nothing can please him but what is foreign', an English writer on tourism declared with some exaggeration in 1831, 'he will find the language, manners, and dress of the inhabitants [of Wales], except in the inns as completely foreign as those of France and Switzerland.'[11]

A distinctive radical political mood in Wales was to grow in the nineteenth century as the impact of agrarian change and industrialisation began to find voice in the growth of a nonconformist politics. As the franchise widened from 1832 onwards so this nonconformist politics gave Wales an increasingly more distinctive kind of radically informed politics from that of England. For the first time since the days of Glyn Dŵr the Welsh began to express political dissent. This discontent was seen in the Merthyr riots of 1831 when a red flag was hoisted, the Chartist riots of 1839 in Newport and the rebellion over toll charges known as the Rebecca Riots (1839–44). The episode in Welsh history which came to focus attention on the language issue and the role of language in Welsh identity came to be known as *Brad y Llyfrau Gleision* (The treason of the blue books). In 1847 a governmental commission of inquiry reported that, despite the policy of assimilation and linguistic annihilation since 1536, Welsh was all too prevalent in Wales. Indeed, it was increasing! The existence of the Welsh language made the Welsh too distinctive from the other members of the British state and was, so the commission reported, a source of considerable educational and economic disadvantage. Welsh was, they concluded, the curse of Wales and a barrier to moral progress and economic prosperity. In the years which followed two things happened: the policy of eradicating Welsh set out in 1536 was intensified and in turn this provoked and stimulated the growth of a nationalist movement. Symbolic of the former was the infamous policy of 'Welsh Not', whereby children would be punished in school for speaking in Welsh. They were fined, punished, and made to wear a sign around their neck on which was inscribed a reminder to them and their fellow young countrymen not to speak the 'old language'. By the end of the nineteenth century around a half of the population of Wales spoke Welsh, and thereafter the proportion was to continue to decline.

The first half of the nineteenth century was to witness a growing sense of cultural identity as may be illustrated by the development of a lively Welsh press, and the nonconformist religious revival. Also important was the antiquarian interest in Wales and the growth of interest in Welsh literature. Lady Charlotte Guest, for example, was responsible for the translation of a collection of important folk tales entitled *The Mabinogion* (1877). Undoubtedly all this had the effect of promoting a sense of romantic national identity, but there was a distinct lack of any political movement as was taking place in Ireland and many other European countries. Indicative of this search for national identity was the attempt to found a new Wales in Argentina (*Y Wladfa Cymreig*) which began in 1865. Although this was something of a failure, as only around 3,000 settlers went to Patagonia, it was a measure of how far, by this time, there was a linkage being made between cultural and political identity and a desire to redefine the relationship between being Welsh and being British. In the forefront of this new movement of national liberation was Michael D. Jones who is regarded as the father of Welsh nationalism.

The key aspect of this emerging sense of political and cultural identity was the central position of language. It is the language that is to be absolutely crucial to the construction of Wales as a nation. As *Y Cymmro* editorialised in 1883:

> If once we lose the Welsh language, that will be the end of us as a nation: the sun of the Welsh people will never rise again; and they will not be heard of any more as a nation but merely as a piece of driftwood that has survived from a wreck that disappeared in the great ocean of oblivion.[12]

This linguistic emphasis which stands in stark contrast to Irish and Scottish nationalism was a problematic basis for a country which was to experience a steady – and seemingly inevitable – decline in the proportion of Welsh people who could speak the language. In addition to this South Wales was on the receiving end of immigration from England and Ireland and elsewhere, which was to further weaken the position of Welsh speakers as a proportion of the people who lived in Wales. In the 1880s, with a bigger electorate (due to the 1884 Reform Act), Welsh politics was to undergo something of a transformation. Welsh Liberalism was radical and pressed for Home Rule. This campaign culminated in the setting-up of an organisation called *Cymru Fydd* in 1886, however it failed to generate the kind of popular support for Home Rule which occurred in Ireland. After a decade *Cymru Fydd* was deeply divided (between north and south) and thus unable to build a national movement. This was especially the case after the death in 1889 of one of the leading Welsh politicians, Tom Ellis. Thereafter the leadership of the Welsh Liberals passed to Lloyd George whose agenda was wider than Home Rule for Wales. In the end, the possibilities of being powerful in a British and world context proved too great a temptation for Lloyd George and he abandoned the cause of Welsh Home Rule. As Gwynfor Evans notes:

> For five years, 1890–95, his brilliance both in the country and in Parliament made the establishment of the nationalist party a real possibility. For five years it was a race between radical nationalism and Briticism. The latter won. The national effort was doomed to failure, and Wales never recovered from it. It would be foolish to blame Lloyd George alone for his failure and for the deterioration witnessed in the years that followed; but some blame must rest on his shoulders and despite his admirable service to England – or Britain – he probably did more harm than good to Wales. In this he recalls Henry VII, four centuries earlier. Their effect on Wales was strikingly similar. Lloyd George tightened the hold of Briticism on Wales at the cost of its Welshness; it led to a long line of young Welsh politicians who saw themselves as second Lloyd Georges, walking the great stage of London and winning personal glory in the 'wider circle of service', as he used to say.[13]

The tension between Britishness and Welshness which Lloyd George embodied was manifest in the regional rivalries that developed during the nineteenth century. The south of the country became a major industrial area and this fostered a division between the agricultural and industrial parts, as well as a division between the increasingly anglicised south and the Welsh speaking heartlands in the north. The 1881 census was to show, for example, that ten per cent of the population of Wales had been born in England. In the industrial south this proportion would have been much higher and also included the growing influx of Irish immigrants. In 1851, for example, it was estimated that there were around 20,000 people born in Ireland living in Wales.[14] This is an important comparison with Scotland and Ireland: for Wales in the nineteenth century was a focus of immigration, not emigration. Cardiff, for instance, was to become one of the first multiracial cities in Britain. So on the one hand, Wales in the latter decades of the nineteenth century was being transformed through industrialisation, immigration and the deliberate assault on the Welsh language, whilst on the other, it was undergoing a political rebirth through the development of a national movement. Inevitably, the path which Wales was to take, therefore, was very different to the nationalist movement in Ireland which was far more united and cohesive.

Kenneth Morgan characterises the period which saw the growth of a radical liberal Wales (1850–70) as a time when a new identity was being shaped, but as the product of a 'fractured consciousness'.[15] Lloyd George is therefore only one part of the explanation of the failure of the national movement to secure a measure of political reform for Wales: the other part has to do with the fact that there was no shared or agreed concept of what being Welsh meant in cultural or political terms. It was difficult, if not downright impossible, to forge a national political movement, if there was no consensus as to what the nation was in the first place, especially when the institutional fabric of Welsh identity was very thin in comparison with the power of British institutions. This tension between Welshness and Britishness has remained central in Welsh politics throughout the twentieth century, when Wales was to produce two other leading 'British' politicians, Bevan and Kinnock, the reluctance to give up the larger British stage was to be all too typical of the position adopted by Lloyd George.

The First World War saw Wales wholly committed to the cause of the empire, now, of course, with their very own Lloyd George as prime minister. Thus in reviewing the development of Welsh national consciousness in the period up to the Second World War one could argue that the achievements were largely, if not wholly, those of securing a greater sense of cultural identity than of attaining a sense of political identity. Nonconformist politics had provided Wales with greater religious freedom; educationalists such as Owen M. Edwards had ensured that Welsh education was improved; and romantics had given Wales a literary revival, but there was little by way of a distinct institutional context for that identity. The Welsh were happy to be British as long as their cultural identity was acknowledged and respected. The period also saw, for the first time however, the emergence of a Welsh political leadership with such people as Henry Richard (1812–88), William Abraham (Mabon) (1842–1922), Michael D. Jones, (1822–98), Tom Ellis (1859–99), and of course, David Lloyd George. In this respect although Wales did not develop a nationalist movement as in Ireland, it did produce an active and increasingly influential political elite who were able to play important parts in British political life. This pattern was to continue in the interwar period with men such as Ness Edwards, Jim Griffiths, Morgan Phillips and Aneurin Bevan, all of whom were major figures in the *British* Labour movement. During the 1920s the Labour Party was to replace the Liberal Party as the dominant party in Wales. The Labour movement provided a powerful institutional focus for Welsh politics, and, as was the case of the Liberal Party, it tended to channel Welsh political identity into specifically British institutions. The leaders who were to emerge out of the Welsh Labour movement (or rather the Labour movement in Wales) were all to be broadly sympathetic to the idea of Wales as a cultural entity, but were generally hostile to the claims for political institutions to give expression to this sense of distinctiveness. Thus, although some members of the party were to be supportive of devolution, the leading figures of Labourism were not convinced of the need for reform in the constitutional position of Wales. It was in this context that Plaid Cymru was founded in 1925 to promote and defend the Welsh language and later, in 1932, to campaign for self-government. But this was not the best time to be campaigning on a nationalist platform. As unemployment grew in Wales and as the threat of war loomed ever larger, the nationalism of people like Saunders Lewis found little popular support. Between 1921 and 1940 some 430,000 people emigrated, which, from a population of under three million, represented a devastating blow to the country. In such times the Labour movement was looking to British and international kinds of solutions, and the idea that political devolution could do something to improve the position of Wales was not one which commanded any real attention. The depression and the world war which followed therefore cemented Wales firmly into the British state, even though the sense of cultural identity was maintained. As the present author has pointed out, the experience of war and the Labour government of 1945–51 was to greatly strengthen the centralist nature of the British state in the way in which a regionalist approach to economic and physical planning was wholly rejected.[16]

The National Question 1945–79

Under Labour governments (1945–51) the national claims of Wales were recognised in administrative terms: in 1946 the Welsh Regional Hospital Board was set up; in 1948 the Wales Gas Board; and in 1948 a Council of Wales and Monmouthshire was established under the chairmanship of Huw T. Edwards. In addition, the government created a Welsh day in the House of Commons, but little else was forthcoming. There were, of course, some who took, contrary to Bevan, a pro-devolutionary position in the party, but for the most part the Bevan line of open hostility to Welsh self-government dominated the Labour Party.

In 1949 a campaign for a Welsh Parliament was launched by *Undeb Cymru Fydd* which culminated in a petition signed by 250,000 people in 1956, but it met with short shrift. As did the attempt by a Labour MP, S.O. Davies, the previous year, to introduce a bill to set up a Welsh parliament. Even so, in 1951 the Conservatives did create a Minister for Welsh Affairs in the Home Office. This institutionalisation of modern Wales continued with the designation of Cardiff as the capital city in 1955. And, in keeping with so much of Welsh history, the position of Cardiff as capital has continued to be an issue ever since. As we shall see later, the aftermath of the 1997 referendum brought the matter to the boil once again. But this rivalry over where the capital should be only serves to demonstrate that, as Hague and Thomas comment:

> The process of industrialisation introduced and exacerbated a range of social divisions, one manifestation of which was contested notions of what being Welsh involved. So, though there might be no historic rivals for the role of capital city of Wales, it was by no means uncontentious which town deserved that kind of symbolic status.[17]

In the 1950s the Council of Wales pushed for more devolution for Wales. This got nowhere with the Conservative government, but at least the inadequacies of the Council prompted Welsh Labour MPs to form a Parliament for Wales Group to press for more extensive reform which would create a democratic body to replace the appointed Council. When the Tories created a Minister of State for Wales in 1957 – or an 'ambassador' for Wales (sic) – and appointed an unknown Welsh Tory (Vivian Lewis, Lord Brecon) to the job it further provoked Welsh Labour MPs to advance a more developed plan for Wales. In 1959 the Labour Party came around to recognising the need for a Secretary of State for Wales; a policy that was implemented by the Wilson government in 1964. This was undoubtedly the most significant development in the political history of Wales for many hundreds of years, as it initiated the process by which Wales began to acquire an institutional structure which continued to grow under both Labour and Conservative governments.

In the years preceding the creation of the Welsh Office there had been a significant renewal of the nationalist movement. This might be dated back to a talk given by Saunders Lewis on BBC Wales radio in 1962 on the fate of the Welsh language. Painting a dismal picture of the decline of the language Lewis forecast the extinction of Wales if drastic action were not taken. This call led to the founding of *Cymdeithas yr Iaith Cymraeg* (The Welsh Language Society) which henceforth was to campaign vigorously for changing the law which had discriminated against Welsh since 1536. This campaign led to the Welsh Language Act of 1967. The campaign of *Cymdeithas yr Iaith Cymraeg* was a turning point in the story of Welsh identity. The Society sought to raise the awareness of people about the impact of Anglo-American culture on the ability of a small country to survive. It also made a clear distinction between cultural and political identity and how one related to the other. What, they asked, would be the point of a self-governing Wales, without its language? The answer it gave was uncompromising:

> ... there would be no reality to a self-governing Wales, even which possessed every possible political institution, if it did not have the Welsh language. Further, it would not have an atom of strength to withstand the Anglo-American influences flooding into it through commercial advertising and in the mass media, nor to resist the worst excesses of the predatory capitalism with which the near future threatens us. In a word, the destruction of the Welsh national identity would be inevitable, despite its political institutions ... If the Welsh language were to die, and so share the fate that is likely to overtake some other numerically small cultures before the end of the century, humanity would be impoverished in the sense that one thread among the thousands that make up the cultural pattern of mankind – whose glory is variety – would be lost. We see this linguistic and cultural diversity also as a defence against the shallowness and corruption of the Anglo-American anti-culture that pours into every corner of the world through the machinery of capitalism. It is in this cultural and national diversity that we see as a means of satisfying man's need for roots.[18]

The founding of the Welsh language society reflected the growing mood of discontent in Wales and Scotland which manifested itself in the growth of nationalist movements in the two countries in the 1960s and early 1970s. The Labour Party was rocked by the success of Plaid Cymru in the 1966 Carmarthen by-election, and later by the performance of the Blaid in the 1968 Caerphilly by-election. In response to the rising tide of nationalism in Scotland and Wales the Labour government set up a Royal Commission on the Constitution, in 1969, which reported in favour of elected assemblies for the two countries in 1973. Under Labour (1974–79) Wales continued to develop its institutional structure, most notably with the acquisition of economic powers by the Welsh

Office, and the establishment of the Welsh Development Agency, the Development Board for Rural Wales and the Land Authority for Wales (1976).

The culmination of the pressure for Welsh devolution came with the 1979 referendum. The 'No' campaign was mobilised around a very clear message: a vote for devolution was a vote for the destruction of Britain, the reduction of Welsh influence in London, and the surrender to Welsh speaking zealots who would take the country over. The anti campaign made for some strange bedfellows: including Neil Kinnock and Enoch Powell. Kinnock's attitude towards devolution echoed the opposition of Bevan, and was not a million miles from the 'unionism' of Powell. For Kinnock, devolution was dangerous and had to be opposed because it made for a weaker working class. Speaking in the House of Commons in 1975 he had argued for a 'unionist' (sic) position, since a 'single nation and a single economic unit' was the best way to 'emancipate' (sic) the class which he represented.[19] It was an argument which played well four years later. At the same time, many local politicians in Wales were against the proposals because they saw a new all Wales body as a threat to the position of local government. The result was confusion, and as John Osmond notes, voters were right so to be:

> Though the official line of the government and the Party in Wales was in favour of the Assembly, neither mounted an effective campaign. The government did not even distribute a leaflet explaining its policy … Moreover, a large proportion of the party's activists, from MPs downward, were actively campaigning against. Of the 23 Welsh Labour MPs at the time, 12 supported the Assembly, but no more than six of these were at all effective in the campaign … After the result was declared, a leader of the all party 'Wales for the Assembly Campaign' … Dai Francis, a Communist and former secretary to the South Wales Miners, accused the Labour Party of 'organised sabotage'.[20]

The 1979 referendum saw the proposal for a Welsh Assembly defeated by four to one. Undoubtedly, there were many reasons why the vote went this way, not the least of which was that when it took place the Labour government was very unpopular, the country was in a mess and in such conditions of uncertainty and division of the Labour Party itself on the issue, a referendum on devolution was almost doomed to the start. If the referendum had been held earlier, the vote may have been somewhat different. Even so, the referendum clearly showed that there was a very weak linkage between a growing sense of *cultural* identity and difference and *political* identity and aspiration, especially when compared to the Scottish vote which showed a majority of favour amongst those who voted.

The sense of gloom was evident in the soul searching which went on in the months and the years following the result. For many it signalled the end of Welsh history, and the nail in the coffin of Welsh identity. To confirm their worst fears the general election result of 1979 gave the Conservatives the largest number of seats in Wales since 1874 – 11. Wales, it appeared was doing the unthinkable: it was turning blue. For some, like Gwyn A. Williams, the referendum result and the implementation of the Conservatives' economic policy represented a low point, if not the end game, of the history of the Welsh people. He grimly concluded that:

> Some kind of human society, though God knows what kind, will no doubt go on occupying these two western peninsulas of Britain, but that people, who are my people and no mean people, who have for a millennium and a half lived in them as Welsh people, are nothing but a naked people under an acid rain.[21]

And yet, others were more hopeful. Whereas Gwyn Williams saw acid rain falling, Kenneth Morgan bravely entitled his history of modern Wales as the *Rebirth of a Nation*! Pointing to the success in Wales maintaining its cultural identity, and the growth of national institutions – even under the Conservatives – Morgan concluded that the story of Wales in the last hundred years has been that of a country which had survived.

> Amidst the cataract of evidence that illustrated British national decline, the Welsh might reflect that their social culture, still flourishing in its many forms form the hill farms of Gwynedd to the steel-works of Gwent, remained a living, distinctive part of the evolution of the British and European world. That culture had survived and had been triumphantly renewed, against all the odds.[22]

Indicative of this surviving against the odds was the fact that no sooner had the Conservatives come to power than the government announced that it would not be going forward with plans to establish a Welsh language TV station. This provoked considerable reaction, not the least of which was the announcement by Gwynfor Evans, a former president of Plaid Cymru, to fast until death unless the government changed its mind. It did, and the channel was launched in November 1982. The shift towards the Conservatives continued, nevertheless, and in the general election of 1983 the Conservatives increased their number of MPs in Wales to 14. However, by 1987 the Conservatives were once again back into single figures (eight) and this fell to six in 1992. In 1997 the Conservative share of the vote slumped to an all time low (20 per cent) – they failed to win one seat in Wales.

Cultural Thinning and Institutional Thickening

In the 1980s it looked as if Wales was becoming far more like England: it was voting for the Conservative Party; and it was becoming more cosmopolitan and more English. Data in 1981 revealed that 17 per cent of the population of Wales was composed of English immigrants. As Giggs and Pattie observe, 18 of the 37 districts in Wales had non-Welsh born populations in excess of 20 per cent, making Wales the most pluralistic part of the UK: in English local government districts only 28 out of 364 areas had foreign-born populations in excess of 20 per cent; in Scotland and Northern Ireland each had only one district where the foreign-born population was higher than 20 per cent.[23] In addition to this, the percentage of the population speaking Welsh had fallen to 19 per cent. By this time the impact of English settlement on Welsh speaking rural areas was further eroding the cultural distinctiveness of the rural heartlands, and adding greatly to the support for the Conservative Party in areas of Wales not known for their attachment to the Tories.[24] In the Thatcher years the industrial heartland of Wales was also to be devastated, as the old industries were dramatically reduced in scale, and in the case of the mining industry all but wiped out. By the 1980s over 96,000 jobs were lost in the coal mining and steel industries alone. In little under a decade Wales went from having an economy largely based on extractive industries to being increasingly a service and manufacturing economy. In large part this has been due to the success of Wales in attracting considerable overseas investment. During this period, however, Wales become not only the land of the rising yen, but the land of the growing quango.

Despite the 'thinning' of Wales in cultural terms, the 1980s also witnessed a *thickening* of the institutional fabric of the country. Under the Conservatives the number of quangos grew dramatically. Indeed, it was this rule by quango and the consequent democratic deficit which was to feature heavily in the subsequent referendum campaign in 1997. The number of executive bodies reporting to the Secretary of State grew to 19, spending over 800 million pounds by the close of the Conservative administration. In addition to this there were a similar number of advisory bodies, as well as tribunals of inquiry and NHS bodies. The significance of this growing network of governance in Wales cannot be underestimated.

The process of institutionalisation in Wales has been slow, when comparison is made with Ireland and Scotland. The result has been that the focus of identity has tended to be directed towards the language, which has proved to be a source of conflict, and towards common traditions which provide unifying national symbols. Sport, for instance, is one of the few areas where Wales can appear on an international stage as a distinct nation. But in so many ways this has served as a substitute for institutional development. As Laura Mcallister notes:

> We in Wales show a lack of unity as a national people in virtually everything other than sport ... sport is an essential element in the composition of most national identities world-wide. In the case of Wales and its history, sport has consistently assumed a proud and special role in our understanding and presentation of Welsh nationhood. Nations like Wales, which lack independent political status, can be seen to have elevated other elements in the equation of national identity as a means of compensation. Wales's dilemma is encapsulated in our enthusiasm for our national sports stars and our general ambivalence to the quest for political and administrative roles to rationalise and protect this sporting independence.[25]

For the greater part of the nineteenth century Wales was practically nonexistent in institutional terms. However, cultural institutions have had an absolutely crucial role in fostering and preserving a sense of national identity. This process of institution building began in 1872 with the creation of the University College of Wales, Aberystwyth and in 1881 with the establishment of a National Eisteddfod and the Welsh Rugby Union. The University of Wales was formed in 1893 and in 1889 the Welsh Intermediate Education Act made special provision for Welsh education. In 1896 a Central Welsh Board was created. This was followed by a Welsh Department of the Board of Education, and the founding of the National Museum, and the National Library in 1907. The dis-establishment of the Anglican Church led to the Church in Wales in 1920. An important youth movement was created in 1922, *Urdd Gobaith Cymru* (The Welsh League of Youth) and in 1937 the Welsh Region of the BBC was created. However, little else was to happen until after the Second World War.

As we noted earlier, the Labour government created the Welsh Regional Hospital Board in 1946, the Wales Gas Board and the Council for Wales and Monmouthshire in 1948. In 1946 the Welsh National Opera was founded. The company started life as an amateur organisation, but grew rapidly to become, by the 1970s, a truly world class opera company. Equally successful in international terms was the Llangollen International Eisteddfod, which began in 1947. This has provided not only a national institution, but one in which Wales can interact with other countries and thereby secure a wider international recognition. The BBC National Orchestra of Wales (NOW) has similarly provided Wales with a symphony orchestra of international repute. In 1967 the Welsh Arts Council was set up and in 1972 the Sports Council for Wales. In political terms the 1960s was important for the creation of the Welsh Grand Committee in the House of Commons (1960) and the Welsh Office in 1964. Following this other public bodies were established: the Welsh Arts Council in 1967; the Wales Tourist Board in 1969 and the Sports Council for Wales in 1971. In the mid-seventies (1975) a Welsh Consumer Council and the Land Authority for Wales was set up. In 1976 a Welsh Development Authority was created. Since the 1960s and 1970s this process of creating national institutions has continued apace. Indeed, under the Conservatives – a party long hostile to devolution – the process actually accelerated. In the 1980s the Welsh office expanded in both the range of responsibilities and the number of personnel, and the number of non-departmental public bodies just grew and grew.

Along with this institutionalisation and administrative integration of Wales has been the formation, for the first time in many centuries, of a Welsh elite *in* Wales and increasingly centred around Cardiff. What we witnessed in the 1997 referendum was, in so many ways, a certain unease with this process: it is very difficult to cheer for the formation of an elite, even if it is your *own* elite, especially when you have a political culture rooted in a dislike of hierarchy and centralism. The 'No' campaign made much of this aspect of devolution by claiming that it would create yet another tier of politicians, jobs for the boyos and reinforce the power of Welsh speakers.

The institutions created in the nineteenth century were not designed to provide for a nation as a whole, but for bits of it. These bits have become increasingly unrepresentative of the majority of people who live in Wales today, but do not see themselves as being part of the Welsh Wales idea of the country. As Gwyn. A.Williams argues:

> In practical terms, most of the institutions of Welsh education which are regarded as central to Welsh identity have been situated within and in response to, regions and ideologies remote physically and ideally from the regions in which the majority of the Welsh lived and had their being. In this serious imbalance, a majority of the Welsh have never been possessed by or entered into possession of , 'their own' national institutions.[26]

What the referendum of 1997 showed was that there is some way to go before a greater majority feel as if they have entered into possession of their national institutions. However, the fact that the new institutions are now more suited to the life of the nation as a whole, demonstrates that institutional attachment or possession is evolving. Consider, for example, the fact that for a long time the 'land of song' lacked any real national institution to give voice (literally) to the myth of being a musical nation for all of the people and not just those who go to the National Eisteddfod. The WNO now performs all over Wales and the world and provides a major national focal point for an important part of the cultural tradition. Again, the fact that one of the most prestigious singing competitions in the world (Cardiff Singer of the World) directs the attention of Wales and the world on the capital gives national direction to an activity which is a significant part of Welsh life. The Wales Millennium Centre, due to be built in Cardiff to celebrate the millennium, will also serve to provide a focus for the nation's performing arts and enable Wales to develop a centre which can serve the whole of Wales as well as enhancing the capital status of the city in a European context. As Geraint Talfan Davies argues, given the fact that the population of Wales is dispersed into small communities, the performing arts (a field where Wales has some strength) really requires a national institution which can create a sense of national purpose:

> That is why a country of small communities also needs a capital and foundation of larger arts organisations. If they are to thrive those organisations need proper facilities, a secure base and audiences large enough to secure viability. That is why the Wales Millennium Centre is a crucial building block in arts provision throughout Wales, and not simply the filler of an important hole in Cardiff Bay's grand plan.[27]

As Wales continues to develop an institutional network we may expect this process to impact on how identity is constructed. This is especially the case when we consider that alongside the process of institutional development the economy of Wales was being internationalised. During the 1980s inward investment from abroad rose to represent 35 per cent of total industrial investment. From 1986 Wales attracted an enormous 20 per cent of inward investment into the UK. All of this means that Wales is now in a very different relationship to the world in the 1990s than in the 1950s or 1960s when the economic relationship with England was dominant. Modern Wales is a country which is very much plugged into a global – rather than a purely *British* economic order.

By 1997, therefore, Wales had acquired what it manifestly lacked throughout its history: an extensive institutional network which could serve to frame and focus national identity in political, social, cultural and economic terms. This process of institutional thickening has to be seen in the context of the 'thinning' of Welsh cultural identity through in-migration, falls in the number of Welsh speakers and the decline and destruction of rural and industrial communities. A good illustration of this is the institutionalisation of the Welsh language. In 1994 the Welsh Language Board (WLB) was established to take, for the first time, a 'national' approach to the language as a whole in the life of the country. (A Welsh Language Board was set up in 1988, but its role was purely that to advise the Secretary of State.) Under the Welsh Language Acts, especially that of 1993, Welsh is more firmly embedded into all aspects of the governance of Wales than at any time in history. Thus, in place of the decentralised and localised policy which characterised the approach to the language issue in the past, Wales now has a far more top-down strategy. The implications of this are profound. In planning, for example, local authorities are increasingly building into their development plans the issue of how given developments will impact on the language. This process was initiated by a Welsh Office circular in 1988 which gave guidance on the formulation of local planning in relation to the Welsh language. However, despite the advice of the WLB to make such linguistic considerations a duty for local government, the Conservative governments' 1993 Act makes no reference to planning and the language. Nevertheless, in 1995 in a draft of the Planning Guidance (Wales): Unitary Development Plans in Wales, local authorities were reminded of the provisions of the 1993 Act which stresses how there must be equality between English and Welsh in the conduct of all public business. This pattern of institutionalisation now extends to many, if not all, aspects of policy making in Wales. Whereas in the 1950s it would have been quite inappropriate to talk about the 'government' of Wales, by the 1990s it is evident that structures and organisations had come into existence which provided venues for policy making and decision making in a 'national' setting. It is ironic that this has taken place less as the result of political nationalism than as a consequence of Conservative new public management.

The 1997 Referendum and its Aftermath

It is important to place the referendum on devolution which took place in 1997 in the context of the process of institutionalisation (and internation-alisation) which had accelerated under the Tories. The Labour government's case for the National Assembly was to make much of the argument that their proposals formed part of an evolutionary process. The White Paper noted:

The establishment of the Welsh Department of the Board of Education in 1907 marked the beginning of administrative devolution in Wales, which gathered pace in the 1960s when the Welsh Office was established with responsibility for local government, housing, and roads. More responsibilities have been added over time ... so that now the Secretary of State for Wales has responsibility for a wide range of public services in Wales ... The services are run directly by the Welsh Office and indirectly through local authorities, health authorities and NHS trusts, and unelected bodies (quangos) like the Welsh Development Authority (WDA), the Further and Higher Education Funding Councils and *Tai Cymru*. Of these, only local authorities are directly accountable to the people of Wales. It is to address this democratic deficit that the Government is now proposing to set up an Assembly for Wales.[28]

Although what was on offer was quite a modest increase in devolved power, especially when compared with the Scottish parliament, in many ways it represented the most significant event in Welsh history since the annexation of the country in 1536. The referendum campaign, and the result itself, provided a fascinating insight into the relationship between cultural and political identity. Above all, the referendum and its aftermath showed that the idea of political identity in Wales remains problematic. The 'No' campaign articulated an idea of Wales as having a distinctive culturally identity, but having no need for a political identity. Significantly, for example, one of the most prominent in the 'No' campaign was a Welsh speaker, one Dr Tim Williams. The argument from the 'No' side was that Wales has done very nicely out of being annexed to England and that devolution – of any kind – would do great injury to Wales. This was a very high level British-Welsh position. The 'No' campaign further exploited the regional divisions in Wales by suggesting that not only would Wales lose out if the Assembly went through, but that different parts of Wales would lose out to one another. The north would be dominated by the south, and the Welsh speaking North would have a disproportionate influence over non-Welsh speakers. Thus the 'No' campaign maintained that if Wales voted for a costly Assembly, Wales would fall apart in regional rivalry, the position of Wales in the UK would be weakened, and money that could have gone to schools and hospitals would go to pay for more bureaucrats and politicians. Wales, it argued, did not need a distinct *political* identity if it was to survive and thrive. The 'Yes' campaign was broader based and better organised than during the 1979 referendum. The key theme of the campaign was the democratic deficit and the need to develop an institution which could enable the governance of Wales to be more coherent and more accountable. This provided for a much wider spectrum of support than devolution attracted in the 1970s. The Association of Welsh County Councils, for instance, backed the assembly, whereas in 1979 the counties had been opposed to devolution. So whereas in the 1970s devolution had been a response to nationalist pressure, in the 1990s devolution in Wales was driven by a growing sense of discontent with institutional arrangements.

On the eve of the vote the *Western Mail* published two pages of readers' letters to represent the spread of opinion in Wales. Typical British-Welsh arguments ran thus: 'be proud of being British and so proud of being Welsh – as I am. A Welsh Assembly can attract only one vote from Welsh people with common sense and that is a big NO.'[29] Amongst the older generation, memories of the War were often important forms of attachment to Britishness:

> I am proud to have been born in Wales, to live here and to have the maiden name of Jones. When I served in the ATS from 1941 to 1946 I was not 'doing my bit' just for Wales but for the United Kingdom and my King ... I shall vote No and as a Welsh woman and loyal British subject, be proud to do so.[30]

The fear of the language issue figured prominently in the 'No' arguments: 'Every Welsh nationalist will vote YES. They will see it as a step in their drive towards independence. The ability to speak Welsh will be a requirement for jobs and homes.'[31] The 'Yes' campaign had to deal with these kinds of arguments about the threat to the British nature of Welsh identity if the 'Yes' vote won. One letter captures this well as it reflects on a day's campaigning:

> An English woman asked if we would be removing our flag from the Union Jack – I had to tell her we are not represented on the Union Jack. A man came to the stall and said he'd just been talking to two women from the 'No' campaign – he asked them what would happen if Wales had a 'Yes' result, and I quote, 'It will be like Bosnia!' ... Someone brought us a copy of a 'No' leaflet being passed around – it stated that 'North Wales would be under the thumb of South Wales' ... As I was leaving , a Welsh speaking woman came up to me and said, 'You will force everyone to speak Welsh. My husband does not speak Welsh.'[32]

Against this view were the voices of Welsh learners, a sign that the language has its supporters as well as its critics. The 'No' campaign was also attacked for using 'racist' arguments to justify the British-Welsh position. A letter which brought these two together came from an English family living in Wales who felt dismayed by the attack made by a prominent 'No' campaigner (Carys Pugh) on one of Labour's Welsh Office team, Mr Peter Hain, for being born in South Africa:

> Both my wife and I were born in England ... According to Carys Pugh we, not
> being Welsh born should have no right to vote or even express our views ...
> Having lived here for the past 48 years ... I think Carys Pugh's views are an
> outrage. Both my wife and I are Welsh learners and have produced three Welsh
> – born children , all grown up and fully fluent Welsh speakers ... It may annoy
> Carys Pugh greatly, but both my wife and I intend to vote 'Yes'.[33]

In the event, the result in the early hours of 19 September was a very
close-run thing. The turnout was lower than expected (50.3 per cent) and the
majority in favour of the Assembly was 0.6 per cent: a majority of fewer than
7,000 votes.

In some senses the vote confirmed the theory that Welsh identity may be
understood in terms of the 'three Wales' model: support for the Assembly was
highest in the Welsh speaking heartland (*Y Fro Cymraeg*) and the old mining
areas (Welsh Wales) than in the more British Wales of the southeast and
Pembrokeshire. However, as Denis Balsom argues, it is simplistic to dwell on
the low level of support that the Assembly attracted. First of all the change in
opinion from 1979 was quite dramatic when only 20 per cent supported the
then proposals. This swing of plus 15 per cent in favour of devolution compares
well with the plus 11 per cent swing in Scotland and was in line with the
steady support for an assembly which has taken place in the intervening years.
Thus although the result was not as apparently dramatic as that in Scotland,
the Welsh result in many ways represents a major sea change in Wales. Balsom
makes the point that:

> It is the nature of the 'Yes' vote which is important. The referendum demonstrated
> an almost unique alliance between Welsh speaking Wales and the traditional
> industrial heartland of Southern Wales. The linguistic divide was bridged by a
> common sense of Welsh identity and purpose ... The pattern of the referendum
> results ... suggests that a sense of Welsh identity remains the unifying factor of
> modern Wales. Far from being divisive, a sense of Welshness, irrespective of
> language can be inclusive and it is the creation of institutions, such as the
> Assembly, which will help engender such a conscious self image and, in time, a
> self-confidence.[34]

At first many commentators dwelt on the divisive aspects of the result
and focused on the 'three Wales'. But this interpretation has to be considered
alongside ongoing research into what the result tells us about Welsh identity
in the late twentieth century. Paul O'Leary has argued that the map of Wales
as being territorially divided is 'wildly inaccurate'. It was, he maintains, not a
question of an east-west divide:

A full 39.3 per cent of 'Yes' votes were cast in the so-called 'No' districts, revealing a much less polarised Wales than reports have suggested hitherto. There can be no question that support for devolution varied from one part of Wales to another. Nevertheless, nearly twice as many votes were cast in favour of devolution in Powys as were garnered in Merthyr Tydfil, yet Powys is shown on the map as a homogeneous 'No' area. In fact, each one of the so-called 'No' areas of Conwy, Wrexham, Pembrokeshire and Powys had larger 'Yes' votes than any of the so-called 'Yes' areas of Merthyr, Blaenau Gwent, Anglesey and Credigion, and it was votes, not districts that counted. In this context, it is as logical to say that it was Monmouthshire (with its 10,592 'Yes' votes) which tipped the balance, as it is to say that the honour belongs to Carmarthenshire. This is not to say that the closeness of the vote ... but the key divisions were not territorial.[35]

The author points out that the result needs explanations other than that simply of the east-west split. Not the least of these, of course are social class differences in a sense of community and in organisational effectiveness. Another factor is that of age: it may be that older voters felt more attached to British-Welshness than did the younger voters. O'Leary's conclusion that we must see the referendum as not so much as a 'confirmation of old and entrenched attitudes so much as a snapshot of an electorate whose attitudes are in flux', seems a sound judgment to make prior to the publication of more detailed research on the result.

Wales in the World

In the past the big nation state was, apparently, the way to go if you wanted economic and political power. As we contemplate the world in the late twentieth century this allure of bigness ain't what it used to be. As Leopold Kohr long ago pointed out,[36] there is much to be said for being small. And there are *more* smaller countries around the Welsh size (three million) now than ever before: 87 countries have populations of under five million, and 58 have under 2.5 million. As the *Economist* argued in commenting on research which casts doubts on the economics of bigness:

Countries with big populations are often politically powerful, but they are not often so prosperous. A glance at a league table of GDP per head reveals a striking shortage of very large countries, and even a middling-large ones, among the names at the top ... littleness is no barrier to wealth: in purchasing-power terms, Luxembourg (population 400,000) has the highest GDP per head. 'Look at

Singapore', says Kenichi Ohmae, a Japanese management guru, who wrote *The Borderless World* ...'Three million people without their own food or water, have grown from a per capita GDP of $1, 000 at independence to $24,000 today ...What matters is leadership and vision.' Even if large size is not actually a handicap, it brings fewer benefits than it once did ... Mr Ohmae is promoting the concept of the doshu republic: a do is a regional unit the size of Kyushu or Hokkaido. 'I want to divide Japan into 11 regions, reducing the role of central government to diplomacy, central banking and co-ordination' ... Elsewhere separatists will take hope. In the past, they rarely thought much about the economic consequences of opting for independence. Now, as their supporters grow richer, they are likelier to vote from the pocket rather than the heart. But today the costs of going it alone are probably smaller than they have been for at least the past couple of centuries.[37]

In which case, as the benefits of being part of a big nation state become more questionable than in the nineteenth century, it is not too far-fetched to maintain that the conditions for devolution and self-government may be getting better: small may indeed become 'beautiful' in the twenty-first century. For a long time one of the main cases against making the linkage between Welsh political identity and cultural identity was that Wales was too small. As this assertion becomes less defensible the impact on how the Welsh see their identity may undergo a significant shift. Again, the context for this has to be institutional: in the EU of the future the role of nation states may become very different to what they have been in the past. Much may be gained by being a well structured region connected into the network of EU institutional processes.[38] If so, then a strong sense of regional identity may be central to the success of Wales in a EU setting. It may pay Wales to be less attached to England and 'Britain' and more able to deploy its sense of identity to maximise its economic advantage. National identity as embodied in Welsh institutions may come to be seen as a powerful resource to be mobilised in the new institutional game of Europe. Taking an institutionalist stance one could posit that, as people in Wales perceive that they can better maximise their interests by redefining and reconstructing their identity, this implies a different kind of strategy than that which was devised in the past.

What was a weakness in this setting, the 'curse' of the Welsh language may now become a blessing. Wales could argue that, in common with a third of the world, it understands what the decline in a language means.[39] It is thereby far better placed in relation to other European (and non-European) countries and historic nations who feel threatened by the spread of Anglo-American culture. The Welsh experience of bilingualism and of the politics of linguistic imperialism may play well in a world in which there is a backlash against the homogenisation of cultures. As Alan Burge argues, this dimension of the Welsh experience endows Wales with a potentiality to relate to a great part of the planet in terms very different to the British state:

> Recent visitors from Guatemala and Africa have found affinity in the Welsh experience as they seek to grapple to overcome being a linguistically and culturally disenfranchised majority in their own country. The nature of Wales today can be a source of learning for many countries trying to come to terms with more than one language and culture within a national boundary.[40]

Wales therefore at the close of the twentieth century is a country in search of itself. One could argue, of course, that this is perhaps a more widespread condition of *la vie postmoderne*, but Wales has been at it for as long as it has existed. As Raymond Williams noted:

> Many of the things that happened, over the centuries to the Welsh are happening, in decades, to the English. The consequent confusion and struggle for identity, the search for new modes of effective autonomy within a powerfully extended and profoundly interacting para-national political and economic system, are now in many parts of the world the central issues of social consciousness, struggling to come through against powerful but residual ideas and institutions ... the flow of contemporary politics is going beyond the modes of all the incorporated ideologies and institutions. The Welsh, of course, have been inside these cross pressures for much longer than the English. And as a result we have had to learn that we need to solve the real contradictions between nationality and class, and between local well being and the imperatives of large-scale systems. Consequently, we may be further along the road to a relevant if inevitably painful contemporary consciousness.[41]

The condition of Wales at the close of the century can now be seen as having a far more global relevance than in the days of Empire. The Welsh experience, as Simon Gikandi has argued, finds a resonance with many other countries who share the culture of colonialism. Writing of Raymond Williams, for example, he notes that:

> Williams is, of course, an important figure in postcolonial cultural discourse not only because he occupies what Radhakrishnan has aptly defined as a subject position that is 'both oppositional-marginal and dominant-central' but also because his experiences mirror those of colonised intellectuals in uncanny ways ... Williams's intellectual journey from the border country of Wales to the

metropolitan centre mirrors the experiences of postcolonial intellectuals moving from colonial periphery to the heart of empire. And in spite of his well-known concern with ideals of community and unifying structures of experience, Williams has been one of the most articulate voices for the perennial condition ... of cultural liminality. Williams's cultural biography begins, importantly and inescapably, at the colonial vanishing point, the juncture at which traditional culture and the mother tongue are lost.[42]

In order to discover himself Williams had, says Gikandi, to pass through the 'eye of Englishness'[43] so as to recapture and reconstruct his own identity as a 'Welsh-European'. Locating this search for Welsh identity in the context of a world composed of many other countries and peoples embarked on a similar journey, imbues the question of what does Wales mean with an international dimension that echoes the search for identity going on in so many parts of the planet. One could argue that the Welsh-British identity was forged for reasons of self-interest. It was obvious to the Welsh that they had much to gain by throwing in their lot with the English as being part of a powerful Britain seemed to offer a great deal more than being little Wales. Furthermore, as Colley has shown, war and rumours of war were potent ways to get the Welsh (and the Scots) to rally around the union flag. Britishness, she argues, was forged by war:

> Time and time again, war with France brought Britons, whether they hailed from Wales or Scotland or England, into confrontation with an obviously hostile Other and encouraged them to define themselves collectively against it ... And increasingly as the wars went on, they defined themselves in contrast to the colonial peoples they conquered, peoples who were manifestly alien in terms of culture, religion and colour.[44]

In the two world wars Wales was bound closer to English Britishness, but as the 'manifestly hostile Other' has become less manifest and less Other, the force of defining a British identity by reference to those who are not 'us', or in terms of those who are against 'us', is weakened.

Conclusion: Constructing a Contemporary Consciousness

The history of Wales in the postwar era, and especially in the so-called 'Thatcher years', may be said to illustrate how, what Raymond Williams called, a sense of contemporary consciousness, is being formed – and very painfully too. The 1997 referendum caused much division. It pushed to the surface many of the fears which underpin the problem of identity amongst the Welsh. It showed the tension between north and south, between the English speakers and the Welsh speakers, and between those who see themselves as having an essentially British political identity and those who define themselves in less unionist terms. But, as Raymond Williams argued, such painful conflict may be necessary if a sense of an identity which is relevant to the present and the future is to be forged. Lacking institutions in which Welsh people could actually have a dialogue about who they are and what they can become, in so many ways has been responsible for the kind of divisions which came out in the referendums of 1979 and 1997. What has so often been manifest in Welsh history is a lack of trust between the different parts of the country: a seemingly inevitable consequence of a lack of political institutions through which trust could be built and enlarged. Thus even after the referendum the (bitter) arguments were to continue with the fierce argument over where the assembly should be sited. The debate on the siting of the assembly was to bring out the regional tensions between north and south, east and west and the old rivalry between Swansea and Cardiff. The National Assembly, to be based in Cardiff, however, will create a place where, for the very first time, people from all parts of the country will be able to come together and engage in an exploration of what Welsh identity means in the context of practical policy making. For the majority of non-Welsh speakers, the issue of the language will have to be explored, and for the Welsh speakers, the issue of an identity which is not rooted in the possession of a language will also have to be discussed. After all, it is not the fact that people who speak Welsh have a strong sense of identity, it is the fact that so many people (the 80 per cent) who do *not* speak the language, consider themselves to be Welsh. This is not to downplay the value of the language, but it is to argue that the new politics which will emerge after the National Assembly will have to find ways of balancing the demands of an essentially multifaceted and very pluralistic identity. In cultural terms it means that the contribution of the Eisteddfod must be seen alongside the contribution of 'American Wales'. And why not? It also means that TV, film, literature and music should reflect what Wales is now, and what Wales could be, rather than dwell on the loss of the Wales of the past and a Wales that never was anyway. The success of rock groups such as Super Furry Animals, Catatonia, Manic Street Preachers and Stereophonics, for instance, illustrate that it is possible to explore and represent Welsh identity through the medium of Anglo-American culture in a lively and accessible form. This may be uncomfortable, if not unacceptable, for some.

Of course, to those who hold the views of someone such as R.S. Thomas, that there is no middle way between a Welsh-speaking identity and a non-Welsh-speaking identity, it may be that the balancing of Wales and *Cymru* may result in considerable tension. But out of this creative conflict a new kind of Wales and a new kind of identity may emerge. It may well be that, as the people of Wales develop more of an institutional life and construct a sense of identity less linguistically structured than in the past, the role of the language in politics will become less central to the definition of identity. The coming of a National Assembly offers the possibility that a national political agenda may develop which is more institutionally driven and is more on a par with the experience of Scotland and Ireland. However, given the strength of the Welsh language it is probable that linguistic divisions will continue to be a key feature of Welsh politics for the foreseeable future. Five hundred thousand Welsh speakers is a sizeable and significant minority population, in British and European terms, despite the decline in the language.

The case of Ireland is instructive on this point, for the country's membership of the European Union has undoubtedly enabled the notion of Irish identity to grow and develop as it becomes a full and active participant in international affairs. Clearly, the identity of a small nation such as Wales is structured by how it relates to other nations, and thence to how it views and perceives itself in the world. Hence, as Christopher Harvie points out, there is a paradox in recent Welsh history:

> ... that while the while the traditional markers of Welsh distinctiveness – the indigenous nature of the population, language, religion – have been either in decline or struggling to hold their own, the international distinctiveness of the nation has increased ... Many more would now follow Raymond Williams in describing themselves as Welsh Europeans, than, say, twenty-five years ago.[45]

In which case, the notion of Welsh identity may in time be reshaped by the European project. This is especially the case when the imperative of defining Britishness in response to threat declines and as the pressure to redefine Britishness in terms of a multi-cultural society increases.

The problem of Welsh identity is also, of course, related to, and in so many ways intertwined with, the conundrum Englishness. For so long Britishness has been, as R.S. Thomas has argued, little more than a convenient mask worn by the English.[46] British history, culture, language, politics, and institutions are English, more than they are 'British'. As Katie Gramich comments, the English ignorance of Wales is 'startling' considering how close the two countries are to one another. She calls for British studies courses in English schools so that English schoolchildren could have the opportunity of learning about the Welsh and the Welsh language, as well as the other Celtic countries. This might be viewed as a something of a fantasy, but 'its realisation would perhaps entail the recreation and redefinition of 'Britain' as a cultural and political entity'.[47] The history of the Welsh is a central part of the story of England and the neglect of Welsh culture in English schools, and in the English dominated media needs to be addressed if Britishness can be reconstructed. And this is, of course, a big if. In so many ways the English have dominated the concept of Britishness, and rendered as second class the place of non-English, British culture. If the English could *reinvent Englishness* as something which exists in a multinational context then the prospects for the Welsh being able to come to a fuller sense of their identity may look more promising than for many generations. This is especially the case for the large number of English immigrants now living in Wales who must become more sensitive to the fact that they are living in a different country and must show respect for the culture and traditions of their host communities.

Perhaps, to use Gikandi's words, it is necessary for the English to boldly go into the 'eye of Englishness' if the question of the identity of the Celtic peoples (including the British-Irish) of Britain and Ireland is to be satisfactorily resolved. The idea of a British-Irish Council, as put forward by the April 1998 Northern Ireland agreement, points towards the creation of an institution in which the Celts and the English can finally get together and explore the relationship between the several countries which comprise our two islands. If we are to reinvent and rethink our identities we need new institutions. Whatever the results of this process will be, the importance for Wales will be immense. So it may be, as the historian David Jones expresses it, that: 'the nation in its fullness is yet to be'.[48] After all:

> The Welsh survived all the crises of their history, remaking their nation time and time again. As Wales seems to experience recurrent death and rebirth, it would almost seem as if the history of the nation is an endless journey back and fore between the mortuary and the delivery room.[49]

Perhaps, the identity of the Welsh may not be lost, as R.S Thomas pessimistically thought, so much as, like the red dragon itself, 'Wales' and '*Cymru*' have never really been found. Perhaps, as the institutions thicken we may find that a sense of Welsh identity will change and prompt a different kind of search. And a final perhaps: perhaps what we can learn from the Welsh experience is that identity is not something which can actually be 'found' or mislaid, but it is rather the object of continuing invention and construction and is consequently the subject of an unending quest. It is when a people stop looking, they have really lost it. And the Welsh are still looking.

Notes

1   R.S. Thomas, 'The Lost' in *No Truce with the Furies*, Newcastle-upon-Tyne, Bloodaxe Books, 1995. Reproduced with permission of the publisher.

2   Book VIII, 'Book of Taliessen' in J. Matthews (ed.), *The Celtic Reader*, Thorson, HarperCollins, London 1995, p. 218.

3   Catatonia, *International Velvet*, Blanco y Negro: 3984 20834 2.

4   For an account of the history of the red dragon see D.J. Davies, *Towards Welsh Freedom*, Cardiff, Plaid Cymru, 1958, pp. 175–183.

5   M. Bruce-Mitford, *The Illustrated Book of Signs and Symbols*, London, Dorling Kindersley, 1996, p. 30.

6   A charming version of this story is recounted in W. Jenkyn Thomas's *The Welsh Fairy Book*, Cardiff, University of Wales Press, 1995, pp. 66–70.

7   A. Zimmern, *My Impressions of Wales*, London, 1921.

8   See D. Balsom, P.J. Madgwick and D. Van Mechelen, 'The Red and Green: Patterns of Partisan Choice in Wales', *British Journal of Political Science*, 13, 1983; D. Balsom, P.J. Madgwick and D. Van Mechelen, 'The Political Consequences of Welsh Identity', *Ethnic and Racial Studies*, 7, 1984; and D. Balsom, 'The three Wales model: the political sociology of Welsh identity, recent electoral trends, pressures for change' in J. Osmond (ed.), *The National Question Again*, Llandysul, Gomer Press, 1985.

9   J. Davies, *A History of Wales*, Harmondsworth, Penguin, 1994, p. 275.

10 J.G. Jones, *The History of Wales*, Cardiff, University of Wales Press, 1990.

11 L. Colley, *Britons: Forging the Nation 1707–1837*, New Haven, Yale University Press, 1992, p. 378.

12 Cited in T. Jones, *The Desire of Nations*, Llandybie, Christopher Davies, 1974, p. 134.

13 G. Evans, *Land of My Fathers: 2000 years of Welsh History*, John Penry, Swansea, 1974, p. 411.

14 Davies, op. cit., p. 385.

15 K.O. Morgan, 'Tom Ellis versus Lloyd George: the fractured consciousness of fin-de-siècle Wales' in G.H. Jenkins and J.B. Smith (eds), *Politics and Society in Wales, 1840–1922*, Cardiff, University of Wales Press, 1988.

16 See W. Parsons, *The Political Economy of British Regional Policy*, London, Routledge, 1988.

17 C. Hague and H. Thomas, 'Planning Capital Cities: Edinburgh and Cardiff compared' in R. Macdonald and H. Thomas (eds), *Nationality and Planning in Scotland and Wales*, Cardiff, University of Wales Press, 1997.

18 'Cymdeithas yr Iaith Cymraeg, Maniffesto', translated by H. Webb, *Planet*, No 26/27, Winter 1974/75, pp. 84–5.

19 Neil Kinnock, cited in J. Osmond, 'Wales in the 1980s' in C.R. Foster (ed.), *Nations without a State: Ethnic Minorities in Western Europe*, New York, Praeger, 1980, p. 48.

20 J. Osmond, 'Introduction' in *The National Question Again*, op. cit., p. xxxvii.
21 Gwyn A. Williams, *When Was Wales? A History of the Welsh*, Harmondsworth, Penguin, 1991, p. 305.
22 K.O. Morgan, *Rebirth of a Nation: A History of Modern Wales*, London, Oxford University Press, 1981, pp. 420–1.
23 J. Giggs and C. Pattie, 'Wales as a Plural Society', *Contemporary Wales: An Annual Review of Economic and Social Research*, Vol. 6, 1992, pp. 25–63.
24 See D. Griffiths, 'The Political Consequences of Migration into Wales' in *Contemporary Wales*, ibid., pp. 77–8.
25 L. Mcallister, 'The Welsh Sporting Dilemma', *Agenda, Journal of the Institute of Welsh Affairs*, Summer, 1997, p. 46.
26 G.A.Williams, op. cit., p. 237.
27 G.T. Davies, 'Beyond the Millennium', *Agenda, The Journal of the Institute of Welsh Affairs*, Winter 1997/8, p. 4. See also *Bread and Roses – The case for the Millennium Centre for the Performing Arts in the Welsh Capital*, Institute for Welsh Affairs, Cardiff, 1996.
28 Cm 3718, *A Voice for Wales: The Government's Proposals for a Welsh Assembly*, HMSO, 1997, p. 7.
29 *Western Mail*, 17 September 1997.
30 Ibid.
31 Ibid.
32 Ibid.
33 Ibid.
34 D. Balsom, 'Assembly Poll Revealed Unity Amidst Diversity', *Agenda, The Journal of The Institute of Wales Affairs*, Winter 1997, p. 13.
35 P. O'Leary, 'Of Devolution, Maps and Divided Mentalities', *Planet: The Welsh Internationalist*, February/March 1998, pp. 7–12.
36 Leopold Kohr was something of a prophet for Wales in the 1970s and 1980s. He adopted Wales as his home for many years and applied his theories to the Welsh context in *Is Wales Viable*, Llandybie, Christopher Davies, 1971. In general see R. Benwick and P. Green (eds), *The Routledge Dictionary of Twentieth Century Political Thinkers*, London, Routledge, 1992, pp. 118–9.
37 *Economist*, 3–9 January 1998, pp. 63–5.
38 See J. Gray and J. Osmond, *Wales in Europe: The Opportunity Presented by a Welsh Assembly*, Institute for Welsh Affairs, and Welsh Centre for International Affairs, Cardiff 1997.
39 See, for example, *New Scientist*, 6 January 1996, pp. 24–7.
40 A. Burge, 'Beyond Europe', *Agenda: The Journal of the Institute of Welsh Affairs*, Winter 1997, p. 48.
41 R. Williams, 'Wales and England' in J. Osmond (ed.), *The National Question Again*, Llandysul, Gomer Press, 1985, pp. 29–30.
42 S. Gikandi, *Maps of Englishness: Writing Identity in the Culture of Colonialism*, New York, Columbia University Press, 1996, p. 42.
43 Ibid., p. 43.
44 Colley, op. cit., p. 5.
45 C. Harvie, 'Wales and the Wider World' in T. Herbert and G.E. Jones (eds), *Post-War Wales*, Cardiff, University of Wales Press, 1995, p. 164.

46   In S. Anstey (ed.), *R.S. Thomas, Selected Prose*, Bridgend, Seren Books, 1995, pp.143–58. On this tension between Wales and Cymru, see R.S. Thomas, *Cymru or Wales?*, Llandysul, Gomer Press, 1992. Thomas makes the point that there is, as far as he is concerned no middle way, no third alternative:

> We are familiar in life with the tyranny of 'either or'. There are certain combative people who try to corner us by asking: 'Which is it, yes or no; black or white?' It can also be the ploy of simplistic persons. 'Come on', they urge, 'it must be one or the other'; whereas the more astute people realise how many shades of grey there can be between black and white. Nevertheless, I chose my title because I cannot in this context see a third or fourth condition. *Cymru* or Wales: there is nothing between (p. 5).

47   K. Gramich, '*Cymru* or Wales? : explorations in a divided sensibility' in S. Bassnett (ed.), *Studying British Cultures*, London, Routledge, 1997, p. 109.
48   J. Davies, *A History of Wales*, Harmondsworth, Penguin, 1993, p. 686.
49   Ibid.

2 The Northern Irish Identity

KAREN TREW

> This is an exciting and questioning time when people are searching for a new way to express their identity ... What you'll find is that more and more people now are talking in terms of a 'Northern Ireland' identity rather than the old stale 'unionist' or 'nationalist' (Corrigan-Maguire, 1994).[1]

> I have no sense of myself as Protestant. I do though have some sense of Northern Irishness of which I am proud – Northern Irishness free of political and constitutional absolutes – Northern Irishness in the way that I had of Northern Englishness when I lived in Manchester (Glenn Patterson, 1995).[2]

The question of identity is seen to be central to academic debate about the conflict in Northern Ireland. Accounts of life in Northern Ireland, ranging from studies of history[3] and politics[4] to those of children's every day activities,[5] tend to include at least one chapter which relates the chosen topic to the development and maintenance of identity in the region. Questions of identity also have a prominent place in public discourse as individuals and their representatives seek to confirm their culture and identity in response to perceived threat.[6]

The conflict in Northern Ireland derives from many interrelated problems. Although there is assumed to be a religious dimension to the conflict it is not a 'holy war'. One way to encompass the complexity of the relationships between the majority of the population who are Protestant and the minority who are Catholic is to describe it as an ethnic conflict. Using a broad definition of the term 'ethnic' Darby argued: 'The ethnic definition is more suitable than other definitions which view it exclusively as a constitutional or religious conflict, or one based on economic, social or cultural inequalities. All of these are part of the problem but none can claim exclusive rights to define it.'[7]

The main advantage for researchers of using the Protestant/Catholic labels to distinguish two communities in Northern Ireland is that these terms seem to correspond to the fundamental reference groups for people living in the region. As the Very Rev. Dr Dunlop, a prominent Presbyterian church minister, indicated in one of a series of articles on identity in the regional evening newspaper: 'Many Protestants do not make a distinction between 'nationalists' 'republicans' and 'Catholics'. The word 'Catholic' serves as a catch-all word for someone who is not 'one of them'.[8] As this community leader recognises, although the Protestant and Catholic labels are denominational they are also assumed to reflect contrasting national identities and political allegiance between nationalist Irish Catholics and unionist British Protestants. He continued his analysis by noting that: 'If it was theology alone, or ecclesiology alone, or even politics alone, it could be dealt with rationally. But in this society these issues are all tied up together with the future of Northern Ireland, which makes the phenomenon complex.'[9]

The Northern Ireland problem is not just about identity. The rhetoric of sectarianism is clearly served by the identification of two clearly defined exclusive groups which are characterised by competing constitutional desires and identities. From the perspective of recent social psychological theories[10] such a scenario can be understood in terms of intergroup processes which serve to increase the divisions between groups and promote cohesiveness within groups. McGarry and O'Leary, who note there are major flaws in liberal readings of ethno-national conflicts which try to find external causes for societal dissensus, argue that: 'Such conflicts are better understood as socio-psychological, rooted in historically established collective identities and motivated by the desire to be governed by one's co-nationals, both for security and for collective freedom'.[11]

Although it is common in Northern Ireland to believe that there is a fault line between two apparently monolithic groups defined by religion, the extent to which dimensions of difference, such as political allegiance and national identity, actually coincide with religious group membership is an area which has attracted empirical research from a range of disciplines.[12] This chapter employs available survey evidence relating to national identity, in order to assess the diversity within the Catholic and Protestant communities in Northern Ireland and the extent to which there is overlap.

National Identities

Those people who were born in the geographical region known as Northern Ireland can legitimately describe themselves as British, because it is part of the United Kingdom and they are British citizens. They can also claim Irish citizenship as they live on the island of Ireland. It is possible to be a British citizen while maintaining an Irish identity in the same way as those born in

Scotland view themselves as Scottish and those born in Wales are Welsh. Alternatively, the person can be a British or Irish citizen and identify themselves as either Northern Irish or Ulster. Ruane and Todd assert that at least three 'cultural' identities,[13] (Irish, British and Northern Irish[14]) exist for both Protestants and Catholics from Northern Ireland. They suggest that these identities are not mutually exclusive but each of them is associated with a distinct imagined community, sense of history and family values. The 'Ulster' identity provides a fourth alternative for Protestants but not for Catholics.

Ulster is one of the four ancient provinces of Ireland and includes three counties which are located in the Republic of Ireland together with the six counties of Northern Ireland. In the past, the term Ulster tended to imply identification with the Northern Ireland as a political region and acceptance of the legitimacy of the devolved government in Stormont. During recent years although the term Ulster remains in use by organisations such as Ulster Television and Radio Ulster, it has gained additional meaning through its use by paramilitary groups such as the Ulster Volunteer Force (UVF) and the Ulster Defence Association (UDA). Like many other terms associated with identity in Northern Ireland, the meaning of the term Ulster is imprecise and its connotations depend on the context. Moxon-Browne noted: 'The term Ulster when adopted as a form of national identity suffers from as much imprecision as the terms British and Irish. In all three cases the geographical implications are a matter for debate. In all three cases the political connotations are a matter for dispute'.[15]

In contrast, Ruane and Todd[16] consider that the meaning of the Ulster identity is clear. It implies identification with the Ulster Protestant people and that: 'For the vast majority of Northern Protestants, the core community is the Protestants of Ulster or Northern Ireland.' However, they further suggest that the Ulster identity is not selected as a primary identification among Protestant survey respondents because of the negative overtones it has acquired. This claim is difficult to support empirically but one of their interviewees noted when asked how she perceived herself : *'I would say 'Ulster' but that sounds too extreme; I won't say Irish for that would only please them [i.e. Catholics]; I will say British for that sounds neutral'*. According to Moxon-Browne,[17] in the mid-1970s the Alliance Party[18] seeing a need to replace the divisive schism between British and Irish nationalism in Northern Ireland with an identity which would unite the two communities: 'toyed with idea of fostering an Ulster identity by adopting new symbols and "Danny Boy" as the new anthem'. One possible reason why they did not actively pursue this idea was that the Ulster identity is unacceptable to the Catholic population because of its historical connections with the Protestant population. Moxon-Browne observed that in the 1970s, the Peace People often 'invoked the unity of the "Northern Irish people", significantly omitting the term Ulster as being too divisive'.[19] The geographical boundaries and political significance of the Northern Irish label are ambiguous which, he suggested,[20] serves to make it less divisive than other possible shared national labels available to Protestants and Catholics. For Catholics, the Northern Irish identity does not legitimise political boundaries or compromise their aspirations to the eventual unification of the island of Ireland, as the term can refer geographically to the northern part of the island of Ireland. Similarly, the Northern Irish identity does not compromise the British identity of Protestants as the term can be seen as derived from 'Northern Ireland', an officially designated region of the United Kingdom.

Nowadays, the Northern Irish label differs from the Ulster label because of the assumption that it is an inclusive identification with both Catholic and Protestant inhabitants of the region. Ruane and Todd suggest that those adopting this identity see Northern Ireland as a 'region of cultural overlap between Britain and Ireland with the Northern Irish identity opening out to Irish, British and possibly European dimensions'.[21]

The Northern Irish Identity

The Northern Irish identity is a new identity and has only been included as an option in surveys since 1986. There are no obvious institutions which promote its growth and very few manifestations of a shared Northern Irish identity. Bryson and McCartney in their scholarly analysis of the use of flags, anthems and other national symbols in Northern Ireland noted that: 'there is no song which is recognised as a Northern Ireland or Ulster anthem, which is not surprising since the residents do not have a shared sense of national identity'.[22] However, the heated public debate in one local council about the use of the term 'Northern Irish' in a £1.5 million government advertising campaign suggests that there may be official support for the Northern Irish label as well as demonstrating the importance of identity in Northern Ireland.

In 1995, in response to the republican and loyalist ceasefires the Northern Ireland Office mounted the 'Time for the Bright Side' campaign consisting of five television advertisements which celebrated the positives of life in Northern Ireland including its scenery, notable achievements, humour, divergence and differences. There were 12 complaints about this campaign. One was from

Ards Borough in County Down, which has a predominantly Protestant population. The members of the Council, with political party affiliations, are all from one of the unionist parties. The minutes of the August 1995 Council Meeting report found that:

> ... some members expressed the view that the current 'Northern Irish Life' advertising campaign funded by the Government was an attempt at propaganda, denying the Unionist population of Northern Ireland their British identity. The term 'Northern Irish' was considered unacceptable as some members felt that, while they lived in Northern Ireland, they were in no way Irish.[23]

Following what seems to be a lively argument the council resolved that a letter should be written to the Northern Ireland Office (NIO) expressing concern with the advertising campaign that 'erodes our identity. We are British, that is our identity and we wish to remain so.' The NIO's reply to the Council's letter, as reported in the Council minutes[24] and the local newspaper,[25] reassured the members of Council who had voted for the resolution that it was no part of the thinking in the advertising campaign to 'deny the Unionist population in Northern Ireland their British Identity'. The letter indicated that:

> The term Northern Irish was used because it had scored a clear majority rating for acceptability among both Catholics and Protestants on whom the campaign had been pretested. The campaign did not trespass into the constitutional debate and it had never been intended that such would be the case. It celebrated divergence and difference under one heading of 'Northern Irish'.

Following a discussion of this letter the Council resolved to write back to the NIO stating that it remains of the opinion that the identity of the majority was eroded by the use of the term 'Northern Irish'. The Ards Borough Council is unusual in displaying a strong reaction to the Northern Irish identity. Conflict and debate have generally been focused on the clash between the British and Irish identities as represented by symbols, such as flags, and rituals such as parades. In this context the Northern Irish identity has largely been ignored. One possible reason why there has been little debate about this new identity is that rather than viewing it as part of a deliberate policy to weaken the link between Great Britain and Northern Ireland, it has been characterised as a frail identity which is used as a label of convenience for survey respondents who remain firmly embedded in their traditional polarised communities. McGarry and O'Leary, for example, suggest that the:

Popular moderation that is often displayed in opinion polls must … be treated with scepticism. Polls are imperfect, especially so in deeply divided territories where respondents may be unwilling to tell the pollster what they really think. They may judge their views to be outside conventional norms, or that their real views, given to a stranger, may put them at considerable risk. The evidence from Northern Ireland is that opinion polls tend to over-emphasise moderation and downplay extremism.[26]

In this chapter, survey evidence is used to establish who chooses the Northern Irish identity, their evaluation of this identity and the reasons why they chose it. This analysis aims to assess whether or not the choice of the Northern Irish label in surveys merely acknowledges a geographical reality or reflects the presence of a salient self-defining social identity which involves identifying with a single community.

Social Attitude Surveys

A question about identity has been included in the 1989, 1991,[27] 1993, 1994,[28] and 1995[29] British Social Attitude surveys carried out in Northern Ireland. In each of these surveys, 800 to 1,000 respondents were asked 'Which of these [terms] best describes the way you usually think of yourself?' and given the choice between 'Irish', 'British', 'Northern Irish', 'Ulster' or 'Other'. Overall, one in five (20.5 per cent) of the sample, in the 1995 survey[30] labelled themselves as Northern Irish, 28 per cent chose the Irish label, eight per cent the Ulster label and 43 per cent described themselves as British. Table 2.1, which shows the findings from the five surveys for Catholics and Protestants, reveals a very consistent pattern for Catholics. The majority of Catholic respondents in each survey described themselves as Irish, but between 23 and 28 per cent in each survey chose to label themselves as Northern Irish rather than Irish and 10 per cent described themselves as British. No more than two per cent of those with Catholic background described themselves as Ulster.

The picture is very different when we turn to the results for Protestants; 66 to 71 per cent of those from a Protestant background chose the British identity. From 26 to 29 per cent of the Protestants defined themselves in terms of the local region in each year but the relative popularity of the Northern Irish and Ulster identities fluctuated for no obvious reason. In 1989, 1994 and 1995 the Northern Irish identity was the more popular choice, whereas in 1991 and 1993 it was the Ulster identity which was more popular with

Table 2.1   Data from Social Attitude surveys

| | Protestant | | | | | Catholic | | | |
| | British | Irish | Ulster | N. Irish | Other | British | Irish | Ulster | N.Irish | Other |
	%	%	%	%	%	%	%	%	%	%
1989	68	3	10	16	3	10	60	2	25	4
1991	66	2	15	14	3	10	62	2	25	1
1993	69	2	15	11	3	12	61	1	24	2
1994	71	3	11	15	0	10	62	0	28	0
1995	67	5	13	14	2	11	63	2	23	1

Protestants. Most recently 14 per cent of the Protestants described themselves as Northern Irish and 13 per cent as Ulster.

In sum, there is no doubt that Catholics and Protestants from Northern Ireland retain distinct patterns of identification. Protestants identify themselves as British, Northern Irish and Ulster but not Irish. Catholics identify themselves as Irish, Northern Irish or British but not Ulster. The majority of the population clearly identify themselves as either Irish Catholics or British Protestants but there is a sizeable minority who are Northern Irish and this group seems to be ignored by the rhetoric of sectarianism. Who are they? The data from the 1994 social attitude survey provides a profile of Northern Irish identifiers.[31] For this analysis the characteristics of Catholics and Protestants who identified themselves as Northern Irish are compared with all of the Catholic and Protestant respondents (see Tables 2.2 and 2.3) in order to establish how similar the Protestant and Catholic Northern Irish identifiers are to each other and to their community group.

As Table 2.2 indicates the Protestant Northern Irish identifiers were younger than all Protestants.[32] They were also likely to be better educated and more likely to be from a non-manual background[33] than all Protestants whereas Catholic Northern Irish identifiers differed very little from all Catholics on these background characteristics.

The data from the social attitude survey also enables us to establish whether the Northern Irish identifiers have common constitutional preferences or whether Catholic and Protestant Northern Irish identifiers share the community preferences of their co-religionists. Respondents were asked, '*Generally speaking do you think of yourself as a unionist [support the union with Great Britain], a Nationalist [support Irish nationalism], or neither*'. As Table 2.3 indicates Catholic and Protestant Northern Irish identifiers tended to conform to their community backgrounds. None of the Protestant Northern Irish

Table 2.2   **Personal characteristic of Northern Irish identifiers as compared with all of the Protestant and Catholic respondents**[34]

	Protestant		Catholic	
	All	**N. Irish**	**N. Irish**	**All**
Age				
18–34	31	43	39	39
35–59	42	41	45	43
60+	27	16	16	18
Social class				
Non-manual	49	59	46	40
Manual	45	36	47	52
Never had a job	6	4	6	8
Education				
Degree/A-level	32	45	33	26
GCSE/CSE	32	33	26	28
None	37	22	41	46

Table 2.3   **Constitutional identity and preferred long term policy preference for Northern Irish identifiers and all Protestants and Catholics**[35]

	Protestant		Catholic	
	All	**N. Irish**	**N. Irish**	**All**
1 Consider self				
Unionist	71	62	2	1
Nationalist	0	0	47	51
Neither	28	38	52	48
2 Long-term policy for Northern Ireland				
Remain part of the UK	87	85	32	27
Reunify Ireland	7	6	56	57
Independent state	1	4	2	1

identifiers were committed to the nationalist constitutional identity whereas almost half of the Catholic Northern Irish identifiers consider themselves to be nationalists.[36] It does seem that although Catholic and Protestant share a Northern Irish identity, the identity encompasses different understandings of the relationship between Northern Ireland, the Republic of Ireland and Great Britain.

Table 2.3 further illustrates the divergence in the national aspirations of Catholics and Protestants. The question they were asked was, '*Do you think the long term policy for Northern Ireland should be for it to remain part of the United Kingdom or reunify with the rest of Ireland?*' Eighty-seven per cent of all Protestant and 85 per cent of Protestant Northern Irish identifiers wanted Northern Ireland to remain part of the UK whereas 57 per cent of all respondents with a Catholic community background and 56 per cent of the Catholic Northern Irish identifiers wanted Northern Ireland reunified with the rest of Ireland.

In sum, the Northern Irish identity is being used by the young, the educated and the middle class. It is particularly widely used by well educated young Protestants.[37] Those Protestants who define themselves as Northern Irish do not differ from other Protestants in their support for the union with Great Britain, while the Catholic Northern Irish aspire to a United Ireland. This could be the potential strength of the Northern Irish identity, which unlike any other identity, can offer a basis for a shared identification by Catholics and Protestant while not threatening the ideological commitments of either.

Evaluation of Identities

Findings from a recent survey,[38] which focused exclusively on identity in Northern Ireland, provide evidence on how the population evaluate their identities. As part of the survey, interviewers asked almost a thousand respondents to select one identity from an array of 12 sociopolitical identities. The majority of Catholics chose to describe themselves as Catholic, Irish or Northern Irish while the majority of Protestants described themselves as British, Protestants or Northern Irish.

All respondents completed a collective self-esteem scale, which assesses how individuals evaluate their membership in a social group, in relation to their chosen identity.[39] The four four-item subscales which combine to produce this overall collective self-esteem scale measure different aspects of collective self-esteem. Private collective self-esteem assesses how good they judge their social group to be (e.g. In general, I'm glad to be a member of this group). Public collective self-esteem assesses how they believe other people evaluate their social group (e.g. In general, others respect this group). Identity Importance is a measure of the importance of group membership to their self-concept (e.g. In general, this group is an important part of my self-image) and membership-esteem assesses how good or worthy a member they feel they are of their social group (e.g. I often feel I am a useless member of this group).[40]

For this analysis, as with the analysis of the social attitude survey data, the Northern Irish identifiers were compared with all of the Catholic respondents. As Table 3.4 shows collective self-esteem was generally positive. Catholics tended to evaluate the Northern Irish identity more positively than Protestants reflecting the general tendency for Catholics to report higher collective self-esteem scores than Protestants. On average, those Catholics and Protestants who labelled themselves 'Northern Irish' did not consider that this identity was a salient and important part of their identity, as demonstrated by their mean scores for Importance of Identity, which were below the neutral point. However, although on average the Northern Irish identifiers had lower mean scores than the survey population, they tended to evaluate their identity positively and to consider that others also evaluated their identity positively as reflected in the mean scores on the private and public self-esteem scales.

Table 2.4   Collective self-esteem scores for all Catholic and Protestant respondents and Catholic and Protestant Northern Irish identifiers[41]

	Protestant		Catholic	
	All (n=572)	N. Irish (n=78)	N. Irish (n=46)	All (n=361)
Private self-esteem	16.6	15.8	16.4	16.7
Public self-esteem	14.9	13.4	13.5	15.0
Importance to identity	12.8	11.6	11.7	13.4
Membership esteem	14.0	13.8	14.1	14.8
Collective self-esteem	58.2	54.5	55.7	59.9

Following the procedure employed by Crocker, Luhtanen, Blaine and Broadnax,[42] the levels of association between the Collective self-esteem subscales were calculated for all Catholic and Protestant respondents and for the Northern Irish identifiers. Table 3.5 shows that there was a small but significant correlation between private and public collective self-esteem for

Catholic and Protestant respondents generally and for Protestant but not Catholic Northern Irish identifiers. According to the symbolic interactionist perspective, a high level of congruence between individuals' private evaluation of their social groups and how they believe others rate these groups is to be expected if people come to see themselves as they imagine others see them.[43] Crocker et al. found that results from both white American and Asian students were consistent with this notion of the 'looking glass self'. However, the results from African-American students did not conform to the predictions of the symbolic interactionists. It seems that the Catholic Northern Irish identifiers in this survey, responded in a similar fashion to African-Americans and separated their own private evaluation of their identity group from how they believed others evaluate the group. As Crocker et al. argued it is possible that the separation between public and private evaluations of the group is adaptive for members of devalued minority groups which have experienced prejudice and negative stereotyping.

Table 2.5   Zero-order correlations between subscales of the collective self-esteem scale for all Protestants and Catholics and Northern Irish identifiers

| | Protestant | | Catholic | |
	All (n=572)	N. Irish (n=78)	N. Irish (n=46)	All (n=361)
Public se/Private se	.41 **	.31 **	.17	.32 **
Public se/importance	.29 **	.10	.40 **	.25 **
Public se/membership se	.25 **	-.01	.25	.37 **
Private se/importance	.47 **	.36 **	.42 **	.50 **
Private se/membership se	.42 **	.31 **	.42 **	.54 **
Membership se/importance	.49 **	.47 **	.40 **	.50 **

** $p<.01$

Overall the Northern Irish identifiers separated how they felt about being Northern Irish, how important this group was to their identity and how good a member they were of the group from how they believed others evaluated this group. It would seem that they isolated others' perceptions of the Northern Irish from their own response to the group rather than using their beliefs about how others saw the Northern Irish as a basis for their own evaluations of the group.

Self-descriptions

Patterns of identity choices, responses to attitude items and psychometric test scores have provided snapshots of the relative attractiveness of different identities for people from Northern Ireland. However, this type of survey data does not provide information on what motivates a person to choose one of a range of possible identities rather than any of the possible alternatives. Open-ended questions can provide this type of information as was demonstrated in a 1997 survey[44] in which 122 students were asked to choose an identity, Irish (chosen by 34 per cent), British (19 per cent) or Northern Irish (47 per cent) and then explain why they chose to describe themselves with this label.

Three themes emerged from the open-ended responses to the question '*Why did you choose this description [Northern Irish] rather than the others?*'. Some of the students chose the Northern Irish identity because they were born in the region and not in any other part of the British Isles. For example:

- '*Because I Don't feel either British or Irish – I am from Northern Ireland*' [a Protestant female student from County Down];
- '*I am from Northern Ireland–I am therefore neither British or Irish but Northern Irish*' [a Catholic female student from County Armagh];
- '*I think people from Northern Ireland are different from people from England, Wales, Scotland and Ireland. We are our own set of people from Northern Ireland so we are Northern Irish*' [a Protestant male student].

Others chose to describe themselves as Northern Irish because they were concerned to be inclusive and not sectarian:

- '*Because I like to think of myself as neutral i.e. not taking sides*' [a Protestant, female student from County Antrim];
- '*I just think of people as all the same rather than their nationality*' [Catholic, female student from County Armagh];
- '*Being Northern Irish means you can dissociate yourself from all the hatred*' [Protestant, female from County Down].

The third theme which emerged from the students' responses was that they had two sides to their identity:

- '*Though I am Protestant I am aware and proud of my Irish ancestry*' [Protestant, male from County Down];

- '*Because we are both British and Irish so Northern Irish is a happy medium*' [Catholic, female from County Armagh];
- '*I think that there is both part of Irish and Britishness in me so I cannot pick one or the other. I am from Northern Ireland, so I class myself as Northern Irish*' [Protestant, female, 19-year-old from Belfast].

Finally, some respondents were very clear about what the term Northern Irish meant to them in the sense of a combination of the themes. As a Catholic male from Bangor, County Down wrote in reply to the question about why he chose to call himself Northern Irish:

- '*Because I don't feel overtly British or Irish and I feel that Northern Ireland's problems would be resolved through people calling themselves Northern Irish and adopting a separate identity of our own ... It gives the opportunity for me to live free of the petty minded sectarianism attached to being either Irish or British*';
- a Protestant female from Lisburn explained that, '*I am from Northern Ireland and not Ireland or Britain.*' For her, the term Northern Irish meant, '*not associating myself with the troubles. Having friends of both religions– Catholic and Protestant and not worrying about the difference.*'

Conclusions

The research evidence clearly confirms the division in Northern Ireland between Irish Catholics and British Protestants. However, this research also suggests that approximately one in twenty of the population choose to describe themselves as Northern Irish rather than either Irish or British. The background of Catholics who identify themselves as Northern Irish does not differ from that of Catholics in general, but Protestants, who identify themselves as Northern Irish tend to be younger and better educated than the general population. Both Protestants and Catholics, who describe themselves as Northern Irish, tend to value the identity, although they do not see it as an important or central part of their self concept. At the same time, most of the Northern Irish identifiers conformed to their co-religionists' preferences in relation to constitutional issues such as whether Northern Ireland should remain part of the United Kingdom or reunify with the rest of Ireland.

The Northern Irish identity can be seen as weak, not only because it is a minority identity which does not command strong attachments, but also because the category is ambiguous and lacks clearly defined attributes. However, it is a new identity which does not have the status of a national identity such as British or Irish. It is possible that its attraction for the majority of the Northern Irish identifiers was that they considered it to be more acceptable to the interviewer, who was a stranger, than the alternatives. In these circumstances it is reasonable to assume that they did not see being Northern Irish as a salient self-defining identity but merely as an acknowledgment of a geographical reality which did not signify either acceptance of the political entity or a shared nationhood. However, it does seem as if some young people, at least, do see themselves as having a Northern Irish identity which involves identification with both the Irish and the British strands of life in the region.

For most people living in Northern Ireland, The Northern Irish identity is now part of an array of acceptable identities for both Catholics and Protestants so that they can describe themselves as either Catholic, Irish and Northern Irish or Protestant, British and Northern Irish.[45] If the circumstances are appropriate, both Protestants and Catholics can acknowledge their common heritage without threatening their strong group allegiances. However, when the sectarian divisions are heightened by violence and threat, it is reasonable to assume that only the small minority will retain their commitment to the shared Northern Irish identity.

Given the current rapidly changing circumstances in Northern Ireland and the political will to find a viable solution which respects both nationalist and unionist concerns, but will inevitably require compromise to succeed, it would be valuable to establish how the peace process impacts on patterns of identification. The availability of both the traditional divisive national identities and the new shared Northern Irish identity to the population of Northern Ireland reflects the complexity of the conflict in Northern Ireland. The search for a permanent peaceful solution in the region has been seen by many commentators as even more difficult than in apparently comparable conflicts such as those in South Africa and the Middle East.[46] Efforts to improve community relations and promote peaceful coexistence in Northern Ireland may be enhanced if the rhetoric and the procedures take account of both the distinctiveness of Catholics and Protestants as well as the shared regional experiences, culture and values reflected in the Northern Irish identity.[47]

Notes

1   Ms Mairaid Corrigan-Maguire, Peace People spokeswoman quoted in the *Belfast Telegraph*, 25 January 1994.
2   Cited in B. Walker, *Dancing to History's Tune: History, Myth and Politics in Ireland*, Belfast, Institute of Irish Studies, 1996, p. 125.
3   E.g. Walker op. cit.
4   E.g. J. Ruane and J. Todd, *The Dynamics of Conflict in Northern Ireland, Power, Conflict and Emancipation*, Cambridge, Cambridge University Press, 1996.
5   E.g. J. Whyte, *Challenging Times: Challenges to Identity: 12 year-olds in Belfast 1981 and 1992*, Aldershot, Avebury, 1995.
6   J. Bardon in 'True Colours', *Omnibus*, 3, 2, pp. 4–10, 1995 noted after the 1995 'Portadown siege' the leader of the Ulster Unionist party, David Trimble MP wrote that: 'we feel that our culture and identity is being crushed, while we have Irish culture rammed down our throats'.
7   J. Darby, *Northern Ireland: Managing Difference*, London, Minority Rights Group, 1995.
8   Very Rev Dr J. Dunlop, 'Labels poisoning our lives', *Belfast Telegraph*, 31 July 1996, p. 15.
9   Dunlop, op. cit.
10 For one of the initial accounts of the application of social identity theory to the Northern Ireland conflict see E. Cairns, 'Intergroup conflict in Northern Ireland' in H. Tajfel (ed.), *Social Identity and Intergroup Relations*, Cambridge, Cambridge University Press, 1982. For a more recent account see K. Trew, 'Social psychological research on the conflict', *The Psychologist*, 5, 1992, pp. 342–4.
11 J. McGarry and B. O'Leary, 'Five fallacies: Northern Ireland and the liabilities of Liberalism', *Ethnic and Racial Studies*, 18, 4, 1995, pp. 837–61.
12 F. Boal, M.C. Keane and D.N. Livingstone, *Them and Us: A survey of Catholic and Protestant Churchgoers in Belfast*, Belfast, Institute of Irish Studies, 1997.
13 The term cultural identity as used by Ruane and Todd, op. cit., is not defined. They specify four cultural identities which coincide with the 'national' identity choices used in recent surveys. Other writers label the identity variants according to religion, politics and nationality e.g. A. Gallagher, 'Social identity and the Northern Ireland conflict', *Human Relations*, 42, 1989, pp. 917–35; K. Trew and D. Benson, *Defining Ourselves: Dimensions of social identity in Northern Ireland*, Belfast, Institute of Irish Studies, 1997.
14 Although little has been written about the Northern Irish identity, Irishness and Britishness provide the focus for many papers and books on Northern Ireland. For example C. Smythe (ed.), *Irishness in a Changing Society*, Gerrards Cross, The Princess Grace Irish Library, 1988; M. Crozier (ed.), *Cultural Traditions in Northern Ireland: Varieties of Irishness*, Belfast, Institute of Irish Studies, 1989; M. Crozier (ed.), *Cultural Traditions in Northern Ireland: Varieties of Britishness*, Belfast, Institute of Irish Studies, 1990.
15 E. Moxon-Browne, *Nation, Class and Creed in Northern Ireland*, Gower, Aldershot, 1983.
16 Ruane and Todd, op. cit., p. 60.
17 Moxon-Browne, 1983, op. cit., p. 5.
18 The moderate Alliance party, which is linked to British Liberal Democrats is supported by both Catholics and Protestants.
19 Moxon-Browne, 1983, op. cit.

20 Moxon-Browne, 'National identity in Northern Ireland' in P. Stringer and G. Robinson (eds), *Social Attitudes in Northern Ireland*, Belfast, Blackstaff Press, 1991.

21 Ruane and Todd, op. cit., p. 59.

22 L. Bryson and C. McCartney, *Clashing Symbols?: A report on the use of flags, anthems and other national symbols in Northern Ireland*, Belfast, Institute of Irish Studies, 1994, p. 20.

23 Ards Borough Council Meeting minutes, 21–22 August 1995.

24 Ards Borough Council Meeting minutes, 23 October 1995.

25 *Bangor Spectator*, 26 October 1995.

26 McGarry and O'Leary, op. cit., p. 849.

27 See Moxon-Browne, 1991, op. cit.

28 See K. Trew, 'National Identity' in R. Breen, P. Devine and L. Dowds (eds), *Social Attitudes in Northern Ireland: The Fifth Report, 1995–1996*, Belfast, Appletree Press, 1996.

29 1995 figures supplied by Paula Devine.

30 The 1995 Social Attitude survey reported by L. Dowds, P. Devine and R. Breen (eds), *Social Attitudes in Northern Ireland: The Sixth Report 1996–1997*, Belfast, Appletree Press, 1997.

31 See Trew, 1996, op. cit.

32 L. Dowds and P. Devine, 'Unleashing the Apathy of a Lost Generation? Community Relations among Young People in Northern Ireland' in Dowds, Devine and Breen (eds), op. cit., analysed the 1995 survey data to examine the extent to which the attitudes of those aged 18–30 who have been born and grown up during the troubles differed from older respondents. They found that the percentage of young Catholics choosing to describe themselves as Northern Irish (28 per cent) differed little from the 31–39 (27 per cent) or 40–59 (25 per cent) age groups but the elderly were least likely to consider that they were Northern Irish (15 per cent). For the Protestants the Northern Irish label was more acceptable to the young with 28 per cent describing themselves as Northern Irish compared with 19–20 per cent of the 31–59 year olds and only seven per cent of those aged 60 or over.

33 The analysis conducted by M. Duffy and G. Evans, 'Class Community Polarisation and Politics' in Dowds, Devine and Breen (eds), op. cit., indicated that the salariat are more likely than the working class to adopt a Northern Irish identity. Middle class Catholics more frequently adopted the Northern Irish identity (30 per cent males, 28 per cent females) than the Protestant middle class (23 per cent males, 22 per cent females), but the Northern Irish identity could not be characterised as a 'middle class label of moderation' as the percentage of Catholic working class adopting the Northern Irish identity (20 per cent males, 21 per cent females) was almost as high as that observed in the Protestant middle class.

34 From Trew, 1996, op. cit.

35 From Trew, 1996, op. cit.

36 Duffy and Evans, 1997, op. cit., note that there was support for the 'Northern Irish for neutrality argument' in their findings that: for Catholics, feeling Northern Irish as compared with Irish was associated with a significantly less nationalist position; for Protestants, feeling Northern Irish rather than British or Ulster was associated with a less strongly unionist position.

37 K. Trew and D. Benson, 'Dimensions of Social Identity in Northern Ireland' in G. Breakwell and E. Lyons (eds), *Changing European Identities: Social-psychological analyses of social change*, Oxford, Butterworth, Heinemann, 1996, and D. Benson and K. Trew, 'Facets of self in Northern Ireland: Explorations and further questions' in A. Wicklund and B.

Oosterwegel (eds), *The Self in European and North American Culture*, Kluwer Academic Publishers, pp. 291–307, 1995 report a survey of 370 university students from Northern Ireland. They were asked to select one identity which would best describe themselves from an array of nine sociopolitical labels. Thirty per cent of the sample selected the Northern Irish label.

38 Trew and Benson, 1997, op. cit.

39 This scale is a modified version of the 16-item scale with a Likert response format of five choice developed by J. Luhtanen and J. Crocker, 'A collective self-esteem scale: Self-evaluation of one's social identity', *Personality and Social Psychology Bulletin*, 18, 1992, pp. 302–18.

40 Overall scale minimum is 16 and the maximum is 80 with a midpoint of 48. Each subscale has potential range from 4–20 with a midpoint of 12.

41 Trew and Benson, 1997, op. cit.

42 J. Crocker, R. Luhtanen, B. Blaine and S. Broadnax, 'Collective self-esteem and psychological well-being among White, Black and Asian college students', *Personality and Social Psychology Bulletin*, 20, 5, 1994, pp. 505–13.

43 G.H. Mead, *Mind, Self and Society*, Chicago, University of Chicago Press, 1934.

44 K. Trew, 'National identity survey', unpublished analysis, 1997.

45 For a discussion of multiple identities see Trew and Benson, op. cit., Ruane and Todd, op. cit. and K. Trew, 'Complementary or conflicting identities?', *The Psychologist*, 1996, pp. 460–3.

46 See B. O'Leary and J. McGarry, *The Politics of Antagonism: Understanding Northern Ireland*, second edition, London, Athlone Press, 1996, p. 354 for a discussion of the three peace processes.

47 See Darby, op. cit., for a more detailed account of the development of community relations policy.

3 'A Good Jew or a Good Englishman?': The Jewish Lads' Brigade and Anglo-Jewish Identity[1]

SHARMAN KADISH

The Jewish Lads' Brigade is the oldest Jewish youth movement in Britain. In 1995 I published a history *A Good Jew and a Good Englishman: The Jewish Lads' and Girls' Brigade 1895–1995*[2] which had been commissioned to mark the centenary. The title chosen was no accident. The self-proclaimed aim of the Brigade has consistently been to inculcate good citizenship and Jewish values into its young members. In writing the book, I set out to answer the question: how successful was the Brigade in achieving this double goal and was this goal in fact achievable, or merely contradictory? My research became a fascinating excursion into an obscure corner of Anglo-Jewish history. Yet it soon became apparent that the history of the Brigade touched upon some of the most sensitive questions which have faced the British Jewish community over the past one hundred years: national identity, assimilation and antisemitism.

'To Iron Out the Ghetto Bend'?

The Jewish Lads' Brigade (JLB) owes its inspiration to Christian uniformed youth movements[3] which mushroomed in Britain in the closing decades of the nineteenth century: chiefly the Boys' Brigade (1883), a nonconformist grouping, and the Church Lads' Brigade of the established Anglican Church (1891). The notion of religion in uniform had originated with the adult missionary society the Salvation Army in 1878. Uniformed youth organisations without the religious component reached their peak with the foundation of the Boys' Scouts by Sir Robert Baden-Powell in 1909. It is safe to assume that the Catholic Lads' Brigade (1896), and the Jewish Lads' Brigade (1895), were sectarian variations on this most British of themes.

The founder of the JLB, Colonel Albert Goldsmid (1846–1904), encapsulated the dilemmas of British and Jewish identity within his own persona. For Goldsmid was a British Army officer, born in India, who discovered his Jewish roots and became a convert to Orthodox Judaism and Chovevei Tsion Zionism. Goldsmid was a 'model Major-General', or at least Lieutenant-Colonel, a conventional military man and a determined Jewish individualist. In short, an Anglo-Jewish eccentric who bucked the trend of assimilation which characterised his social class.

The Jewish Lads' Brigade was inaugurated in the East End of London on 16 February 1895. The official object of the movement was: 'To instil into the rising generation, from earliest youth, habits of orderliness, cleanliness, and honour, so that in learning to respect themselves they will do credit to their Community.'[4] JLB officers, both in London and the provinces, were overwhelmingly drawn from the English born Anglo-Jewish upper and middle classes – the so-called 'West End' Jews. The majority of the JLB Companies, by contrast, were situated in the immigrant working class neighbourhoods, above all, in the East End of London.

The phenomenon of the educated upper classes 'going down the East End' to 'elevate the condition of the people' was characteristic of late Victorian England. The 1880s and 1890s were the heyday of university settlements and public school missions, of Fabian Socialism and the birth of the Independent Labour Party. The uniformed youth movements too set out to do their bit to alleviate the appalling social conditions of the urban poor and to 'improve' them through education and training. With their healthy regime of fresh air and exercise, the Brigades promoted a double agenda. On the one hand, they epitomised the public school code of conduct, perpetuated through the universities and officers' mess. Their high minded leaders created a forum for working class youth to escape, at least temporarily, the squalid existence that was the lot of juvenile labour. Fair play and sportsmanship could counteract poverty. On the other hand, the Brigade movement may be seen as an agency of social control. Healthy recreation would help protect the young from crime and vice and, perhaps more importantly, protect society from delinquency, class conflict and the spread of 'dangerous' socialist doctrines.

Goldsmid, like his more famous contemporary, Baden-Powell, had much the same aims in mind. However, the JLB had an additional objective, which may be summed up in that celebrated phrase 'to iron out the ghetto bend',[5] in other words, to turn working class and foreign born Jewish youth[6] into fit and respectable 'Englishmen of the Mosaic persuasion'. Like other Anglo-Jewish institutions of the period, such as the United Synagogue (1870), the Federation of Synagogues (1887), the Jewish Board of Guardians (1859), the Jews' Free School (originally founded in 1732), the Brigade – and indeed the Jewish youth club movement as a whole – functioned chiefly as an agent of Anglicisation of the Yiddish speaking East European refugees who flooded into the country after 1881.

In 1897 the *Jewish Chronicle* extolled the virtues of Brigade training: 'The narrow-chested, round-shouldered, slouching son of the Ghetto becomes converted with extraordinary rapidity into an erect and self-respecting man, a living negation of the physical stigma which has so long disfigured our race.'[7] Arguably, Anglo-Jewry had an even greater incentive than other sections of the population to keep its 'lower orders' in tow: the fear of antisemitism. The advent of a new immigrant community filled 'the [Jewish] establishment' with unease. After all, their quest for social acceptance had been crowned, only comparatively recently, with the symbolic achievement of political emancipation in 1858. Unchecked immigration of foreigners provoked anti-alien sentiment. Organised Labour, anxious to protect its members from unfair competition for housing and jobs, was just as susceptible as the Tory Right. Growing agitation to end Britain's 'open door' policy on immigration bore fruit in the 1905 Aliens Act which was, in practice, targeted at East European Jewish refugees who were the only significant immigrant group of the period (if one leaves aside the Irish). The distinction between anti-alienism and antisemitism was a fine one. It is therefore understandable that Anglo-Jewry should have been concerned to absorb the newcomers with as little fuss as possible. Encouraging adaptation to English ways would help ensure the 'good name' of British Jewry in the eyes of society at large. The JLB was an expression of 'native' Jewry's enduring faith in the Emancipation Contract and was, at bottom, a defence against antisemitism.

The Anglo-Jewish gentlemen who staffed the Brigade saw nothing incongruous in seeking to 'graft' English public school values onto a population which came from an entirely different tradition, with a vibrant cultural life of its own, and who lived under economic and social conditions which were not at all comparable. Yet, in one vital respect, the JLB differed from the Church Brigades upon which it was modelled. The JLB has been seen as the Jewish equivalent of the 'muscular Christianity' fashionable in the late Victorian period. But if this was indeed the case, the Judaism which it was supposed to espouse, was of an essentially secular nature. JLB activities were not punctuated by Bible reading and hymn singing. Whilst, in the early years at least, the basic requirements of Jewish observance were respected, they were never emphasised. Religion was equated with moral rectitude and social action. This attitude may be explained by the overriding objective of the movement: Anglicisation. The officers and gentlemen who ran the Brigade no doubt felt that the sons of immigrants in their charge got 'enough' Judaism at home. Their educational and cultural requirements were more than adequately catered for by parents, *melamdim* (teachers) and *Rabbonim* (rabbis). The function of the JLB, as we have seen, was to inculcate *English* values.

The Role of Religion

The annual summer camp, which brought lads and officers together for a week or 10 days under canvas, revealed a great deal about the JLB's attitude towards religion. In the early years camp was run on Spartan and highly regimented lines. In this regard JLB camp was little different from those run by the other Brigades, Volunteers and Territorials with whom they shared the camp site on farmland near Deal.[8] Indeed, there was little distinctly Jewish about the JLB camp. Certainly, a Camp chaplain was usually, but not always, in attendance. A 'parade for prayer' took place every morning before breakfast and every evening, including of course on *Shabbat* (the Jewish Sabbath). Friday night and Saturday morning services were held in the open field, weather permitting. At Deal in 1900: 'A hollow square was formed, at the western side of which a pulpit was erected of drums, covered by a Union Jack, and the colours of the Brigade, a flag of white and blue.' In the morning, the chaplain conducted a shortened form of service and read an extract in English from the week's *sedra* (Portion of the Law). A *Torah*[9] scroll was only brought down for special occasions, such as the very first *barmitzva*[10] celebrated at camp – in the *barmitzva* year of the Deal camp itself, in 1908. The chaplain never failed to deliver a sermon on the importance of 'king and country, race and religion'. The 1900 Lytham camp took place during the Three Weeks, the traditional period of mourning for the destruction of the Temple in Jerusalem: 'On Saturday evening, being the eve of the Fast of Av, the Book of Lamentations was intoned, and on Sunday morning the full service for the Fast was read.' In 1903, 'boys wishing to fast were given facilities to do so'. At first it was decreed that, 'under no consideration should the canteen be opened on Saturday'. However, in 1901 the camp authorities relented and sanctioned the issuing of tickets which could be exchanged in return for refreshments. This was to get around the religious prohibition of trading on the Sabbath.

The overall impression given by camp orders, regulations and minutes, is that religious requirements were treated in a more and more perfunctory fashion as the years passed. It should be noted in this connection that boys were not accepted for camp under the age of 13, i.e. *barmitzva*. Catering arrangements at camp were not up to the stringent standards of *kashrut* (kosher food laws) which would be required by Jewish organisations approved by the Chief Rabbinate today. Yet, these apparently satisfied the more relaxed standards which prevailed in Anglo-Jewry in the days of Hermann Adler.[11]

On the Sabbath at the 1899 camp, after Revd Cohen had 'read the service … The whole of the day was given to sport etc., no drill taking place'. Official sports matches were not generally gazetted, but informal cricket games, including officer *vs* lads challenges, did take place on Saturday afternoons. Boys were also expected to participate in the daily 'bathing parade' even on the Sabbath, contrary to Orthodox religious law. By the early 1920s there are instances of JLB participation in sports competitions with non-Jewish clubs taking place on Saturday afternoons. This was somewhat ironic, given that one of the original motivations for the founding of the Jewish Athletics Association, to which the Brigade belonged, was to facilitate sports fixtures on Sundays and weekday evenings and thus avoid public desecration of the Jewish Sabbath.

The JLB Employment Bureau was designed to help working boys to keep the Sabbath. However, this rationale was apparently not very compelling in 1905:

> The applicant shall be asked whether he is prepared to work on Saturdays and if so whether his parents have any objection, and no other question on this subject is to be put to him. Best efforts shall be made to obtain him employment whether he is prepared to work on Saturdays or not.[12]

This was hardly a ringing endorsement of the sabbatarian principle. It would have been inconceivable for a church organisation to permit its members to work on Sundays.

Even before the First World War, the Brigade came under fire for apparently sacrificing Jewish tradition on the alter of social acceptance. In 1910, an observant West End Jewish benefactor of the movement wanted a reassurance that JLB lads would 'turn out good Jews as well as good Englishmen'. Whilst an immigrant rabbi in Liverpool complained bitterly about cricket matches and written scoring taking place on *Shabbat*. He pointedly asked the question: 'whether any Christian school or Church Brigade would arrange cricket games on Sunday?'. The boys' parents who were 'mostly orthodox Jews' would, he asserted, 'resent this organised Sabbath desecration by their children'. However, a generational clash between immigrant parents and their British born sons, between the demands of religious observance and the lure of the wider society, was undoubtedly beginning to make itself felt.

Militarism, Muscular Judaism and Zionism

Parental distrust was largely focused on a more obvious aspect of Brigade work. The *Jewish Chronicle* reported in 1899 that: 'Some of the foreign Jews in Manchester seemed to view the movement with suspicion, evidently finding it difficult to realise that an organisation which practises military drill, carries arms and bears a military title, can yet be an entirely private and self-directed affair.' In Leeds there was tangible 'local prejudice' and in Hull this opposition was put down to 'fear amongst the foreign element that the lads are being trained to become soldiers'.[13] Military training: drill, discipline, uniform, the carrying of dummy rifles, the introduction of shooting practice (1908) and the leadership role played by career soldiers, all combined to create a military air in the JLB. Indeed, the emergence of the Brigade movement as a whole has been seen by historians as symptomatic of a preoccupation with national efficiency, race deterioration and imperial defence in the years before the First World War. The arms race with Germany was reinforced by attempts on the part of the War Office to incorporate the Brigades into the national Cadet Force which acted as a feeder for the British Army. Anxious to demonstrate their loyalty to the country which had granted them emancipation, the British Jewish elite had evolved a veritable tradition of military service, of which Colonel Goldsmid was the personification. Viewed from the Ashkenazi religious and cultural perspective of eastern Europe, on the other hand, the Army was a decidedly un-Jewish profession. In Tsarist Russia, military service meant forcible conscription, brutal repression and often conversion to Christianity. It was something to be avoided at all costs – even upon emigration to the West.

In the interests of self-preservation, the immigrants were wise to shun the JLB. Despite frequent denials that it was a 'militaristic' organisation, the fact remains that it employed a military style of training and was convinced of the educational value of such a regime. On the outbreak of the First World War, 80 out of a total of 90 JLB officers volunteered for Army service. Thirty-eight of them never returned. Five hundred and thirty-five names appear on the

JLB Roll of Honour of war dead. This figure accounts for almost one third of all British Jews who died for their country in 1914–18.

After 1918 the JLB, in common with the Christian Brigades, suffered from the public revulsion against militarism which swept the nation in the wake of the Great War. The retention of khaki uniform was 'the real bogey', not to mention the continued, if sporadic, association with the Cadet Force and by extension with the War Office, throughout the 1920s and 1930s. In this respect, the JLB followed the policy of the Anglican Church Lads' Brigade. The Nonconformist Boys' Brigade, on the other hand, severed its link with officialdom in 1924. The historian of the Brigade movements in general has drawn a contrast between the expansion of the Boys' Brigade in the interwar period, as compared with the other Brigades which, he claims, went into permanent decline. The JLB had a total membership of about 2,000 by the late 1920s. Certainly, over half this number (1,200 in 1927) attended summer camp – an impressive figure. The fact remains however, that total Brigade strength had been halved from its pre-1914 peak of 4000. This decline may be attributed in large measure to the key decision to cooperate with the military – a calling which went out of fashion during this period.

Throughout the 1920s the Jewish Lads' Brigade leadership, now led by 'the two Ernests', Ernest Halsted (Hallenstein) and Ernest Joseph – both of whom had been involved almost from the beginning – made a point of disavowing 'militarism' at almost every public opportunity. The JLB was a movement entirely devoted to 'social' ends. According to a loyal rank and file member in 1922:

> Members of the J.L.B. ... pride themselves ... on being 'better than other men'. They are distinct from their school fellows in clean boots, well-brushed hair and clothes ... they are assiduous, punctual and tidy, never walk about with their hands in their pockets, nor in other people's, and are always smart in appearance. They are sportsmen in the best sense of the word, and have a strong sense of discipline.

Nevertheless, parental resistance in the primary immigrant neighbourhoods remained a problem. The editor of the Yiddish daily *Di Tsait* (*The Jewish Times*) was prevailed upon to advertise the advantages which membership of the Brigade bestowed but, in doing so, felt obliged to emphasise that '*Di Yidishe Brigade iz nisht kein a militerishe organizatsia*' (the Jewish brigade is not a military organisation), and that by joining, youngsters would not be turned into soldiers. Phil Glickman from Manchester, for one, was not convinced. In 1927 he wrote to the *Jewish Chronicle*:

> to protest against the existence of the Jewish Lads' Brigade Movement, with its ridiculous mimicry of the British Army. It is really a repetition of the pre-war militarist doctrine that Might is Right; and for Jews to band themselves together for the inculcation of such pernicious teaching into mere children is deplorable in the extreme.

He attacked 'all the snobbery of difference in rank' perpetuated by the Brigade: 'If this is not militarism', he declared, 'I should like to know what is.'[14]

By the 1930s the JLB was being increasingly challenged by both the appearance of rival youth groups and by the politicisation of Jewish youth especially in the East End of London. In 1898, at the Second Zionist Congress, Dr Max Nordau made his famous call for the physical education of the Jewish people. *Muskeljudentum,* which had received practical expression in the creation of the first Jewish sports club in Constantinople in 1895 – the same year as the JLB was founded in London – now became incorporated into the political Zionist movement. Out of the largely German *Judische Turnerschaft* movement evolved the Maccabi Union (1921) as an integral part of the Zionist Organisation. In 1932 the first Maccabiah or 'Jewish Olympics' was held in Palestine and in 1935 Maccabi headquarters were transferred from Nazi Germany to London under the presidency of Selig Brodetsky. Henceforth, Maccabi was to compete with the JLB, Scouts and Clubs in providing sports activities for Jewish youngsters in Britain. Moreover, in 1929 *HaBonim* (The Builders) was set up by Wellesley Aron as a conscious effort to inculcate a Jewish, if not religious atmosphere, into club culture. Within a few years *HaBonim* had become militantly Zionist; Hebrew was interspersed with English as the language of command, lectures were held on aspects of Jewish history and culture, summer camp became *Hakhshara* – agricultural training with a view to settlement on *Kibbutz* in *Eretz Yisrael* (the Land of Israel). By 1939 HaBonim boasted 4,000 members – twice as many as the JLB.[15] The activities of the Zionist youth movements were stimulated further in the late 1930s with the influx of refugees from central Europe.

Zionism was becoming fashionable amongst young Anglo-Jewry and its image was arguably more democratic. A contrast has been drawn between the 'Old Order' as represented by the Association *for* Jewish Youth (1927) – and the Brigade closely linked with it – and the Federation *of* Zionist Youth (1935) created by the young people themselves.[16] The Zionist groups encouraged ideological debate and political activism. They competed with the Communist Party and its Young Communist League for the allegiance of young Jewish radicals in the East End and the working class districts of Manchester, Leeds and Glasgow. Communists and radical Zionists shared a common desire to make a stand against the Fascists. The Battle of Cable Street (October 1936) became a symbol of working class Jewish disaffection with the lukewarm attitude of established political parties and the 'low-profile' adopted by the Board of Deputies of British Jews.

Nor did the Brigade, or at least those elements which controlled Brigade policy at London Headquarters, regard Zionism as a solution to antisemitism nor, indeed, as recommendable in itself. By the 1930s, its official religious affiliation with the mainstream United Synagogue notwithstanding, the JLB had developed strong links with the Liberal Synagogue. This was a tendency shared with other Jewish youth organisations notably Basil Henriques' Bernhard Baron Settlement and Lily Montagu's West Central Clubs. In those days, such links were significant given that the Liberal Synagogue had become, in the opinion of Geoffrey Alderman, 'a religious refuge for anti-Zionists in the inter-war period'.[17] Harold Cohen, a leading benefactor of the Brigade in Liverpool and a member of the Liberal Synagogue in London was, according to *The Times*, 'on more than one occasion' reported to have said that:

> He was not ... what for want of a better term was called a Zionist, but for all Jews fortunate enough to live under the aegis of the British Empire ... it could only be good to assist those Jews who still suffered great disabilities, and even persecution, in some other European countries. It was for them that the work in Palestine was intended.[18]

In an age of ideologies, the JLB stuck to its tried and tested formula: the inculcation of discipline and good citizenship. As for the problem of antisemitism, E. Royalton Kisch, summer camp commandant in 1928, declared:

> There are ... reasons which lead to an anti-Jewish feeling here, and one of them is ... the undisciplined and un-Jewish behaviour of some of our fellow Jews ... Unnecessary showiness of dress; extravagant public displays, intolerance of the views and feelings of others, disrespect of persons and institutions, money-lending and sharp practices in commerce are unfortunately not rare ... We are a conspicuous minority and always in the limelight ... and the bad impression caused by the wrong-doings of the ten bad men reflects ten-fold upon the many *Minyanim* (prayer quora) of good Jews.

This speech came dangerously close to an apologia for the antisemites, whose brand of racial prejudice was far nastier than anything which had confronted the Brigade in its early days.

In the aftermath of the Battle of Cable Street, Harold Lion, officer commanding the London Regiment declared:

> The Jews are as worthy citizens as anybody else in this land. We have been disgusted and shocked at the things that have been going on in the East End. They are most undeserved and I am afraid it has been a case of Jew-baiting.

> I feel there is nothing like speaking one's mind. Ninety per cent. of our fellow Jews are as good a type as anyone else. It is that minimum which belongs to no organisation at all who cause trouble. If we can get every member of the Jewish community into the brigade or a club or some similar organisation, I am sure that through the training we give them we shall have no antisematism [sic] whatsoever.

Following an impressive display mounted by the Brigade in March 1937, Lord Reading wrote in glowing terms to Lion:

> I am sure that it must be a lasting satisfaction to you and your officers to realise that your hard work is not wasted but is successfully supplying the best possible answer to antisemitism.

> In any case this temporary wave of artificially engendered hostility will pass, but the results of your labours will remain for all to see in the physical and moral development of the next generation.

The assumption that antisemitism could be cured by 'good behaviour' on the part of Jews permeated down through the ranks of the Brigade. In an issue of the Brigade journal *The Advance* published soon after the coming to power of Hitler in Germany in 1933, Captain P. Levy of the Tottenham Company wrote under the heading 'Anti-Semitism' as follows:

> We Jews in England are fortunate to live in a country which has always been extremely tolerant ... The English have always treated the Jews well; the Jews have, in their turn, always striven to show how they recognise this just treatment ... by force of example we should demonstrate how unjust and how unreasonable attacks on Jews really are. The charges that the Nazis bring against the Jews can be refuted only in one way: by actually showing that the Jew is neither treacherous, nor deceitful, nor unscrupulous in his greed for gold, nor mean and cunning, nor lacking in any of the nobler motives which the Nazis deny of all Jews ...

> ... I would urge upon you the necessity of always living an upright and chivalrous

life, as only through such example can antisemitism be *permanently* [sic] destroyed.

The idea that Hitler was amenable to 'gentlemanly' behaviour and the claims of 'justice' was hopelessly naïve. English public school notions of sportsmanship and fair play were to be swept away in the maelstrom of the 1930s and 1940s. Captain Rubby Risner who had grown up with the Brigade and who was something of a writer in its journals, spent a few weeks in Germany in November 1934. Judging from his testimony published in *The Advance* the following spring, the experience had been nothing less than traumatic. 'Unfortunately,' he wrote, 'the accounts given in the Jewish Press are more or less true ... The Jews are completely segregated and ostracised.' (This, before the imposition of the Nuremberg Laws in 1935.) On one occasion, Risner attended a concert held in a grand synagogue:

> The orchestra of thirty sat on a platform just in front of the Ark (the men wearing their skullcaps) and rendered a fine interpretation of Schubert, Mozart, Haydn, Beethoven ... Thus by playing to Jewish audiences first-class Jewish musicians are able to eke out a livelihood in the Germany of today.

Yet, even Risner clung on to his faith in human nature:

> I came away from Germany with the conviction that if only the common people were given *a sporting chance* [author's italics] – before the youth have been poisoned by the teaching [of Nazism] – there will yet be a chance for German Jewry to regain their lost status.

'But,' he added 'the Jews themselves are very pessimistic.'[19]

Nor did it do for the Jew to attract attention to himself by being overly successful. In 1936 the Brigade took the decision to withdraw temporarily from competing for the Prince of Wales Boxing Shield. The Brigade had won this trophy an almost embarrassing number of times since its inception in the early 1920s. This remarkable success was attributed: 'To the fact that other cadet units could not compare, age for age, with the Jewish boys in physique and fitness, and to the fact that greater care was lavished upon their children by Jewish parents.' The decision to withdraw may have been hailed as sportsmanlike, but was governed too by other motives. As the veteran Commanding Officer of the Manchester JLB (E.C.Q. Henriques), put it: '[We do] not go out for 'pot-hunting', and, indeed, there was a danger in the Jewish clubs always being so successful, so much so that jealousy was perhaps created and non-Jewish clubs would not enter the competitions.' The Brigade evidently did not subscribe to the philosophy of Benny Leonard, the American Jewish lightweight champion of the world, who asserted that 'the Jewish youth of America should learn the art of boxing, because the ability to handle your fists is perhaps the best insurance against antisemitism'.[20] In December 1939, soon after the outbreak of the Second World War, the notorious English Nazi radio propagandist Lord 'Haw-Haw' described the JLB as 'the greatest of Jewish sports organisations,' and as in control of British sport.

Still less did the Brigade wish to engage in any form of political activism. In April 1933 an organisation styling itself the 'Jewish Lads' Brigade anti-Fascist Group' distributed leaflets outside Camperdown House[21] calling upon members to demonstrate at the May Day rally in Hyde Park. The flyer, signed by the committee's chairman Joe Levy and secretary Miss Green, was headed 'JEWISH LADS' BRIGADE. WHAT ARE WE DOING AGAINST HITLER'S MURDER GANG?' The answer was provided by Ernest Halsted and his colleagues who swiftly brought an injunction to stop the anti-Fascist committee from printing and disseminating 'defamatory' material in the name of the JLB. In their evidence, the Brigade submitted that it had '...no political object, and was entirely opposed to any form of political agitations [sic] and to the spreading of Communism and class hatred among its members.' Nevertheless, the rather curious spectacle of a Jewish organisation silencing anti-Nazi activity hit national headlines. Perhaps the JLB's stance was not so remarkable after all. They were simply following the example set by the Board of Deputies in the 1930s.

There is some evidence however, that grassroots JLB members engaged in political activity, despite the disapproval of Headquarters. Motel Robins, long time Brigade Archivist, recalls:

> If my memory serves me well, and it does, many a demonstration which took place East of Aldgate Pump mainly consisted of alerted members of the working class, Communists, Socialists, and many ... Jewish 'teenagers'. They always had a band, which consisted mainly of members of the JLB D[rum &] Fife & Bugle Band – of course in MUFTI. If the upper crust were aware of this, I shall never know, but who knows, perhaps the Nelson Eye existed amongst those who cared. Most youth club members took part in the struggle against Fascism. I cannot recall any demonstration taking place at that time organised by the big whigs of the Jewish Community.[22]

Englishmen of the Mosaic Persuasion

By the 1930s, the JLB, with its emphasis on patriotic service to the state, had become the natural home for those 'Englishmen of the Mosaic Persuasion' to whom Jewish nationalism was anathema. This was perhaps ironic given the proto-Zionist activities of founder Colonel Goldsmid. As Harold Lion, a member of the West London Reform Synagogue and future Brigade Commandant, put it in 1934 in a speech at the Oxford Union:

> I for one am a British Jew and whilst I have every sympathy with the trials and tribulations of our co-religionists abroad, my loyalty is to England and it seems to me a pretty poor sort of loyalty that discredits its country where one earns one's living, has been educated and had all the advantages of imperialism in the true sense of the word ... I do not want you to misunderstand me as being anti-Zionist; perhaps the better way of putting it would be to say that one is pro-British.[23]

Certainly, as far as Brigade work was concerned, the political views of the leadership were not made overt. Yet they inevitably permeated down. From the outside, the Brigade was perceived as a non-Zionist and, at times, anti-Zionist organisation in the 1930s and 1940s. Leopold Greenberg, the Zionist editor of the *Jewish Chronicle* once wrote: 'I was surprised to find ... that the J.L.B. band could not play *Hatikvah* [the Zionist anthem]. Is it that in the Brigade Jewish Nationalist feelings are quelled or kept submerged? Someone in authority might care to state what attitude the J.L.B. takes up on this question.'[24]

No response was forthcoming from the Brigade on this point. Moreover, there is little doubt that the impression that the JLB was unsympathetic to Zionism was reinforced in the years immediately after the end of the Second World War. This was largely on account of the controversial political career of the new Commandant, Louis Gluckstein (1897–1979), outside his Brigade work. Tall and distinguished, Gluckstein sprang from the family which helped found both the Salmon & Gluckstein tobacco company and J. Lyons & Co. – of corner-house teashop fame. Educated at St Paul's School and Lincoln College, Oxford, Louis became a barrister, colonel and was Conservative MP for Nottingham East between 1931–45. Later on, he was to serve on the London County Council and was elected Chairman of the Greater London Council in 1968. Through Gluckstein, the Brigade connection with the Liberal Synagogue was perpetuated. He succeeded Claude Montefiore as president and, as its representative on the Board of Deputies, played a prominent role in the abortive battle at the Board to secure legal recognition for Liberal Judaism for the purpose of appointing marriage secretaries.[25]

Much more important, however, in the context of the present discussion, in 1939 Gluckstein voted with the government in favour of the MacDonald White Paper which severely curtailed Jewish immigration into British Mandatory Palestine, effectively blocking one of the major escape routes from Hitler's Europe. Moreover, in the final years of the Mandate, Gluckstein joined Basil Henriques as a founder member of the Jewish Fellowship (1944–48) which has been described by Gideon Shimoni as 'the last stand of anti-Zionism in Anglo-Jewry'.[26] During the war, this grouping had taken part in fighting a rearguard action at the Board of Deputies to prevent the 'takeover' by the Zionists and the adoption of the 'Biltmore Program' (1942) for Jewish statehood.

Gluckstein was Commandant of the JLB for the 10 years between 1945–55. Under his leadership, even behind the scenes the subject of Zionism was studiously ignored. One can search in vain through the JLB minutes for 1948 for some mention of the creation of the State of Israel – a momentous event in modern Jewish history by any standards. By contrast, in November 1948, the Brigade immediately sent a telegram of congratulations to their Majesties King George VI and Queen Elizabeth on the birth of a grandson and Heir Apparent Prince Charles, later Prince of Wales. This reluctance to accept the new political realities persisted and, arguably, was reinforced by the experience of the Second World War and the Nazi Holocaust. One-third of world Jewry had been wiped out in the Nazi genocide. But throughout the 1950s the JLB carried on as if nothing had changed. This was no doubt symptomatic of the 'collective amnesia',[27] induced by guilt feelings which enveloped Anglo-Jewry in the immediate postwar period.

It was not until the late 1950s that the JLB came to terms with, and finally embraced the State of Israel. But the process took a decade and was not completed until after Gluckstein's departure from office. In 1958 the Israeli Ambassador to London, Eliahu Elath, inspected the JLB camp at Walmer. The invitation was extended by Commandant Harold Lion, but the initiative had come from Jonas May. Headquarters Committee 'applauded the news', welcomed the anticipated publicity, and invited the Ambassador to write the foreword to the annual report. His flattering words concerning the 'noble tradition of the Brigade' carried an unconscious irony. It was just as well that the Ambassador had been insufficiently briefed on the history of the Brigade. In any case, bygones were bygones.

As CO London Regiment, Josh Manches was responsible for introducing the playing of *HaTikvah* in the late 1960s 'because of the pressure from parents who found it very, very odd …' that the anthem was omitted. He recalled:

> I was the first person that introduced at our camp playing … *HaTikvah* … I remember so clearly that Swaythling [Brigade Commandant the Third Lord Swaythling] was very much opposed to it … he said that we are a British unit here and we don't play the national anthem of foreign countries … Certainly, we did not want to give the impression that we were under any instructions or any control from Israel … The only time we ever played at camp before that the Israeli national anthem was when we had their Ambassador … Swaythling said that that's the time when you play[ed] the national anthem, a foreign national anthem …[28]

By Manches' time, a public demonstration of affection for Israel no longer posed a psychological threat to the stability of Anglo-Jewish life.

Ironically, even today the Brigade leadership is reluctant to recall Gluckstein's anti-Zionist record.[29] In the end, though, apparent ideological neutrality may have been a strength to the JLB. Whilst other youth organisations, including Zionist ones, have gone in and out of fashion, the Brigade has endured. It may be speculated that the existence of a religiously pluralistic and outwardly non-ideological movement like the Brigade suites well the character of the Anglo-Jewish community. Despite the conflicts, by and large, the JLB has managed to reconcile some of the tensions between British and Jewish identity.

Notes

1   A shorter version of this paper was presented at the conference 'National Identity, Assimilation and antisemitism in France and Britain in the 19th and 20th Centuries', University of Haifa, 14–15 May 1997.

2   S. Kadish, *A Good Jew and a Good Englishman: The Jewish Lads' and Girls' Brigade 1895–1995*, Ilford, Vallentine Mitchell, 1995.

3   See J. Springhall, *Youth, Empire and Society: British Youth Movements 1883–1940*, London and Connecticut, Croom Helm, 1977; M. Rosenthal, *The Character Factory: Baden-Powell and the Origins of the Boy Scout Movement*, London, Collins, 1986. A biography of Colonel Goldsmid has appeared since the centenary history of the JLB was published: E. Lehman, *The Tents of Michael: The Life and Times of Colonel Albert Williamson Goldsmid*, Maryland, University Press of America, 1996 and see my review in the *Jerusalem Post Literary Supplement*, 22 May 1997, p. 5.

4   Quoted from original JLB Pocket Book in JLB First Annual Report pp. 33–4. The Brigade archives have been deposited at Southampton University Library.

5   The earliest mention of this phrase which I have been able to trace is in the Report of the Royal Commission on Alien Immigration in 1902.

6   Youth which the *Jewish Chronicle* once notoriously referred to as 'the slouchy guttersnipes who loaf about the lanes and alleys of the East End', *Jewish Chronicle*, 8 July, 1898, p. 19.

7   *Jewish Chronicle*, 12 February 1897, p. 17.

8   Other Jewish youth groups, such as Brady Street copied the format of the JLB camp.

9   The five books of Moses.

10 The age of religious majority.

11 Hermann Adler (1839–1911), succeeded his father Nathan as Chief Rabbi in 1891, having been delegate Chief Rabbi since 1879.

12 *Jewish Chronicle*, 24 August 1900, pp. 12–3; 10 August 1900, p. 17; 7 August 1903, pp. 16-7; JLB GEN/79 Camp Sub-committee Minutes 1898–1910, 21 May 1900, 11 July 1901; JLB GEN/16 'Report of 1899 Camp' [anon.]; JLB Minutes 23 January and 6 February 1905.

13 S. Bunt, *Jewish Youth Work in Britain*, London, Bedford Square Press, 1975, pp. 46–7; *Jewish Chronicle* and *Jewish World*, 12 August 1910, plus editorial comment in latter; *Jewish Chronicle*, 4 August 1911, p. 12; *Jewish Chronicle*, 11 August 1899, p. 25; JLB Annual Report, 1902–3, pp. 14–5.

14 *Jewish World*, 5 November 1919; L/Sgt R. Risner, Bayswater Company JLB, 'From Strength to Strength', *The Reveille*, December 1922, pp. 10-1; *Di Tsait*, 11 March 1922; *Jewish Chronicle*, n.d., December 1927, January 1928 (JLB press-cuttings book, JLB Archives).

15 On 'Muscular Judaism' see *inter alia*: G. Eisen, 'Zionism, Nationalism and the Emergence of the Judische Turnerschaft', *Leo Baeck Year Book*, Vol. 28, 1983, pp. 246–62; entries on 'Nordau' and 'Maccabi World Union' in *Encyclopaedia Judaica*. I am grateful to Professor Richard Cohen of the Hebrew University who first suggested a possible link between English 'Muscular Christianity' and Nordau's 'Muscular Judaism' in a discussion on my paper at the World Congress of Jewish Studies, Jerusalem, June 1993. On Jewish youth organisations see especially D. Mendelsson, 'The Development of a Pioneering (*Hechalutzti*) Youth Movement from 1929–48' [HaBonim], unpublished Hebrew University MA thesis (English draft kindly loaned); M. Kalman, 'Young Zionism and Jewish Youth in London between the wars', unpublished Cambridge MA dissertation (kindly loaned); H. Silman-Cheonig, *Wellesley Aron: Rebel with a Cause*, Ilford, Vallentine Mitchell, 1992.

16 Bunt, op. cit.

17 G. Alderman, *Modern British Jewry*, Oxford, Clarendon Press, 1992 p. 353.

18 *The Times*, 28 July 1936.

19 JLB Archives GEN/5; 'Jew-baiting', 'Cutting from local press' [Woolwich], JLB press cuttings book, 6 November 1936; 16 March 1937, JLB LETT/2; *The Advance*, May–June 1933, pp. 5,7, April–June 1935, p. 3.

20 *Jewish Chronicle*, 27 March, 8 May, 11 September 1936 on boxing; 8 December, on 'Haw-Haw'.

21 JLB headquarters.

22 See *The Times*, *Evening News*, *Star*, 1 May 1933. Motel Robins to Charles Kay (former Brigade Secretary), 5 January 1993, kindly passed on to the author. In a letter written since the publication of *A Good Jew and a Good Englishman*, Lazarus Sheridan recalled the differing attitudes towards political activism on the part of members of the JLB and of the Hutchison House Club for Working Lads which shared premises at Camperdown House in the 1930s:

The most important difference in the two organisations became clear at the height of the Fascist marches, The Hutch boys, in the main, became very political and left wing. A meeting of the Hutch boys was called by the Managers who urged the boys to keep away from the great demonstration, now known as the Cable Street Battle, that was to take place. It was a very angry meeting, and the boys expressed themselves strongly! Many Hutch and JLB lads played a part in that battle.

He added: 'I agree with you that the Officers of the JLB were naïve in their philosophy as to the cause of antisemitism.'

Letter to the author, 6 October 1997 and see L. Sheridan, *King Sol*, London (publisher not known), 1939.
23 Cited in Bunt op. cit., ch. 3.
24 *Jewish World*, 22 August 1929.
25 Since Chief Rabbi J.H. Hertz had finally (despite some measure of accommodation during the war years) set his face against the Liberals as 'persons professing the Jewish religion', Glucktein's efforts proved fruitless. Like the Reformers before them (in 1856) the Liberals were obliged to seek redress through parliament with a special Marriage Act in 1958. See Alderman *British Jewry*, op. cit. and *Jewish Chronicle*, 19 November 1954; 2 November 1979 (obituary).
26 G. Shimoni, 'The non-Zionists in Anglo-Jewry, 1937–48', *Jewish Journal of Sociology*, Vol. 28, 1986, pp. 89–115.
27 Alderman, *British Jewry*, op. cit., p. 310.
28 Taped interview with the late Josh Manches, 22 December 1993, Southampton University Library.
29 See *Jewish Chronicle*, 26 August and 2 September 1994; G. Alderman, 'Anglo-Jewry and its Present Discontents', *Jewish Quarterly*, Summer 1995, pp. 21–5, esp. p. 24.

4 Issues of Identity through the Synagogue: British Jewish Women in the late Twentieth Century

MARLENA SCHMOOL

Introduction

This chapter is concerned with a particular form of identity, namely Jewish identity and more specifically the identity of British Jewish women. These issues have not been much researched despite a worldwide expansion of gender and women's studies over the past 20–30 years that has brought forward a vast literature on American Jewish women. This has expanded the range of Jewish sociological research undertaken in the United States since the late 1950s but in neither field has there been a parallel Americanisation of British Jewry. Indeed the number of Jewish academics and scholars who have worked consistently in these areas in Great Britain since the 1960s may be counted in tens – if that. Only two large scale surveys of Jews were carried out in Britain before the 1990s, both of them drawing on American experience. They are Krausz's survey of Edgware Jewry[1] and Kosmin's study of Redbridge[2] and both were constructed as community studies which incorporated questions pertaining to Jewish identity. In this they followed the pattern set down by such pioneering work as Goldstein's Survey of the Jews of Rhode Island.[3]

For this author, as a practitioner of British Jewish social science, the reasons for such a lack are not difficult to find. They relate to three circumstances that we repeatedly confront and that seem to combine in a peculiar way. As far as I am aware these research issues have not been greatly aired in respectable print but they form a regular subtext whenever Jewish researchers confer. First there is widespread agreement that British Jewry is at bottom if not anti-intellectual then certainly non-intellectual in its organised aspects. This is not of course to ignore the very many historians, scientists and thinkers who have brought honour and recognition to the community but it is to indicate that their professional interests and achievements are rarely in the field of the social sciences of the Jews. This may be a result of the minimal British audience for these topics as compared with the vast numbers of American Jewry or could indicate lack of the philosophical predisposition of smaller European communities towards ideological issues. But beyond this there seems to be a historical pattern growing from the British understanding of education as a means to an end, as something that shows material results. Moreover, while Jewish learning looks to a different result – to development of man's holiness and learning as a way to becoming a more observant Jew – it nevertheless echoes this British instrumentalism to some extent. Two conventions could here have reinforced one another. The late nineteenth century Jewish immigrants to be discussed later were subjected to a secular education system that taught reading, writing and arithmetic to fit them for the job-market of the time. Perhaps British social class divisions did not encourage an opening of the mind for penniless newcomers and their children. Then again after World War II Britain did not have an equivalent of the GI Bill to provide returning soldiers with a university education that would compensate a generation of men for a disrupted youth and lost opportunities. From the Jewish point of view any discussion of possible outcomes is, unfortunately, speculative but it is unquestionable that the community did not establish a cadre of scholars who concerned themselves with British Jewry nor did it develop a tradition of social assessment at a time when it needed so to do.

Secondly, this lack is compounded by past reluctance of the community through its leaders and organisations to invest in the social research which would help in basic planning. The process here reinforces itself circularly. If there had been a tradition of self-examination and academic enquiry then leadership would have found money to support research. In fact, there were a handful of small-scale numeric assessments of community at irregular intervals before 1939. Furthermore in the middle of World War II a proposal was put to the Board of Deputies of British Jews that it should undertake a properly designed statistical study in order sensibly to confront the outcomes of the upheavals experienced by the community during the war. This suggestion was never acted upon but some four years after the war a study was carried out by Neustatter[4] which provided a statistical benchmark that went unchallenged for some 20 years. Research on any continuous basis therefore began only in the mid-1960s when the Board of Deputies[5] established its Statistical and Demographic (now Community) Research Unit initially to monitor the community numerically. These studies have continued until today and have also expanded to embrace wider surveys and evaluations, undertaken both by the Unit and other organisations. The steady preaching and application of researchers and their protagonists have slowly engendered an understanding that research is indispensable in accurately describing community and in anticipating its needs. This attitudinal shift has been helped by generational changes where both lay and professional leaders in the community are now disciples of an educational system which has inculcated the value of information for decision-making.

Thirdly, until 1993, British Jewish women were especially under-researched, if not ignored, because of their limited representation in those mainstream Jewish organisations that promote studies. Decisions about what to study were for the most part arrived at by men; the committees which plan and oversee research have had few women members. As it takes some years to reach positions of authority within the institutional structure of British Jewry, these men were also for the most part older and likely to disregard the fact that more than half the British Jewish population has been female over the past 45 years[6] and unheeding of the feminist currents which were affecting British Jewry by way of general society.

The overall situation has changed in the 1990s and there have been three major studies[7] since 1991 all of which incorporated the core identity questions. These were the Membership Review of the United Synagogue[8] (fieldwork in 1991), the survey commissioned by/for the Review of Women in the British Jewish Community (fieldwork 1993) and the Institute for Jewish Policy Research's study of the Social Attitudes of British Jews (fieldwork 1995). As a member of the research teams responsible for all three studies, I can testify to the care taken to ensure that each study covered consistent central elements of identity. As is clear from the titles of the studies, the middle one concerned itself only with women; it focused on their position, experiences and requirements as Jewish women. Its database, which is described in greater depth later in this chapter, therefore provides an opportunity to examine many aspects of the lives of British Jewish women and in particular to relate them to Jewish identity.

We must, however, begin by asking why women's involvement came to the fore as a crucial discussion area within the Jewish community. Until the appearance of modernity, which affected the numerous Diaspora communities at different rates over the past 200 years, within orthodox Judaism throughout the world gender roles of men and women were well-defined and separated into different spheres of influence. A division was established between the home and the synagogue/study house: the public arena was for men and the private for women. This pattern was reinforced as Jewish communities came into contact with nineteenth century bourgeois family models and slowly embraced them[9] but was at variance with the working life of East European women in their small communities.[10] However on coming to Britain immigrant women and their daughters adapted to this 'modern' form as British Jewry became steadily more middle class.

Not all women were content to accept these limitations. In the course of this century, slowly at first but at an accelerating pace over the past twenty or so years, women have come to assert themselves in relation to the synagogue, i.e. in respect of the man's sphere of influence. This began with the birth of liberal synagogues[11] which *ab initio* allowed women a public voice and whose example was eventually followed by the reform synagogues.[12] Then since about the mid-1970s younger women, including the orthodox, have been motivated and influenced by feminist thought originating mainly from the United States and by better and more widespread Jewish education for women of all ages; both these trends have meant attenuation of the institutionalised role differentiation. The affects have been cumulative. Women are less and less willing to accept traditional restrictions and look to play a stronger role in the decision-making processes of communal institutions. By definition in Britain this assumes they will participate more extensively in synagogue affairs and for such involvement to have real meaning, women must see the synagogue as an arena for personal activity beyond the now almost-defunct Ladies' Guild.[13]

While Jewish awareness of woman's place and importance has in part been enhanced by the influence of secular feminist thought, it nevertheless has important religious reverberations in the community. Its consequence comes from woman's preeminent role in socialising successive generations into Judaism and the fact that the steady movement of women towards wider communal involvement has established an alternative model for their successors. Essentially, as for British women generally, new modes of thought have provided British Jewish women with choices and opportunities beyond marriage and the family. Furthermore, in the past two decades Jewish women have shown an increasing readiness to intermarry and cohabit.[14] Home and community no longer fulfil Jewish women *en masse* – if they ever did. A community anxious about its future must therefore provide the rising generations of well-educated women with those public outlets for Jewish identity that are permitted to other aspects of their personalities. It is against this background that appraisal of the attitudes and identity of British Jewish women must be set.

This chapter therefore begins by examining the concept of Jewish identity and explaining how it has been measured and analysed. In doing so it draws on the findings of the Review of Women in the British Jewish Community including both subjective and objective approaches to identity. This discussion is set in the context of British Jewish, particularly demographic, development and current international concerns about future of world Jewry. Since the main institution of Diaspora Jewry throughout the centuries has been the synagogue, particular attention is paid to how women's identity relates to their attitudes to the synagogue today and what this may mean for British Jewry as it reaches the twenty-first century.

Measuring Jewish Identity in British Jewish Women

Essentially Jewish identity, like any other, is a socio-psychological construct; it is not a fixed entity but rather develops over time and with life's experiences.[15] However, its meaning is often taken for granted and Jewish identity studies have for the most part disregarded the technical psychological understanding of the term.[16] Sociological quantitative research processes by their nature demand a rigor that makes it inappropriate for the psychological aspects to be covered simply by asking, for example, 'on a scale of 1–10, how Jewish do you feel'. While such questions have indeed been asked, normally they simply accompanied enquiries about the core beliefs, basic practices and links between Jewish people – without seeking deeper meaning or substance. This triad of elements has been studied since the late 1950s in the (mainly) American surveys mentioned in the introduction. A range of factors was selected for those studies on the basis of Jewish norms and subsequently they evolved into a minimal yardstick for assessing adherence to community and religion. This covered belief, practice and ethnic feeling and has come to be used internationally on the premise that Jews everywhere may be expected to follow a common rule.

In the main, because American studies were related to community planning, the sampling unit was the household and 'identity' was taken as a catch-all for strength of household commitment to the principles and structure of the organised Jewish community. In 1993 the Review of Women in the British Jewish Community tailored the basic format so that questions were directed to women as individuals rather than as spokeswomen for a household. Although a household address was chosen for the postal survey (by which means this research was carried out), the contact letter was directed to one *named* woman with specific methodological adjustments to ensure wide age coverage[17] and the index was extended to take in personal perceptions and attitudes. The Review itself was promoted by the then-new Chief Rabbi, Dr Jonathan Sacks, who declared himself eager to encourage the involvement of women in communal affairs and who had previously, under the banner 'Traditional Alternatives', spearheaded a conference focusing on women's issues. The Review was partly prompted by his understanding that social currents had clearly influenced Jewish women, particularly their take-up of the educational opportunities afforded by the expansion of universities, their appreciation of feminism and the rising incidence of divorce. All three trends were considered to contain negative effects for a community which looked to its women Jewishly to socialise the growing generations.

The Women's Review primarily adopted the yardstick by asking about adherence to *ritual observances*: lighting of candles on a Friday night, attending a *Seder* (Passover meal), maintaining a kosher home, fasting on the Day of Atonement, frequency of synagogue attendance and refraining from driving or travelling on the Sabbath. These items were scored for strength of observance and amended by a negative score allotted for taking part in seasonal activities at Christmas time, such as hanging up stockings. Commitment to core *religious tenets* was assessed by respondents checking, in a list of statements expressing issues of Jewish interest, how far they agreed with belief statements relating to: a) God's centrality to Judaism; b) the Jewish people's special relationship (covenant) with God; c) God's place in the creation of the World; and d) the efficacy of prayer. *Sense of peoplehood* (ethnicity) was examined by questions about communally structural elements such as proportion of Jewish friends, and synagogue and organisation memberships. At the psychological level this index covered the respondent's feeling of closeness to other Jews and degree of personal Jewish awareness, together with her evaluation of: a) Jews' ability to rely only on Jews; b) whether Jews should only marry within the group; c) the importance of the survival of the Jewish people; and d) the unity of Jewish people throughout the world.

The responses for ritual, belief and peoplehood were scored and summed for each respondent. The individual scores for the three dimensions were added and averaged to provide a single personal score as an index of 'identity'. A crosscheck on what this index implies for respondents themselves was provided by a subjective religious self-assessment scale. For this, respondents were asked which one of five labels best described their position as regards Jewish religious practice. The choices were: non-practising (i.e. secular), just Jewish, progressive (e.g. liberal, reform) 'traditional' (not strictly orthodox) and strictly

Orthodox (e.g. would *not* turn on a light on Sabbath) and responses neatly allocated the women into the four distinct groups delineated below.

Each subjective group showed strongly patterned combinations of the components which were selected for identity measurement.[18] The strictly Orthodox women, as would be expected, have full commitment to Jewish practice, a commitment which is driven as much by belief as it is by the wish to express ethnic identity. Traditional women observe ritual practices less rigorously and have moderate to low levels of belief, yet they show high levels of ethnic identity. Non-Orthodox – just Jewish and progressive – women, while admitting to a religious identity and showing high levels of ethnicity, nevertheless have low levels of ritual practice and belief; and secular women exhibit practically no belief or practice but still have strong levels of ethnic identity. Thus when comparing groups we can see that only the ethnic element contributes markedly to overall Jewish identity.

Background to the Contemporary Jewish Community

British Jewry is a community based on immigrants. Its modern history is usually dated from 1656 with the settlement in London of a small group of Sephardi Jews. This reintroduction of open Jewish life into Christian England involved no more than a score of families.[19] They were quickly followed by co-religionists of Ashkenazi stock coming either directly from Germany or again via Holland.[20] The community continued to grow slowly and by 1800 it numbered between 20,000 and 25,000.[21] By the early 1880s when an escalating influx from Eastern and Central Europe was given extra impetus by the passing of the antisemitic May laws in Russia in 1882, England was home to a little over 60,000 Jews.[22]

Immigrant and native-born alike lived mainly in London. Originally they concentrated in the Spitalfields and Aldgate/Whitechapel areas at the eastern boundary of the City of London but with slow migrations of the more affluent to the northern areas of Hackney and Stamford Hill and of the socially aspiring to Bayswater and Maida Vale in the west. Between 1880 and 1914 the flow into the area of first settlement, within walking distance of both Liverpool Street station and the London docks, was to confirm the 'East End' as the heart of a new British Jewry composed of Ashkenazi proletarian immigrants and their first-generation British-born children. This was the basis of a fivefold growth in British Jewish population by 1914,[23] a direct and indirect consequence of Jewish participation in the nineteenth century mass migrations from Europe. The direct consequence was the immediate addition to British Jewry of the Jews who settled here and the indirect was natural increase accruing to marriages between immigrant men and local Jewish women (who might otherwise have remained spinsters) and from immigrant women who had larger families than their British-born co-religionists.

The response of the socially-integrated Jewish establishment to this demographic challenge may be summed up as an attempt 'to turn the immigrants into Englishmen of the Jewish persuasion' and if this was not possible for the adults then certainly it was to be attempted for the children.[24] From the point of view of the acculturated British Jewish community, the acceptance they had laboured long to earn and had earned by 1871, seemed threatened by newcomers with strange customs who did not readily blend into the late-Victorian English scene. An ethos of cultural imperialism permitted these attempts to mould the incomers to a pattern of private religion, maintained in the home not in the street, where attendance at synagogue on Saturday mirrored church attendance on Sunday. This cautious view of religion as selected public rites was a far cry from the vibrant Judaism of the *shtetl* (East European Jewish village) that the immigrants had left behind and not unnaturally the activities of the Establishment met with reaction and opposition.[25] For their part, the immigrants must have experienced what would now be termed 'culture shock'. They came from countries where they had lived in self-contained societies and while there had been migration from rural to urban areas within Eastern and Central Europe, the immigrants were for the most part only a generation away from rural life in small villages.[26] The move to the smoky industrial tenements and overcrowded houses of East London must have been traumatic.[27]

The immigrants brought with them a sense of mutual responsibility which, notwithstanding its place in the religious values of the longer-settled, was a particularly marked element in the immigrant way of life and may be seen as a form of proto-ethnicity. It expressed itself in institutions such as *hevrot* (small prayer groups), *landsmanschaften* (organisations of people originating from the same village or area) and friendly societies (whose functions very gradually integrated with those of older agencies such as synagogue burial societies), as well as in the sharing of scarce household space with acquaintances and kin from *der heim* (the home). This influx has provided the demographic core of British Jewry throughout the twentieth century. No later immigration has been large enough greatly to colour the broad trends of British Jewish development. Concomitantly their values and the patterns of Jewish identity that emanate from them have formed the cornerstones of the modern British community.

Between 1918 and 1950 British Jewry grew in numbers from some 300,000 to over 400,000, Since the mid-1950s there has been a steady contraction in core numbers caused by both strict demographic decrease and diffuse social movement away from the community.[28] British Jewry, in common with other western Jewish communities, has had to face the paradox that acceptance by host communities has been at the cost of widespread rejection of Jewish religious and cultural values and of physical departure from the community.

Populations are not static and British Jewry is at present reaching the end of a demographic period that has its roots in the late nineteenth century. Later inflows of refugees in the 1930s and immediately after World War II, and between 1956 and the 1970s with incomers from for example Egypt, Hungary, Aden and Iraq, were not large enough to change the long-term demographic nature of community. However their synagogues and associations remain identifiable elements in the communal framework. Similarly the more recent influx of Israelis is strongly noticeable in particular areas of northwest London[29] and an unnumbered but substantial South African immigration has also become part of contemporary British Jewry. Neither group has established a distinct structural position in the community; rather both have been absorbed into its existing institutions.

The predominant influences on the present demographic structure of British Jewry have been the mass-immigration of the late nineteenth century and the youthful nature of the immigrants. It is important that this migration was limited to a relatively short time-span and that both adult women immigrants and the generation brought as infants to Britain showed high levels of fertility. The succeeding generation adapted immediately to then-current British, middle class patterns of low fertility and families born to the cohort of Jewish women marrying after about 1925 were almost half the size of the previous generation.[30] Native-born British Jewry did not thereafter replace itself and the tendency has, in the main, continued until today.[31] Only with the increase, over the past 25 years, in numbers of those who meticulously observe Jewish law has a substantial section of any age-cohort emulated the birth rate of the 1880–1920 immigrant women. Strict natural decrease has been accompanied by changing social forces[32] which have also occasioned numeric loss to the community. These include less, or at least postponed, synagogue affiliation and a low rate of synagogue marriage. These societal influences produce a Jewish social erosion that matures into a strong dynamic.

In 1995, the British Jewish core population was estimated at some 285,000 persons.[33] Just under two-thirds lived within the geographical boundaries of

Greater London and the remainder were either in smaller communities or spread as individuals through the regions. While there are strong long-established communities throughout northern England, when seen with a broad brush the concentration of British Jewry within (Greater) London has always been its most marked geographic feature. Within this population as a whole, women account for approximately 55 per cent.[34] Outside London, the proportion of Jewish women rises to 57 per cent as a result of the migration experience and age-structure of smaller communities. Given this majority position and women's traditional socialising role, changes in their attitudes to community become crucial.

Community and Identity

Late twentieth century British Jewry centres around synagogues which have largely been organised through the Chief Rabbinate and those synagogues which recognise its authority. The *Jewish Year Book*[35] explains that the Chief Rabbinate developed from the position of the rabbi of the Great Synagogue in London in the early eighteenth century. He was acknowledged initially as the spiritual leader of the London *Ashkenazi* (East and Central European) community and recognition gradually spread to the regions and overseas. Today his official designation is Chief Rabbi of the United Hebrew Congregations of the Commonwealth. The *Sephardi* (Spanish and Portuguese) congregations have their own spiritual head. Self-evidently the Chief Rabbi's authority does not stretch to progressive synagogues but nevertheless the very existence of the Chief Rabbinate causes outside society[36] to perceive British Jewry as monolithic, although the media publicity given to communal disagreements and wrangles in recent months[37] is no doubt affecting this image. However, while the myth of unity does not hold within the community, widespread awareness of variety is counterbalanced across-the-board by an ignorance of communal size and definition that assumes estimates of Jewish population are restricted simply to those who belong to a synagogue. This interpretation is ill-founded: of the 285,000 estimated core population, approximately 72,000 households and a further 19,000 individuals are affiliated to over 350 synagogues.[38] Assuming 2.4 persons per household, these two elements cover approximately 67 per cent of the delineated population. The remaining 33 per cent includes individuals who may have strong communal affiliation through organisational and/or family ties as well as those socially or geographically removed from any kind of formal Jewish commitment or activity. Responses such as 'I think of myself as belonging to my parents' synagogue in ...' were fairly regular when enrolling unaffiliated respondents for the Women's Review and many women who are not synagogue members will be numbered among the approximately 24,400 members of the women's organisations which provide non-synagogal avenues to community involvement.[39] Furthermore, unaffiliated men and women include some who have not *yet* decided to join a synagogue and catalysts such as the death of a friend or relative may edge individuals into synagogue membership. The ratio of synagogue members to estimated population is upheld by findings of the Institute for Jewish Policy Research's database[40] which showed that 70 per cent of respondents (all aged over 18) were synagogue members.

Naturally indirect methods of estimating population do not bring in all who might self-identify as Jewish if asked directly. It is clear that beyond the 'estimated unaffiliated' revealed by comparisons of various data sets are the 'unestimated unaffiliated' who would come to light only, for example, in a statutory census.[41] Techniques of estimation suggest that high proportions of 'unestimated' may be young and have a sense of Jewish identity based on criteria other than those in the yardstick.[42] That these younger people may be omitted from calculations reinforces the observation that the decision to join a synagogue comes mainly in later adulthood. The age-structure of synagogue members confirms a strong coincidence between synagogue membership and marriage/child rearing. Although synagogue (or any) marriage is not a *sine qua non* for parents who wish to join a synagogue, *in this context* it becomes a comprehensive index of communal identity levels, attesting to commitment to community and its institutions at a key life-cycle stage. Thus the declining synagogue marriage rate recorded over the past 40 years[43] reflects not only the changing demographic structure of British Jewry but also the religious and secular social forces to which the community has been exposed.

Since the mid-1980s the cumulative outcomes of these social forces have generated communal concern about the continuing vitality of world Jewry. The anxiety has engaged Jewish leaders and communal professionals internationally in a sustained dialogue with academics working in the field.[44] More parochially the intensified interest in identity issues and in British Jewish women's views of their community may be construed as growing in part out of these worries. The importance of identity, particularly that of women, had been brought forward earlier by Kosmin and Levy. Writing about the Redbridge Jewry of the late 1970s they found a 'gender bias in belief ... especially interesting when seen in terms of practice. Those rituals which are observed most are home-based, traditionally the realm of the woman'. Kosmin and

Levy linked these home observances to a desire, particularly among women, to transmit Jewish values and knowledge.[45] This transmission is a handing over of Jewish identity; supremely for all concerned about the future of the Jewish people the driving imperative has become this transmission of conviction and heritage to succeeding generations. This process has usually been expressed as 'strengthening Jewish identity and ensuring Jewish continuity'.

Whatever its absolute strength, intuitively we would expect identity to be its strongest at certain stages in life or at particular times of the year when the Jewish aspects of an individual's life and character may resonate more. In this way also identity is a dynamic force rather than a static entity. Certainly, communal officers and leaders have for years assumed this dynamic when noting the strong coincidence between the birth of children (or their reaching school age) and formal attachment to a synagogue. The importance of the cyclical rhythm for women was underlined in Goodkin and Citron's work for the Women's Review.[46] They begin their analysis by reporting that 'a large number of affiliated women countrywide [wished] to express thanks to God at key events in their life and the lives of their families'. It is at these times that religion and community at their best have provided the support, interest and comfort which serve to reinforce identity.

An analogous seasonal relationship is shown by the religio-ethnic involvement of High Holyday 'three times a year' synagogue attendance and by annual participation in a *Seder*. With historically poor levels of Jewish education and consequently of Jewish knowledge, such activities among Jews aged about 35 and over may be interpreted as signs of group, or ethnic, commitment rather than of religious, or spiritual, depth. Very many congregants of these ages do not readily understand the orthodox synagogue services attended by the majority of British Jewry; nor is it clear to what extent the Passover meal is more than simply a festive family gathering if it lacks recitation or understanding of the *Haggadah* (Passover prayer-book, literally 'Telling').

Just as they have been concerned about the passing on of Jewishness, those charged with ensuring that a historic chain is not broken have simultaneously been preoccupied with the attractions of an open, liberal society and its implications for the community.[47] One response has been a concerted effort to extend the availability of full-time Jewish education so that in 1996 43 per cent of British Jewish children aged between five and 17 were receiving Jewish day-school education compared with 20 per cent in 1975.[48] But for very many young Jews the years between 13 and school-leaving have been, and to a large extent still are, devoid of formal Jewish learning. At the very time when the ideological map of adult life is being established, Jewish input is almost totally social. The intellectual questioning endemic to personality development at these ages may be deprived of answers from a Jewish perspective. As a result Judaism can come to be construed as legalistic and specifically lacking guidance on morality and ethics; this may engender a distance between Jewish and other aspects of life. The gap may become increasingly difficult to close and Judaism will be further marginalised if Jews then seek responses to life's questions in secular and other religious traditions rather than recognising and valuing a Jewish moral framework which transcends ritual. Additionally, with later age at marriage and family formation, the time lengthens between an individual's own Jewish socialisation and that of her/his children, and the mechanisms and memories drawn on to reinforce Jewish socialisation become attenuated. The process of cultural and identity transmission may thus require more effort at an individual level and become more problematic at a communal one.

Women in the British Jewish Community

I turn now to data from the quantitative survey for the Review of Women in the Community which, as has been explained, examined women's experiences of, and attitudes towards, community and did so conscious that, especially 'orthodox', women were feeling disenchanted with the organised community and its synagogue-centred institutions, and were re-evaluating their role in it. Of two samples examined in the Women's Review I concentrate here on the purposeful sample of women synagogue members which was designed to represent and reflect the attitudes of synagogue-affiliated women as a whole. The sample was designed to cover women in numbers large enough to permit, with statistical certitude, in-depth examination of specific groups, such as those in the main geographical areas and in separate synagogal groups.[49]

Of the 1,125-strong sample of synagogue affiliated women, 58 per cent lived in the Greater London area and 42 per cent were from the Regions; 57 per cent were members of Orthodox synagogues and 43 per cent belonged to the progressive movement.[50] The group was mainly married or had been so in the past: 82 per cent were currently married (a further two per cent cohabited), six per cent were widowed and five per cent divorced; 89 per cent had children. The age range was wide, 17 years to 94[51] with a mean age of 47.7 years. London-based and progressive women were slightly younger than the Orthodox or those in the regions. One-third of the sample was under 40 years of age.

The women were well-educated and worked outside the home. Thirty-six per cent had 'A' level or equivalent and 26 per cent had attended university; 20 per cent of the Orthodox and 39 per cent of progressive members had a degree. Overall, 58 per cent of synagogue members were in (mainly part-time) paid employment. Of those not gainfully employed, 61 per cent were homemakers and 27 per cent had retired (presupposing earlier employment). Community links were also maintained by organisational involvement (52 per cent had attended at least one communal event in the year prior to the study) and by residential location (25 per cent considered they lived in a very Jewish area and a further 38 per cent felt their home area was moderately Jewish).

When we look at respondents' perceptions of their Jewish identity – as described in the discussion on measuring identity – we find 44 per cent were non-Orthodox (30 per cent progressive and just Jewish 14 per cent) followed by 43 per cent choosing traditional. At the ends of this self-identity continuum were four per cent secular (non-practising) with nine per cent strictly Orthodox. It must be repeated here that all these women were formally affiliated to a synagogue. Secular and just Jewish are communally identifying individuals not those from the perimeters whose links with any formal Jewishness or communal activity may be very tenuous. This becomes clear when we analyse the subjective identity categories separately in relation to synagogue membership. Looking first at progressive synagogue members, we discover that whereas two-thirds self-identify as progressive and 15 per cent as just Jewish (i.e. fall into the non-Orthodox category),16 per cent say they are traditional and the remaining five per cent are secular (non-practising). On the other hand, among members of mainstream Orthodox synagogues, over one in five allots herself to a less orthodox subjective category: five per cent progressive, 14 per cent just Jewish and three per cent secular.

It must also be recognised that while fee-paying synagogue membership was the sample-base, such affiliation indicates only the barest identification with a congregation. It need not mean that a woman attends synagogue with any regularity nor need it imply either spiritual or social satisfaction with the synagogue attended. For women, both attendance and satisfaction can be more problematic than for men since attendance is not incumbent on a woman according to *Talmudic* (orthodox Jewish) law and because membership has traditionally been vested in a man/husband who will usually make the final selection of synagogue. Nevertheless, the synagogue to which a woman (and her family) belongs will be a primary gateway to the formal community and her experiences there may be expected to colour her view of the community as a whole. Those synagogal experiences will in turn influence her sense of satisfaction with a particular congregation, a satisfaction which may itself depend on frequency of attendance, or vice versa. It should therefore be noted, and borne in mind, that only ten per cent of the sample we are discussing had attended a synagogue service 'once a month or more' in the year prior to the study. In line with calendar-linked ritual observance, 39 per cent had attended 'once or twice' but 29 per cent had not attended at all.

Life-cycle and Calendar

Quantitative postal surveys do not readily permit examination of life-cycle effects. However as there is naturally a strong relationship between life-cycle and age, it is possible to try and use age illustratively as a proxy for life-cycle. In this instance, patterns of attendance at a *Seder* and the frequency of a woman's attendance at synagogue (where incidence varies across the year) have been selected as examples of calendar-linked practices and correlated with age and identity. The results of these analyses are set out in Table 4.1 which gives correlation coefficients between four variables: age, measured identity, and the chosen calendar-linked practices. The questions (and answers) used to discover the extent of the latter were:

At Passover, do you attend a *Seder* meal at home or elsewhere?:
every year; most years; some years; never.

In the past year how often have you attended a synagogue service?:
not at all; once or twice (e.g. on Day of Atonement); on a few occasions (e.g. festivals, *Yahrzeit* [annual memorial for dead parents]); about once a month; most Sabbaths or more often.

Two points about the analyses and index need explaining here. First, attendance at synagogue and at a *Seder* are both normally incorporated in the identity index. However, for analytical purity, they have been excluded in these background correlations. Second, I have separated out women who self-identify as strictly Orthodox and they are not included in tables because, as explained above, these women produce very high scores on all identity components. The inclusion of this group in tabulations (although it is not

Table 4.1 Correlations between age, identity, and calendar-linked practices of synagogue members excluding strictly Orthodox

	Age	Identity	*Seder* attendance
Age	1.00		
Identity	0.174	1.000	
Seder attendance	0.109	0.372	1.000
Synagogue attendance	-0.006	0.316	0.361

numerically large) would cloud the picture, overstating the situation within the majority group. Any marked differences between the two sectors are noted in the commentary.

The values given in Table 4.1 are all statistically significant except for the correlation between age and synagogue attendance. The lack here of a statistically noteworthy relationship reflects what can readily be noticed about British Jewish women in the synagogue every Sabbath. This relationship could be high or low without varying with age but in fact frequent attendance of all ages is low; familiar faces are *proportionately* fewer at High Holydays or celebrations. At older ages this may be because it can be physically difficult for women to get to a synagogue (and among the older mainstream Orthodox those most likely to wish to attend may be those who are least ready to travel to synagogue). There are special attempts to attract absent younger age-cohorts but in most congregations younger women without families are not noticeable attenders, and it takes a strong commitment for a mother of very young children to sit with them and keep them quiet throughout highly structured services – orthodox or progressive. For the strictly Orthodox there is the added consideration that a child cannot be carried or pushed to synagogue. Therefore, unless a woman goes to service at a different time from her husband or has older children with whom to leave infants, she is prevented from attending. Thus for all age groups there are practical explanations for women's absence which very broadly may be extended to suggest that there is no significant life-cycle effect on synagogue attendance.

The weak but nevertheless significant correlation between age and *Seder* attendance indicates that older women were less likely to attend the traditional Passover gathering. In the light of the demographic structure of the community this is not too surprising. British Jewry has been geographically mobile within Great Britain and many parents, or widowed mothers, live some distance from their children. Although anecdotal evidence points to families getting together at this time of the year, distance, age and infirmity (or even emotional resistance to participating in a celebration which seems a shadow of earlier enactments) means that younger adults are more likely to be present at a *Seder*. This would seem to be a life-cycle, or generational, effect.

The analysis in Table 4.1 shows that the strongest relationships involve measured identity, especially those between 1) identity and *Seder* attendance, and 2) identity and synagogue attendance. This is unexceptional because an identity measure which takes in a range of psychological and cognitive factors in addition to basic practices is likely to be a firm indicator of level of ritual observance. Indeed a glance at the strictly Orthodox patterns shows how this interpretation holds good. When the correlations between the four variables are examined for this Jewishly punctilious sector, there is no significant correlation between any two variables. In this case the lack of a significant correlation reflects high identity scores and wide adherence to the two calendar-linked practices that are spread across all ages.

For the 1,000-strong sample who were not strictly Orthodox there was, on the other hand, a significant correlation between age and identity, albeit not a strong one. The correlations therefore underline that whereas the strictly Orthodox of all ages have a strong identity (embracing all its components), for the remainder identity levels increase with age. This correlation amongst more secularly-acculturated women may of course reflect a conservatising life-cycle effect where older women 'return to religion' but other possible explanations also come to mind. Age may be masking a generation-related consistency; older women who were brought up in practising households hold to accepted beliefs throughout their lifetime. Another explanation may be that those women of earlier generations who did not accept historical, conventional Jewish mores may have in one way or another excluded themselves from the Jewish community – or at least from its synagogal face.[52] This would restrict the identity profile of older age cohorts to those with higher scores, and this outcome would show in the correlation.

But ultimately, the sample is a static snapshot. It cannot be developed to include non-respondents nor can it be viewed as a film over time to indicate the levels of identity of older women when they were younger.[53] It is therefore a moot point whether belief, practice and sense of peoplehood have become more or less important for women as they have grown older.

Identity and Attitude to Synagogue

As was explained in setting the framework for this discussion, the changing position of women in Jewish society is seen as one of the crucial issues facing British Jewry. How women feel about the synagogue today and react to it is one aspect of this change, and just as identity is a significant correlate of the synagogue attendance patterns of most Jewish women so measured identity may be expected to correlate with their overall approach to the synagogue. This correlation will be important to community since women with high identity scores may be more involved in a synagogue simply because they have the knowledge and experience to make them feel comfortable there and *vice versa*. The 1993 survey included a range of statements of opinion about synagogue life designed to uncover some underlying attitudes and help throw light on the phenomenon. The statements drew on comments often voiced about synagogues and women's place therein and respondents were required to indicate the extent of their agreement/disagreement with each using a five-point scale. The statements, listed in the random order used on the questionnaire, and the replies of all except the strictly Orthodox are set out in Table 4.2 below. These pointers allow us to judge what synagogue members feel about certain aspects of synagogue life and how attitudes relate to overall Jewish identity.

As background to these analyses, it should be noted that 81 per cent of the major group of synagogue members considered it was equally important for boys and for girls to attend synagogue regularly,[54] compared with only 19 per cent who felt such regular attendance was more important for boys. We are therefore in the main examining a group who basically feel that women and men should attend synagogue at the same rate despite the fact that, as mentioned earlier, a woman is not obliged to attend services. This ratio in itself therefore suggests a move away from traditional norms.

The eleven statements set out in Table 4.2 encapsulate a range of issues which move from the material (I don't feel comfortable going to synagogue because I don't really have the right clothes), through the political (Women should have equal representation with men on all synagogue committees) and social (People who run synagogues sometimes make others feel like outsiders), to the devotional (I find it very difficult to express myself spiritually in synagogue).

If we take a very broad brush simply to describe strongly defined attitudes, within this group 92 per cent are comfortable with their attire in a synagogue, 91 per cent disagree that synagogues should be mainly for men, 89 per cent

Table 4.2   Attitudes towards synagogue of all except strictly Orthodox

	N= 100 per cent	Agree strongly	Agree	Are not certain	Disagree	Disagree strongly
			Percentage who			
I wish there could be more explanation during the service	959	20	45	9	23	2
Synagogues should be mainly for men; women can express their Jewishness in other ways	978	1	4	5	40	51
I feel myself to be a stranger in the synagogue	979	7	16	9	46	22
There is no need to change the way synagogues are organised; as a woman I am happy with the present arrangements	972	4	30	17	31	18
People who run synagogues sometimes make others feel like outsiders	981	21	46	10	19	4
The idea of 'all women' prayer groups is out of step with Jewish values	972	11	29	29	22	9
Men should be asked to prepare food for synagogue social occasions just as often as women	985	16	40	14	26	4
I find it very difficult to express myself spiritually in synagogue	973	10	28	16	40	7
Women should have equal representation with men on all synagogue committees	979	39	50	6	4	1
I don't feel comfortable going to synagogue because I don't really have the right clothes	980	1	3	3	47	45
Synagogues are mainly for families; unmarried people feel excluded	973	3	12	20	42	23

feel women should have equal representation with men on committees and 65 per cent wish for more explanation during the service. On a less pleasant issue, 67 per cent consider that those running the synagogue sometimes make others feel like outsiders although 68 per cent do not themselves feel strange in the synagogue and only 15 per cent feel that synagogues are mainly for families.

The strictly observant respondents display a different attitudinal profile. Only 68 per cent disagreed that the synagogue was a male province, and conversely only 32 per cent are looking for equal representation or 26 per cent seeking explanations during services. On the other hand a lower proportion (42 per cent) feel that synagogue dignitaries make others feel outsiders; a mere two per cent feel strange in the synagogue and only six per cent agree that the synagogue is mainly for the family.

The essentially differing synagogal orientations of strictly Orthodox and other synagogue members are summed up by the fact that approximately two out of three (64 per cent) strictly Orthodox agreed that, as women, they were happy with the way synagogues are organised while just under half that proportion (34 per cent) in the not strictly Orthodox group felt this way.

In order to reach a deeper understanding of the sentiments being expressed, a factor analysis was conducted on the correlations of the 11 statements. This process brings out underlying patterns or factors in the data. Two such factors were extracted from the attitudes set out in full in Table 4.2 above, and seven of the 11 attitudes are shown as contributing in different degrees and different combinations to each factor. Table 4.3 below, contains abbreviated versions of the seven statements with the extent to which each statement loads on the two factors. This loading shows the correlation between each element (statement) and the underlying factor. The four highest loading statements for each factor are given in bold.

Table 4.3   Factor loading matrix for synagogue attitudes

Attitude statement	Factor 1 Loading	Factor 2 Loading
I feel myself to be a stranger ...	**.78**	-.06
I find it difficult to express myself spiritually ...	**.55**	.02
I wish there could be more explanation ...	**.52**	- .04
There is no need to change the way ...	**- .47**	**- .46**
Women should have equal representation ...	.06	**.66**
Synagogues should be mainly for men ...	.11	**- .51**
Men should be asked to prepare food ...	.09	**.50**

The characterisation of these data is to a degree a matter of personal interpretation. In this instance I have taken as a guide the statement loading highest on each underlying factor, which is effectively a continuum of the combination of loading attitudes. I would on this basis suggest that the first factor may be termed *familiarity* and the second a *wish for democracy*.

The attitude which by a large margin loads most on the familiarity factor says 'I feel myself to be a stranger in the synagogue' (which as we have seen attracts fairly high levels of disagreement) and this is followed at a far less marked level by a group of attitudes which express closeness to/distance from the synagogue. A similar factor is found among the strictly Orthodox but it is constructed in a slightly different way. The 'stranger', 'spirituality' and 'explanation' statements load on the factor but not the wish for change. It is replaced by the statement which says 'I don't feel comfortable going to the synagogue because I don't really have the right clothes'. This last statement loads fairly strongly (0.6) on the factor, ranking higher than the desire for explanation.

The desire for change is repeated in the second factor where the 'change' statement loads with approximately the same strength as for factor 1. However, in this case it is grouped with those statements that relate to women seeking formal representation in the synagogue and to the extension of men's role to a 'domestic' involvement in synagogue affairs. The elements of the continuum here seem to be expressing classic feminist demands for equality or a 1990s 'partnership marriage' syndrome.

Table 4.4   Correlations between factors, identity and age

	Familiarity	Democracy	Identity
Familiarity	1.00		
Democracy	0.319	1.00	
Identity	0.155	0.14	1.00
Age	0.022	0.093	0.174

The next step is to examine the relationships between these two latent factors and between them, identity and age. The question to be addressed is what, if any, relationship exists between the strength of Jewishness and these underlying factors. The strictly Orthodox have again been excluded on account of their normatively strong and consistent Jewish lifestyle. The results of the analysis are set out in Table 4.4 which shows a weak, insignificant correlation between *familiarity* and *democracy*. These two factors express different understandings of the synagogue but the relationship between them is distributed randomly throughout the sample. On the other hand the correlations between identity and the two factors, *familiarity* and *the wish for democracy*, are both statistically significant.[55] Neither relationship is particularly strong although that between *familiarity* and identity is stronger than that between *democracy* and identity. This indicates that measured levels of *familiarity* and *democracy* both increase with objectively measured identity. As a higher *familiarity* score implies greater ease within the synagogue environment clearly this correlation is to be anticipated. In contradistinction, given the wording of the key statement in the *democracy* factor, an increase on this continuum accompanying an increase in identity suggests that more highly identifying women may have a lower desire for a change in the traditional synagogal role of women.

The Future?

The assumption underpinning my analyses has been that women's changing attitudes to the synagogue (and by implication to the community) are critical to the future of the British Jewry. This is not simply to infer, as is sometimes done, that lack of Jewishly focused socialisation (as historically provided at home) will add to the numeric decline confirmed by the demographic statistics. It also has qualitative attributes: as women's attitudes change, the character of Jewish experience that they transmit to their sons and daughters will be affected. A simple manifestation of this is that in an era when children no longer expect to 'do as I say, because I say so' Jewish parents have to educate themselves more in order to give convincing responses – e.g., when asked by teenagers 'why should I come to synagogue at New Year when we don't go for the rest of the year'. For women, who as a class were for centuries denied Jewish education when at least a minimum was assured for men, this is a greater step than for men; but it is a step that is being taken by Jewish women of all religious outlooks. Twenty-eight per cent of a sub-sample in the Women's Review had attended some form of Jewish adult education in the three years prior to the survey. Moreover, a glance in a classroom at Jewish evening classes shows their appeal for women and younger women particularly adopt attendance at such classes as a way of relating to community.[56] However, education is a two-edged sword: it may reinforce but it can also lead to questioning, expectation and argument.

The data presented in this chapter show that there is a strong relationship between identity and familiarity with the synagogue and a parallel relationship between identity and a wish for more women's involvement in this public arena, an involvement that is not confined to domestic duties. Both *familiarity* and public participation (that I have named the *wish for democracy*) call for an understanding and knowledge of Jewish affairs, which may be built up through experience and/or by more formal training and education. These underlying factors at first sight seem to be contradictory responses to contemporary synagogue life but this is of course entirely probable. Women may feel at home in an environment and may at the same time see its shortcomings. Conversely, the desire to change a public space from which you have previously been excluded may require the confidence which comes from familiarity. To this extent the two underlying factors will interlock.

The main implication of this convergence for community rises from the fact that the women who become involved in synagogue affairs have high levels of Jewish identity; they are activists[57] who will work and campaign for issues that they find important and they are increasingly using the synagogue as a vehicle to improve Jewish women's status. They are supported in this by a *zeitgeist* which encourages such activity. Indeed, the Women's Review on whose database this chapter is based authenticated much of this activity. It gave a voice on issues like *get* (Jewish divorce) and *agunah* (the chained wife) which reverberate internationally but which have yet to be resolved in line with modern women's expectations of married life. The challenge to rabbis and communal leaders comes here from Orthodox and traditional women who are most affected by these issues. At the same time at a micro-level increased women's interest and involvement in synagogue life has led to less headline-catching changes. These include new formats for the *bat-mitzvah* ceremony which mean that a girl approaching puberty is given personal public recognition as an individual, not as the member of a group. This valuing will be carried through life and influence how women now growing to adulthood will assess their Jewish identity and place in the community in years to come.

As individual identity changes, so the sum of these changes is expressed by a shift in communal identity. In the British experience highly Jewish immigrants were persuaded or wished to transform themselves into accepted British citizens. The most recent identity research[58] shows that one in every three Jewish adults feels him/herself to be equally British and Jewish and equally at home with Jews and non-Jews; a successful outcome of the historical process. However, success for one generation may be reappraised with hindsight by a future generation that recognises what has been lost and that selects those elements of the past which they wish to preserve. It is this current redefinition and reassessment which makes identity development such an absorbing issue for the Jewish community.

Notes

1 E. Krausz, 'The Edgware Survey: factors in Jewish identification', *The Jewish Journal of Sociology*, Vol. 11, 1969, pp. 151–64.
2 B.A. Kosmin and C. Levy, *Jewish Identity in an Anglo-Jewish Community*, London, Board of Deputies of British Jews, 1983.
3 See for example S. Goldstein, *The Greater Providence Jewish Community: A Population Survey*, General Jewish Committee of Providence, 1964; B. Horowitz, *1991 New York Jewish Population Study*, New York, UJA-Federation, 1993.
4 H. Neustatter, 'Demographic and other statistical aspects of Anglo-Jewry' in M. Freedman (ed.), *A Minority in Britain*, London, Vallentine Mitchell, 1955.
5 Under prompting from the Institute of Contemporary Jewry of the Hebrew University and the three British Jewish scholars who were indeed interested in Jewish sociological research.
6 In 1986 I proposed low-key research into women's involvement in Jewish organisations as a background to understanding communal volunteerism. One elderly member of the Community Research committee baldly asked why we needed to know about women. The research was eventually carried out in the early 1990s, see M. Schmool, 'Women in the Organised British Jewish Community', *Journal of Jewish Communal Service*, Vol. 71, 1995, pp. 170–9.
7 S. Kalms (chairman), *United Synagogue Review; A Time for Change*, London, United Synagogue, 1992; M. Schmool and S. Miller, *Women in the Jewish Community: Survey Report*, London, Women in the Community, 1994; S. Miller, M. Schmool and A. Lerman, *Social and political attitudes of British Jews: some key findings of the JPR survey*, London, JPR, 1996.
8 The largest synagogal group in Britain. It is London-based and mainstream orthodox.
9 For discussion of this issue see P.E. Hyman, *The Emancipation of the Jews of Alsace*, New Haven and London, Yale University Press, 1991.
10 T. Richman, *Konin*, London, Penguin, 1996.
11 Founded by Lily Montagu in 1909.
12 Jackie Tabbick inducted as first British woman rabbi in 1976. Today there are 18 women serving in the Progressive Rabbinate.
13 Ladies' Guilds are women's social and cultural committees in synagogues. See Schmool, op. cit., p. 175.
14 Miller, Schmool and Lerman, op. cit., p. 12.
15 For discussion of this issue see P. London and A. Hirschfeld, 'The Psychology of Identity Formation' in D.M. Gordis and Y. Ben-Horin (eds), *Jewish Identity in America*, Los Angeles, Wilstein Institute, 1991, pp. 31–50. This volume as a whole is a rounded introduction to the whole topic.
16 The most notable exception is S. Herman, *Jewish Identity: A Social Psychological Perspective*, London, Sage Publications, 1977.
17 See Schmool and Miller, op. cit., Appendix A for full methodology.
18 For full discussion of this relationship see Schmool and Miller, op. cit., chapter 2.

19 C. Roth, *Short History of the Jewish People*, London, East and West Library, 1953, p. 326.
20 V.D. Lipman, *A Social History of the Jews in England, 1850–1950*, London, Watts and Co., 1954, p. 8.
21 Ibid.
22 V.D. Lipman, *A History of the Jews in Britain since 1858*, Leicester, Leicester University Press, 1990, p. 12.
23 Ibid.
24 R. Livshin, 'The Acculturation of the Children of Immigrant Jews in Manchester, 1890–1930' in D. Cesarani (ed.), *The Making of Modern Anglo-Jewry*, Oxford, Blackwell, 1990, pp. 79–96.
25 Geoffrey Alderman, *The Federation of Synagogues 1887–1987*, London, The Federation of Synagogues, 1987.
26 See Hyman, op. cit., passim.
27 See S. Waterman and M. Schmool, 'Literary Perspectives on Jews in the Early Twentieth Century' in R. King, J. Connell and P. White (eds), *Writing Across Worlds-Literature and Migration*, London, Routledge, 1995.
28 S. Haberman and M. Schmool, 'Estimates of the British Jewish Population 1984–88' in *Journal of the Royal Statistical Society, Series A*, Vol. 158, Part 3, 1995, pp. 547–62.
29 The 1991 Census indicated 12,195 Israeli-born residents in Great Britain on census night of whom 43 per cent were in the London Borough of Barnet: M. Schmool and F. Cohen, *Patterns and Trends at the Turn of a Century – A Profile of British Jewry*, London, Board of Deputies of British Jews, 1998.
30 B.A. Kosmin, C. Levy and P. Wigodsky, *The Social Demography of Redbridge Jewry*, London, Board of Deputies of British Jews, 1981.
31 Board of Deputies' Annual compilations of vital statistics, 1965 to date.
32 It is important to note that these changes affect Jews as part of the general population, not simply because they are Jews.
33 Schmool and Cohen, op. cit., 1998.
34 Compared with 51 per cent for the general population of England and Wales.
35 London, Vallentine Mitchell, 1996, p. 7.
36 In my professional capacity, I am frequently called upon to explain to journalists and other enquirers that the Chief Rabbi does not speak for all British Jews and that there are other religious viewpoints with their own institutional networks within British Jewry.
37 For example the extended press coverage in 1997 about the Chief Rabbi's actions following the death and memorial to the Reform Rabbi Hugo Gryn.
38 M. Schmool and F. Cohen, *British Synagogue Membership in 1996*, London, Board of Deputies of British Jews, 1997, p. 11.
39 Schmool, op. cit., p. 174.
40 Miller, Schmool and Lerman, op. cit., p. 19.
41 And even then it is clear from the religion question on other censuses, for example in Australia, that a number of Jews would not self-identify.
42 Haberman and Schmool, op. cit., p. 559.
43 S.J. Prais and M. Schmool, 'Statistics on Jewish Marriages in Great Britain: 1901–1965', *The Jewish Journal of Sociology*, Vol. 9, 1967, pp. 149–74.
44 See, for example, S. DellaPergola, 'An overview of the demographic trends of European Jewry' in J. Webber (ed.), *Jewish Identities in a New Europe*, London and Washington, Littman Library of Jewish Civilisation, 1994.

45 Kosmin and Levy, op. cit., pp. 15–6.
46 J. Goodkin and J. Citron, *Women in the Jewish Community: Review and Recommendations*, London, Women in the Community, 1994, p. 1.
47 For example, J. Sacks, *Will we have Jewish grandchildren?*, London, Vallentine Mitchell, 1994.
48 Board of Deputies' Annual compilation of education statistics, 1998. In 1996, a further 24 per cent attended supplementary classes, in many cases solely to equip them for a *bar/bat mitzvah* (attainment of religious majority) ceremony.
49 Additionally, a snowball sample was collected of women who did not have formal synagogue membership in order to see how their experiences and attitudes differed from synagogue members.
50 I.e. they were members of synagogues attached to Reform Synagogues of Great Britain, Union of Liberal and Progressive Synagogue and the Assembly of Masorti Synagogues.
51 Despite efforts to keep the population covered to 18–70, see Schmool and Miller, op. cit., 'Methodology'.
52 This is certainly happening today within an open, pluralistic Britain. Part of the Women's Review involved searching for unaffiliated women many of whom had only slight, social links to community. See Schmool and Miller, ibid. This self-selection on affiliation makes it very difficult to design a completely random sample of British Jewry; see Miller, Schmool and Lerman, op. cit., p. 19.
53 Although the questionnaire did include a broad question about the religious character of the home in which the respondent grew up this was not extensive enough to provide the information that would be needed to answer this point.
54 In this instance 'regularly' was left for the respondent to define for herself. Less than one per cent thought it was more important for girls.
55 As is the correlation of age and identity as discussed above.
56 Schmool, op. cit., p. 177.
57 M. Schmool, *Organisation and Affiliation*, unpublished paper presented at seminar for Women in the Community, London, 1994.
58 Miller, Schmool and Lerman, op. cit.

5 Paths and Pitfalls in the Exploration of British Bangladeshi Identity

ROD CHALMERS

Introduction

The Bangladeshi community in the United Kingdom numbers some 200,000.[1] In recent years it has been the focus of increased attention both by academic researchers and by statutory and voluntary agencies concerned with the provision of services to large groups of people generally recognised as disadvantaged. In the definition of Bangladesh as an independent state, and in the definition and self-definition of the British Bangladeshi community, language has always played a significant role. However the way in which language has been investigated by outsiders, and presented by insiders, has perhaps been simplistic. Long-standing recognition of the need to address linguistic issues has not led to any widespread understanding of the specific situation of the vast majority of British Bangladeshis who originate from the Sylhet District of northeast Bangladesh. Indeed misleading information still has an alarming currency.

The aim of this chapter is to look at the place of language in the formation of British Bangladeshi identity. It will, however, become apparent that the intrinsic interest of the study of language within the Bangladeshi community is overshadowed by pressing areas of practical concern directly related to the understanding, or misunderstanding, of linguistic identity and needs. Any researcher in this field will rapidly become aware that language is an issue not only of great importance but also of great sensitivity. I propose to argue that underlying the technical issues of linguistic definition is a deeper ambivalence towards the recognition and representation of diversity within the Bangladeshi community.

Language, Identity and the Media

Language is central not only to the identity of many British Asian communities but also to their evaluation by the mainstream media. In particular, language usage is frequently taken as a measure of commitment to integration within British society. A recent full page feature in the *Observer*, entitled 'Blaming the Asians', is illustrated with a large photo of Asian boys studying in a mosque with the 24-point caption 'Your Pakistani taxi driver may speak English with a Yorkshire accent, but his children won't – they're too busy learning Urdu'.[2] The photo, and repeated references to attitudes towards language – be it lack of ability in English, or excessive ability in Urdu – strongly reinforce the article's argument that for Asians in Bradford 'many of the ghetto walls are of their own building'. Criticism of a continuing preference for 'traditional dress', and bemusement at the ability of even 'bright girls' to cope with the concept of arranged marriage, is underlined by reference to a linguistically demonstrable clan mentality: 'The family language goes on being Punjabi, or Bengali. The children learn Urdu as a stepping stone to the Arabic that's essential for the recitation of the Koran – an hour or two each day at the mosque, boys and girls; English doesn't get much of a look in.'

Meanwhile, young Bangladeshis of Camden and Westminster gained their fifteen minutes of fame in November 1996 courtesy of the *Evening Standard*. In a two-page spread entitled 'Asian teenage gangs terrorising London'[3] a head teacher breaks his silence on 'tribal battles' in inner London schools and 'conjures up an almost apocalyptic vision of unrest'. The head teacher's argument, as summarised by the *Evening Standard*, runs through the standard litany of disadvantage faced by Bangladeshi families, highlighting the fact that 'most children never speak English at home and their parents, largely from poor peasant stock, may often not be literate in their own language'. The pejorative choice of vocabulary – to describe the tribal battles of the children of peasants – is perhaps unexceptional in an article such as this. The introduction of implied value judgments on the basis of parents' linguistic ability is more noteworthy.

In response to the *Evening Standard* article a press release, headed 'Unwarranted demonisation of Bangladeshi teenagers in London' was issued jointly by the Bengali Workers Association, Camden Race Equality Council and the Marylebone Bangladesh Society.[4] The reference to illiteracy among Bangladeshi parents had clearly been noted and the majority of the press release was devoted to responding to this comment rather than the arguably sensationalist journalism. The Bangladeshi youths involved were described as having 'internalised the ethos and macho bravado-spirit of their white peers, whose parents and families also suffer from a high level of disadvantage and deprivation and who in spite of 125 years of literacy have so little control over their teenage children'. Specifically addressing the implied criticism of the article, the press release emphatically states that 'illiteracy of parents by itself has hardly ever significantly affected literacy achievement of pupils in any age or country but it is their socioeconomic status and expectation and skill of teachers and school environment which influence literacy and academic achievement of pupils much more significantly'.

The head teacher concerned was accused of having been 'rather dishonest in blaming everyone else but himself and his mainly monolingual teaching staff for failing successive generations of children learning English as a second language in the absence of adequate representation of linguistic and cultural role models at all levels in his teaching staff'. Despite the prominence accorded by the coverage in the *Evening Standard*, the issues raised, particularly in regard to education, are not in the least new.

Interestingly, both the head teacher in question, Michael Marland of North Westminster Community School, and the Marylebone Bangladesh Society were involved in giving evidence to the Home Affairs Committee's inquiry into Bangladeshis in Britain which reported in 1986. In its memorandum to the committee the Marylebone Bangladesh Society stated that 'it will be seen that the question of language is highlighted in each section. Therefore it must be concluded that this is a major factor for consideration'.[5] Here language is not seen as an unalloyed source of pride but as a potential obstacle to participation in wider British society. The perceived problem is not, however, confined to a lack of fluency in English but can also extend to a disregard for the *type* of Bengali spoken. Another organisation, the Dawatul Islam (UK and Eire), targeted more directly the source of its frustration when it complained in its memorandum that British Bangladeshi mothers and children 'cannot even understand proper Bengali except the Sylheti dialect'.[6] Here we see some public airing of an internal tension which we will examine at more length below.

Language in Bangladesh

The birth of Bangladesh could hardly have been a more dramatic demonstration of the power of linguistic nationalism. The independence movement could be justified in economic and political terms but it was born of mass mobilisation in defence of the Bengali language. The struggle for secession from Pakistan became a focal point for overseas Bangladeshis, particularly in the United Kingdom. Not only did this process redefine their homeland in the eyes of the world but it also forced the recognition of a distinct British 'Bengali' or 'Bangladeshi' community.

The significance of unity around a common language should not be underestimated. Language Day, a tribute to the 'Language Martyrs' who died in 1952 campaigning against the attempted imposition of Urdu as a national language, is still celebrated annually. Blood has been shed for the Bengali language. Furthermore, Bengalis may justly lay claim to one of the subcontinent's supreme literary languages. From Rabindranath Tagore to Kazi Nazrul Islam and his successors in present-day Bangladesh, the breadth and vigour of the Bengali 'Great Tradition' can seem almost overwhelming.

The strength of a Bengali identity, and a cohesive Bangladeshi identity, is to some extent dependent on the power of this tradition. The linguist Monica Klaiman has pointed out that for the majority of Bangladeshis 'the basis of their Bengali identity is not genetic and not religious, but linguistic and the bulk of the population perceives commonality of language as the principal basis of its social unity'.[7] This assertion, however, leads us to a seemingly paradoxical situation for, as the same researcher observes, 'although throughout the Bengali-speaking area a single, more or less uniform variety of the language is regarded as the standard dialect, the bulk of speakers have at best a passing acquaintance with it'.[8]

The great tradition has itself been woven from the many strands of lesser traditions. Debate still continues about the distinctiveness of nineteenth century literary Hindu and Muslim Bengali, while linguistic inquiry into modern Bengali has almost always been underpinned by reliance on an understanding of the immense regional diversity of the language. The scholars whose names dominate the history of scientific investigation of Bengali have all involved themselves to some extent in researching its dialects.[9]

Sylheti and Diversity within the Bangladeshi Community

The huge predominance of Sylhetis of Bangladeshi origin amongst migrants to the United Kingdom has only served to highlight this diversity. For the mother language of the vast majority of both British and Bangladeshi Sylhetis is significantly removed from the Bengali now recognised as standard.

Camden's *Bangladeshi Residents' Survey*, concluded emphatically that 'the Bangladeshi population in Camden is very much a Sylheti population'.[10] Ninety-seven per cent of respondents stated that both of their parents were born in the Sylhet district of Bangladesh. Issues surrounding choice of language were highlighted not only in the results of the survey but even in the process of its compilation. Given a choice of three languages in which to answer the questionnaire, 65 per cent of respondents opted for Sylheti, 22 per cent for English and only one per cent for Bengali. A total of 97 per cent of respondents stated that they could speak Sylheti 'very well' with the figure for the younger, 16–24 age group, standing at 100 per cent. The corresponding total for Bengali was only 69 per cent. Interestingly, the survey twice emphasised that Sylheti has no written form.[11]

The survey is also revealing in terms of self-identification. While 95 per cent of respondents in the Camden survey opted for the national category, stating that they always see themselves as Bangladeshi,[12] Sylheti was the clear second choice, with 86 per cent identification, higher than the totals for Muslim, British-Bangladeshi and Bengali, a label with which only 34 per cent of respondents always identified.

I have elsewhere presented outlines of Sylheti grammar and phonology and highlighted key structural distinctions between Sylheti and standard Bengali.[13] It is not my intention to revisit those technicalities. At this stage it should, however, be mentioned that Sylheti has a substantial literary tradition, in a script of its own, which was maintained by at least one printing press until the war of independence of 1971.[14] Indeed, Sylheti language is occasionally referred to as the 'Nagari' language from the name of its script, Sylheti Nagari. Even a recent business guide to Sylhet devotes some space to a description of Sylheti Nagari, commenting that 'although the cultivation of Nagari has now diminished, it has not been lost'.[15] In the 1860s Maulvi Abdul Karim of Sylhet returned from a visit to Europe to establish a Sylheti Nagari printing press: the publication of dozens of Sylheti books from presses in Sylhet and Calcutta followed.[16] The arrival of the printing presses, however, represented perhaps the final chapter of a tradition which dates back to at least the fifteenth century[17] and whose most famous author was active earlier in the nineteenth century.[18]

It is also important to note that Sylheti is distinctive enough for writers and speakers to have proposed that it should be considered a language in its own right. This suggestion may lack widespread support but is nonetheless alarming to many Bengalis. A recent letter to the *Camden New Journal* highlights a feeling of resentment among non-Sylhetis:

Whatever the council is doing is for the Muslims who migrated from East Pakistan which became Bangladesh. This has polarised between the Bengalis from West Bengal and Bangladesh. The council must know that the requirements of the Bengalis with a Sylheti dialect is very special compared with those who speak in standard Bengali. The council should review its policy towards Bangladeshis to contain polarisation with a view to improve the common objectives for the Bengalis. This would begin with the teaching of the Bengali language in standard Bengali, not the Sylheti dialect.[19]

Language is, of course, a focal point for wider issues. The 'polarisation' that so concerns the author of this letter echoes the title of the only general study of the stratification of Bangladeshi society in Britain, Fazlul Alam's *Salience of Homeland: Societal Polarisation within the Bangladeshi Population in Britain*. Alam neatly summarises his own conclusions on language and the stratification of Bangladeshi migrants: 'I overcame the difference of dialect (most restaurant personnel speak Sylheti dialect having come from the district of Sylhet) with the help and understanding of educated persons among them. I can claim to have been "accepted" and "placed" in the community of the people grouped here as the "Economic migrants".'[20]

Alam's analysis emphasises economic and educational status to the exclusion of any serious consideration of regional and ethnolinguistic identity. His work, however, clearly reveals that a division of Bangladeshi migrants by either economic or regional criteria would produce a near identical majority group of Sylhetis. This throws some light on the relationship between Sylhetis and other, generally educated and middle class, Bengalis who have often been looked to as 'community experts'.[21] In terms of class stratification, Alam concludes that 'segregation is not the effect of the British class structure, rather it is the accommodation of the Bangladeshi class structure within the existing British system'.[22] The nexus of low socioeconomic status and low linguistic and cultural status is far from insignificant.

Pejorative attitudes to Sylheti and its speakers may not frequently appear in print but there is no shortage of anecdotal evidence to indicate that they were and are prevalent. *Bangladeshi Children in Tower Hamlets*, a recently published guide for teachers, notes that 'there is considerable prejudice against Sylheti by standard Bengali speakers and this is reflected in the attitudes of some Bengali teachers in Britain who are not from Sylhet. It is quite common for young Sylhetis to internalise some of this prejudice against Sylheti and somehow feel that Sylheti is inferior'.[23] Meanwhile a researcher wishing to investigate any aspect of Sylheti must be prepared for dismissive reactions from non-Sylheti Bengalis. Sylheti literature, if its existence is even acknowledged, is 'ancient history' while the spoken language is at best 'just a dialect' not worthy of attention in its own right.

Some observers have moved towards drawing wider conclusions from a distinction initially manifested in language. Greg Smith, a researcher with the Linguistic Minorities Project of the mid-1980s, perhaps took the argument to its limits in stating that 'Sylhet has a historical and linguistic tradition which is in opposition to that of the hegemonic centralist tradition of Bengal and Bangladesh. Furthermore, the recent history of Bangladeshi migration, settlement and community development in Tower Hamlets, which has taken place in the context of an unequal and racist society, has led to a high level of political awareness in the British context, and to a restatement of ethnolinguistic identity on the part of many local Sylheti-speaking people'.[24]

While this restatement of ethnolinguistic identity proved far from decisive, Smith was writing at a time when it appeared that the Sylheti issue might play a serious role in reshaping community activism and representation in Tower Hamlets. Discussion of educational issues, especially through the organisation Bangladeshi Educational Needs in Tower Hamlets (BENTH), provided a forum for debates on language status. Smith observed that 'the conflicts between the radical pro-Sylheti sections of the local community on the one hand, and the professional pro-Bengali elites from outside have become more sharply polarised, with the pro-Sylhetis gaining the upper hand at the 1984 AGM of BENTH'.[25] However, only months later BENTH itself suffered an acrimonious schism which led to its collapse.[26] The most significant legacy of this conflict has probably been a continued reluctance to allow any resurfacing of potentially divisive language issues.

Recognising Sylheti

BENTH had nonetheless addressed some pertinent areas of concern. However minimal public discussion of Sylheti language might become, its relevance to educational achievement could not be diminished. A report in the BENTH Bulletin of January 1984 had accepted that there was 'little scope for the presence of the [Sylheti] dialect in teaching materials' but insisted that 'there should be a proper recognition of the children's dialect as far as the use of language for communication purposes is concerned and it should be possible to promote children's dialect specially in the pre-literacy stage'. This, a well-reasoned point that accorded with the emerging norms of educational practice in relation to bilingual learners, emphasised that the recognition of linguistic realities had to take place in a context broader than intra-community politics. Specifically, enhancement of educational practices and achievement depended on informing the practices of statutory institutions.

Yet these institutions have had to grapple with complex questions of identity without access to basic information. The Home Affairs Committee resorted to classifying Sylheti-speakers as Bengali-speakers while simultaneously stating that a Sylheti-speaker would 'have difficulty understanding a Bengali interpreter'. Its report proceeded to state categorically that Sylheti has no written form. This led the committee to refer to Bengali whenever written communication was discussed although it had already established that 'most of Britain's Bangladeshis are not literate in Bengali'.[27]

How did the committee arrive at its judgments? It was only on the final day of evidence-taking that Sir Edward Gardner, the Chair, decided to investigate the question of language status with Mr Wilson, an assistant undersecretary from the Home Office. As a man with no direct knowledge of Sylheti, Mr Wilson was clearly in difficulty when asked to clarify whether Sylheti should be viewed as a language or a dialect. His assessment that 'the Sylheti dialect has in it accretions from the languages of those people ... from places like Burma and South India' is at least misleading; the committee, however, accepted his conclusion that Sylheti is a dialect, based largely upon his assessment that 'Sylheti cannot be written down. I think that is an important factor in establishing whether something is a language or a dialect'.[28]

This inexpert testimony was supplemented by a Home Office memorandum to the committee which explained that 'Most Bangladeshis in this country ... speak a dialect of Bengali – Sylheti – which has no written tradition'.[29] In fact the Linguistic Minorities Project had already noted that 'a few [Sylhetis] are beginning to campaign to raise the status of Sylheti, pointing out the existence of an earlier Sylheti literature in a distinct script'[30] while Smith went into more detail.[31] Articles on the subject had been appearing in the local press in Tower Hamlets for some time. *Bangalee Shomachar* of August 1984 offered a poignant lament for the declining Sylheti literary tradition: 'Only because of the lack of practice and research the Sylhetti Nagri is beginning to disappear. In the villages and towns of Sylhet today books written in this language still provide food for excitement and thought in people's minds.'[32]

Not only had news of Sylheti literature failed to reach the Houses of Parliament but no individual or organisation was eager to correct any misimpressions. The dismissal of a well-developed and fascinating literature was even supported, although presumably inadvertently, by the Commission for Racial Equality.[33] The low premium placed on linguistic information is well demonstrated by Manchester City Council which had only managed to arrive at the unsurprising conclusion that 'Bangladeshis are largely Bengali rather than Urdu speaking'.[34] The Department for Education and Science did hint, in parentheses and without elaboration, that Sylheti 'is regarded by some as being not a dialect but a language in its own right'.[35] However this statement is typical of most publications from the 1980s to the present day: suggesting that the 'Bengali-speaking' community might not be entirely homogeneous but unable, or unwilling, to pursue the suggestion beyond a parenthetical comment.[36]

Even the professionals of the Linguistic Minorities Project found themselves in trouble. Realising half way through their Adult Language Use Survey (ALUS) that a different approach would have to be adopted for the 'Bengali-speaking' community, they revised their questionnaire only to come into conflict with their own interviewers:

> Our aim had been to produce a version which would be easily understood by most people with Bangladeshi or Indian Bengali backgrounds living in England, including Sylheti speakers with little experience of formal schooling. Six months later some of the London Bengali-speaking interviewers forcefully expressed their disapproval that certain phrases had been translated into 'such poor Bengali'. It may have been the surprise at seeing colloquial and regional forms in print for the first time that produced this reaction. [37]

Greg Smith subsequently recognised that 'our decision [for the ALUS] to treat speakers of Sylheti and Bengali as a single linguistic minority now appears to be based on a gross over-simplification'.[38] Limited academic work on Sylheti which was produced in the 1980s[39] received little attention and remains unavailable.

The Practical Implications

It was against this background that Michael Marland gave evidence to the Home Affairs Committee on the relationship of language and educational achievement. His evidence may be credited with persuading the committee to report that 'it is argued that general language ability, including ability to learn English, is enhanced by better command of one's first language, and more particularly by literacy in that first language. Her Majesty's inspectorate appears to accept this view'.[40] Taking into account the advice of community organisations it went on to recommend that 'Bangladeshi pupils, where they are numerous, should have the opportunity, especially at secondary level, to study Bengali instead of one of the more traditional foreign languages ... we recommend that, wherever possible, Bangladeshi pupils be given the opportunity to study their mother tongue at school'.[41] However his answers to the Committee's questions, and its subsequent recommendations, illustrate a basic misunderstanding of the Sylheti/standard Bengali relationship. An extract from one of his answers outlines the core of his argument:

> ... many of these pupils [who leave school unable to communicate in English] are not literate in their language, which is Sylheti. It is obvious that the basis of reading, which is the phoneme/grapheme relationship, the sound and the shape of the letter, is much harder to learn in your second language for those who have not yet learned it in their first language ... I would like to suggest that discussion of the teaching of English has to go alongside ... with the teaching of their home or community language, Sylheti.[42]

The recommendation is fundamentally sound except, of course, that Sylheti is no longer a written language. Regardless of the past achievements of Sylheti literature, Mr Marland's advice depends on the resuscitation of a near-extinct tradition. Few would dispute that the mastery of the phoneme/grapheme relationship in one's mother tongue forms the basis of reading ability, yet for Sylheti-speaking children this raises more questions than it answers. While the study of standard Bengali certainly has much to offer, it cannot equate to literacy in the mother tongue (and in this context mother tongue can mean nothing but the language naturally learnt and spoken from the earliest age). A Sylheti-speaker learning standard Bengali must learn more than a dozen new phonemes, not to mention new grammatical rules and vocabulary.

If the recommendations of the Home Affairs Committee are to be endorsed it is for reasons other than functional efficacy in supporting the acquisition and development of literacy. Most Sylheti parents want their children to be able to read and write standard Bengali. The children themselves have much to gain: access to a broad and highly developed written culture, literacy in the world's sixth largest language, the enhanced ability to maintain and develop ties with Bangladesh, and participation in a national culture and identity. However, while the *taught* 'mother tongue' or 'community language' of Sylhetis is always standard Bengali, it is clear that if future generations of

Sylhetis retain any *spoken* home language other than English, it will be Sylheti, rather than standard Bengali.

This point is rarely, if ever, raised in public or institutional discussion of mother tongue education although 'potential for achieving much higher standards' in Bengali education has been noted by Tower Hamlets.[43] It is not, however, lost on teachers of Bengali. For participants on the first accredited course for Bengali teachers in Britain, which recently concluded at the Institute of Education, the relationship between Sylheti and standard Bengali was a major concern. The teachers were all non-Sylheti Bengalis, their pupils almost entirely Sylheti.[44] They had access to no resources which could help them address the difficulties they face in teaching Bengali as a mother tongue to children who generally do not speak it as a mother tongue. Yet despite these teachers' enthusiasm for learning more about Sylheti, its very inclusion as a topic on their course had been vigorously opposed.

For those with no direct knowledge of Sylheti or Bengali the situation remains confusing. Recent guidance for teachers in Tower Hamlets attempts to arm English-speaking teachers with some basic linguistic facts:

> Sylheti children, particularly in the early stages of learning to speak English, may display errors which occur as a result of applying grammatical rules from Sylheti/Bengali to English ... it is likely to be useful for teachers to be aware of the main grammatical differences between Sylheti/Bengali and English: ... the third person pronoun is the same for masculine and feminine gender. Verb inflection usually signals gender ... Bengali uses gender for neutral/natural nouns e.g. sun [masculine]; moon, river [feminine] ... [45]

While this is a selective quotation, it is illustrative of the continuation of misunderstanding. For none of the definitive-sounding statements is true of Sylheti, and only one holds good for standard Bengali. Indeed at first glance this, combined with the points not quoted, adds up to a reasonable description of Hindi or Urdu. Yet for most English-speaking teachers this is the most reliable information available. The problem reaches beyond the world of education. Those concerned with improving communication with the Bangladeshi community through interpreting, advocacy or translation services are similarly hindered by this information deficit. The Camden survey identified strategies, including increased use of audio tapes and videos, to target Sylheti-speakers.[46] In general, however, provision across statutory services from NHS Trusts to local authorities has yet to be informed by detailed analysis of actual communications needs.

Conclusion

From the tensions of regionalism within Bangladesh itself to the emergence of a modern British Bangladeshi identity language is a key factor. This chapter may have stressed the more problematic aspects of Bengali linguistic diversity but there is no picture to be painted in black and white. The consideration of Sylheti without reference to standard Bengali would be as pointless as an examination of the state of Bengali in Britain which ignored the linguistic heritage of the vast majority of the Bengali-speaking community. Most interestingly, the avoidance of public discussion of Sylheti language issues which appears so striking in the British context is not at all in evidence in Sylhet itself.

The cultural, political and linguistic dynamics between Sylhet and the central institutions of Bangladesh and Bengali are far from being frozen in opposition. Sylhetis at home and abroad played a significant role in the war of liberation leading to the creation of Bangladesh and in the language movement that preceded it. It was, indeed, a Sylheti, General Osmani, who led the Mukti Bahini freedom fighters in the armed conflict with Pakistani forces. Today the Kendriya Muslim Sahitya Samsad in Sylhet maintains its dual role as the chief repository of Sylheti literary texts and as the publisher of Bangladesh's oldest Bengali literary journal, *Al-Islah*.[47]

Sylheti language is of intrinsic interest as well as being of relevance to broader linguistic concerns. Minute local variations in the forms of Sylheti spoken in different households are evidence of resilient links and loyalties to localities far more specific than Sylhet District as a whole, let alone Bangladesh. Meanwhile the state of Sylheti in Bangladesh and Britain can shed light on issues as diverse as the development of New Indo-Aryan vowel systems[48] and the emergence of clearly defined *koinés* among migrant speech communities.[49] Analysis of the history of the Sylheti script and literature could call into question simplistic approaches to traditions of literacy within Bangladeshi communities.

The exploration of Bangladeshi identity has much to gain from addressing questions of language more directly. Many issues, such as the extent to which the inspirational linguistic nationalism leading to Bangladesh's independence is still relevant to British Bangladeshis, would bear further investigation. Meanwhile the continuing prevalence of prescriptive, rather than descriptive, definitions of ethnolinguistic identity should concern us all.

Notes

1 Although writing before the most recent census, C. Peach, 'Estimating the growth of the Bangladeshi population of Great Britain', *New Community* 16 (4), 1990, pp. 481–91, outlines some problems in assessing demographic data relating to British Bangladeshis which remain relevant.

2 K. Whitehorn, 'Blaming the Asians', *The Observer*, 9 March 1997.

3 'Asian teenage gangs terrorising London', *Evening Standard*, 13 November 1996.

4 Bengali Workers Association, Camden Race Equality Council and Marylebone Bangladesh Society press release, 'Unwarranted demonisation of Bangladeshi teenagers in London', 19 November 1996.

5 Home Affairs Committee, *Bangladeshis in Britain*, 3 vols, London, HMSO, 1986, III, p. 47. This report will henceforth be referred to as *HAC*.

6 Ibid.

7 M.H. Klaiman, 'Bengali' in B. Comrie (ed.), *The Major Languages of South Asia, the Middle East and Africa*, London, Routledge, 1990, p. 75.

8 Ibid., p. 94.

9 Noteworthy studies of regional Bengali, and Sylheti in particular, from within the mainstream of Bengali linguistics include A. Caudhurī, 'Śrīhaṭṭer Bhāṣā', *Bhāṣā*, Calcutta, 1974, pp. 32–3; S.K. Chatterji, *The Origin and Development of the Bengali Language*, Calcutta, 1926, repr. London, Allen and Unwin, 1970; G. Grierson, *Linguistic Survey of India, Volume 5 Part 1*, Calcutta, Government of India, 1903; Ā.H. Dānī, 'Śrīhaṭṭa Nāgarīr Utpatti Bikāś', *Bānlā Ekāḍemī Patrikā*, Vol. 1, No. 2, 1364 B.S., pp. 1–72; M.A. Hai, 'Sileṭi', *Parikram*, Vol. 2, No. 7, 1962, pp. 587–90; Ś.P. Lāhiṛī, 'Sileṭi Nāgarī Lipir Utpatti o Kramavikāś', *Bānlā Ekāḍemī Patrikā*, Vol. 3, No. 1, 1366 B.S., pp. 32–42, *Sileṭi Bhāsātattver Bhūmikā*, Dhaka, Bangla Academy, 1961, 1368 B.S., and 'Sileṭer Āñcalik Bhāṣāy Vyavahṛt Katakgulo Dhātu o Kriyāpad', *Bānlā Ekāḍemī Patrikā*, Vol. 23, No. 2, 1385 B.S., pp. 138–82; Maniruzzaman, 'Cākmā Prabād o Sileṭi Nāgarī Parikramā', *Bānlā Ekāḍemī Patrikā*, Vol. 6, Śrāvan-Āśvin, 1388 B.S., pp. 25–43, *Studies in the Bangla Language*, Adiabad, Adiabad Sahitya Bhaban and Bhasha Tattva Kendra, 1991, and *Upabhāṣā Carcār Bhūmikā*, Dhaka, Bangla Academy, 1994; M. Śahidullah (ed.), *Bānlādeśer Āñcalik Bhāṣār Abhidhān*, Dhaka, Bangla Academy, 1993 (1965); Nilmadhav Sen, 'Some Dialects of Bangla Desh – An Outline', *Indian Linguistics*, 33 (2), 1972.

10 London Borough of Camden and the Institute of Education, *Camden Bangladeshi Residents Survey*, London, 1996, p. 9.

11 Ibid., pp. 20 and 22.

12 The 'ethnicity question' introduced in the 1991 census has come under criticism for its reliance on categories based more on nationality than ethnicity. The Camden survey would tend to suggest that 'Bangladeshi' is one national category which is largely acceptable to respondents.

13 R. Chalmers, *Sylheti: a regional language of Bangladesh*, ENBS/EC Research Paper No. 5/6–96, Bath, European Network of Bangladesh Studies, University of Bath, 1996 and *Learning Sylheti*, London, Centre for Bangladeshi Studies, 1996.

14 For an overview of the Sylheti Nagari script and Sylheti literature see Chalmers, *Sylheti: a regional language of Bangladesh*, pp. 22–5. Works by local authors examining Sylheti language, literature and folk tradition include M. Āfzal and S.M. Kāmāl (eds), *Habigañj Parikramā*, Sylhet, Habigañj Itihās Praṇayan Pariṣad, 1994; H. Ākbar, *Lok Sāhitye Sileṭ*,

Sylhet, Jālālābād Lok Sāhitya Pariṣad, 1995; M.K. Ālam, *Sileṭer Āñcalik Bhāṣā o Lok Sāhitya Prasaṅga*, Sylhet, Mrs Mamtāz Khorśed, 1994; M.Ā. Ālī (ed.), *Silaṭ Ekāḍemī Patrikā*, Sylhet, Sylhet Academy, 1979, and *Caryāpade Sileṭi Bhāṣā*, Sylhet, Tāiyībā Prakāśanī, 1993; S.M. Ālī, *Hazrat Śāh Jālāl o Sileṭer Itihās*, Dhaka, University Press, 1988 (1965); S.M. Ālī, 'Sileṭī', *Parikram*, Vol. 1, No. 6, 1962, pp. 472–76; G.Ā. Caudhurī, *Sileṭi Nāgarī Parikramā*, Sylhet, Jālālābād Lok Sāhitya Pariṣad, 1978, and *Lok Sāhityer Kathā*, Sylhet, Jālālābād Lok Sāhitya Pariṣad, 1988; F. Rahmān, *Sileṭer Marmī Saṅgīt*, Sylhet, Rāgib Ālī, 1993; N. Āarmā, *Śrihaṭṭa Sāhitya Pariṣader Itikathā*, Sylhet, Jālālābād Lok Sāhitya Pariṣad, 1994.

15 Ā.H. Mānik and K.Ā. Rauph, *Sileṭ Gāiḍ*, Dhaka, The Business Post Publication, 1993, p. 42.

16 G.Ā. Caudhurī, op. cit., pp. 32–9.

17 The first recorded Sylheti author is Sañjay Kāśīrām Dās (referred to by Rizvi, op. cit., p. 313, as Sanjay Laur), who translated the greatest Sanskrit epic poem, the *Mahābhārata*. Following Dās, the early fifteenth century writer Bhābānanda, said to be of Habiganj, produced the *Haribaṃśa*, a work which S.M. Ālī, op. cit., pp. 170–1, finds remarkable for the number of Sylheti words it contains which remain in currency today.

18 Sylheti literature perhaps reached its peak with the publication of four works by Sādek Ālī (born in 1801 as Gaurkiśor Sen). Foremost among them is *Hāltunnabī*, a life of the prophet; *Mahabbatanāmā* is a love story; *Hāśar Michil* considers the day of judgment and the afterlife; and *Raddekuphur* offers a comparison of Hinduism with Islam, an autobiography and a sketch of society (S.M. Ālī, op. cit., p. 174).

19 Letter from Sunil Kumar Pal, *Camden New Journal*, 6 March 1997.

20 F. Alam, *The Salience of Homeland: Societal Polarisation within the Bangladeshi Population in Britain*, Coventry, Centre for Research in Ethnic Relations, University of Warwick, 1988, p. 5.

21 Cf. Greg Smith, *Language, Ethnicity, Employment, Education and Research: The Struggle of Sylheti-speaking People in London*, CLE/LMP Working Paper No. 13, London, University of London Institute of Education, 1985, p. 40.

22 Alam, op. cit., p. 45.

23 *Bangladeshi Children in Tower Hamlets: A Guide for Teachers*, London Borough of Tower Hamlets, Humanities Education Centre, p. 16; cf. Smith, op. cit., p. 37: 'in Tower Hamlets just as in Bangladesh the vernacular values and culture of the Sylhetis is largely ignored, devalued and suppressed'.

24 Smith, op. cit., p. 11.

25 Ibid., p. 40.

26 See Inner London Education Authority, Education Committee Policy Co-ordinating Sub-committee Report by Education Officer 7.4.85.

27 *HAC* I: 13.

28 Ibid., III: Q454.

29 Ibid., II: 206.

30 Linguistic Minorities Project, *The Other Languages of England*, London, Routledge and Kegan Paul, 1985, p. 44.

31 Smith, op. cit., pp. 20ff.

32 Quoted by Smith, op. cit., p. 40.

33 *HAC* III: 10: 'The Sylhetis have their own dialect, which has no written form'.

34 Ibid., II: 27.

35 Ibid., II: 195.

36 Other British publications from the mid-1980s onwards have, to greater or lesser degrees, addressed the Sylheti/Bengali issue. J.V. Boulton, 'Bengali' in C. Shackle (ed.), *South Asian Languages: A Handbook*, London, Occasional Papers X, External Services Division, SOAS, 1985, p. 45 summarises that 'Sylheti, the dialect they [working class UK Bengali-speakers] mainly speak, is so far removed from Standard Bengali that Sylheti-speaking infants addressed in Standard Bengali often make virtually no response, since they see little or no similarity between the dialect they speak and the Bengali of the educated'; Y. Choudhury, *The Roots and Tales of the Bangladeshi Settlers*, Birmingham, Sylheti Social History Group, 1993, p. 9 touches on the question of language: 'Although officially Sylhet is supposed to be a Bengali speaking area, the local tongue is actually a mixture of Bengali and Assami, with many words of Arabic, Persian and Turkish origin, to some extent it may be considered as a unique language in its own right' while his *Sons of the Empire: oral history from the Bangladeshi seamen who served on British ships during the 1939–45 War*, Birmingham, Sylheti Social History Group, 1995, p. 40 includes the intriguing tale of a Bengali from Chittagong lodging with a Sylheti family in 1947: 'At the beginning I was not able to understand the Sylheti language so they spoke to me in Hindi'; V. Edwards, *The other languages: a guide to multilingual classrooms*, University of Reading, Reading and Language Information Centre, 1996, p. 14 contains slightly updated information: 'Other languages and dialects are also spoken within Bangladesh, including Sylheti which is used by most Bangladeshi settlers in the UK. Sylheti, however, does not have a well developed written tradition, and Bengali is the medium of instruction both in schools in Bangladesh and in community-run language classes overseas'; E. Gregory, 'Cultural assumptions and early years' pedagogy: the effect of the home culture on minority children's interpretation of reading in school', *Language, Culture and Curriculum*, 7 (2) describes Sylheti as 'a strong dialect of Bengali which has no written form'; Jyoti Husain, 'The Bengali Speech Community' in S. Alladina and V. Edwards (eds), *Multilingualism in the British Isles*, Vol. 2, London, Longman, 1991, deals with the linguistic status of Sylheti in some detail and also points out that 'Mother tongue teaching is a highly sensitive and important issue for the Bengali community. One of the key questions for this, as for many other linguistic minorities, is the variety which should be taught. There is a widespread expectation that children in Britain, as in Bangladesh, should be taught standard Bengali. However, many Bangladeshis argue that greater recognition should also be given to Sylheti both as a medium of instruction and for the language support of bilingual learners in the mainstream curriculum'; Michael Mobbs, *Britain's South Asian Languages*, London, Centre for Information on Language Teaching and Research, 1985, p. 26 notes not only the distinctiveness of Sylheti but also one of the difficulties in recognising it: 'a large proportion of Bengali speakers in Britain are from Sylhet district in the northeast of Bangladesh, where the vernacular (Sylheti) differs considerably from Standard Bengali. When asked about their mother tongue, many Sylheti-speakers in Britain tend to identify themselves as 'Bengali' speakers, implying the standard language, even if their everyday speech is Sylheti'.

37 Linguistic Minorities Project, op. cit., p. 154.

38 Smith, op. cit., p. 24.

39 Anil Sinha's pioneering *Spoken Sylheti Bengali*, Tower Hamlets Adult Education Institute, unpublished, 1985 was used in classes for English-speakers and revised versions were produced; D. and N. Spratt, *The Phonology of Sylheti Bangla*, Summer Institute of Linguistics, unpublished, 1987 is a fundamentally sound technical analysis but it appears

to have enjoyed only limited circulation; as far as I am aware only one work emerged from the universities: A.K. Azad, *Aspects of code-switching amongst young people of the Sylheti-Bengali minority group in East London*, unpublished MA dissertation, School of Oriental and African Studies, 1989.

40 *HAC* I: 65.

41 Ibid., I: 68. This contrasts with the traditional approach of immersion in English and isolation of the mother tongue, cf. M. Martin-Jones, *The Sociolinguistic Status of Minority Languages in England*, London, Linguistic Minorities Project Working Paper, 1985, No. 5, p. 7: 'In the post-war period with the arrival of many of the newer linguistic minorities in Britain, language education practice continued to be dominated by a broadly assimilationist outlook.'

42 Ibid., III: Q354.

43 London Borough of Tower Hamlets, *Review of Mother Tongue provision in Tower Hamlets 1994–95*, 1995, p. 10.

44 The same scenario was encountered by R. Warner, *Bangladeshi is my Motherland*, London, Minority Rights Group, 1992, p. 9 and is probably indicative of the general situation.

45 *Bangladeshi Children in Tower Hamlets: A Guide for Teachers*, p. 20.

46 *Camden Bangladeshi Residents Survey*, p. 26; 'It is important that interpreters should in most cases communicate in the Sylheti dialect of Bengali ... The Council needs to be innovative in the use of audio and video tapes (in Sylheti) in providing information and promoting issues ...'.

47 Recent Bengali publications which take pride in Sylhet while celebrating its position within Bangladesh include S.M. Kāmāl, *Bāṅlār Ādhyātmik Rājdhanī*, Sylhet, Samīkaraṇ Prakāśanī, 1991, which refers in its title to Sylhet as the 'spiritual capital of Bangladesh', Ś.K. Kayes, *Bāṅlā Sāhitye Sileṭ*, Vol. 2, Sylhet, Dolā Prakāśanī, 1989 whose subject is Bengali literature in Sylhet, and T. Mohāmmad's three works *Sileṭer Juddhakathā*, Dhaka, Sāhitya Prakāś, 1993, *Bhāṣā Āndolane Sileṭ*, Dhaka, Sāhitya Prakāś, 1994 and *Sileṭer Duiśat Bacharer Āndolan*, Dhaka, Āgāmī Prakāśanī, 1995 which cover the war, language movement and political history of Sylhet.

48 Cf. Chalmers, *Sylheti: a regional language of Bangladesh*, p. 19 and C.P. Masica, *The Indo-Aryan Languages*, Cambridge, Cambridge University Press, 1991, p. 109.

49 Maniruzzaman, *Upabhāṣā Carcār Bhumikā*, p. 328, raises the possibility of the development of London and Birmingham varieties of Sylheti.

6   The Search for Wholeness: The Construction of National and Islamic Identities among British Bangladeshis

JOHN EADE

Identity, Identification and National Heritage

At the end of August 1997 Diana, Princess of Wales, was killed in a Paris car accident. The public outpouring of grief surprised and intrigued those who were critical of the media hype surrounding the divorced partner of a British royal. One of the issues raised in newspaper debates about the public reaction in Britain was the prominent involvement of non-Establishment groups including 'ethnic minorities'. Although journalists were inevitably selective in their choice of people to interview it was surprising to see young Asian men expressing their sorrow at the loss of the 'English rose' and a black man on his knees before Buckingham Palace gates sobbing his eyes out. The death of this one British woman also touched people around the world and her funeral became a global media event with broadcasters estimating an audience of 2.5 billion.[1]

The relevance of these events to a discussion of Bangladeshis in Britain lies in: a) the ways in which national grieving involved ethnic and other minorities in a highly visible way; and b) the repeated references to identity, both personal and collective. These minorities were insisting on their contribution to a debate about national identity – the subject of a public discourse which long preceded Diana's death. The commemoration of the 'People's Princess' established a recurrent theme – the search for a new collective unity to overcome the fragmentation of British society. A letter by a woman expressed the theme succinctly: 'Despite being an anti-royalist I realised that I was grieving not for Diana alone. Along with genuine sadness, I experienced the joy of shedding my old cynicism and fragmentation – and of feeling a real sense of belonging at last.'[2]

This desire for wholeness, for a personal and collective unity, is integrally related to conventional notions about identity. The unity of identity is usually associated with a state of being which is rooted in some long-standing essence which establishes the distinctiveness of an individual or a group. National identities are, therefore, widely understood as grounded in a heritage which stretches back into the mists of time. The tendency is to combine an essentialist definition of identity with a primordialist assertion of historic fixity. Such a tendency suggests that those who 'truly belong' to the group are those who are long established members and define what are the central beliefs and values of the group. Newcomers are treated with reserve until they conform to those core cultural traditions. It is usually their assimilated children and grandchildren who are accepted as they slough off their outsider inheritance.

Since the 1960s this 'melting pot' model of national integration has been challenged, first in North America and then in Britain. Those contributing to anti-racist and multicultural movements on both sides of the Atlantic advocated a pluralist model of society which allowed for the retention of newcomers' cultural traditions within the wider political and economic structure. They pointed to the increasing heterogeneity of nation-states created by global migration since the end of the Second World War and the positive impacts which immigration has made on traditional discourses and practices both for the 'indigenous' population and the newcomers. The public debate about British identity has been shaped, in large part, by the controversy over immigration and the changing character of British society. This discourse concerning a collective identity also overlaps with the emergence of another debate about identity in the context of the individual, the self and psychological integrity.

The growing interest in identity issues across the Western world since the 1960s has led some commentators to focus on migrants and other transnational groups in their exploration of the changing and heterogeneous character of nation-states.[3] Here I want to concentrate on Stuart Hall's arguments in particular[4] and apply them to the discussion of British Bangladeshi identities.

Identity and Identification

Hall prefers to use the term 'identification' rather than 'identity'. He argues that identity suggests a fixed entity which people possess whereas identification indicates a process of identity formation which thereby allows for change and contestation. An individual is always in the position of becoming rather than simply being. Identification refers to a process whereby identities are constructed but these identities are neither homogeneous nor permanent.

Old and New Ethnicities

These general formulations concerning identity are related Hall's claim that the migration of people from former colonial countries to Britain has resulted in ethnicity becoming split between 'the dominant notion which connects it to nation and "race"' and 'what I think is the beginning of a positive conception of the ethnicity of the margins, of the periphery'.[5] New ethnicities, developed by this country's 'ethnic minorities', challenge fixed notions of a homogeneous national community and link these minorities to other parts of the world, especially the 'Third World'. Ethnicity – a concept which 'acknowledges the place of history, language and culture in the construction of subjectivity and identity [6] – has to be located within specific contexts of unequal power and knowledge relations where dominant definitions of national identity are challenged by ethnic minorities'.

The New Politics of Representation

Hall locates these developments within a change in 'black cultural politics'. He suggests that there has been a shift 'in the politics of anti-racism and the postwar black experience' which has entailed moving from 'the innocent notion of the essential black subject' to 'the recognition of the extraordinary diversity of subjective positions, social experiences and cultural identities which comprise the category "black"'.[7] There is emerging a new politics of representation based on the realisation that 'black' is a 'politically and culturally *constructed* category' (emphasis in the original).[8]

Essentialism and Power

One of the major attractions of Hall's position lies in its non-essentialist approach towards the political and cultural construction of identity which challenges most conventional anthropological analyses of Britain's 'ethnic minorities'. His influence can be seen in the writing of another highly perceptive commentator, Avtar Brah, who carefully explores the ways in which gendered differentiation interweaves with constructions of racial, ethnic, class and national difference. She welcomes Hall's attempt to 'retrieve ethnicity from racialised nationalist discourses'. Nevertheless, she points to the gendering of ethnicity and the lack of any guarantee that 'their non-essentialist recuperation will simultaneously challenge patriarchal practices unless this task is made a conscious objective'.[9] Dominated groups may assert 'a seemingly essentialist difference' when they 'appeal to bonds of common cultural experience in order to mobilise their constituency'. Some feminists have welcomed this practice of 'strategic essentialism' as long as 'it is framed from the vantage point of a dominated subject position'.[10] However, the assertion of essentialist differences between communities for specific strategic purposes can lead to a number of analytical problems for sociological and anthropological observers as the debate between Benson, Eade and Werbner illustrates.[11]

These general formulations within the academic arena of cultural studies, feminism and anti-racism have made a contribution to leftist political debates concerning the changing nature of British society and the challenge of 'Thatcherism' during the 1980s in particular. However, they usually lack the empirical depth provided by anthropological investigations of specific local ethnic minority communities. As yet there are very few published studies which combine the strengths of both approaches although the research carried out by Les Back[12] and Claire Alexander[13] graphically illustrate what can be achieved by drawing on both perspectives. My discussion of developments within Tower Hamlets does not aspire to the richness of empirical material generated by this kind of ethnographic research. Yet my account does suggest what might be achieved through the crossing of various academic borders in the study of local politics where social identities are diversely constructed by 'newcomers' and 'natives' through the use of public space.

Bangladeshis in Tower Hamlets: Local and Global Relations

Between 1961 and the national census of 1991 the Bangladeshi population in Britain has increased dramatically and is forecast to be the most rapidly expanding ethnic minority group of the 1990s. From an estimated and highly approximate 6,000 in 1961 the number of Bangladeshis rose to approximately 22,000 in 1971, to a more definite 64,561 in 1981 and to 162,835 in 1991.[14] In other words, between the emergence of Bangladesh in 1971 and the 1991 census the numbers of Bangladeshis living in this country have increased more than sevenfold. Its very young demographic profile means that those numbers will continue to increase rapidly throughout the 1990s.

The rapid growth of the British Bangladeshi population has been accompanied by its highly concentrated geographical location. Over half the Bangladeshi population is settled within the Greater London area and a quarter of British Bangladeshis are to be found in one London borough – Tower Hamlets. While community organisations, journalists and researchers have provided some information about the various Bangladeshi settlements scattered across the United Kingdom it is not surprising that most studies and reports have focused on Tower Hamlets. This borough contains the largest concentration of Bangladeshi businesses and community facilities as well as the most numerous and lively political activists. Tower Hamlets continues to act as a powerful magnet attracting Bangladeshis from other parts of the country despite the manifold and well documented socioeconomic problems confronting Bangladeshis and the borough's other working class residents.

The involvement of Tower Hamlets' Bangladeshi residents in identity issues provides rich opportunities for analysing the ways in which local and more global solidarities interweave. This is a topic which has attracted a number of writers who have pointed to the wider context of political and economic relations within which specific local issues and struggles must be placed.[15] There is a temptation in investigations of local political and cultural processes to remain within the confines of borough, metropolitan and nation-state boundaries. The studies of Bangladeshi migration to this country[16] and research undertaken within the country of origin itself[17] clearly reveal the dangers of remaining within the narrow confines of local and national boundaries. While specific beliefs and practices demarcate each level of political and cultural activity those beliefs and practices are influenced by what is taking place at other levels. Thus what may appear to be a peculiarly local issue may be deeply influenced by what is taking place elsewhere. To describe the issue as a local event is to accord it an autonomy which does not properly exist. Such is the case even when the people involved fervently regard it as an intensely local event.

The interweaving of local and more global processes across different levels of people's beliefs and practices may be more easily perceived when issues involving new settlers are discussed. The virulent forms of indigenist claims to locality by some white residents in the Isle of Dogs to the south of the borough, for example, would appear to present a rigid separation between the local and the wider world.[18] The 'cricket test' proposed by the narrow nationalism of certain ethnic majority politicians fails to include the ways in which Bangladeshis and other ethnic minorities have engaged in local political and social institutions and thereby changed understandings of what locality means for others as they have become residents themselves.

The growing Bangladeshi engagement with British urban life has coexisted with close ties to the country of origin. The research by Katy Gardner and other anthropologists writing about New Commonwealth migration to Britain[19] reminds us of the dangers of making ethnocentric interpretations of 'ethnic minority' settlement. A preoccupation with the institutions of the white British majority can dangerously underestimate the continuing significance of the social, cultural and political traditions which settlers brought with them even as the first generation is joined by a second and a third generation. These traditions are subtly changed as ethnic minority citizens across Britain adapt to life in this country and to changes taking place within their country of origin and other parts of the world which are important to them.

Periodic visits to the 'homeland', communication with absent relatives and friends by letter and telephone, exchanges of photographs, home videos, newspapers, films and radio programmes may combine with continuing economic ties and marriage alliances to sustain a close identification with Bangladesh. At the same time the migration of relatives and friends to the oil-rich states in the Middle East may also strengthen the sense of being part of an Islamic community which extends far beyond the nation-state boundaries of Bangladesh and which potentially links them to other Muslims within Britain and the 'western world'. Clearly the issue of identity which could be expressed in such questions as : 'what is my identity?' and 'with whom do I identify?' is complicated in a world where the personal identity of any individual consists of multiple, overlapping and sometimes contradictory social identities.

Community Politics in Postwar East London: The First and Second Generation of Settlers

As we have already seen, by 1960 the estimated number of Bangladeshis in Tower Hamlets and other areas of Britain was minute. Approximately 6,000 – almost exclusively adult males – were scattered across the country's urban, industrial centres. While there is some evidence that the nucleus of London's Bangladeshi community had already formed in what became the borough of Tower Hamlets it is also apparent that *lascars* had found work in the factories, foundries, cafes and shops of towns and cities across the Midlands and northern England.[20] During the 1960s up until the creation of an independent Bangladesh in 1971 the size of the British Bangladeshi population may have increased almost fourfold and during the 1970s the rate of increase was almost threefold.[21] In Tower Hamlets Bangladeshis were already well established in the heartlands to the west of the borough. Across Spitalfields, St Mary's, St Katharine's and Weavers wards the availability of cheap, privately-rented accommodation in relatively large numbers enabled them to establish a presence which began to influence local politics.

What we know about Bangladeshi community leaders during the post-Second World War period up to the creation of Bangladesh indicates that they were not only closely involved with political and cultural developments within East and West Pakistan but were also aware of economic opportunities in post-Second World War Britain. Aftab Ali, one of the most celebrated activists, focused on labour organisation within the Indian Seamen's Union before the Second World War, became vice-president of the All India TUC in 1939 and served as a member of the Bengal Legislative Assembly between 1937 and 1944. He pursued his political career in the eastern wing of Pakistan after the partition of British India but continued to represent the interests of his fellow Sylhetis playing a key role in encouraging *lascars* to find employment within Britain during the 1950s.[22] Aftab Ali was not surprisingly involved in the most influential community organisation during the 1950s and 1960s – the Pakistan Welfare Association (PWA). Its first major public meeting was held in Tower Hamlets during 1954 to challenge the visiting Pakistan Foreign Minister over the problems experienced by East Pakistanis in gaining access to Britain.[23]

East Pakistani leaders within the PWA largely focused their efforts, therefore, to lobbying representatives of the Pakistan state, to continuing 'the "welfare" functions that had always been so important – the letter writing, form-filling, etc'.[24] These leaders also established discreet links with influential British politicians such as Peter Shore, a local MP and a future minister in Labour governments during the 1970s. The Association played no obvious part in the political life of the three boroughs which formed the new borough of Tower Hamlets in 1965. The Labour Party dominated the political and administrative apparatus of these boroughs although its ward party structure had become largely moribund. The process of chain migration from clusters of villages within the East Pakistan district of Sylhet ensured that the newcomers' political interests were principally shaped by what was happening in their country of origin. Consequently, the politicisation of community leaders was shaped by:

> Their growing consciousness of the mass movement for autonomy in East Pakistan, a movement that was born with the Language Martyrs [students shot

in Dhaka on February twenty-first 1952, while protesting at the government attempt to enforce the use of Urdu in place of Bengali] and was to lead eventually to the liberation struggle and an independent Bangladesh in 1971.[25]

These political developments led to the splitting of the PWA into two factions and the creation of the Bangladesh Welfare Association (BWA) whose interests were even more closely tied to the growing Bangladeshi population of Tower Hamlets. The BWA established its office in Spitalfields where almost half the borough's Bangladeshi residents were concentrated by 1971.[26]

Yet it would be misleading to over emphasise community leaders' involvement in political developments within their country of origin. The Association's awareness of wider political campaigns over racism was reflected in its collaboration with the Campaign Against Racial Discrimination during the 1960s. With the increase in attacks on Bengali settlers the BWA also affiliated to the Joint Council for the Welfare of Immigrants in 1968 and a year later the Association: 'launched a new campaign against racial attacks. A register was kept of all reported attacks that took place in the area. The police were informed of suspicious congregations of "teddy boys" in the locality.'[27] Although the BWA remained largely inactive during the 1970s community leaders continued to mobilise Bangladeshi residents over particular local issues such as housing, racism and a Bangladeshi community centre.[28]

Before the late 1970s, therefore, community leaders in Tower Hamlets looked in two directions – a) to their country of origin which, after 1970, was a newly independent nation-state engaged in often turbulent political and social conflict and b) to the British nation-state where Bangladeshis were gradually moving from being temporary to permanent settlers. Wives and dependants were arriving and a second generation of community leaders was emerging which would engage much more directly and actively with British political and community institutions. While remittances still flowed back to the Sylhet villages the demands of living in Britain became more insistent and the pressure to campaign for a greater share of local resources increased. At the same time 'white' activists and state institutions became more closely involved with the demands of Bangladeshi and other single interest groups.

While there was no inevitability in the way in which Bangladeshi issues entered the local political arena it is interesting to note that the first highly-publicised struggles focused around housing and racial violence. These struggles centred on Bangladeshi access to public urban space – in terms of improving conditions in the privately rented sector, entering local authority accommodation and being safe from attacks both within the home and in the streets. At the same time the particular concerns of Bangladeshis could be linked to other struggles pursued by local political and community activists.[29] Bangladeshi activists developed the kinds of alliances and essentialist interpretations of community which Brah and Werbner, for example, have discussed in a more general context. [30]

During the mid- and late-1970s attempts were made by left-wing activists within the Labour Party and Far Left political organisations to establish 'socialist' campaigns which would bring together local 'working class' constituencies fragmented by racial, ethnic, gender and national differences. These attempts met with very limited success. One of the many obstacles preventing the development of any large-scale socialist campaign was the gulf between the political and cultural priorities of white radical activists and those espoused by the first generation of Bangladeshi community representatives. Between 1978 and 1986 a degree of convergence occurred between white activists and certain second generation community leaders which largely benefited a revitalised local Labour Party. At the same time a 'white backlash' against the alliance appears to have played a crucial role in the party's first electoral defeat since the 1930s.

Two important and related themes emerged during the 1978–86 period. One is the proliferation of Bangladeshi community organisations. The second is the way in which this proliferation encouraged the second generation activists to challenge the leadership which first generation settlers assumed was theirs by right of seniority and connections with Bangladeshi and British politicians and administrators. Street demonstrations against racial attacks during the borough election year of 1978 were the stimulus for the entry by second generation activists into local political and administrative institutions. This was a process which was encouraged and financially assisted by left-wing leaders within the local Labour Party, the Greater London Council and the Inner London Education Authority.[31] The second generation activists contributed to an anti-racist campaign which challenged, among others, the 'Thatcherite revolution' triggered by the Conservative victory over the Labour Party in the national elections of 1979.

The community organisations which received state funding during this period usually described themselves as serving the interests or needs of those who had migrated from the recently independent state of Bangladesh. Their official functions served to foster an identification with Bangladesh. The BWA now had to compete with these new organisations in the quest for representatives from the Bangladesh High Commission as well as from the local state at annual general meetings, Language Day, Martyrs Day and

Independence Day. Yet with the waning of official enthusiasm for the secular ideological foundations of Bangladesh the calls to satisfy Islamic needs became more insistent in Tower Hamlets. During 1983 the issue of religious education for Muslim students at local state schools, for example, was raised in a bulletin published by Bangladeshi Educational Needs in Tower Hamlets, a community organisation funded by the Inner London Education Authority. Moreover, allegations that left-wing Labour leaders were opposed to the development of Islamic religious centres aroused strong feeling in certain local wards before and during the 1986 borough election.[32]

The entry of Islamic issues into the local political arena was, once again, the product of both local and more global developments. In Tower Hamlets and across the country there was an increasing demand for Islamic provision in terms of worship, education, food and other elements of lifestyle. In the borough the Bangladeshi population expanded almost threefold again between 1981 and 1991 and a more balanced and settled network of families was requiring (and being encouraged to demand) public support for a range of Islamic facilities. These local issues were accompanied by the expansion of political Islam both in Muslim-majority Bangladesh and across the globe. Developments such as the Iranian revolution, the assertion of the power of oil-rich Gulf states, the conflict between Israel and its Arab neighbours and *The Satanic Verses* saga encouraged people to locate their specific local interests within more global contexts. The interconnections between these different contexts were made even more apparent when local mosques were repaired, new ones constructed with money from Bangladesh, Saudi Arabia and Pakistan or news was received from Bangladesh about relatives migrating to jobs in the Middle East.[33]

The 1986 borough election saw not only an historic defeat of the local Labour Party but it also ushered in a period of decline for Bangladeshi community organisations and encouraged more Bangladeshi activists to look for political opportunities beyond the left-wing Labour networks. Second generation Bangladeshis were able to continue defining and representing Bangladeshi interests by gaining employment in local state agencies which provided public services to local residents – a process which had begun during the early 1980s. Employment in the private sector also continued to be important with some community activists following their elders as entrepreneurs in the garment industry, the small shopkeeping sector and the catering trade. These economic activities sustained the social and political links with Bangladesh as entrepreneurs competed with one another for the custom of their predominantly Bangladeshi clients or maintained a respectable distance from their non-Muslim customers. 'Protecting the honour' of the rapidly expanding numbers of wives and female dependants became a persistent theme in male discussions about life in Britain. Another associated theme concerned the alleged decline in moral standards involving members of the emergent third generation.

By the time the Labour Party returned to power in 1994 the second generation Bangladeshi activists who were elected as councillors operated in a much more variegated world of political and cultural allegiances than was evident during the late 1970s. Three generations of Bangladeshis had emerged with diverse interests which were shaped by local and more global involvements. A politics of representation had developed where people were far more aware of the kinds of complexities created by the interweaving of class, race, ethnicity and gender, for example, which we outlined at the beginning of this chapter.

These complexities defied the popular model of social identities as fixed entities which individuals possessed through their membership of specific groups classified through such homogenising and reifying terms as the Bangladeshi ethnic minority and the Muslim community or, more subtly, through the hybrid categories of Bangladeshi Muslim, Bengali Muslim and British Bengali. Furthermore, the politics of representation did not simply involve the unmediated expression by activists of the needs and interests of specific groups united by some social and cultural essence. Yet in spite of these complex divisions and mixtures the popular model of social identities as fixed, essentialised and discrete units deeply influenced the ways in which activists represented 'their community' to others as the following section will reveal.

Constructing Identities and the Second Generation: The State and Several Nations

Political Representation and Community Identity

Anthropologists have emphasised the powerful influence of ties which South Asian settlers in Britain have maintained with the villages from which so many migrated. These ties sustain social status differences, family and kinship networks, patterns of marital arrangements and religious affiliations which distinguish them socially and culturally from the majority population.[34] Continuing links with countries of origin played a central role in providing the ethnic, cultural resources on which South Asian and East African Asian settlers have successfully drawn despite the structural disadvantages of class inequality and racial prejudice. An analysis of the process of identification, from this perspective, is directed towards these distinctive local social and cultural ties rather than more macro-level institutions of British society.

This anthropological tradition clearly reflects important aspects of the everyday life of British Bangladeshis and other 'ethnic minorities'. It shows the limitations of sociological accounts which focus on racialised disadvantage and the structural deprivation of the inner city areas in which many minorities still find themselves. Anthropological perspectives help to explain the upward socioeconomic mobility enjoyed by some South Asian and East African families and their migration from the inner city.

While the debates between anthropologists and sociologists sometimes suggest a sharp polarisation and opposition in perspectives, studies of local areas actually draw on both traditions. When the process of identification is approached it is evident that political discourses concerning identity at local and more global levels influence the ways in which social and cultural identities are understood in everyday life (see, for example, Centre for Bangladeshi Studies, 1994). Popular discussions about identity have been informed by the growth in public debates about what the meanings of such terms as 'English', 'British', 'European', 'Bangladeshi', 'Asian' and so on. This reflexive process of 'becoming' rather than simply 'being' has involved British Bangladeshis as a settled population has emerged extending over two and, more recently, three generations. As we have already seen the second generation have played a crucial role in the development of this continuing debate about identity. Here we will focus on a particular stage in the local politics of representation – the early and middle 1980s – a period during which many of the contemporary themes were established.

The Bangladesh Youth Front and the British State

During the late 1970s the second generation activists had already established youth centres and football clubs. The expansion of state funding for local community initiatives during the late 1970s and early 1980s enabled these activists to acquire public support for existing and new community organisations across Tower Hamlets. By the mid-1980s Bangladeshi organisations had proliferated across the country and their articulate representation of 'their community' can be gauged by the extensive reports which they produced for the House of Commons Home Affairs Committee inquiry, *Bangladeshis in Britain, 1986–87*. This political process of representation entailed constructing the 'Bangladeshi community' in terms of the material needs which the British state could provide as well as contributing to group solidarity among Bangladeshi settlers. When these organisations produced their annual reports, for example, they frequently described their contribution in both these areas. The Bangladesh Youth Front, for example, a well known organisation which used the facilities of a long-established community centre in Spitafields, described its aims and objectives in its 1981–82 report as:

(a)   To work towards creating unity and helping consolidation of young people of Bangladeshi origin as a component part of the Bengali speaking ... young people in the United Kingdom.
(b)   To develop young people as a social and economic force in the community to enable them to deal specifically with problems relating to:
- Education
- Employment opportunities and Equal rights
- Housing
- Social Welfare amenities and recreational opportunities
- Emancipation of the Bengali speaking young women with special attention to those of Bangladeshi origin.
(c)   To provide [an] office, meeting place and a centre for the members of the Front.
(d)   To support initiatives aimed at improving the level and quality of religious education for the members of the community.
(e)   To work towards a multi-racial and multi-cultural society and in this regard to cooperate with and coordinate activities with organisations having similar aims with special reference to organisations of the ethnic minority communities.

After letters of support from the representatives of other community organisations and political institutions the Annual Report proceeds to describe the problems which Bangladeshis faced in gaining fair access to state resources concerned with health, housing, unemployment, interpreting and legal institutions. Racism is a recurrent theme and, while the borough is described as 'a poor and depressed area', the Front argues that this 'does not mean that adequate services should not be maintained'. The youth organisation did not have any power but it 'had all the responsibility to look after the needs of many Bengalis'. This commitment to service was detailed in the following way:

As a youth organisation the Bangladesh Youth Front has arranged camping holidays, outings, various sports and games – outdoor and indoor cultural functions, drama performances, gymnastic activities, physical exercises, feast, festivals and many other things. As a responsible and active Bengali organisation, the Bangladesh Youth Front also makes an important contribution to the general welfare of the local Bengali community in areas such as: Welfare Rights, education, immigration, housing, income tax and health and provides local organisations with interpreters, as well as going with Bengali people to local government departments, courts, police stations, hospitals, clinics, doctors etc. to assist and act as interpreters. The Bangladesh Youth Front also makes a valuable contribution to the wider community, by participating and co-operating with other local groups.

Bangladeshi identity was constructed here in terms of a political process whereby a particular community organisation a) represented the needs of the Bangladeshi community to the British state and b) attempted to satisfy those needs through a combination of voluntary work and state-funded activities. The organisation's aim of creating unity among Bangladeshi youth as a distinct category within a 'multi-racial and multi-cultural society' would be achieved through a heavy reliance on the assistance of such British state institutions as the local borough council and the GLC, as well as more general community organisations funded by the state.

The activities of the BYF continued a tradition of welfare work which the Pakistan Welfare Association had established during the 1950s and 1960s and which the Bangladesh Welfare Association had failed to sustain vigorously during the 1970s. Community leadership was a familiar means whereby adult males were able to extend their social and economic influence among fellow migrants. Formal accounts such as the BYF's annual report were directed largely at a non-Bengali audience of political and administrative functionaries closely associated with the state outside the community. Given the descriptions of social and cultural life in the Sylheti villages from which most British Bangladeshi settlers came there would have been a considerable gap between these political constructions of the 'community' and the everyday under-standings of Bangladeshis. However, there is a *prima facie* case for claiming that the process of communication between community activists and those who used their services has narrowed this gap over the years. The expansion of community organisations like the BYF during the late 1970s and early 1980s accelerated this process which was given further momentum by involvement in all the other aspects of settlement within this country, especially the creation of a third generation 'born and bred' in Britain during the 1980s.

Radical perspectives contend that the intimate association between state and nation is the product of ideological work whereby the interests of hegemonic groups based on class inequality are generalised to the 'national community'. In the BYF's report we can see this association at work through the provision of state funds to encourage Bangladeshi youth's experience of the wider society. Participation in 'camping holidays, outings, various sports and games' continued a tradition which extended far beyond the post-Second World War settlement of Bangladeshis. It invoked memories of youth work among groups of earlier settlers in the area – Jewish and Irish in particular. Significantly, the BYF occupied a community centre whose origins were rooted in the attempt of Jewish activists to 'Anglicise' the second and third generation of East European Jewish settlers during the 1920s and 1930s. Bangladeshi activists were aware that racialised differences shaped their struggle for more equal resources but, understandably, they were usually not prepared to bite the state hand which nourished their particular organisation.

State, Nation and Bangladeshi Community Organisations

The problematic relationship between state and nation also underlay the celebration by these emergent community groups of the young nation from which their elders had migrated. The East Pakistan crisis of 1970–71 had sharply divided members of the Pakistan Welfare Association and the ineffectiveness of the BWA during the 1970s was partly due to the factional conflicts which were generated by the bitter divisions created during 1971 and the early days of the new nation. These factions were intimately associated with political struggles in Bangladesh between supporters of Sheikh Mujibur Rahman, the country's first prime minister, and his Awami League party, on the one hand, and the Awami League's opponents, which included those who had supported a united Pakistan, on the other.

One of the major ideological pillars of Bangladesh was a formal commitment to 'secularism'. Awami League supporters rejected the way in which appeals to Islamic identity had been used to strengthen Pakistani unity between 1947 and 1971. The conflict between secularists and Islamicists continued during the 1970s, however, and the bitterness between political factions was deepened by such events as the assassination of Sheikh Mujib and his immediate entourage in 1975 and the moves by subsequent leaders in Bangladesh towards other Muslim-majority countries, especially those in the Gulf and the Middle East.

Most second generation activists in Tower Hamlets appear to have been sympathetic towards the Awami League. Some of them had been closely involved in student politics during 1971. They were joined by others who left Bangladesh after struggles with resurgent Islamic student organisations during the late 1970s and 1980s. Their ideological commitment to secularism enabled them to appreciate the interests of left-wing leaders within the local Labour Party, the GLC and ILEA which became major sources of community organisation funding between the late 1970s and 1986. Although they did not directly criticise the state regimes which followed the overthrow of Sheikh Mujib, they continued to remind their supporters of the original ideological commitments by the Awami League during the creation of the new nation. As we have seen above in the BYF's aims and objectives they included references to the religious needs of Bangladeshi settlers in Britain but they also dominated the distribution of state funds to youth organisations. In the process they marginalised the efforts of explicitly Muslim groups which operated in the area such as the Young Muslim Organisation.

The work of continual nationalist remembering was pursued through the public functions which community organisations held across Tower Hamlets and elsewhere. The major events in the national calendar are Martyr's Day (Bengali Language Day), Bangladesh Independence Day and Victory Day. These were commemorated through public meetings in the premises used by particular organisations or in local meeting halls. The events usually consisted of speeches, the distribution of commemorative literature and food, as well as some form of entertainment (singing, instrumental playing, dancing and poetry readings). The 1986–87 annual report by the Bengali Mahila Samity, one of the few women's groups in Tower Hamlets, provides a succinct summary of the organisation's contribution to this work of remembrance:

Social Events

Mahila Samity has taken a lead over the last few years in organising various social events. We have celebrated Bangladesh Independence Day on 22nd March this year and also Victory Day [16th December] and Martyr's Day [21st February, Bengali language day]. These functions were well attended.

A radical interpretation of the lessons to be learned from these commemorative functions was set out in the 1984 annual report of the Federation of Bangladeshi Youth Organisations (FBYO). In a section devoted to 'days of political and cultural significance' the report declared that:

There is a great deal of Bangladesh here within the Bengali community in Britain. A sense of identity and knowledge of one's roots and heritage are of the essence for the Bengali community, particularly the second and third generation of young Bengalis.

It is only through a proper understanding of political history and the role of British cultural imperialism in Bengal, that our youngsters can gain the kind of confidence they need to stand up to the forces of oppression in society.

The report then proceeded to describe three commemorative days – Independence Day, Martyr's Day, Victory Day and Bengali New Year. Independence Day was placed within the context of 'imperialism' and the activities of Pakistan, China and the USA. Its contemporary relevance and commemoration was outlined in the following way:

The impact of the liberation war of 1971 was instrumental in building up the confidence and sense of identity of British Bengalis. The Federation observed independence day by having a seminar/discussion followed by a cultural function.

The FBYO annual report emphasised a theme which other community groups also established – the significance of the Bengali language for Bangladeshi nationalism. Martyr's Day provided the context for the celebration of this theme:

The right of a people to express themselves in their own language can not be questioned. In 1952 workers, students and peasants took to the streets of Dhaka and other cities defending this right. The then government of Pakistan tried to [impose] Urdu as the national language and this was met by the resistance of the people. Many lives were lost as brutal forces of coercion opened fire on demonstrations. The Federation observed this day by a simple ceremony at the Berner Club in remembrance of those who gave their lives on 21st February, 1952.

The allegation of continual intrusion by outside forces on Bangladeshi affairs was repeated in the discussion of Victory Day. The delivery of social justice promised by the successful completion of 1971 liberation was shattered 'with the murder of Sheik Mujibur Rahman at the hands of the CIA using reactionary Bengalis linked to the army'. This dark picture was lightened, however, by the last anniversary to be described – Bengali New Year – whose 'theme is one of looking forward with optimism'.

The FBYO's close association with the Awami League was made even more obvious to outsiders by its 1986–87 annual report. Here a detailed account of a visit by Sheikh Hasina, the daughter of Mujibur Rahman and the leader of the Awami League opposition to the current military regime. At a meeting with '45 specially invited Bengali women activists' at the Montefiore Centre in Whitechapel, Sheikh Hasina claimed that:

> The biggest problem and obstacle in the path of women [in Bangladesh] is the Military Junta. If free and fair elections were held [she] believes that the Awami League would have won and formed the Government. In the last 12 years of Military rule, there has been no development for women. However, changes can be made for women. During the rule of Sheikh Mujibur Rahman, women's education was free up to class 8, [there were] quota systems for women and in admissions to Universities and Colleges. The most important thing Sheikh Mujib achieved was to restore to society rape victims who were earlier abandoned by their families and society, compelling the victim to turn to prostitution in order to survive.

Islam and Nation: The Young Muslim Organisation

These organisations were not hostile to Islam. Indeed, we have already seen the BYF's advocacy of measures which would improve 'the level and quality of religious education' for British Bengalis. Yet by the mid-1980s they had established a dominance within the circle of publicly funded Bangladeshi community organisation which effectively marginalised local groups receiving support from Islamic foundations.

The Young Muslim Organisation (YMO) was one community group which was able to mount a sustained challenge to this marginalisation of Islamic activities. The YMO was supported by an international organisation – the Dawatul Islam – which had established bases in other areas of Britain and had long been active in what was now Pakistan and Bangladesh. The YMO's aims were clearly outlined in its 1987 anniversary publication. It set itself against 'the melting pot of British culture' and western values and sought to establish a 'Muslim nation' in the conviction that 'Islam offers total salvation – which is eluding almost every nation and individual on the surface of this earth'. Its programme was summarised under five headings:

• Dawah: To d[i]ss[e]minate the message of Islam particularly to the young people.

- Organisation: To organise those who accept this message under the banner of the YMO.
- Education and Training: To impart Islamic education to the members of the YMO and train them to give correct leadership.
- Social Services: To provide various services to the needy members of the society irrespective of colour and race.
- Salvation of the Humanity: To fight against all injustices to bring peace and salvation to the humanity at large.

The YMO paid great attention to providing extramural educational support as well as the usual sporting and recreational facilities. It also encouraged young people to attend its annual leadership training camp in order 'to create correct leadership and provide guidance to the community'.

The YMO's activities were shaped by the teachings of Sayyid Abul A'la Mawdudi. Mawdudi's hopes of establishing a Muslim nation had not been realised in Pakistan and many dismissed the relevance of his ideas to the British context. However, Dawatul Islam and its associated youth organisation found a measure of support from urban lower middle class residents in Pakistan and Bangladesh. In Tower Hamlets the YMO attracted some dedicated activists who were attending higher education programmes. Moreover, the organisation found favour within the local ILEA youth office which had played such an important part in the state funding of Bangladeshi youth groups.

An indication of the YMO's engagement with its opponents in local community politics can be gleaned from an article describing the YMO's development in the 1987 publication. Abdur Razzaq Siddiqi, a barrister, explained how the YMO participated in the 1981 BWA's election of officers. The YMO supported a motion to include a highly symbolic Islamic saying into the BWA's constitution despite opposition from those who used 'the most weird of arguments'. Siddiqi claimed that:

> The glaring fact that Bangladesh is a Muslim country, and virtually all members of Bangladesh Welfare Association are Muslims were simply being ignored. The rock solid unity of YMO and their unshakeable conviction in the rightness of the proposal eventually unnerved the opponents. The enemies of Islam were defeated, and the name of Allah was written at the top of the BWA Constitution for the first time ever.

The contention that Bangladesh was 'a Muslim country' was not strictly correct since approximately 14 per cent of the nation's citizens were non-Muslims, mainly Hindus. Nevertheless, Abdur Razzaq Siddiqi expressed a widespread belief that the Bangladeshi national community should be defined in terms of Islam and that the almost exclusively Muslim population of British Bengalis should affirm their Islamic identity in a non-Muslim country through such important community organisations as the BWA.

The YMO remained the only Islamic youth group in Tower Hamlets to gain local state support during the 1980s. It continued to be outnumbered by the many Bangladeshi community organisations which emphasised secular issues but it also benefited from both the declining influence of those organisations during the last 10 years. It benefited further from the increasing political influence of Islamic representatives in Bangladesh and other Muslim-majority countries as well as in Britain. At a local level the decline of secularist community organisations was triggered in the mid-1980s by the eradication of the GLC and ILEA and the Liberal Democratic Alliance's defeat of the Tower Hamlets Labour Party. At the same time the public presence of Islam was dramatically announced by the opening of the East London Mosque with Saudi and Pakistani financial support as well as the development of other mosques, prayer halls and Islamic educational centres (*madrassahs*) across the borough.[35] These developments involved the Islamicisation of local public space as well as fostering links with a global Islamic community (*ummah*) where a Muslim nation could be seen as transcending particular nation-state boundaries.

Conclusion

This chapter began with a discussion of the reaction to Princess Diana's death and the way in which different people's reactions can be interpreted in terms of a search for wholeness and integrity. This search can be seen as performing a crucial role within the process of identity formation. Public displays of emotion by women and 'ethnic minorities' during the aftermath of Diana's death showed to a vast television audience what academic research has long confirmed to a more limited audience – that the search for wholeness and identity crosses diverse social and economic boundaries. Minorities play a central rather than a marginal part within the long-standing debate about identity (political, cultural and personal) across Britain.

The public debate about political identity involves reflections about the changing character of the British nation-state. The settlement of people from Britain's former colonies has been the focus of an attention which far exceeds their numbers. 'Black and Asian' settlers have clearly challenged exclusivist notions of Britain's national heritage. The search for wholeness is complicated by the existence of strikingly different social and cultural practices. The creation of 'new ethnicities' and hybrid, diasporic communities challenges the tendency to see British identity as rooted in some essential national heritage which links the present to a distant past. Identities are continually being made. We are engaged in processes of identification where, as Stuart Hall reminds us, change, contestation, heterogeneity and mixture are the key features rather than fixity, consensus, homogeneity and purity.

The main body of this chapter concentrates on the representations and practices by Bangladeshi community organisations which reveal the emergence of a hybrid sense of being both British and Bengali/Bangladeshi. At the same time community activists were still influenced by nationalist discourses which explained the creation and survival of Bangladesh in essentialist terms. Bangladesh was born out of a struggle whose origins went back in time to the early 1950s and the 'language movement'. Some extended the roots of the contemporary Bangladesh nation-state into a much further distant past.[36] Although the articulation of a British Bangladeshi/Bengali identity reflected an awareness of the implications of settlement in this country the hybrid consisted of two separate, coexisting identities rather than a blend of elements. The coexistence of separate traditions was further nurtured through the community organisations' celebration of Bangladeshi national commemorations and continuing involvement with political developments in the country of origin.

The Islamic background of Bangladeshi settlers added another, crucial element to the representation of British Bangladeshi needs. While an elision could be made between the nation-state of Bangladesh and Islam through the claim that Bangladesh was a 'Muslim country', the presence of Hindus and other minorities within the country of origin was thereby ignored. The Young Muslim Organisation's rejection of western values and 'the melting pot of British culture' suggested that their view of Islamic identity did not allow for the kind of change, contestation and mixture envisaged in the discussion of transnationalism, new ethnicities and black cultural politics. The YMO's programme appeared to be based on another essentialist conception of identity where Islam held the promise of salvation for the whole world regardless of national and individual differences.

Some community representatives were well aware of the complexities caused by the engagement between different political, social and religious beliefs and practices. They described well the desire to cooperate with British, Bangladeshi and Islamic institutions. Yet while people's lives were caught up with change and mixture, activists' interpretations of identity still emphasised the juxtaposition of essentialised traditions rather than a true hybrid of mixed elements. A challenge to these traditions through the demonstration of a more complex reality may not lead to their overthrow, however. The quest for wholeness may result in a deeper attachment to what people perceive as the deep history and the fixed destiny of their particular nation whether, in this context it be Britain, Bangladesh or Islam.

Notes

1 *Evening Standard*, 6 September 1997.
2 *The Guardian*, 10 September 1997.
3 See H. Bhabha (ed.), *Nation and Narration*, London and New York, Routledge, 1990; U. Hannerz, 'Cosmopolitans and locals in world cultures' in M. Featherstone (ed.), *Global Culture: Nationalism, Globalization and Modernity*, London, Sage, 1990; S. Hall, 'New ethnicities' in J. Donald and A. Rattansi (eds), *Race, Culture and Difference*, London, Sage, 1992; S. Hall, 'The question of cultural difference' in S. Hall, D. Held and A. McGrew (eds), *Modernity and Its Futures*, Cambridge, Polity and Milton Keynes, Open University Press, 1992.
4 See Hall above.
5 S. Hall, 'New ethnicities' in Donald and Rattansi, 1992, op. cit., p. 258.
6 Ibid., p. 257.
7 Ibid., p. 254.
8 Ibid.
9 A. Brah, *Cartographies of Diaspora: Contesting Identities*, London and New York, Routledge, p. 126.
10 Ibid., p. 127.
11 See S. Benson, J. Eade and P. Werbner, 'Asians have Culture; West Indians have problems: Discourses of race and ethnicity in and out of anthropology' in T. Ranger, Y. Samad and O. Stuart (eds), *Culture, Identity and Politics*, Aldershot, Avebury, 1996.
12 L. Back, *New Ethnicities and Urban Culture*, London, UCL Press, 1996.
13 *The Art of Being Black*, Oxford, Clarendon Press, 1996.
14 J. Eade, C. Peach and T. Vamplew, 'The Bangladeshis: the encapsulated community' in C. Peach (ed.), *Ethnicity in the 1991 Census*, London, HMSO, 1996.
15 See J. Eade, *The Politics of Community*, Aldershot, Avebury, 1989; J. Eade, 'Bangladeshi community organisation and leadership in Tower Hamlets, East London' in C. Clarke, C. Peach and S. Vertovec (eds), *South Asians Overseas: Migration and Ethnicity*, Cambridge, CUP, 1990; J. Eade, 'Nationalism, community and the Islamization of space' in B. Metcalf (ed.), *Making Muslim Space in North America and Europe*, Berkeley and London, University of California Press, 1996; J. Eade, 'Identity, nation and religion: educated young Bangladeshis in London's East End' in J. Eade (ed.), *Living the Global City*, London and New York, Routledge, 1997; C. Rhodes and N. Nabi, 'Brick Lane: a village economy in the shadow of the city?' in L. Budd and S. Whimster (eds), *Global Finance and Urban Living*, London and New York, Routledge, 1992; M. Keith, 'Making the street visible:

placing racial violence in context', *New Community*, 21 (4), pp. 551–65, 1995; J. Jacobs, *Edge of Empire: Postcolonialism and the City*, London and New York, Routledge, 1996.

16 See S. Carey and A. Shukur, 'A profile of the Bangladeshi community in East London', *New Community*, 12 (3), pp. 405–29, 1985–6; C. Adams, *Across Seven Seas and Thirteen Rivers: Life Stories of Pioneer Sylhetti Settlers in Britain*, London, THAP Books, 1987; Y. Choudhury, *Roots and Tales of the Bangladeshi Settlers*, Birmingham, Sylheti Social History Group, 1993; Y. Choudhury, *Sons of the Empire*, Birmingham, Sylhet Social History Group, 1995; J. Eade, op. cit.

17 See K. Gardner, 'International migration and the rural context in Sylhet', *New Community*, 18 (3), pp. 579–90, 1992; 'Mullahs, miracles and migration: travel and transformation in rural Bangladesh', *Contributions to Indian Sociology*, NS 27 (2), pp. 213–35, 1994; *Global Migrants, Local Lives: Travel and Transformation in Rural Bangladesh*, Oxford, Clarendon Press, 1995.

18 See P. Cohen, 'All white on the night? Narratives of nativism on the Isle of Dogs' in T. Butler and M. Rustin (eds), *Rising in the East: The Regeneration of East London*, London, Lawrence and Wishart, pp. 170–86, 1996, and P. Cohen, 'Out of the melting pot into the fire next time: imagining the East End as city, body, text' in S. Westwood and J. Williams (eds), *Imagining Cities: Scripts, Signs, Memory*, London and New York, Routledge.

19 V. Saifullah Khan, 'Asian women in Britain; strategies of adjustment of Indian and Pakistani migrants' in A. De Souza (ed.), *Women in Contemporary India*, Delhi, Manohar, 1975; P. Jeffery, *Migrants and Refugees*, Cambridge, Cambridge University Press, 1976; H. Tambs-Lyche, *London Patidars*, London, Routledge, Kegan and Paul, 1980; P. Werbner, 'The organisation of giving and ethnic elites', *Ethnic and Racial Studies*, 8 (3), pp. 368–88; R. Ballard, 'The political economy of migration: Britain, Pakistan and the Middle East' in J. Eade (ed.), *Migration, Labour and the Social Order*, London, Tavistock, 1987; A. Shaw, *A Pakistani Community in Britain*, Oxford, Basil Blackwell, 1988; P. Werbner, *The Migration Process: Capital, Gifts and Offerings among British Pakistanis*, New York, Oxford and Munich, Berg, 1990; R. Ballard, 'The emergence of *desh bidesh*' in R. Ballard (ed.), *Desh Bidesh: The South Asian Presence in Britain*, London, Hurst and Co., 1994.

20 See Adams, op. cit. and Choudhury, op. cit.

21 See Eade, Peach and Vamplew, op. cit.

22 See Adams, op. cit.

23 Ibid, p. 58.

24 Ibid, p. 55.

25 Ibid.

26 A. Asghar, *Bangladeshi Community Organisations in East London*, London, Bangla Heritage, 1996.

27 Ibid, p. 129.

28 Ibid, p. 131.

29 See J. Eade, *The Politics of Community*, Aldershot, Avebury, 1989 and 'The political construction of class and community in Tower Hamlets' in P. Werbner and M. Anwar (eds), *Black and Ethnic Leadership: The Cultural Dimensions of Political Action*, London, Routledge, 1991.

30 See Brah, op. cit. and P. Werbner, 'Essentialising the other' in T. Ranger, Y. Samad and O. Stuart (eds), *Culture, Identity and Politics*, Aldershot, Avebury, 1996.

31 See Bethnal Green and Stepney Trades Council, *Blood on the Streets*, 1978; Eade, 1989, op. cit.; Tower Hamlets Trades Union Council, *No More Blood on the Streets: How to Fight Fascism and Racism*, 1994.

32 See Eade in Werbner and Anwar, op. cit.

33 See Gardner, 1995, op. cit and Eade, 1997, op. cit.

34 See R. Ballard and C. Ballard, 'The Sikhs: the development of South Asian settlements in Britain' and V. Saifullah Khan, 'The Pakistanis: Mirpuri villagers at home and in Bradford' in J. Watson (ed.), *Between Two Cultures*, London, Tavistock, 1977; P. Bhachu, *Twice Migrants: East African Sikh settlers in Britain*, London and New York, Tavistock, 1985; Shaw, 1988, op. cit.; Werbner, 1990, op. cit.

35 See J. Eade, 'Nationalism, community and the Islamization of space in London' in B. Metcalf (ed.), *Making Muslim Space in North America and Europe*, Berkeley and Los Angeles, University of California Press, 1996; R. Home, 'Building a mosque in Stepney', *Rising East*, 1 (1), pp. 59–77, 1997.

36 See J. Eade, 'Nationalism and the quest for authenticity: the Bangladeshis in Tower Hamlets', *New Community*, 16 (4), pp. 493–503, 1990.

7 Identity, Age and Masculinity amongst Bengali Elders in East London

KATY GARDNER

Of course a lot has changed. I came here as a young man and now I'm worn and beaten. My legs have gone, it's not the time for me. My time is over.[1]

Introduction

By the late 1990s there can be little doubt that many of the descriptions of 'minority communities' and 'ethnic boundaries' written over the 1970s and 1980s appear overly static and essentialist.[2] Whilst many of these rightly emphasise the importance of the 'sending' society on the cultural adaptations of migrant communities within Britain, the impression is often given that the 'home' culture is the polar opposite of 'away'. However, as is increasingly clear, instead of simply arriving in places such as Britain with their cultural identities intact, global migrants and their children occupy a third space, where counter narratives of belonging are formulated.[3] Rather than falling 'between two cultures'[4] second and third generation settlers have hybrid identities which they choose between according to the shifting positions they occupy.

Terms such as 'hybridity', 'global migrants' and the 'new ethnicities'[5] clearly have much to offer in the analysis of contemporary global cultures. But by focusing our attention on the myriad cultural choices and identities facing individuals there is a danger of moving too far in the opposite direction, of producing generalised accounts which say little about the ways in which identity is structured by particular historical contexts, as well as a variety of social and cultural factors. Whilst writers such as Paul Gilroy have rightly drawn attention to the ways in which Britain's 'black' settlers[6] have forged a compound culture from disparate sources, we also need to indicate how the identities and cultures of different settlers are affected by a range of historical, environmental and individual factors.

160

In what follows I hope to show how the identities of one specific group of British settlers – first generation male migrants from Sylhet, Bangladesh – whilst certainly multiple, fluid and frequently contradictory, are also closely tied to the stages they have reached in the life-cycle. This in turn is affected both by cultural norms and specific economic and political conditions in Bangladesh as well as in Britain.

As we shall also see, we should not assume a simple transition from 'sojourner' to 'settler' during these men's lives. Nor should we expect them to represent the stable and traditional culture of 'home' as opposed to the increasingly hybrid cultures of children and grandchildren born in Britain, although at a superficial level this may appear to be the case. It is true that as they reach the end of their lives many elders stress the importance of their Muslim and Bangladeshi[7] identities. But whilst they may now appear to be the representatives of 'traditional Sylheti/Muslim ways', this may not always have been the case.

Instead, the relationship between *desh* (home) and *bidesh* (away) has never been simple; it is both continually re-evaluated, and contingent upon different historical and social contexts. Whilst many elders subscribe to what is frequently termed 'the myth of return'[8] this often involves a highly complex array of emotions, imaginings and positions, which are continually fluid, for relationships with Britain and Bangladesh, and perceptions of relative belonging, have shifted in different directions over their life cycles.

As we shall also see, statements about the *desh* are as much a way of thinking and speaking about elders' identities in Britain and their aspirations and fears for the future as they are an objective reflection of conditions in Bangladesh. Whilst they may dream of returning 'home', they can never go back to the place they originally left, for the processes of globalisation and modernity in which both they and the societies they left behind are caught up, have irredeemably changed them both. In the words of Stuart Hall : 'Migration is a one way trip. There is no home to go back to.'[9]

Background

The research on which this chapter is based was carried out at St Hilda's East Community Centre in Shoreditch, which runs a day centre for Bengali elders.[10] The majority of the elders have had strokes or are in other ways disabled and unable to look after themselves adequately during the day.[11] Whilst most are men, the centre caters for a growing number of women, reflecting the changing demography of the Bengali population in East London. St Hilda's also provides support services for the elders' carers, all of whom are women. I should add that not all of the people attending St Hilda's are 'elderly' in the sense that the white majority might understand the term. Although most have reached the stage in their life-cycle which, it is generally agreed, qualifies them to become a *murubbi* (elder),[12] the actual ages of *murubbi* ranges from the early 40s to the late 80s.[13] A small minority have experienced strokes tragically early in their lives, but although still in their 30s also have the beards and *lathi* (walking sticks) which denote the status of a *murubbi*.

All of the elders included in the research are Muslims originating from rural Sylhet. Although they have much in common, there is also considerable diversity between them. Some arrived in Britain in the 1930s and 1940s as *lascars* (sailors), others in the 1960s as employees of Britain's heavy industry; some came from relatively rich and educated backgrounds, whilst others were illiterate and landless. In Britain, some have spent all their time living in Tower Hamlets employed in the garment industry, whilst others have travelled all over the country working in a range of occupations. Some have wives and children living in Bangladesh, others have wholly reunited their families in Britain (all, it should be noted, have at least one wife in Britain). The list of differences could of course continue.

Whilst themselves far from homogeneous, the elders also have particular characteristics which are not necessarily generalisable to other older Bengalis in East London. All are in need of support above and beyond what their families and friends are able to provide, a reflection of both the gravity of their physical conditions and also in some cases the failure (for a variety of social and economic reasons) of their family members to look after them. All are dependent to a greater or lesser degree upon what is left of the welfare state. None are in employment, and all are housed in council accommodation. Because of their physical health and the circumstances which have forced them to seek help from a public agency, many express negative feelings about their present and future lives. Not surprisingly, regret and loss were a frequent theme in many of our interviews. But whilst comprising a group with specific characteristics, in many ways the elders at St Hilda's embody the recent history of Bengali settlement in London. Through their individual histories, the wider picture emerges.

A Short History of Bengali Settlement

South Asians have of course been settling in Britain for many hundreds of years,[14] a history intimately connected to that of British colonialism. Bengalis, in particular, gained a reputation over the late nineteenth and early twentieth century as *lascars* or sailors, working on British ships which carried goods from Calcutta to around the world. Some of the elders have fathers and grandfathers who were lascars, a few worked on the ships themselves. The vast majority however first came to Britain in the 1950s and 1960s when the second phase of migration to *Bilhati*[15] took place. Prompted by a labour shortage after World War Two, the British authorities actively encouraged labour migration from its previous colonies, and thousands of migrants began to arrive, an era which is described in more detail elsewhere.[16]

Arriving as young men in the postwar period, most lived and worked in northern cities such as Birmingham and Oldham, finding employment in heavy industry. Some went directly to London, working in the garment trade as pressers or tailors. Usually living in lodging houses with other Sylhetis, this was a period of unremittingly hard work, a major factor shaping the men's identities. As much money was saved each month as possible, and sent back to Sylhet. According to conventional accounts of this period, the men were 'sojourners' rather than 'settlers'.[17]

Over the 1970s and into the 1980s conditions started to change. Britain's heavy industry was in decline, and after losing their jobs in the north many Sylheti men moved to London to seek employment in the garment or restaurant trades. Even more significantly, perhaps, an increasing number started to bring their wives and children to the UK. Compared with other South Asian groups,[18] British Bengalis have experienced family reunification relatively late; many of the elders' wives at St Hilda's have only been in Britain since the mid- to late 1980s, some for as short a time as one or two years. This process of reunification is often explained as resulting from changes in British immigration law, which made movement between Britain and Bangladesh more difficult.[19] As we shall see, however, elders tend to explain their decisions to bring their families to the UK in terms of the stages they had reached in their life-cycles.

Whilst it is important not to represent the Bengali community in Tower Hamlets in wholly negative terms, there can be little doubt that as a population they have many problems. Living in one of the poorest and most socially deprived boroughs in London, they face high levels of unemployment and are largely dependent upon the council for housing, frequently living in overcrowded and damp accommodation. Racism is a continual problem, and for a short period in the 1990s gained official expression with the election of BNP candidate Derek Beacon in the Isle of Dogs. Recently too, crime levels within the community have been rising: the result of a small minority of young men involved in drugs and gang related activities.

Individual Histories and the Life-cycle

In what follows I shall argue that the identities and perceptions of *desh* and *bidesh* of the first generation Sylheti elders have depended to a large degree upon the stages they have reached in their life-cycles, as well as the wider historical context. As we shall see, the elders' identities and cultural positions are highly fluid, and show few indications of a lineal progression over time from being a wholly Bangladeshi sojourner to a hybrid settler. Whilst today often representing themselves as defenders of 'proper' Sylheti ways against wayward youth, this is more a result of their age than a fixed position vis-à-vis what is presented as 'traditional'.

Young, Free and Single: The 1960s and 1970s in Britain

Let us start with elders' accounts of their first years in Britain. For all, these were times of relentlessly hard work, a theme which came up again and again in the interviews. Abdul Wahed,[20] for example, came to Britain in the early 1960s, and was employed in Birmingham and Worcester in various factories. As he puts it:

> I came here to work. The thing I did the most of was work. I remember the most about work … I did this kind of work or that kind of work … work, work and more work. During the holidays, when everyone gets time off, the people from our country they'd say 'what's the point'?

In answer to the question 'Did you miss your family'? Jamil Ahmed replies:

> I used to sleep, eat, work and sleep. Get up in the morning and work and work. I would just work and work, save and count my money.

Work was not however always readily available, so most men were highly mobile, moving from place to place in search of employment. As Dorus Khan tells us:

At least these days you can get some kind of work, but when I first came here you'd sometimes spend a whole year sitting and waiting, all the while looking and looking. In London [compared to the other cities he lived] you'd only get about £5. How can you eat from that? And then there's your family, your mother and father left behind to provide for. I've spent all my life with these things on my mind, working, being redundant – it's gone along like that.

Many elders recount these days not only in terms of the hardships and deprivations they involved, but also the fun that was to be had as single young men living with other Sylhetis or South Asians in lodging houses. Talking about his days in Blackburn, one told us:

I was on my own. I was a single young man. There were other single young men, like me, *goondas* [hooligans], they'd come round. It was like a little group of us *goondas*.
Q : So you were a *goonda*?
Oh yeah! We were. We did a lot of things, but forget that. [He smiles.] It used to be one pound then [the cost of a prostitute].
Q : One pound!
Yeah [he laughs loudly]. We'd all sit around and someone would say, 'Let's go and get a girl and poke her. It's Saturday night!'
Q : Saturday out for the boys then?
Yeah [he laughs loudly again]. In the middle of all that I'd shout 'I'm first!' Allah, we did so much.

Other pleasures were more innocent:

It was a happy time. I sometimes went to the cinema. In those days the cinemas were much better in this country. They showed much better things, even from Bangladesh.
Q : Where did you go out to [on your days off]?
Just out. Two friends or four friends, we'd go out together, maybe to the cinema, or a coffee-bar or something.

Some of the elders had white girlfriends. A minority married and had children with them.[21] These clearly did not see themselves solely as 'sojourners' in Britain. Instead, their roles and identities were various and shifting. Looking back, Abdul Sayed blames his relationship with a non-Muslim on his lack of religious observance during this period of his life:

I was a broken Muslim. I had a white woman. I never lost my religion but then I never really prayed or anything. That was how I lived. She never said to me not to pray ... but you understand that that was a particular time for me. Everything was work, work, nothing else.

Other men comment upon how their employment stood in the way of being a 'proper' Muslim. The lack of places to pray was an influential factor, as were the types of work in which some were involved. One elder, for example, recounts how, as he approached middle age, his friends suggested he should sell his share of a restaurant in which alcohol was served, for this interfered with his religiosity. I shall return to the issue of the increasing Islamisation of the Bengali community in the next section.

Despite some regrets about their unIslamic ways, most of the elders look back on these days as happy times, in which they fulfilled their roles as workers and providers whilst enjoying considerable freedoms. Interestingly, many express nostalgia for these 'good old days' in Britain, arguing that British people were more friendly and accommodating than they are today. A common explanation for this is that the Bengali presence in Britain was far smaller:

In those days the English used to see us as their own. But then slowly the number of Bengalis increased and now they hate to look at us with both eyes. They can't tolerate our name.
Q : Were there not many Bengalis at that time?
No, it depended on the area ... now [he raises his voice] there are ONLY Bengalis. You can't see any English and you can't get any *maiya* [love, affection] from them.

Today, if you were to ask anyone on the streets to show you the direction they'd probably deliberately show you the wrong way. But in 1964, once, I was on the bus and I ended up in Stratford. I got out and of course couldn't recognise anything. So I asked a policeman ... and they took me to a bus stop and waited with me, and asked other people who was going my way. One customer who used to eat at my uncle's restaurant took responsibility for me, taking me all the way back to my usual bus stop and home. He was really kind. The police, then, were really kind. Men and women, were all kind. Nowadays it is not like that.

These comments may reflect changing race relations in Britain, although there is little evidence that the white majority were any less racist in the 1960s and 1970s than they are today. Certainly they refer to a time when unskilled work was more plentiful, and since most Bengali families had yet to be reunited, there was less competition between them and other groups for council accommodation and other state benefits.[22] But it is also significant that this is the way that the elders chose to represent and remember the Britain of their more youthful days, for memories are not fixed, but are as much fluid responses to present circumstances as to the imagined past.

It would be frivolous to argue that young Bengali men in this period navigated multiple and hybrid identities in the same way as their offspring today. What I do contend, however, is the notion that during this period their identities were stable, or that they saw themselves solely and simply as 'Bangladeshis' abroad.[23] Indeed, many tell of confused feelings on their return to Bangladesh:

> Q : How did it feel to go back?
> Everything felt different. The people especially looked really dark, and going to the toilet made me feel sick. After a few days it got better. But the food – the rice had grit in it, and the salt too. That also made me feel sick.
>
> I was not sure how I felt anymore. It felt weird. I liked Britain and in Bangladesh the people looked different, darker ... but it was my place of birth.

After a long period away, some found to their surprise that they were treated now as foreigners, no longer truly belonging at 'home' either:

> So much had changed after 18 years. I can remember not being able to find this road I was looking for, it was all so different. And the people around our house, ooh, they thought I was such a beautiful fruit. I couldn't sit in the local bazaar in peace, I was always surrounded.

The Establishment of Family and Community: The Late 1970s to 1980s

For many of our informants the late 1970s and 1980s was a period in which their lives became increasingly orientated towards family, community, and a more strongly Muslim identity. During this time many Bengali men brought the wives and children they had acquired on their trips back to the *desh* to Britain. Various reasons have been suggested as to why Bengalis reunited their families at this stage rather than earlier. Changes in immigration laws, which increasingly threatened the ability of families to move freely from Britain to Bangladesh, were certainly important. The ages of some men's children was also influential, for according to British law once they reached the age of 18 they would no longer be allowed entry into Britain. In some cases, men waited until the marriages of their older daughters in Bangladesh before bringing the rest of their families to Britain. Other explanations for the reunification of families over this period may be found within Bangladesh, which by the late 1970s showed few signs of economic or political stability.

But the main reason cited by the elders for bringing their families to Britain during this phase involves both the development of the Bengali/Muslim 'community' in Britain, and their own life cycles. In earlier years, many elders explained to us, Britain was not a suitable place for their wives and children. But as the numbers of Muslims increased, and mosques, *madrasas*, and halal butchers were established they began to feel that their families would be more protected and catered for than previously. The 'snowball' effect of the growing Bengali community was also important: the more Bengalis settled in specific pockets of the country, the more Bengali shops and services were set up, and the more comfortable people felt about their families coming to Britain. As the wife of one elder who came to Britain unusually early in 1958 comments:

> At first I didn't like it here, mainly because I was so alone. Then slowly Bangladeshi women came here and I used to mix with them and became friends with them. So it wasn't so bad after that.

The growing sense of 'community' in Britain was linked to another change during this phase: movement from industrial cities such as Birmingham and Oldham which had earlier provided employment, to London, where there were more facilities and provisions for Muslim Bengalis. The main reason for this was economic. Over the 1970s employment opportunities for unskilled workers in heavy industry began to fall drastically. Forced to find new economic niches, many Bengalis sought work either in the bourgeoning 'Indian' restaurant trade, or the garment industry based in Tower Hamlets. Interestingly, this shift often involved moving from ethnically 'mixed' environments, such as factories, where in the words of one old man:

> Whichever person sees the empty place will come and sit next to you. You can't say : 'Hey! ... go and eat with your own *jaat* [people/race]!' If you did you'd quickly lose your job.

By comparison, the Tower Hamlets garment and 'Indian' restaurant trades tend to employ mainly Bengali or South Asian workers. The move to London is generally described in positive terms by elders and their wives. London is preferable to elsewhere in Britain, they say, because the Bengali community is larger. As Asia Khatun, who has lived in Birmingham, Manchester and London comments:

> For me London is the best ... Here I can mix with everyone. I consider all the

people from my country as my own brothers and sisters. I think of them as my relatives.

The growth of the Bengali community in Tower Hamlets is also associated with the increasing Islamisation of British space over the 1970s and 1980s.[24] Increasingly, specific areas of Britain were becoming viable places in which to be a Muslim. In Tower Hamlets for example, not only is the East London mosque a striking example of Middle Eastern architecture, but with its prominent position on the Whitechapel Road, and the broadcast of its *azan* (call to prayer), it is a graphic claim to British space by local Muslims.[25] I suggest that this is one reason why many elders during this period placed an increasing stress on their Muslim identities.

Q : What does it feel like being a Muslim in Britain, before and now?
Now you can see – it feels like every road there is a mosque. Before there was no value attached to it. People prayed if they felt like it, if not they didn't bother. Some didn't even care. People now pray more, in mosques and at home. We even have visits from *mouluanas*, they come from the *desh*, they go from here. It is going well.

Nowadays we have mosques in many places, now for Muslims it's easy and secure. Before, we didn't have mosques – just one or two room affairs ... now the government has allowed for many mosques ... Everything has changed. There are mosques in so many places that you can pray everywhere.

Combined with the growing establishment of Islam and the 'Bengali community' in Britain, another reason for family reunification is the stage that the men had reached in their own life-cycles. As many carers explained, their husbands sent for them because they were growing older and needed women around.

Q : Why do you think your husband brought you here two years ago?
He'd lost all his strength and the English woman had left him. Now who was going to look after him? Earlier he cooked and fed that woman, but now he's housebound so I have to do it [he had a stroke]. Tell me, is that justice?

Old Age and Disability: The Late 1980s and 1990s

So far I have argued that the identities and perceptions of our informants changed over time, partly as a result of historical conditions within Bangladesh and Britain, but also because of changes within their own life-cycles. Although the majority would always have talked of themselves as being 'Bangladeshi'[26] as they have grown older I suggest that many are increasingly rejecting the more 'Western' elements of their lives, 'returning' to an imagined Bangladesh, and as elders, defending what they now represent as 'traditional' Muslim ways. These changes are largely to do with the developments outlined above: as many men approached late middle age, their wives and children joined them and they moved from smaller communities in the industrial heartlands of Britain to Tower Hamlets, which as a community was far larger and better catered for. The two men married to English women divorced them, and sent for their Bengali wives in Sylhet.

Wider changes within Britain may also have been influential. The recession of the 1970s and the continuing shrinking of heavy industry brought large scale unemployment to unskilled or semiskilled workers. This led many British Bengalis to move to London and change their occupations. It may also have contributed to increasing resentment within some quarters against the newcomers who were (wrongly) perceived as having taken jobs and housing from whites. The official endorsement of racist sentiments expressed in the speeches of figures such as Enoch Powell over the 1960s and 1970s, the activities of organisations such as the National Front, and increasingly draconian immigration legislation which made it quite clear that (non-white) people from the old colonies were no longer welcome, all contributed to the growing sense expressed by elders that Britain was a less and less friendly place. Given their labelling by the white majority of 'foreigner' and 'other', it is hardly surprising that many became increasingly focused on being Bengali and Muslim, and as old age and death approached, on returning to the *desh*.

As we have also seen, the increasing self-identification as 'British Muslims' is closely tied to the growing Islamisation of pockets of Britain. It is also connected to wider changes both locally and globally. There is not the space here to adequately describe these but they include the growing influence of *Tabligh Jamaat*[27] (mentioned by several elders as important to their lives), the increasing Islamisation of the Bangladeshi state (at least, until the recent election of the Awami League), the Gulf War, and the Salman Rushdie affair.[28] As John Eade points out in his discussion of nationalism within the Bengali community in Tower Hamlets, political discourses at both local and global levels increasingly encouraged the articulation of Islamic forms of solidarity rather than those based on secular allegiances or identities over the 1980s.[29] More generally, processes of globalisation and the formation of diaspora have often led to a heightened sense of 'otherness' and alienation which make the apparent unambiguity of Islam increasingly attractive for displaced groups.[30]

All of these factors are important reasons why Islam appears to have become increasingly central to the lives of our informants over the last few decades. I would however like to suggest another: their ages and physical health. Whilst being physical facts, these are culturally constructed. The status of 'elder' for Muslim men from rural Sylhet involves particular meanings and practices. As most elders explained to us, being a *murubbi* is not so much a matter of reaching a particular age, but of assuming the position of a knowledgeable and pious person, who earns respect through his or her behaviour. Once elder children are married and a man's working life finished, the time has come for *Haj*, religious contemplation, and for some, missionary work for the *Tabligh Jamaat*.

Combined with this, the experience of having had a stroke and becoming physically incapacitated, has led many elders to examine their spirituality and relationship with God. As they are all too painfully aware, death may come soon. All have also been forced to stop working, usually because of their health, but also because of unemployment in Tower Hamlets. For men for whom work was so central to their identities, this can come as a huge blow, and contribute to feelings of depression and inadequacy. As Abdul Wahed graphically describes it:

> Now there is no work and I sit and sit at home, my arse is sore, please forgive my rudeness. What can I do? I can't sit at home all the time and I can't work, my doctor won't let me. I'll probably just die suddenly. That's my story I'm telling you. I can't say much more [he laughs].

> Those times [of work and fulfilment] are finished. Now all I can do is sit at home and pray. All day long I have to sit at home asking for this or that. How long can one do that?

All the elders we interviewed were dependent upon the welfare state for housing and benefits, either in the form of disability allowances or old age pensions. So far as we were aware none had any other income, besides what children sometimes contributed.[31] This, plus the availability of free medical care in Britain has led many to express complicated feelings about returning to the *desh*. Whilst the majority dream of return, for practical reasons this is often not possible. As we were frequently told, the economic insecurity of Bangladesh, plus the cost of medical care often means that there is little real choice between London and the *desh*, especially for those who are wheelchair bound or who need regular medication.

> At the moment, Baba forgive me for saying this, but this country is best for me. Why? Because [back] in the *desh* I can't work, I'm blind, no-one would have me ... I do have about four acres of land in Bangladesh, and I know lots of people who could sharecrop it, but it doesn't always work. What if all the crops get washed away?

As the following quotes show, the presence of children who have no intention of leaving Britain also means that some elders stay here against their will.

> I do see this country as my own, but I'll tell you. When we first came here all we thought about was working for about four or five years and then going back. How could we go back? That was all we worried about. Now we don't have that, this country is partly our country ... Now that we have our families here, that is what has caused us to be stuck here. We cannot go back.

> I thought I would work and retire, go back to Bangladesh, settle and live out the rest of my days religiously. Now I cannot go back. It looks like I'm going to stay and die here. Only Allah knows. If my sons cared they would notice and send me back but they have not done anything.

> [Our children] will never go back to Bangladesh. They won't go back. ... My little daughter said: 'I'm not going back to the *desh.*' I said: 'Why not, my dear?' She said: 'If I go back to the *desh* I can't do anything. There are mosquitoes everywhere, flies – I can't even get a drink of water.'

The yearning for the *desh* expressed in the above quotes (and reflected in most of our other interviews) is, I suggest, tied partly to the ages of the speakers, who have always imagined Bangladesh as the place they would eventually retire to and be buried in. But it is also connected to changing conditions within Britain, which most elders perceive to be increasingly violent, unfriendly and lacking in economic opportunity. Growing unemployment in Tower Hamlets has almost certainly contributed to this view, as has the increasing centrality of 'race' in local political discourses.[32]

The disaffection expressed by many elders is also connected to changes within the Bengali community. Here, in Britain, they say, the younger generation no longer give them the respect which as *murubbis* is their due. As children are less able and willing to comply with what are presented as 'traditional' ways, (which may include marrying who their parents wish, observing 'proper' Muslim ways, and returning to Bangladesh with them) many elders look back to an imagined time when their status as older people would have been higher. Their relative power over children has been affected by material conditions as well as changing cultural mores. Whilst in rural Bangladesh parents usually control land and property until their death, when it is divided amongst their sons, in Tower Hamlets most elders have few resources which their children are waiting to inherit. The following quotes sum the effects of this up well:

> This country has different laws. They [the younger generation] can seek their own path and not even bother to tell their father. We have had this way since our forefathers. Each has in turn provided for the other. But in this country I'm not really providing for them, the government is, so they owe me nothing and I can no longer expect anything from them.

> Before, the *murubbis* used to be the decision makers in the *shomaz* [society]. They would be consulted, judge things. No-one bothers to ask *murubbis* now. Do you understand? That's a major change in our *shomaz*.

A second, but equally important factor is the provision of housing in Tower Hamlets, where it is council policy not to allow extended families to be rehoused.[33] Since there are very few four or five bedroom flats available, parents find that as their children grow up and their families expand, overcrowding has become a major problem. When one of them has a stroke and can no longer get access to a second or third storey flat, the need to be rehoused becomes even more pressing. Council policy means that parents are now very unlikely to be rehoused with their children. The every day care and contact that they might have expected from their extended families in Bangladesh is, for practical reasons, increasingly unlikely to be available in London.

Combined with these material changes, many elders perceive the younger generation as becoming ever more wayward.[34] Growing up in Britain, some (but by no means all) of their children vociferously reject the 'traditional' ways which their parents appear to represent. Their relative lack of authority comes as a bitter blow to some fathers:

> I have the one son. If I say 'do your *namaz*', he'll say: 'I'll pray if I want to pray.' If I hit him I'm in trouble and if I say anything I'm in trouble ... They were born into a Muslim house. He should learn *namaz*, fasting ... but when I see him eat at *eefta* [the end of the fast] I don't know if he's been sticking to it or not.

Before, we would never have smoked in front of a *murubbi*. That would have been considered a great insult to their status and dignity. But now they light up in front of you, and even push you aside to let them by. Nowadays it's all about showing off. I look at them and I think : 'You **** sons of ****, we're here too.' [In my day] we never went near *murubbis,* just in case they thought we were being ill mannered. Now we have to salaam the youths! Day, night, everything has changed. In my forty years here, everything has changed.

Tradition and The *Desh*: Imagined Return

I suggest that the cultural hybridity of their children has pushed some elders into an increasingly intransigent position vis-à-vis their own identities. The more 'mixed-up' the second generation appear to them to be, the more some fall back upon the notion of a pure Sylheti culture, which their generation represents. As one elder puts it:

> They are not like me, their brains work differently. They are not like me, they are more like the English people. They cannot speak, they do not know our ways. They only know what the computer says.

In this context, 'tradition' is something which has arisen out of contemporary conditions. This is not to say that it has no relation to customary ways in Sylhet, but rather its construction in the lives of elders in Tower Hamlets is as much a response to life in Britain as to some unchanging and fixed set of laws to be found in Bangladesh. After all, many elders have spent nearly all of their adult lives in the UK, and as we have seen did not themselves always follow the 'proper' ways which they now advocate.

As Paul Gilroy has pointed out, the idea of 'tradition' in black political discourse can form a refuge from 'the maelstrom of modernity'[35] and the threats this poses for the 'coherence of the racial self'.[36] Rather than understanding tradition as oppositional to modernity, Gilroy suggests that it can be seen as a way of speaking about the: 'apparently magical processes of connectedness that arise as much from the transformations of Africa by diaspora cultures as from the affiliation of diaspora cultures to Africa'.[37]

Whilst Gilroy is talking of what he terms 'racial communities' and specifically, the Afro-Caribbean diaspora, similar observations might be made for the Bengali community in Tower Hamlets.[38] For the older generation a major element of this involves a re-imagining of 'the *desh*' as the place where they belong and will ultimately return to. Whilst it is certainly true that many elders always planned to return to Bangladesh, we need to understand the urge to return and the ways in which different groups of people represent the *desh* as resulting from specific historic, cultural and social factors. Return is often a myth[39] but it is a myth which is continually changing and which fulfils the varying needs of people over their life-cycles.

As they reach the end of their lives, I suggest that the idea of the *desh* takes on particular symbolic qualities for many elders, who construct it as the opposite to Britain, a place to which they are profoundly linked and which is 'of their blood'.[40] As many elders stressed during their conversations with us, Bangladesh is both the place where they were born, and where they wish to die. The following quotes are typical:

> I can never say Bangladesh is bad. It is the land of my birth and I must adore it.

> It's my own country, it's the land of my birth.

This does not necessarily mean that even if they could, all elders would return to Bangladesh, for many hold various and contradictory attitudes towards it. Whilst the majority spoke of the *desh* in loving and idealised terms, many described it a few minutes later as a place of economic insecurity, crime and corruption in which it was no longer practically possible to live. Rather than being the place where they will actually return, statements about the *desh* are therefore a way of expressing alienation towards London.

> I haven't been to Bangladesh for 13 years, but if I do go I don't think I'll feel like coming back. I won't feel like leaving the *shonar desh* [golden land] again. This country is not a country. I didn't understand these things before. I once stayed here for a stretch of eighteen years.

> This time if I go, my intention is to never come back. Only if Allah wants me to will I return [to UK]. The earth in which I've buried my father is where I want to be buried. That's the promise I'm going to make myself before I go. I'll have a return ticket, [but] if I die then I'll find peace.

However they may imagine the *desh*, many elders realise there can be no simple 'going back', for processes of modernity and globalisation have transformed both them and Bangladesh. This sense of no return was perhaps the most poignant theme of our interviews:

> Bangladesh is full of *shoytans* [devils]. My heart cries out for it, but I don't want to go.

> We are in-between now. Even if you are Bangladeshi, if you went back to live there it wouldn't be possible. You are not seen as the same. You cannot fit into their society. That is why this country is better for us now.

Conclusion

Rather than being fixed or stable, the state of migrancy: 'involves a movement in which neither the points of departure nor those of arrival are immutable or certain'.[41] Our research at St Hilda's indicates the degree of this uncertainty. Whilst the quotations have been selected to illustrate certain points and may therefore appear to tell a coherent story, the elders frequently contradicted both themselves and each other throughout the various interviews they kindly gave us. Whilst people are by nature contradictory, some of this internal confusion is, I suggest, a product of the diasporic condition. Migration involves profound contradiction and conflict[42] and this generation, more than others, embody and express the pain this causes. Caught between the opposing ideals of family togetherness and economic aspiration, love of the *desh*, and the practical needs for economic and medical support, it is hardly surprising that many feel an overwhelming sense of loss as they enter the last years of their lives.

> I have lost everything. I have lost my sons, they refuse to acknowledge me as their father. In Bangladesh they would have washed my feet and looked after me by earning a wage. My daughter is married to a rich man, but she can't come here … It's all losses.

In this chapter I have attempted to show how highly complex identities and attitudes towards *desh-bidesh* have changed over the lives of first generation Sylheti settlers in Britain. This is partly a result of general historical circumstances, but also the stages which they have reached in their individual histories. Alongside others (such as gender) I suggest that age is a major factor in the structuring of identity.

The importance of what we might think of these 'micro' factors, such as age, in influencing peoples' identities is however often lost in discussions of 'macro' processes of modernity and globalisation, which (it is implicitly assumed) have a top-down effect on peoples' lives and cultures. But whilst these certainly influence the conditions in which people live and the ways in which they see themselves, to understand the choices which they make and constraints which face them, we need to also consider specific economic, political, and personal factors. These push and pull people in many ways; no-one is simply swept helplessly along by global cultural processes over which they have no choice or control. Whilst in many senses caught within historical circumstances, the elders at St Hilda's are active agents: the spirit of opportunism and enterprise with which most have led their lives is testimony enough of that.

Notes

1   Elder at St Hilda's Community Centre, Shoreditch.
2   Informed by social anthropology, this body of work describes particular ethnic minorities and their cultural adaptations to life in Britain. Whilst providing some valuable insights, one problem with these accounts is that they tend to overly focus on the 'other' and on cultural strategies which appear to have been imported from the 'sending' society, whilst ignoring the wider British context, the rapidity of cultural change, and the multiple identities which people chose between. J. Watson's edited volume *Between Two Cultures*, Oxford, Basil Blackwell, 1977 is a good example. For a more detailed discussion see J. Eade, 'Muslims in a "green and pleasant land", or who belongs where?', *Critical Survey*, 7 (2), 1995, pp. 172–82.
3   H. Bhaba (ed.), *Nation and Narration*, London, Routledge, 1990, p. 300.
4   Watson, op. cit.
5   S. Hall, 'New Ethnicities' in J. Donald and A. Rattansi (eds), *Race, Culture and Difference*, London, Sage, pp. 252–9.
6   Gilroy's analysis focuses upon Black or Afro-Caribbean groups, rather than Asians. See P. Gilroy, *The Black Atlantic: Modernity and Double Consciousness*, London, Sage, 1993, p. 15.
7   Most elders use this term to describe themselves, as opposed to Bengali or British-Bengali.
8   M. Anwar, *The Myth of Return: Pakistani Migrants in Britain*, London, Heinemann Educational Books, 1979.
9   Cited in I. Chambers, *Migrancy, Culture, Identity*, London, Routledge, 1994, p. 9.
10 The project, 'Ageing and Death amongst British Bengalis' was funded by the Leverhulme Trust, to whom I am extremely grateful. The interviews with male elders cited here were carried out by Mutmahim Rouf.
11 Levels of heart disease and diabetes, both of which may lead to disability, are particularly high amongst British Asians, see S. Ebrahim and S. Hillier, 'Ethnic minority needs', *Reviews in Clinical Gerontology*, 1, 1991, pp. 195–9.
12 The marriage of adult children.
13 Most members of this generation are vague about their actual ages, although well able to quote the dates of birth cited on their passports.
14 See R. Visram, *Ayahs, Lascars and Princes: the story of Indians in Britain 1700–1947*, London, Pluto Press, 1986.
15 A local rendering of the phrase 'Old Blighty'.
16 See K. Gardner, *Global migrants, Local Lives: travel and transformation in rural Bangladesh*, Oxford, Oxford University Press, 1995; C. Adams, *Between Seven Seas and*

Thirteen Rivers, London, Tower Hamlets Arts Project, 1987, and more generally, S. Castles, H. Booth and T. Wallace, *Here for Good: Western Europe's New Ethnic Minorities*, London, Pluto Press, 1987.

17 R. Ballard, 'The emergence of desh pardesh' in R. Ballard (ed.), *Desh Pardesh. The South Asian Presence in Britain*, London, Hurst and Co., 1994, pp. 11–3.

18 See R. Ballard (ed.), *Nation and Narration*, London, Routledge, 1990.

19 See Gardner, op. cit., pp. 47–9; and H. Summerfield, 'Patterns of adaptation: Somali and Bangladeshi women in Britain' in G. Buijs (ed.), *Migrant Women: Crossing Boundaries and Changing Identities*, London, Berg, 1993 pp. 85–7.

20 In order to respect the privacy of our informants, all their names have been changed.

21 Out of a total of 21 households included in the research, two men had definitely previously had English wives. There may be more who did not care to tell us about it.

22 An important source of tension, exploited by the BNP in their successful election campaign on the Isle of Dogs in 1993, was competition over housing.

23 This label was of course far from straightforward during this period, with East Pakistan fighting a war of independence from West Pakistan and proclaiming itself Bangladesh in 1971.

24 For accounts of this process in North America and elsewhere in Europe, see B. Metcalf (ed.), *Making Muslim Space in North America and Europe*, Berkeley, University of California Press, 1996, pp. 217–33.

25 For more details see J. Eade, 'The Islamisation of Space in London in Metcalf, op. cit.

26 Or before 1971, 'Pakistani'.

27 *Tabligh Jamaat*, a Muslim missionary organisation based in Tower Hamlets.

28 See T. Modood, 'British Asian Muslims and the Rushdie Affair' in Donald and Rattansi, op. cit., pp. 260–278 and Eade, 'Muslims in a "green and pleasant land" ...', op. cit.

29 J. Eade, 'Nationalism and the Quest for Authenticity: Bangladeshis in Tower Hamlets', *New Community*, Vol. 14, 4, 1990.

30 See A. Ahmed and H. Donnan (eds), *Islam, Globalisation and Post-Modernity*, London, Heinemann Educational Books, 1994.

31 Contributions to household incomes by adult children in employment cannot always be relied upon.

32 Key events include the racially motivated murder of Altaf Ali in 1979, and more recently, the attack on Kuddis Ali in 1992, on Muktar Ahmed in 1993, and the election of the BNP candidate Derek Beacon in 1993.

33 Personal communication from Anne Turton, Tower Hamlets Council, November 1996.

34 A feeling probably shared by most older people in Britain!

35 Gilroy, op. cit., p. 187.

36 Ibid.

37 Ibid., p. 199.

38 Gilroy is of course describing a particular political discourse which has arisen out of slavery, and in many ways is radically different from those of the South Asian diaspora.

39 Anwar, op. cit.

40 For a further discussion of the link between blood and land in Sylheti culture, see Gardner, op. cit., pp. 65–97.

41 Chambers, op. cit., p. 5.

42 Gardner, op. cit., p. 111.

8   Caribbean Identities and the British Context: Creolisation as a Common Framework

PHILIP NANTON

This chapter is concerned with the historical, social and political construction of Caribbean identities both in the Commonwealth Caribbean and among the black Caribbean origin population in the United Kingdom. It explores ways in which the population of Commonwealth Caribbean countries and those of Caribbean descent resident in Britain challenge a range of imposed identities. In what follows I argue that it is possible to locate common characteristics of Caribbean identity shared between the two localities through creolisation. The term creolisation is used to suggest a process which forces the dominant culture into negotiation, or compromise, or the process of subversion of the dominant culture, through a 'bottom up' process. The operation of the process is shown to apply not only in the Caribbean region with which it is associated but also in the United Kingdom.

The Caribbean comprises 32 million people living in the 16 independent and 10 non-independent states. Their political status varies from colonies like the islands of Anguilla and the Turks and Caicos to the partly autonomous Puerto Rico and the six Netherlands Antilles islands. Around two-thirds of all Caribbean peoples speak Spanish, some six million people speak English and five million people speak a French-based creole.[1] In the context of the Anglophone Caribbean, which is the focus of this chapter, further complications and variations abound. They arise from the history of the region as a society of immigrants who have over the years brought a diverse range of racial and cultural influences to their island societies. These features are overlaid with the facts of the genocide of the indigenous Arawack and Carib populations; colonialism and exploitation characterised by white European and American economic domination; African slavery; Asian indentured labour and skewed land and other resource ownership. Land ownership was for a long time dominated by a small, local, predominantly white, political and economic elite. This elite has, in the latter part of the twentieth century, broadened to include those from diverse ethnic backgrounds. A long history of outward migration to a wide range of destinations, evidence of more recent return migration and circulatory migration contribute further to the picture of diversity. Thus it is often not difficult to discover exceptions to most statements that begin with the specific claim 'Caribbean identity is ...'.

European colonial domination and colour stratification, emanating from the region's history of slavery, have traditionally been used to inform discussion of the structure of Caribbean society.[2] Caribbean societies are ethnically more diverse than the essentially dual representation, suggests. Poor whites were not uncommon in the region before slavery was institutionalised and they have remained small but significant groupings in islands as diverse as Martinique, St Thomas and Barbados.[3] Abolition of slavery and the ensuing search for alternative sources of labour prompted, between 1840–1920, the importation of several hundred thousand indentured labourers from India, China and Dutch Indonesia to Guyana, Trinidad, Cuba and other countries to a lesser extent.[4] Between 1880–1920, the region also experienced the immigration of small numbers of Syrians and Lebanese. In Trinidad by 1980, from a total population of 1,055,763, those of Indian origin comprised 40.7 per cent and those of African descent 40.8 per cent.[5] Since the middle of the twentieth century, white landowners in the region have been increasingly replaced by landowners from more diverse backgrounds, with the state becoming the dominant landowning force in many island societies.

In the wake of such diversity, a discussion of identities among the Caribbean born population in Britain, alongside that of the population in the Caribbean, would at first glance appear to be attempting to bridge a divide which is now too wide and increasing with each year. As the migration to Britain from the region in the late 1940s and 1950s increased and then declined, analysis of identity in each locality has become geographically specific. There would thus appear to be no mutual benefit arising from analysis which attempts to compare identity formation in the Caribbean and in the United Kingdom. The problem, then, is how to proceed to make and justify my proposed link? *Prima facie*, the urbanisation of increasing proportions of populations in both localities provides a basic common feature to the experience of the Caribbean population both in the Caribbean and in the United Kingdom.

The experience of Jamaica, Trinidad and Tobago and Puerto Rico illustrate a common trend in the region with the exception of Cuba, which imposes strict limits on urban residential construction. In Jamaica the urban population grew from 42 per cent of the total in 1970 to 53 per cent in 1990. An annual urban growth rate between the years of 1980 and 1993 of 1.9 per cent was recorded. In 1990, Kingston accounted for 53 per cent of the total urban population, dwarfing all other Jamaican cities. The result was massive employment, housing and other problems. In Trinidad, the urban population as a percentage of the total population rose from 63 per cent in 1970 to 71 per cent in 1993; an annual increase of 2.2 per cent was recorded between the years 1980 and 1993. Puerto Rico's urbanisation increased from 58 per cent of the total population in 1970 to 73 per cent in 1993.[6]

In the UK the Caribbean migrant is essentially a metropolitan based inner city population. The migrant Caribbean population settled predominantly in London and other metropolitan centres. Whereas only one quarter of the total population lived in Greater London, the West Midlands, Greater Manchester and West Yorkshire, 80 per cent of the Caribbean population did so.[7]

The urban shift for migrants to the United Kingdom is perhaps more dramatic and geographically extended. However, one common problem of identity for each population in their respective locality may be a similar one. Gordon Rohlehr has suggested that the post-modern Caribbean identity is essentially caught between a memory of the folk experience and the increasing reality of urban life.[8] This involves coming to terms with the gap between the communal folk heritage and the modern anomie of the city in both situations.

The debate that this chapter addresses is that underlying the diversity and separateness of the Caribbean population in the region and the Caribbean origin population in the United Kingdom, it is possible to locate a common framework for the notion of identity within the context of creolisation. In tracing the outline of a creole model it is important to avoid the simple rhetorical appeal which will place creole diversity in opposition to purity or homogeneity. Creole identity as presented here involves the subversion of dominant structures, the establishing of authentic ways of operating in a society. These ways of operating grow out of local experiences and what Brathwaite has called 'the local folk tradition'.[9] It is possible to trace the outline of this process both in the context of the Caribbean and the Caribbean's United Kingdom Diaspora. To carry out this task the chapter is divided into two parts. The first section outlines the features of politically imposed or conferred identity both in the Caribbean and in the United Kingdom. The second section proceeds to locate a creolised identity which is characterised by subversion of dominant structures and the establishment of alternative lifestyles. This approach has some affinities to that adopted both by Stuart Hall[10] and Paul Gilroy[11] to the extent that they emphasise the production of new syncretic identities. However, I argue that a number of features of the UK Caribbean origin population, in particular its continued mobility and state dependency, challenge the broad application of the notion of diaspora which Hall and Gilroy adopt.[12]

The burgeoning number of studies of the notion of identity can be located within two focal points of analysis which appear to serve almost as alternative and implicit definitions for the term. One perspective has explored the way that shared meanings in societies are maintained. In the other, boundaries are drawn between the divide of 'self' and 'other' and at times imposed, often by the state, and conferred through relations of power.

As Cohen has noted: 'Discussions of Otherness have undoubtedly helped in understanding the general processes of identity formation at national and international levels. Definitions of the "other" are helped by identifying who is not like us, thus who we reject as "different".' Cohen's observation, that the nation is always being shaped and the other, though not necessarily the same other, is always being excluded, appears apposite, capturing the essence of the dynamism in the concept of national identity.[13]

My focus on national identities and 'otherness' is intended to signal that the analysis here will be grounded in an examination of a number of historically specific processes in which negotiations with the state plays a central part.

Conferred Identity

Caribbean Historical Identities

British consciousness of the Caribbean 'over there' has not always been dominated by tourist brochures. Alternatively, the Caribbean origin population 'over here' in Britain has not always been perceived within the confines of the threatening, shiftless, metropolitan immiserated black youth. Such features of imposed identity are figures of convenience which are far too circumscribed, hiding a conferred identity subject to considerable change. If one asks, to which West Indian 'other' reference is being made and in what historical period, a number of different pictures of conferred identity emerge. An historical reading suggests that the West Indian 'other' was certainly different but not necessarily always a negative other. An apprehension of this 'other' changes dramatically from one period to another as social and economic conditions alter. In effect, the imposed notion of the West Indian 'other' shifts dramatically from flattery to disdain. To illustrate my argument I will draw briefly on the centuries of British colonialism and domination in the English speaking Caribbean. Such an endeavour suggests also that national identities in the region are a relatively recent creation.

In the seventeenth century, the Caribbean islands which Britain seized, quickly became a mixture of frontier settlements for the soldiers who expropriated them and booty to be traded between competing metropolitan plunderers. In Jamaica, for example, when the colony was founded, the social historian Pares noted that, 'it was laid out regiment by regiment, here we are told the regiment of Colonel Barry planted, and there the regiment of General Doyley'.[14] It is something of a cliché to record that St Lucia was known as the Helen of the West Indies because it changed hands so often between the French and the British metropolitan powers when peace treaties were drawn up. By the middle of the eighteenth century the massive, if short lived, windfalls which accrued from sugar plantations and which were flaunted in England, created in the minds of those in England the proverbial notion 'as wealthy as a West Indian'. Pares again illustrates how the Pinney family from Dorset made a fortune in the West Indies over a period of 150 years. The family then returned to Dorset to resettle in the countryside that they had for a time vacated. In this way the West Indies financed a number of 'English' family fortunes.

Both Pares[15] and Ragatz [16] recount the story of the encounter between a wealthy Jamaican planter, George III and his prime minister. While driving out near Weymouth the King and his prime minister met a pretentious equipage with many outriders in grand liveries. When the King heard that the ensemble belonged to a Jamaican, he is reputed to have exclaimed 'Sugar, sugar hey? – all that sugar! How are the duties hey Pitt, how are the duties?' Thus, for George III, there was no sense that these grandees were anything other than his subjects and so liable to taxation. As recently as the nineteenth century the islands had little or no character as countries.

Indeed, they appear to have existed in the British mind more as centres of British wealth creation. Mill expressed this association between England and the Caribbean islands in the following way:

> There is a class of trading and exporting communities on which a few words of explanation seem to be required. These are hardly to be looked upon as countries, but more properly as outlying agricultural and manufacturing establishments belonging to a larger community. Our West Indian colonies, for example, cannot be regarded as countries, with a productive capital of their own. If Manchester instead of being where it is, were on a rock in the North Sea (its present industry nevertheless continuing) it would still be a town of England, not a country trading with England ... The West Indies in like manner, are the places where England finds it convenient to carry on the production of sugar, coffee and a few tropical commodities.[17]

However close Mill perceived the association, this perception was soon to change. After the 1820s and the collapse of the second boom in the price of sugar, the fear of increasing costs resulting from the abolition of slavery, growing difficulties in obtaining property sales of plantations because of high mortgages encumbering estates, and the abandonment of certain estates, a dramatic change occurred in perceptions about the fabulously wealthy West Indian and the value of a close relationship with the area. The change is to a less flattering more disdainful view of a locale where various forms of colonial cheats and idlers are located and on whose population 'civilisation' needed to be imposed. One reason for the distancing and dismissive attitude was the worsening relationship between absentee landowners and the colonial community. Whenever absentee landlords tried to make claims on their estates in the West Indies colonies, Pares noted that: 'Nothing could altogether counteract the tendency of the colonial communities to favour interests of the resident debtor against those of the creditor in Europe. Every creditor found that "*les absents ont toujours tort*".'[18]

At the same time, 'mother country' perceptions did not inhibit a sense of local self identity. The Caribbean social historian Lewis has drawn attention to the sense of a 'colonial aristocracy' that developed among Barbadian planters in the latter half of the seventeenth century. He suggested that this viewpoint represented 'the beginnings of an emergent sense of collective planter identity' rooted in their divergence of interest from the British mercantilists, and as such was distinct from the popular nationalism of the twentieth century.[19] The records of planter-led Assemblies in most territories also testify to their sense of distinctiveness caused by a feeling of unfair dealings by interests in England.

The notion of the region as a centre of colonial laziness can be identified behind Colonial Secretary Grey's policies at the time of the abolition of slavery. Grey was anxious to implement policies which he saw as overcoming a lack of interest in work among the newly freed masses. In 1834, Lord Rippon outlined a number of policies to which Grey was attracted. They involved various forms of taxation on colonial populations, for example taxes on slaves' provision grounds and laws against vagrancy. In Grey's words 'the design of these proposals was to substitute for the direct coercion of the whip by which Negroes had hitherto been impelled to labour'.[20] With the economic collapse of sugar and the decline of the West Indies as region of strategic importance to metropolitan powers, a further change can be identified in the perception of the Caribbean 'other'. A form of minimal welfare ideology became established in the last 20 years of the nineteenth century. For example, in

1885, the first locally initiated land settlement policy in the British West Indies was put into effect in St Vincent. In 1889, the first officially sanctioned land settlement scheme was established following the Report of the West Indies Royal Commission. This was just one of many enquiries into what became established as the West Indian problem of poverty, unemployment and mal-administration. Perhaps the most well known report was the Moyne Report, compiled in the 1930s. It was not published till 1945 because of fear of disruptive social unrest should its contents, which itemised the circumstances of poverty in the region, become widely known during the war effort.

Historically, then, it is possible to identify a number of important changes in perception of the West Indian population under British rule. In policy terms the blunt instrument of conquest was followed by the coercion of slavery and subsequently the mission to institute the work ethic by other means ('civilisation') through taxation and law and order measures. By 1900 these concerns began to give way to welfare considerations, however inadequately put into practice. After 1945, the incorporative features of welfare ideology were minimally established but quickly began to give way to the ideology of development with a significant role for the state. Welfare ideology was never totally discarded. It has remained, for example, a feature of the protected banana market in Europe, the agreement for which is to end in the year 2000.

It has been necessary to skip through the centuries of colonial domination in order to illustrate the changing pattern of conferred Caribbean identities 'over there'. A process of change is also apparent in the conferred identities in Britain. The shift has been from a range of separate island identities[21] to an increasingly commonly recognised racialised and politicised notion of a 'black' identity. The latter has come to be articulated by British officialdom and is a common form of self description of the Caribbean origin community.

Conferred Caribbean Identity in Britain

In the second half of the twentieth century the Caribbean origin population joined a wider stream of migrants who, from the perspective of national policy analysis, became the collective 'ethnic minorities' in Britain. Once legally entitled to settlement, these groups obtain full formal participatory democratic rights of citizenship. Policy responses were broadly twofold. On the one hand, immigration controls began steadily to be tightened, from the early 1960s, primarily targeting sources of non-white immigration. On the other hand, by the mid 1960s central government had begun to give official support to local authorities most affected by immigration and to set up the first national non-government organisation to help coordinate 'integration'. In a mere thirty years the generally accepted term of description 'West Indian' had shifted from island identity and loyalty to the current variant between 'Black', 'Black-British' and the official census term 'Afro-Caribbean'. The regular documentation of racial discrimination in Britain through a variety of social surveys[22] and the recognition of systematic bureaucratic practices as institutional racism provide independent authoritative evidence of the extent of rejection and exclusion experienced by this population.

During the 1960s, however, it was widely believed among policy makers that the course of time and the workings of the education system would change the new generation of immigrants into Black Britons who would maintain only superficial differences from the indigenous majority. In the education service it was assumed that this process would be advanced when schools educated mainly children of immigrants born here rather than those who had been brought to join their families. In health and welfare, provision also reflected assimilationist views. Services saw clients distinguished only by the problems they presented. These attitudes represented the now much criticised 'colour-blind' approach. Thereafter a black perspective articulated these issues with growing confidence as problems of a racist society which required from each person a race conscious response. Policies, however, have not, on the whole, been racially or ethnically specific. Instead they have concentrated on apparently race neutral programmes. These have, however, provided considerable scope for interpretation and ministerial guidance so that they can be more specifically directed. I have elsewhere argued that whether or not it was intended, a climate fostering recognition of ethnic and racial differentiation became so pronounced that an orthodoxy could be identified. The development of ethnic categorisation in the 1991 census and ethnic monitoring of work forces by public sector employers, the establishment of some 30 years of centrally directed ethnic specific grants to local government for educational and community programmes for minority communities have reinforced these tendencies.

Policies have increasingly categorised members of ethnic minorities according to administrative labels, reducing them to the single dimension of their 'ethnic origin' and obscuring the process of change and adaptation within and across groups.[23] Essentially, these developments have encouraged the attention of UK-based analyses away from a number of paradoxes of Caribbean identity in the United Kingdom. One such paradox is the increasingly apparent diversity of this community. Observers for a time preferred to emphasise a collective, politically attuned black British identity, developed painfully among the first generation and accepted by later generations arising out of the years of racial exclusion and discrimination in the United Kingdom.[24] However, it is possible to identify a variety of responses to the situation experienced by the Caribbean community in Britain. These experiences challenge racialised notions of identity and demonstrate a resilient creolisation.

Creolisation

As suggested above, creole identities involve the subversion of dominant structures and the establishing of authentic life styles in a society which grows out of local experiences. Nettleford has explained the process in the Caribbean in the following way:

> If the British imperial power *governed* for those 300-odd years under colonialism, it was the ordinary people who *ruled* ... *The* language(s) religious expressions, kinship patterns, artistic expressions, even the indigenous mode(s) of production, distribution and exchange, as well as the native organisation of action groups with recognised leaders, all had their own intrinsic logic often forcing the establishment to either resist or appropriate them in order to control them.[25]

This Caribbean identity, Nettleford goes on to point out, is 'rooted in the exercise of the creative imagination and intellect *by the people from below* and is central to the ethos of the postcolonial Caribbean'.[26]

Bolland has similarly offered a positive critique of creolisation in the Caribbean context and suggests that it be adapted to take account of opposition within the society. Thus he suggests a definition of creolisation as 'a process of contention between people who are members of social formations and carriers of cultures, a process in which their own ethnicity is continually re-examined and redefined in terms of the relevant oppositions between different social formations at various historical moments'.[27]

A similar version of Bolland's interpretation of creole identity has been applied by Harney in his literary analysis of Caribbean identity in the contemporary United Kingdom. Harney has used as evidence the novels of Sam Selvon which were set in Britain around the 1950s Caribbean migrant boom. He demonstrates through Selvon's use of language, character and 'serious playfulness' the robust nature of the creolising process. Moses, the main character in *The Lonely Londoners*, for example, changes his attitude from nostalgia to a tougher world encompassing view of his life in London as he comes to terms with change. All this is conveyed through an uncompromising use of 'dialect' or nation language and descriptions of 'liming' conveyed with a *joie de vivre*. The robust challenge to London life displayed in the novel, Harney argues, although not without its problems, illustrates how West Indian men (sic) can hold can hold their own in a metropolitan context. In this way they have produced a popular culture that withstands colonial pretensions, ethnic root searching and even nationalist invention.[28]

The process of subversion in the Caribbean has taken a variety of lasting forms. One of the most widespread has involved a challenge to the dominant land owning plantation system and imposed colonial cultures. Among small holders the pattern of land ownership often described as 'family land' has been described as a resistant response to dominant Caribbean agrarian relations.[29] At the same time a sense of identity is derived from the ownership of land. Wilson, for example, suggests that land ownership is the prime basis of social identity in Caribbean societies.[30] Family land holdings are essentially small plots, the ownership of which resides in a range of extended kin who may live both in the country or abroad. Besson has demonstrated how ex-slaves throughout the Caribbean obtained freehold land where ever possible and created family land to maximise these freehold rights in the face of plantation engineered land scarcity. Social anthropologists have demonstrated that family land involves both a symbolic indication of belonging, as well as representing a short term economic asset.[31] However, because the land is often not put into agricultural production, conventional development ideologies are constantly challenged and disrupted.[32]

Migration can be similarly identified as a major Caribbean strategy which, as Jolivet argues, became one of the foundations of creole identity.[33] That is a form of rejecting anything associated with slavery society and later a path to social advancement.

Thomas-Hope has illustrated this range of movement within the Caribbean as soon as opportunities permitted freedom from ties to the land.[34] The presence of the Caribbean origin population in Britain owes much to Britain's long involvement with the region from its days of plunder, mass Carib expulsion and British settlement to its exercise of imperial and colonial rule over substantial parts of the region. Island societies were suppressed to the extent that as soon as travel was possible an important focus for the population was emigration.

In 1966, an estimated 60 per cent of the Caribbean population came to Britain from Jamaica alone. Primary immigration effectively ended in the late 1960s and since the mid-1960s population growth has come from natural increases in Britain. Between 1973 and 1982 net migration from the Caribbean to the United Kingdom totalled only 1,800. This was a negligible number compared to the 1950s and compared to the estimated Caribbean origin population in Britain which totalled 520,000 in 1982. By 1991, however, this total had declined to 499,000.[35]

Peach, comparing 1981 and 1991 UK census totals of people born in the Caribbean, argues that over the past three decades, return migration has become a growing phenomenon. He has identified a decrease of about 97,000 over a twenty-two year period, or a loss of 4,400 persons per year.[36] In 1995, Byron estimated that around one-tenth of the Caribbean migrants to the United Kingdom had already returned to their birth places and that up to one-third may be expected to return to the island where they were born.[37] The evidence of return is also supported by increasing numbers of pensions paid into Caribbean countries by the United Kingdom government. In 1982 the total number of pensions paid in the Caribbean was 8,903. By 1995, the number of pensions paid into Jamaica alone amounted to 19,088.[38] Additionally, Segal has noted that 'return' is not necessarily a single journey. Qualitative ethnographic research has begun to demonstrate increasing evidence of a pattern among some Caribbean migrants of circulatory migration.[39] That is, persons who migrate regularly and frequently over sustained periods of time between Caribbean and overseas places of stay on a legal basis.

From the above data it appears that different trajectories of identity are becoming increasingly apparent among the Caribbean community in Britain. One divide may be identified on the one hand as an inward focus towards a sense of 'the black community' competing for resources in a form of community politics within the metropolitan context of its location. Community politics is defined here as a continuous process of negotiation for resources between black and ethnic minority community associations and government around policy and distributive justice. The aim of the negotiation is to combat racism, discrimination and disadvantage. Community group politics had its origin in the early years following immigration. In the 1980s it was given a major boost with positive action by many local councils to encourage and support non-white community associations with funds. These associations are non-profit making organisations which were developed within minority ethnic communities in the wake of migration of the 1950s and 1960s. Their precise number is difficult to estimate. One official estimate suggests some 488 run by people of Caribbean origin. Small has described the origin and key features of these associations in the following way:

Black organisations emerged in response to specific needs such as discrimination, poor housing and indifferent education. Many have remained local. Most do not have a specific policy to exclude white people, but at the same time they do not actively go out of their way to encourage them.[40]

A number of issues which were taken up at the local level were in time reflected in national campaigns. Those concerned with policing were taken up by the Afro-Caribbean communities. Ethnic minority communities have organised caucuses on their own behalf within, for example, professions and trade unions and this has been mirrored in the campaign for 'black sections' within the Labour Party which began in the early 1980s.

Participation in politics in Britain on 'community' terms suggests a settled population determined to participate in a future Britain on their terms. Simultaneously, the abandonment of settlement and return to the Caribbean indicates a restatement of a geographically specific form of Caribbean identity. The existence of these two trajectories became increasingly overt when Bernie Grant, Member of Parliament raised the issue of reparation for Caribbean returnees who wanted to go back to their homelands. At least one critic within the community was of the opinion that, despite the hardships experienced in Britain, those opting for return were avoiding their responsibilities of United Kingdom citizenship. He argued that 'citizenship does not only imply privileges it also implies duties and responsibilities ... The least of a citizen's obligations is to remain a citizen instead of threatening to cut and run every time the going gets tough'.[41]

The unifying political challenges taken up by the 'community' in Britain does not necessarily represent a homogenous community. Among those who remain in Britain, class and residential divisions are becoming increasingly apparent, with division noticeable between the immigrant generation and those generations now born in Britain.[42]

Those who return to the Caribbean from Britain would appear to be further creolised. Thomas-Hope has observed from her survey of the ways in which migration was evaluated in the Caribbean that two contrasting perceptions of return migration persisted. The dominant positive view across all classes in the three islands that she surveyed, (Jamaica, Barbados and St Vincent) was that successful migration 'related to a combination of material and cultural improvement. Material gains and changed behaviour patterns were the main expectations of the criteria of success'. In contrast, she also noted:

The chief exception to this positive view about the benefits of migration was felt to be exhibited by those persons who had returned from Britain and about whom there was the general feeling that *they come back from England crack.* The onset of a high incidence of neurosis, described as *nerves,* was believed to occur among those who went to Britain.[43]

Returnees from Britain then would appear to be perceived, by those who have not taken up the migration option, as a form of rich outcast challenging for influence and resources. The, not unusual, epithet of 'madness' used to describe returnees is perhaps an attempt to control their growing influence as increasing numbers of pensioners with regular incomes from abroad dare to come back and join health queues, complain about inefficiency and generally stand out as a distinct group competing for influence in the islands that they left many years ago. Signs of their growing influence, for example, are that both Jamaica and Barbados have now established official agencies for the reception of returnees back into those two countries respectively.

Conclusion

The issues which test the creolisation process in the Caribbean and in Britain exhibit considerable differences. In both localities, however, they have in common the underlying feature of urbanisation. Beyond the surface differences the challenge to the status quo and the establishment of new lifestyles which emanate from local experience are common features represented in each locality. I have illustrated this process in the Caribbean through the challenge to land holding patterns and the contrary experience of return migration. In Britain community participation politics, literature and lifestyle variations illustrate this challenge. Thus, it appears that what we are witnessing in Britain is a population too long identified as a singular grouping and who are increasingly dividing along a number of distinct lines. The evidence here suggests that members are making up their minds and coming to different conclusions about who they are and where they should be located. Both processes represent ongoing challenges to the established structures. They challenge both the forms of participation in politics and the notion of an identifiably black British community which is permanently settled.

This chapter suggests that in Britain, explanations of Caribbean identity and its formation firstly suffer from an historically shallow framework, secondly they suffer from being too restricted and thus often unable to explain contradictions and developments which arise when actors break out of confining structures. Thirdly, they often ignore a fundamental driving force of identity and identity formation, that is its emotional element as in return migration. Application of the notion of creolisation, which is long established in the context of the Caribbean, enhances attempts to locate the shifting patterns of Caribbean identities in both Caribbean and United Kingdom contexts.

Notes

1   A. Segal, *Migration and Development in the Caribbean*, Annual Meeting of the American Association of Geographers, Charlotte, North Carolina, 1996.
2   M.G. Smith, *The Plural Society in the British West Indies*, Berkeley and Los Angeles University of California Press, 1965.
3   D. Lowenthal, *West Indian Societies*, London, Oxford University Press, 1972.
4   B.C. Richardson, 'Caribbean Migrations 1838–1995' in F. Knight and C. Palmer (eds), *The Modern Caribbean*, Chapel Hill, University of North Carolina Press, 1989.
5   S. Vertovek, 'Oil boom and recession in a Trinidad Indian village' in C. Clark, C. Peach and S. Vertovek (eds), *South Asians Overseas: migration and ethnicity*, 1990, p. 90.
6   World Bank, World Development Report, Washington, DC, 1995.
7   C. Peach, *The Caribbean in Europe, contrasting patterns of migration and settlement in Britain, France and the Netherlands*, Research Paper No. 15, CRER, University of Warwick, Coventry, 1991.
8   G. Rohlehr, *The Shape of that Hurt and other Essays*, Port-of-Spain, Longman, 1992.
9   E. Brathwaite, *The development of Creole society in Jamaica, 1770–1820*, Oxford, Clarendon, 1971.
10 S. Hall, 'Cultural identity and Diaspora' in J. Rutherford (ed.), *Identity: Community, Culture, Difference*, London, Lawrence and Wishart, 1990.
11 P. Gilroy, *The Black Atlantic: modernity and double consciousness*, London, Verso, 1993.
12 P. Nanton, 'The Caribbean Diaspora in the promised land' in A.J. Kershen (ed.), *London the promised land?: the migrant experience in a capital city*, Aldershot, Avebury, 1997.
13 R. Cohen, 'Fuzzy frontiers of identity: the British case', *Social Identities*, 1, 4, 1995, p. 3.
14 R. Pares, *A West India Fortune*, London, Longman, Green & Co. Ltd., 1960, p. 3.
15 R. Pares, 'Merchants and planters', *The Economic History Review*, Supplement no. 4, London, Cambridge University Press, 1954, p. 16.
16 L. J. Ragatz, *The fall of the planter class in the British Caribbean 1763–1833: a study in social and economic history*, New York, Appleton-Century Co., 1928.
17 J.S. Mill, *Principles of Political Economy* (Peoples edn), Longmans, Green, Reasder and Dyer, London, 1868, Bk. 3, ch. 25, sec. 5.
18 R. Pares, op. cit., 1960, p. 44.
19 G. Lewis, *Main Currents in Caribbean Thought: the historical evolution of Caribbean society in its ideological aspects, 1492–1900*, Johns Hopkins University Press, Baltimore and London, 1983, pp. 72–5.
20 E. Grey, *The Colonial policy of Lord Russell's Administration*, Vol. 1, London, Richard Bentley, 1853, p. 19.
21 D. Lowenthal, 1978, op. cit.

22 W. Daniel, *Racial discrimination in England*, Harmondsworth, Penguin, 1968; D.J. Smith, *Racial disadvantage in Britain*, Harmondsworth, Penguin, 1977; C. Brown, *Black and White Britain: The Third PSI Survey*, London, PSI/Heinemann, 1984.

23 P. Nanton, 'The new orthodoxy: racial categories and equal opportunity policy', *New Community*, 15, 4, 1989, pp. 548–64.

24 S. Hall, C. Critcher, T. Jefferson, J. Clarke and B. Roberts (eds), *Policing the Crisis: Mugging, the State and Law and Order*, London, Macmillan, 1978.

25 R. Nettleford, *Inward stretch outward reach: a voice from the Caribbean*, London, Macmillan, 1993, p. 118.

26 Ibid., p. 119.

27 O.N. Bolland, 'Creolisation and creole societies: a cultural nationalist view of Caribbean social history' in A. Hennessy (ed.), *Intellectuals in the twentieth century Caribbean, Volume 1, Spectre of the New Class: the Commonwealth Caribbean*, London, Macmillan, 1992.

28 S. Harney, *Nationalism and identity: culture and the imagination in a Caribbean Diaspora*, London, Zed, 1997, p. 95.

29 J. Besson, 'A paradox in Caribbean attitudes to land' in J. Besson and J. Momsen (eds), *Land and development in the Caribbean*, London, Macmillan 1987.

30 J. Wilson, *Crab antics: the social anthropology of English speaking Negro societies of the Caribbean*, New Haven, Yale University Press, 1973.

31 Besson, op. cit.; S. W. Mintz, 'The Caribbean Region' in S.W. Mintz (ed.), *Slavery, Colonialism and Racism*, New York, Norton, 1975.

32 J. Besson, op. cit.; H. Rubenstein, 'Folk and mainstream systems of land tenure and use in St. Vincent' in J. Besson and J. Momsen (eds), *Land and Development in the Caribbean*, Warwick University Caribbean Series, London, Macmillan, 1987.

33 M.J. Jolivet, 'Migrations et histoire dans la Caraibe francaise', *Cahiers de l'ORSTOM*, 21; S. Condon, 'Migration and identity: the case of Caribbean migration to France', paper presented to the Annual Conference of the Society for Caribbean Studies, Oxford, 1994.

34 E.M. Thomas-Hope, 'The Establishment of a Migration Tradition: British West Indian movements in the Hispanic Caribbean in the Century after Emancipation' in C.G. Clark (ed.), *Caribbean Social Relations*, Monograph Series no. 8, University of Liverpool, Centre for Latin American Studies, 1978.

35 J. B. Rose, N. Deakin, M. Jackson, V. Preston, M. Vanagi, A. Cohen, B. Gaitskell and P. Ward (eds), *Colour and citizenship: a report on British race relations*, London, Oxford University Press, 1968.

36 C. Peach, 1991, op. cit.

37 M. Byron and S. Condon, 'A comparative study of Caribbean return migration from Britain and France: towards a context dependent explanation', *Transactions of British Geographers*, New Series, 21, 1991.

38 Department of Social Security, International payments of Returned Pensioners and Widow Benefit Allowances, Newcastle, 1995.

39 A. Segal, 'Locating the Swallows: Caribbean Recycling Migration', paper presented at the Caribbean Studies Association, Annual Meeting, San Juan, Puerto Rico, 1996, p. 2.

40 V.S. Small, *From arts to welfare: a bibliography of the black voluntary sector*, London, Sia., 1993, p. 10.

41 M. Phillips, 'Home is where the struggle is', *The Weekly Journal*, 14, 10, 1993, London, p. 15.

42 V. Robinson, 'Inter-generational differences in ethnic settlement patterns in Britain' in P. Ratcliffe, *Social Geography and Ethnicity in Britain*, London, HMSO, 1996.

43 E. M. Thomas-Hope, *Explanation in Caribbean Migration*, Warwick University Caribbean Studies, London, Macmillan, 1992, pp. 84–5.

PART TWO
EUROPEAN, AFRICAN AND
AMERICAN IDENTITY

9 German Identity after Reunification

EBERHARD BORT

In Germany, a difficult historical heritage, responsibility for two world wars, the resultant uprootedness of large streams of refugees, the nightmare of the Holocaust, and forty years of partition, have disrupted traditions in which a common German identity could be grounded. No other European seems to have as many problems abroad admitting to his or her nationality than the German – particularly young Germans in countries where they speak the guest country's language.[1]

When, on 3 October 1996, the sixth anniversary of Germany's unification was commemorated, it took the form of a sober stocktaking rather than a celebration. The great enthusiasm following the fall of the Berlin Wall on 9 November 1989, the grand promises of 'blossoming landscapes' (Kohl) in the East within months or, at the utmost, a few years, had given way to a feeling of disenchantment, questioning the success of the unification process. Six years after Unification, East Germans produced only 60 per cent of what they consume. The *Economist*, in a special 'Survey of Germany', found that 'people on both sides of the former border feel disenchanted, even bitter'.[2] Soaring unemployment of 16 per cent in the East, and rising costs in the West – the bill topped one trillion marks by the end of 1996 – soured the celebrations. North-Rhine-Wesphalia's prime minister, Johannes Rau, of the German Social Democratic Party (SPD), speaking at Düsseldorf on 3 October 1995, offered a bleak but fitting resumé:

> Despite the fall of borders and walls within Germany, reservations and prejudices have made some invisible gulfs wider and deeper. What separates thinking and feeling of people on both sides of the old border sometimes prevails. Many are still meeting as strangers.[3]

Undoubtedly, 1989 was a revolutionary landmark. Incorporating the former German Democratic Republic (GDR) not only added 16 million East Germans to the 63 million West Germans, and pushed the frontier of the European

197

Union further East, it meant an unprecedented experiment ending over 50 years of authoritarian rule for the territory of East Germany.

West and East were compelled to redefine themselves, in a period of shifting ground. Both had been frontier states, privileged to an extent within their blocs, endowed with a special position, at the dividing line of a bipolar world order, permanently focused upon from the outside. This can be seen most clearly in the changes of attitude in (West) Berlin, where the Wall has all but vanished – and with it not only the grief and suffering it had brought, but also that sense of being special, and the symbol of the Berlin spirit of endurance and freedom. Nowhere else can the unification process be observed and characterised so clearly as a coming to terms with normality.[4]

The rapidity of the unification process (was it an *Anschluss*?) was spurred by arguments of a disintegrating GDR economy and the heavy social costs of internal German migration, but owes – in retrospect – perhaps more to the interest of West German elites in institutional continuity and to Chancellor Kohl's grasp of tactical electioneering.[5] Internal migration was slowed down, but certainly not stopped, neither by Economic and Currency Union on 1 July 1990, nor by Unification on 3 October.[6] By mid-1996, over 1.6 million people, most of them young, talented, able to work and enterprising, had migrated from East to West;[7] under 500,000 from West to East. Five hundred and fifty thousand East Germans, a figure that has stabilised on a very high level, are commuting daily from East to West for work.[8]

There was no time for a two-way communication, no interest in an analysis of mutual identities. 'Unification has amounted to a straightforward western take-over,' wrote Tony Paterson in the *European*, 'with West Germans filling top jobs in the main banks and businesses and in government.'[9] Unification was, in essence, a conservative project: West German interest in continuity met East German material aspiration for change, and they seemed to fit like hand in glove. Legally speaking, it was the incorporation of the GDR into the Federal Republic in the form of five new *Länder*, under Article 23 of the Basic Law (West German constitution), eschewing any deeper constitutional discussion and rendering unnecessary a referendum on the matter.[10] This was seen at the time, as Harold James commented, 'as the supreme demonstration that the West did not intend to learn or adopt anything from the East'.[11]

Differences in Identity: Federal Republic of Germany and German Democratic Republic

Looking at German identity after reunification, we must first take a brief glance at the differences in identity between the former Federal Republic of Germany (FRG) and the former German Democratic Republic, based on the experience of different economic and political and social systems, different cultures, different ideologies, different education and socialisation, different attitudes to (German) history, etc.; but also at the similarities: both were mainly grounded, albeit to varying success, in material and social security ('DM patriotism'), rather than other, historically more problematic identity-markers.

In West Germany, identity was experienced as problematic, caught in the tension between historical continuity and discontinuity. The construct of 'Stunde Null' in 1945 was to suggest a completely new beginning; yet denazification was a cumbersome process, and lots of ex-Nazis made it into the corridors of power in the new Federal Republic. Material well-being became the rationale behind West Germany. 1950s' restoration and the *Wirtschaftswunder* provided the West Germans with their most efficient means of identification: the Deutschmark. Walter Stützle, editor-in-chief of the Berlin daily *Der Tagesspiegel*, has put it in a nutshell: 'The Germans love the D-mark as if it is the thing next to God. For around half the population, losing the mark is akin to losing part of their identity.'[12]

Western integration, with EEC and NATO as its cornerstones, became the *sine qua non* of German foreign policy. Lacking full sovereignty until 1955, the elites of the Federal Republic had to look to the Western powers; through Western integration, Daniel J. Goldhagen has recently argued, value systems of the Western allied powers became assimilated and eventually internalised in the Federal Republic.[13] Culturally speaking, unease was a prevailing factor, resulting in the inclination to escape into 'ersatz' identities.

1968 became a pivotal year of change for the Federal Republic; social and political reforms and the subsequent integration of the student movement into the political centre-left, including the rise of the Greens in the 1980s, produced a high degree of contentment and identification with the Federal Republic of Germany's institutions, while markers of national identity – like the flag, or the national anthem – still met with a good and, in the eyes of many, healthy degree of scepticism and irony, if not with outright embarrassment.

A 1991 study came to the conclusion that 'the emotional identification with abstract institutional achievements of the polity has, in Germany, reached practically the same level as Great Britain'.[14]

In East Germany, official, state-regulated and decreed national identity (anti-fascist, socialist, internationalist) separated the GDR from the German past and absolved East Germans *ex cathedra* of coming to terms with the Nazi heritage.[15] Socially, 'The GDR provided cradle-to-grave security, but did not prepare them for freedom, choice, uncertainty and wrenching changes in almost every aspect of their lives'.[16]

Private identity, creating and using niches outside state-control, created cultural spaces, circles of trust, and resulted in deep and widespread mistrust of political institutions, whose double-speak was seen through, as public discourse decreasingly reflected public and private reality. That the system lasted as long as it did, is due to two main factors: one is the importance of the GDR for Russia and the Eastern bloc (as the FRG was the frontier state of the West), and the fact that the regime bought a degree of loyalty by the provision of what the *Economist* survey termed 'cradle-to-grave security'.

When the economy crumbled in the 1980s, the protests grew. Yet equating the protest movement with the economic difficulties of the GDR would be too simplistic. Helsinki 1975, the Biermann affair, Gorbachev, Solidarnosc in Poland, and Charter 77 in Czechoslovakia – all contributed to the formation of a democratic opposition in the GDR which, in the 40th year of the 'peasants' and workers' republic', erupted in mass demonstrations and led to the peaceful revolution culminating in the fall of the Berlin Wall in the autumn of 1989.[17] Against West Germans, East German's had always been defensive, realising that they were regarded by them, at best, as poor relatives. Travelling abroad, particularly in the Eastern bloc states which they could easily travel to, they were treated as second-class Germans, as they could not oblige with the coveted Deutschmark!

External and Internal Perspective

Analysing German identity after unification, furthermore, external and internal perspectives and approaches have to be taken into account, even if external and internal perspectives do interact and cannot be totally separated.

External perspectives involve two subsets of questions:

a) what does Germany stand for;

b) how are the Germans perceived from the outside?

In other words: have, in the eyes of the world, Germany and the Germans changed since 1990, and – if the answer to this is yes – what impact do these changes have for the relationship with Germany and for its international role? Assessments have varied, from Conor Cruise O'Brien's apocalyptic view of the new Germany as the 'Fourth Reich' compounding 'pride about the Holocaust', 'expulsion of Jews, breaking off of relations with Israel ...' and 'a statue of Hitler in every town ...',[18] or Margaret Thatcher's verdict, revealed in her *Downing Street Years*, that a unified Germany would be 'simply much too big and too powerful',[19] to Will Hutton's much more favourable characterisation of the new Germany as 'a liberal democracy of benign intentions', dismissing the 'mythical Fritz who has long since disappeared'.[20] Or, to put it differently, from the country which draconically tightened its asylum laws and experienced thousands of violent attacks on minorities by skinheads and neo-Nazis, and whose loyalties to democracy and its institutions may, even after 40 years of the Bonn republic, not be fully trusted, to the acceptance of Germany as a rooted democracy, with a degree of what Habermas and Sternberger have termed *Verfassungspatriotismus*,[21] the consistent advocate of European integration, championing a model of federal decentralisation and social solidarity.

'At first sight,' the *Economist* contended, 'the united Germany looks like a blown-up copy of the former West Germany ... The political landscape still looks remarkably similar, although... below the surface it is being transformed. Germany's policies towards the rest of the world appear unchanged.'

It went on to point out that:

> Germany, having accepted the finality of Poland's borders at last, for the first time in its history has clearly defined borders not disputed by anyone. It has no destabilising minorities abroad, and is making no territorial claims.[22]

Assessing the new Germany, the verdict of the *Economist* survey was: 'Western upholstery has been frayed, but the furniture is unchanged.'[23] A contrary position is taken by the journalist Tony Paterson: 'Unification has changed Germany fundamentally. It has prompted questions about the country's role, not only in Europe but on the global stage.'[24]

Undoubtedly, the expectations of Germany's partners have risen. Deployment of troops on the Balkans, to take one example, has been welcomed as Germany accepting its share in international responsibility. This is sometimes used, particularly by the right, to argue for a new foreign policy, more outspokenly in the German 'national interest', doing justice to Germany's grown 'international responsibility'. 'Germany has become, without being prepared for it, a sovereign state,' runs the argument of Karl-Heinz Bohrer and Kurt Scheel, 'and can no longer, for better or worse, play the special part of the old Federal Republic.'[25] They would like to see Germany leave behind what Volker Rühe has called the former West Germany's 'culture of restraint',[26] expressed in the popular image of Germany being an economic giant, but a political dwarf.[27] Yet, the Berlin historian Michael Kreile asks, is this not implying a distorted image (*Zerrbild*) of the foreign policy of the old Federal Republic. Had it not – as far as sovereignty goes within the framework of the European Communities – acted as if it was a sovereign state for decades?[28]

Germany's role in advocating the single currency and further European integration, as well as enlargement of EU and NATO towards the East, is a sign of continuity rather than the assumption of a new role. Tony Paterson's 'fundamental change' theory, quoted above, seems at least questionable.

Internal perspectives on an all-German, but necessarily also on an East versus West level, defining identity with Hermann Glaser as 'the plural of individual agreements with objects and persons, "territories" and values', again comprise two subsets of questions:

a) how do the Germans see themselves;

b) how do the Germans define their international role?

Unification had 'winners' and 'losers', in both East and West. Is there any substantial GDR-nostalgia? *Ossi vs Wessi*? How 'high' is the 'wall in the heads'? What is the level of content with developments, from a purely personal to a national perspective? After over one trillion Deutschmarks in transfer payments from West to East, is unification seen as a success or a failure? What are the parameters of such an assessment – comparison of the East's performance in closing the gap with the West; or comparison with other reform states in East Central Europe, like Poland, the Czech Republic or Hungary.

'The *Wende* ... was no merger, it was a take-over; and in many ways it worked.'[29] A German-British research survey conducted by the London-based German-British Foundation over two years (1994-95) came to interesting results.[30] Generally speaking, the survey concluded, Germany was en route to normality:

•   86 per cent East Germans favour private enterprise;
•   62 per cent see improvement in their household's welfare;

- 70 per cent are 'very' or 'rather' content with their situation;
- 75 per cent are positive about the market economy;
- 65 per cent are positive about the political system;
- 72 per cent are optimistic about the future.

Interestingly enough, the question 'Do we need a strong leader?' was answered more affirmatively in the West (25 per cent 'yes') than in the East (20 per cent 'yes'). Yet, a considerable 21 per cent of respondents in the East were found in favour of abolishing parliament.

If one compared these findings with figures from the new Eastern democracies, it became even more clear-cut that East-Germans were en route to Western 'normality'. The question concerning the desirability of a strong leader elicited the following 'yes'-ratings:

- 77 per cent of Belorussians;
- 71 per cent of Slovenes;
- 66 per cent of Bulgarians;
- 52 per cent of Ukrainians;
- 41 per cent of Poles.

Abolishment of parliament is favoured by one-third to nearly half of the Ukrainians, Belorussians, Poles and Bulgarians. Only Czechs and Slovenes have around 50 per cent contentment with the economic development in their countries – all others' contentment rate is way below.

But, the survey also showed that only 24 per cent of all East Germans think they have been treated justly in the unification process, and concluded that Germany was indeed en route to normality, but that it would still need a long haul to finally achieve it. To add to an uneven picture, Rainer Zitelmann, the conservative publicist, mentioned in a commentary that now an alarming three quarters of the East German population declare that they have no trust in democracy.[31]

Gerhard Schmidtchen, a social psychologist, was given the task by the German federal government in 1993 to analyse attitudes of young people in the East. In his published findings, Schmidtchen compares Western data with his analysis of 5,500 persons aged 15–30 who were interviewed in Leipzig. On the whole, values and goals of these young people are uncannily similar to those of their Western counterparts: social engagement and personal development are generally regarded more important than financial security, good jobs, and family. Moreover, two-thirds of the interviewees opposed any form of *Ostalgie* (GDR nostalgia), but one third still feel alienated in the new Germany.[32]

Opinion polls show that more than half of the easterners think they are being treated as second-class citizens. Elections showed the existence of deep divisions between East and West: 'An invisible political wall split Berlin along its old Cold War dividing line yesterday, with ex-communists reclaiming the leading role in the east and the conservative Christian Democratic Union (CDU) dominating the west.'[33]

Rainer Eppelmann pointed out a dilemma, 'In October 1990, we East Germans moved into the common home; most of the Federal Germans have grown up in it.'[34] While most West Germans were satisfied that they 'had won the war of ideologies',[35] two-thirds of the people in the new *Länder* still consider themselves first and foremost 'East German' which, incidentally, is matched by about 40 per cent of those in the old *Länder* considering themselves as predominantly 'West German'. A survey among people aged 50 plus found that Eastern identification with the new Germany is still deficient: 86 per cent of that group feel to be in limbo: they do not want the GDR back but do also not feel at home in the Federal Republic.[36]

Listing similarities and dissimilarities in East and West would, roughly, look like this. Similar opinions would concern:

- to be sceptical about the economic situation;
- a negative stance regarding the Euro;
- unemployment as the biggest problem (94 per cent in the East/87 per cent in the West).

The differences are to be found in:

- the worry about foreigners (50 per cent West/30 per cent East);
- levelling living standards a problem (15 per cent in the West/56 per cent in the East);
- worry about national debt (60 per cent in the West/21 per cent in the East);
- taxation as burden (67 per cent in the West/47 per cent in the East);
- worry about future of pensions (72 per cent in the West/53 per cent in the East).[37]

Fritz Vilmar and Wolfgang Dümcke have coined the term 'structural colonisation' for the unification process.[38] They argue that the precipitated economic union was economically disastrous, motivated largely by electioneering tactics, not by economic needs. Unsolved property questions and 'old debts' are identified as hindering Eastern economic initiative and development. What they call the 'Treuhand sell-out of Eastern companies' – rather than any sustained attempt at consolidation and privatisation – often to Western companies, had as its main effect that those Western companies got rid of potential competitors. Unemployment, they contend, was not combated with a second labour market; on the contrary, what has developed in terms of a second labour market is now being reduced, which makes prospects for the mass unemployed even gloomier. The transfer of one-trillion Deutschmarks from West to East has, in their analysis, not led to sustainable economic structures in the East. Most of it was spent in order to avoid financial and social collapse: 215 billion DM for unemployment benefits; 139 billion DM in social subsidies; 121 billion DM filling the deficit of the Treuhand. Only 109 billion DM went into infrastructure, and only 71 billion DM into manufacturing investment.

Despite this devastating analysis, Vilmar and Dümcke identify a competing process of 'structural (economic) colonisation' and 'democratisation', offering the cautious hope that the process of democratic self-determination will prevail in the end.

On the positive side, one could also tick the fact that 45 per cent of Federal infrastructure investment in East Germany between 1990 and 1996 went into transport infrastructure: 65 billion DM have provided 11,000 km of new roads, 4,500 km of rail tracks have been laid. The emerging priority for rail development is reflected in the 34 billion DM invested in the railways, against 17 billion DM for road investment, and one billion DM for waterways.

Seventeen current projects with a total value of 67.5 billion DM are also reflective of that policy: of the 18 billion DM already spent, 13 billion were for rail improvements, five billion went into roads.[39] The telecommunications network in east Germany is now better than that of the old FRG.[40]

People of the GDR: Immigrants or Partners?

In the words of Rainer Eppelmann, GDR defence minister in the Maiziere government and now vice-chairman of the ruling Christian Democrats, ex-GDR people are 'immigrants' whose integration will take three generations' time: 'The first generation is self-reflective and reclusive; in the second generation this encapsulation brings about internal conflicts, and only in the third generation assimilation will happen.'[41]

The Social Democrat Prime Minister of Saxony-Anhalt, Reinhard Höppner, stated the counter-position when he insisted that the East Germans were not immigrants. They had come, he said, as partners into the united Germany, and now everything depended on the West's acceptance of them as equal partners.[42]

Yet, that is exactly what West Germans seem more than reluctant to do. Christof Dieckmann came to the conclusion that West Germany does not want the East German experience to become part of its own history.[43] The playwright Heiner Mueller, shortly before his death in 1995, summed it up thus: the more Easterners and Westerners get to know each other, the less they like one another.

'King Kurt of Saxony',[44] CDU-minister president Kurt Biedenkopf, Helmut Kohl's old rival, pointed out in a much-quoted letter to the German Chancellor that 'in the light of recent developments the impression is inevitable that increasingly central Eastern interests are being sacrificed in favour of West German interests'.[45] In this stance, he is supported by Gert Poppe, a veteran civil rights activist and now a Green MP: 'The end of the GDR meant also the end of the old FRG. Hardly anybody in the West believes this, but the process of change has already begun, whether the old inhabitants want it or not.'[46]

An 'Elite Study' conducted by Potsdam University among elites East and West, revealed different values, independent of party leanings: West German elites want a liberal state, representative democracy and are hardly prepared to forego rights of freedom, self-determination and participation in favour of an expansion of the state sector; East German elites favour a state system, which aims at state control and initiative in as comprehensive a way as possible as well as at safeguarding the individual against social risks. East Germans seem to be prepared to trade freedom against security, autonomy against guardianship.[47]

Wolfgang Thierse, the leading East German Social Democrat, pointed out the contrast between the 'work orientation' of East Germans and the 'leisure orientation' of West Germans.[48] Sixty-one per cent of East Germans identify themselves as working class, whereas that figure is miniscule in the West. Thierse also identified women as the losers of unification. They are hardest hit by unemployment; child-care, preventive health-care, free birth control, a liberal abortion regime, continuing education and training for women as much as men have all suffered in the new political dispensation and the market-oriented economy. The thinning-out of child-care institutions, especially, makes for a complete change in lifestyle. The liberal abortion law of the GDR has been replaced by the more restrictive version of the West.

Thierse also laments the fact that positive institutions of the GDR were not even considered to be integrated into a unified Germany. A striking example of this is the abolition of polyclinics which worked more efficiently and were less costly than the West German system of hospitals.

More importantly, perhaps, the experience of the democratic revolution of the East German people has not become a constituent factor of the new Germany. Civil rights groups and *Wende* activists have either been absorbed into the Western political and cultural machinery, or were marginalised. Christoph Meckel, another leading Eastern Social Democrat, drew the conclusion that: 'The historic experience of the Germans that their unity in a democratic community is rooted in a constitutive act of self-determination, has not been consciously grasped by many.'[49]

A German Identity?

Is there *a* German identity? Or are there plural German identities, layers, different manifestations of German identities, regional and historical, cultural, East and West, all-German, competing, complementing each other, in flux, which can be seen as a reflection of the unfinished business of Unification itself, and within the European processes and insecurities of the 1990s? On the macro level, the question of 'ever closer union' in Europe and the fate of the currency project will have inevitable repercussions for Germany's role in Europe and its self-perception. Although the Maastricht criteria have bolstered the nation state as the central player in the European political theatre (fiscal policies, budgetary cuts, etc.), there is still a strong undercurrent of regionalism in Europe which reinforces the political identity of the federal states of Germany.

Some of Germany's old and new *Länder* are historic units, with strong regional identities; others are constructs of the postwar period. On the whole, it is astonishing how much Germans have come to identify themselves with their *Land*, even if it was artificially created only 50 years ago. The *Wirtschaftswunder* and its attendant 'feel-good factor' and conscious measures of identity-building, like *Land* festivals (garden festivals, cultural festivals, etc.), have superseded, if not supplanted historical affiliations. Other *Länder* can invoke the long historical perspective. Biedenkopf has said of Saxony that '[a] thousand years of history binds this region, like Bavaria, and differentiates it from many of the other regions in Germany'.[50]

In one respect, at least, there has been a significant convergence between

East and West. The bleak, or realistic, economic outlook – economic growth in the East in 1997 below the Western rate; the East's catching-up process, after peaking at just 53 per cent of the West's economic power, having obviously petered out[51] – is shared by Easterners and Westerners alike. A Forsa poll revealed that a majority of 51 per cent (of over 1,000 in that survey) were now convinced that it will take another 10–20 years to complete unification.[52]

Germans have, of necessity, become more introspective, more preoccupied with themselves since Unification. Demands for accepting greater responsibility, in Europe and globally, are voiced from the inside as well as from the outside. Some of these demands have already been met and have, tentatively, transformed German foreign and security policy. 'Germany is in the middle of redefining its role in Europe and in global affairs,' wrote Helga Welsh and Donald Hancock in 1994:

> A reluctance toward leadership born out of the legacies of two world wars and understandable anxieties on part of its European neighbours meet with increasing expectations to accept leadership roles, particularly so on the part of public officials in the United States. However, increased burden sharing – for example in multilateral peacekeeping operations and in financial assistance – ultimately has to lead to increased decision sharing. The acceptance and reconciliation of these unfolding developments may prove to be difficult – for Germany as well as its international partners.[53]

The prevailing economic difficulties of the unification process have forced a new debate about the way this process has been going. The multitude of claims, from Biedenkopf to Thierse and Poppe, that 'the united Germany is not an enlarged Federal Republic – it is something new',[54] are in themselves a sign that the new Germany is widely perceived as just that: an enlarged, but only slightly changed, version of the old West Germany.

Thus, on the whole, I would maintain that as a conservative project of assimilating East to West, chances and options Unification could have offered for innovation and reform were not used. The 'lack of consequences' of Unification has been analysed by Wolf Lepenius who characterised it as a 'self-congratulatory festival' of West German elites. But German Unification is still, as the *Observer* put it, 'work in progress'[55] and far from complete, and as the 'self-congratulatory' element gives way to critical and self-critical analysis, German identity is still in the process of – in that most ambiguous of terms – being forged.

Notes

1 Ian Traynor quotes one such example in 'confused and afraid: being German today', in the *Guardian*, 20 November 1996.
2 *Economist*, 'A Survey of Germany', 9 November 1996.
3 Quoted in H. Breuer, '"Das Trennende im Denken lebt fort": Nachdenkliche Töne bestimmen den Festakt zum Tag der einheit', *Die Welt*, 4 October 1995.
4 See A. Tusa, *The Last Division: Berlin and the Wall*, London, Hodder & Stoughton, 1996.
5 See H. Wiesenthal, 'Die neuen Bundesländer als Sonderfall der Transformation in den Ländern Mitteleuropas', *Aus Politik und Zeitgeschichte*, 40, 1996 (27 September), pp. 46–54, in particular pp. 47–8.
6 For an analysis of the effects of the currency union of 1 July 1990, see S.F. Frowen and J. Hölscher (eds), *The German Currency Union of 1990: A critical assessment*, London, Macmillan, 1997.
7 'Der Geschmack der Freiheit', *Der Spiegel*, 4 November 1996.
8 See H. Glaser, 'Deutsche Identitäten: Gesellschaft und Kultur im vereinten Deutschland', *Aus Politik und Zeitgeschichte*, 13–14, 1996 (22 March), pp. 32–41, p. 33; and 'Zahl der Pendler nimmt ab', *Die Welt*, 11 October 1995.
9 T. Paterson, 'Challenges of a new world role', *European (Special Report: Germany)*, 12 December 1996.
10 See P.E. Quint, *The Imperfect Union: Constitutional Structures of German Unification*, Princeton University Press, 1996.
11 H. James, 'The landscape that didn't blossom', *Times Literary Supplement*, 13 June 1997, p. 6.
12 Quoted in Martin Jacques, 'Germans unite in heated agreement', *Observer*, 17 November 1996; the same report disclosed not only that more than half the German population are against the single currency, it also quoted a Berliner's statement, backing Stützle's analysis: 'The Deutschmark is part of my German identity.' See also D. Staunton, 'Save our Deutschmark', *Irish Times*, 9 June 1997, stating that in Germany now 'more than two thirds of the population is [sic] against the project' of a single European currency.
13 D.J. Goldhagen, '"Modell Bundesrepublik": Nationalgeschichte, Demokratie und Internationalisierung in Deutschland – eine Preisrede', *Süddeutsche Zeitung*, 15 March 1997.
14 W. Weidenfeld and K.-R. Korte, *Die Deutschen – Profil einer Nation*, Stuttgart 1991, pp. 132–3.
15 On this division of historical heritage, see C. Dieckmann's compelling essay, 'Deutschland: Ost und West driften wieder auseinander', *Die Zeit*, 20 June 1997.
16 *Economist*, 'A Survey of Germany', 9 November 1996.
17 For an account of the terminal years of the GDR, see C.S. Maier, *Dissolution: The crisis of Communism and the end of East Germany*, Princeton University Press, 1997.
18 C.C. O'Brien, 'Beware, the Reich is Reviving', *The Times*, 31 October 1989; reprinted in H.James and M. Stone (eds), *When the Wall came down: Reactions to German Unification*, London: Routledge, 1992, pp. 221–3; p. 223. In an article in the Austrian journal *Europäische Rundschau*, in 1993, Conor Cruise O'Brien again predicted the imminent rise of a German 'Großmacht' less and less interested in 'Western integration': 'Die Zukunft des "Westens"', *Europäische Rundschau*, 93/2, pp. 19–28.

19 Quoted in *The Economist*, 'A Survey of Germany', 9 November 1996. The new Germany, with its 80 million people, has 22 per cent of the EU population, and produces 28 per cent of the EU's GDP (1995).

20 W. Hutton, 'The Enemy is now within', *Observer*, 9 February 1997.

21 See J. Gebhardt, 'Verfassungspatriotismus als Identitätskonzept der Nation', *Aus Politik und Zeitgeschichte*, B 14/93 (2 April), pp. 29–37.

22 Ibid.

23 Ibid.

24 T. Paterson, 'Challenges of a new world role', *European*, 12 December 1996.

25 K.-H. Bohrer and K. Scheel (eds), *Deutschland in der Welt, Merkur* special edition, Vol. 48, No. 9/10, 1994, p. 749.

26 Quoted in the *Economist*, 'A Survey of Germany', 9 November 1996.

27 See also M.S. Lambeck, 'Deutsche Interessen', *Die Welt* (leader), 20 June 1997.

28 M. Kreile, 'Verantwortung und Interesse in der deutschen Außen- und Sicherheitspolitik', *Aus Politik und Zeitgeschehen*, 5/1996, 26 January 1996, pp. 3–11; p.3.

29 *Economist*, 'A Survey of Germany', 9 November 1996.

30 B. Conrad, 'Die geeinte Nation ist auf dem Weg zur Normalität', *Die Welt*, 16 February 1996.

31 R. Zitelmann, 'Gefährliche Grenze', *Die Welt*, 5 July 1997.

32 G. Schmidtchen, *Wie weit ist der Weg nach Deutschland? Sozialpsychologie der Jugend in der postsozialistischen Welt*, Opladen, Leske + Budrich, 1997.

33 K. Liffey and T. Heneghan, 'SPD inquest follows Berlin poll disaster', *Scotsman*, 24 October 1995.

34 R. Eppelmann, 'Zur inneren Einheit Deutschlands im fünften Jahr nach der Vereinigung', *Aus Politik und Zeitgeschichte*, 40–41, 29 September 1995, pp. 8–12; p. 9.

35 *Economist*, 'A Survey of Germany', 9 November 1996.

36 *Sozialreport 50 plus*, conducted by Wohlfahrtsverband Volkssolidarität (1,084 citizens over 50 years old), quoted in D. Schütz, 'Zukunftsangst im Osten wächst', *Die Welt*, 20 December 1996.

37 Emnid poll for n-tv quoted in R. Zitelmann, 'Probleme Ost – Probleme West: Was Deutsche denken: Ähnlichkeiten, aber auch große Differenzen', *Die Welt*, 4 January 1997.

38 F. Vilmar and W. Dümcke, 'Kritische Zwischenbilanz der Vereinigungspolitik: eine unerledigte Aufgabe der Politikwissenschaft', *Aus Politik und Zeitgeschehen*, 40/96, 27 September 1996, pp. 35–45; in particular pp. 39–43.

39 'Umschwung Ost: Bonn forciert Ausbau der Bahn-Strecken', *Die Welt*, 10 December 1996.

40 *Economist*, 'A Survey of Germany', 9 November 1996.

41 Quoted in U. Ahlers, 'Auf der Suche nach der DDR-Identität', *taz*, 17 May 1996.

42 Quoted in C. Dieckmann, 'Die Ossis: Fremdlinge im eigenen Haus', *Die Zeit*, 24 May 1996.

43 Ibid.

44 T. Paterson, 'King Kurt is the people's friend', *European*, 5 September 1996.

45 Quoted in M. Lesch, 'Biedenkopf sorgt sich um die CDU-Wähler im Osten', *Die Welt*, 11 December 1996.

46 Quoted in B. Conrad, 'Die Deutschen haben Grund zur Zuversicht', *Die Welt*, 7 January 1997.

47 *Der Spiegel*, 4 November 1996.

48 W. Thierse, 'Fünf Jahre deutsche Vereinigung: Wirtschaft – Gesellschaft – Mentalität', *Aus Politik und Zeitgeschehen*, 40–41, 1995, 29 September, pp. 3–7, especially pp. 6–7.

49 In R. Süssmuth and B. Baule (eds), *Deutsche Zwischenbilanz*, Landsberg, Olzog Verlag, 1996, quoted in B.Conrad, 'Die Deutschen haben Grund zur Zuversicht', *Die Welt*, 7 January 1997.

50 T. Paterson, op. cit.

51 U. Müller, 'Sieben Jahre danach', *Die Welt*, 9 November 1996.

52 'Die Einheit ist gelungen', *Die Welt*, 9 November 1996.

53 H.A. Welsh and M.D. Hancock, 'Beyond Unification' in M.D. Hancock and H.A. Welsh (eds), *German Unification: Process & Outcomes*, Boulder, Colorado, Westview Press, 1994, pp. 313–21; p. 319.

54 K. Biedenkopf, quoted in B. Conrad, 'Die Deutschen haben Grund zur Zuversicht', *Die Welt*, 7 January 1997.

55 M.Jacques, 'Germans unite in heated agreement', *Observer*, 17 November 1996.

10   Immigration, European Integration and the Representation of Migrant Interests

ANDREW GEDDES

Introduction

Every six months, and sometimes more frequently, the heads of governments of EU member states gather within the grandly titled European Council. The purpose of these meetings is to 'steer' the EU and plot the course for future developments. These meetings, and their consequences, are quite often discussed in terms of transport-based analogies – comparing the movement towards closer economic and political integration to a train ride is a particular favourite. Thus, so the analogy goes, the heads of governments are on a train; they are not too certain what the destination is, but they are fairly sure they will like it when they get there. Not all the member states are enjoying the trip quite so much: the British and Danish governments, for instance, have bought tickets for the train, but would often seem to prefer that it was heading in a different direction.

The 'passengers' on this train are the heads of government acting on behalf, or so they suppose, of the people's of Europe. A major problem for the EU is that it is often perceived as technocratic, elitist and disconnected from the interests of its citizens. These problems of representation and representative-ness are compounded for the more marginal members of society in EU member states, particularly migrants and their descendants. Many migrants are not even citizens of the state in which they reside and EU law makes it very clear that if they are not citizens of a member state then they are not usually entitled to the rights and freedoms bestowed by the Union's treaties. These problems are compounded by a lack of clarity as to what actually are 'migrant interests' at EU level. This has been a problem bedevilling the European Community

Migrants Forum (ECMF) which was set up by the Commission to provide a veneer of consultation alongside the developing immigration and asylum policy provisions of the EU. The ECMF does not, though, seem to have carved a clear and distinct role for itself at European level.

As the heads of government progress from meeting to meeting the view of the final destination becomes slightly clearer. Since the mid-1980s there has been particularly rapid progress with plans laid for a single market with a single currency and a significant social dimension. The plan for creation of a single market has contributed to raising of the salience of immigration-related issues[1] at EU level. Whether or not these developments are harbingers of a common EU policy is an open question, after all the metaphorical train's destination is not clear. A common EU policy would, for instance, imply a far greater degree of supranationalisation, with concomitant expansion in roles for supranational institutions such as the Commission, European Parliament and European Court of Justice, than is currently the case. As it stands, member states have maintained a fairly tight intergovernmental grip on decision-making in these areas. The institutional structures and decision-making procedures rest power with the Council of Ministers and minimise the role of the Commission, Parliament and Court.

This intensification of policy cooperation over the last ten years or so has important implications for migrants and their descendants in EU member states. In this chapter, I survey links between policy and institutional developments and, what is a rather neglected area in analysis of EU immigration policy development and EU politics more generally, the scope for representation of migrant interests. The chapter's basic argument can be stated quite simply: supranational level institutional structures and decision-making procedures have implications for the structure of political opportunity and the scope for participation and representation of migrant interests. If, for instance, institutional structures are designed to shield decision-makers from the glare of scrutiny and accountability by charging secretive intergovernmental institutions with decision-making powers then there is likely to be only limited scope for political participation and representation by groups affected by policy development.

The most recent port of call for the heads of government (they tend to stop in only the prettiest European cities, although they have also been to Birmingham) was in June 1997 in Amsterdam. The Amsterdam summit concerned itself with drafting new Treaty provisions, including provisions for free movement, immigration and asylum policy. At the time of writing the Treaty awaits ratification.

Towards Fortress Europe?

There are important connections between national level policy developments and the EU responsibilities. It is not surprising that national level emphases on restrictions on the numbers of migrants, particularly from less economically developed countries, are reflected in the intergovernmental deals that underpin integration. The bargains negotiated at Maastricht and Amsterdam, for example, put in place structures to manage immigration-related issues which prioritise restriction of the numbers of immigrants, particularly those from less economically developed countries. This reflects long-standing national policy preferences in older countries of immigration; and rather more recent policy preferences in new countries of immigration in southern Europe. The broad parameters of the EU's legal remit tend to reflect lowest common denominator policy-making because they are based upon unanimity. The key point about such a policy is not that it exactly reflects the viewpoint of the most recalcitrant member state, but that the range of possible outcomes is decisively influenced by the stance of the most reluctant.

Examination of national policy preferences is crucial because they underpin intergovernmental bargaining processes which determine the scope and direction of integration. When we apply this insight to immigration policy we encounter what could be called the 'received wisdom' about immigration policy and politics in European countries; namely that policies in EU member states are restrictive and that these restrictive immigration policies engender social exclusion of settled migrants and their descendants. The result is that immigration and immigrants themselves (the definition of 'immigrants' is often very broad and incorporates people of immigrant origin whether they themselves are immigrants or not) become public policy problems (based on a rather boiled down conceptualisation of the immigration problem as one of numbers of immigrants) to which the solution to the problem (defined as one of numbers of immigrants) is restriction. Consequently, immigrants become objects of policy rather than actors in the political process. These formal and symbolic processes of exclusion contribute to political marginalisation.[2] National level policies and EU developments are connected in the sense that landmark decisions about the scope and direction of European integration are decisively influenced by the preferences of member states. Thus, it is argued, 'fortress Europe' is built. A problem with the exclusion argument is that its culmination would seem to be repatriation of immigrants as a consequence of ever tighter restriction which engenders ever greater levels of exclusion. The fact that large scale deportation of immigrants has not occurred has prompted a challenge to the 'exclusion' perspective from what could be called a 'citizenship' perspective which focuses on the implication of extension of legal, social and political rights.[3]

If we just adopt as our focus the grand intergovernmental deals that underpin European integration we may lose sight of the *effects* of integration. It has been argued that European integration can have effects which are not explained by recourse to analysis of national policy preferences because the effects of integration were not intended by member states at the time when particular decisions to integrate were made. Unintended consequences may arise from the ceding of legal powers to supranational institutions with concomitant development of institutional autonomy and, associated with this, enhanced agenda-setting capabilities of EU institutions. Integration can, therefore, lead to the opening of 'gaps' in member state control which enhance the role of supranational institutions, and other non-state actors.[4] In this way, the European polity is reshaped and the dominance of the member states challenged. Much recent research into European integration has attempted to map the development of a new European polity and changing patterns of governance. However, when we seek to apply these perspectives to immigration policy we encounter the tight intergovernmental grip on decision-making held by the member states.

Consequently, in issue areas related to immigration policy the gaps into which supranational institutions could seek to expand their policy-making role as a result of legal powers bestowed by the EU's legal framework appear to be very small, if not nonexistent. Decision-makers in the Council are relatively insulated from democratic oversight. This insulation has occurred by design not accident. It reflects both a desire to extract sensitive immigration-related issues from mainstream political debate and thereby seek depoliticisation, as well as a wider problem of the EU's 'democratic deficit'. In spite of the draft Treaty of Amsterdam's provisions on what is called 'transparency', many aspects of EU decision-making remain decidedly opaque.[5]

The notion of 'fortress Europe' has become central to many analyses of EU immigration policy. The member states, it is argued, are busily constructing the external ramparts of the fortress and these ramparts – as a consequence of their problematisation of immigration and immigrants – contribute to internal social and political exclusion within the fortress.[6] But if the term 'fortress Europe' is to have more than rhetorical value it needs to be operationalised rather more specifically than is sometimes the case. It tends to be used to denounce European integration and, thereby, contributes to a Eurosceptic rhetoric associated with the political left. Two evaluative criteria are of particular relevance for more specific consideration of the policy-related dimensions of the putative European fortress. First, the creation of fortress Europe implies the consolidation of restrictive immigration policies and, second, a move beyond national-based restriction to increased regulatory competence at supranational level.

Restrictive Policies

The ability to regulate movement of people is a good indicator of state power (or sovereignty) construed in Weberian zero-sum terms. This implies maintenance of effective regulation over who can or cannot enter a country. Over the last 20 years West European countries – particularly the post-colonial and post-guestworker countries, such as Britain, France and Germany – have sought ever tighter restrictions on immigration. In this endeavour they have been less successful than the more fervent advocates of control had hoped because numbers of immigrants and, more recently, asylum-seekers, have remained relatively high. Immigration has become a social and political problem which European countries have found difficult to manage. Migration continued after states ceased recruitment of migrant labour following the economic recession of the early 1970s. International human rights laws protecting, for instance, the rights of the family render control of secondary immigration – mainly family reunification – problematic. More recently, the numbers of asylum-seekers, who are also extended a measure of protection under international law, have increased. States have, though, drastically tightened their asylum procedures to make asylum far more difficult to obtain.

The seeming disjunction between the rhetoric of tight control and continued immigration has prompted the formulation of two hypotheses which are seen as encapsulating a contemporary paradox underpinning the politics of immigration. First, a 'convergence hypothesis' notes similarities in response to immigration in receiving countries measured in terms of policy instruments, public reactions to immigration (generally hostile) and immigrant integration policies. At the same time, a 'gap hypothesis' addresses the lacuna between restrictive policy *goals* and *outcomes*. As the gap between restrictive goals and actual outcomes increases it is argued that the end result is greater public hostility towards immigrants (with knock-on effects for settled immigrants and their children).[7]

Castles has remarked upon an apparent breakdown of migration regulation in the 1990s as a result of the increased numbers of asylum-seekers fleeing war, famine, ethnic persecution or ecological disasters; many of these asylum-seekers do not fall within the definition of political persecution provided by the 1951 Geneva Convention.[8] Joppke has argued that the response to the asylum crisis has been for states to reassert their sovereignty as a means of controlling asylum-seeking.[9] The best example of this reassertion of sovereignty, Joppke argued, was in Germany where the previously liberal provisions of the 1949 Basic Law were significantly tightened by the new law of 1993. Tightened asylum procedures in EU member states which, for example, recognise 'safe third countries' and 'safe countries of origin', have drastically reduced the numbers of asylum-seekers and the numbers of successful applications. Interestingly, though, the German response emerged in the context of an increasingly integrated European policy framework. The Germans appear to have 'reasserted' their sovereignty by integrating something which is, of course, wholly compatible with a non-zero sum notion of state sovereignty.

The impact of what has been called the new phase of mass migration has been keenly felt in new countries of immigration in southern Europe. These countries constitute the southern ramparts of the putative European fortress. Both legal and clandestine immigration continue to have structural importance to certain sectors of southern European economies and southern European economies still display a need for foreign labour in economic sectors (typically lower paid) where it can be difficult to find workers. This is not to suggest that southern European countries are distinguished from northern European countries by their reliance on undocumented migrant workers. It is, of course, the case that there are also unscrupulous employers prepared to hire cheap undocumented migrant workers in 'older' countries of immigration too. If, though, there is a continued need for migrant labour to plug labour market gaps, will southern European countries be complicit in the construction of fortress Europe? The strong clandestine sectors (or 'black economy') in southern Europe mean that dual labour market principles apply with the result that demand for cheap labour can coexist with relatively high unemployment. Labour market requirements may militate against effective operationalisation of tight controls. When combined with the geographical characteristics of southern European countries, and underdeveloped administrative structures, external frontier control is rendered problematic.[10] Discussion of a southern European migration regime does, though, need to be placed on a firmer footing. In what ways is it distinct, if at all, from migration policies pursued in northern European countries? If the differences are operationalised in terms of geographical, economic and bureaucratic factors then it needs to be specified how these factors impact upon a distinct southern European regime which both distinguishes southern European countries from each other, and differs from a 'northern' regime.

Discussion of connections between immigration policies and their knock-on effects for already-settled immigrants and their descendants has also engendered debate between those who argue that restrictive immigration policies prompt social and political exclusion and those who argue that there is a structural liberal democratic tendency towards expansive immigration policies and the social and political inclusion of migrants: a 'politics of exclusion' versus a 'politics of citizenship'. This could be seen as presenting us with an overstated restriction/expansion, exclusion/inclusion dichotomy which does not capture what could be called 'differential incorporation'. There is clear evidence that migrant and migrant origin groups are among the most disadvantaged members of European societies, but these patterns are not uniform.

Connections between restrictive policies and social exclusion are particularly associated with Marxist influenced analyses of immigration policy and politics which link relations of production and the regulation of scarcity in capitalist societies with a dialectic of inclusion and exclusion. Social exclusion is generated because the regulation of scarcity in capitalist society necessitates signification and categorisation in order to typify individuals and consign them to a place in the social order. One aspect of signification is categorisation based on phenotypical and cultural differences. The attendant development of racist ideologies justifies subordination of immigrant workers on the basis of supposed 'racial' inferiority. Migrants, thus, 'threaten' external borders and constitute an internal 'threat' to the 'national culture', whatever that may be. This twin-track threat perception clearly affects the developing security profile of the European Union. The best representation of this is the Schengen Agreement which imposes external and internal security measures. These general processes of inclusion and exclusion are, of course, diffused through differing historical, social, political and institutional contexts, but at a basic level, processes of exclusion are similar.[11]

Perspectives on exclusion have been challenged by those who argue that the trends are actually towards expansive policies and inclusion of migrants and their descendants. Freeman, for instance, argues that liberal democracies have an inherent structural tendency towards expansive policies.[12] The structural features of liberal democracy identified as relevant in this respect are: free constitutions founded on individual rights; competitive party systems; and regular elections which lead to optimal policies derived from the preferences of individual voters who are assumed to be utility maximisers with perfect information. This model of liberal democratic immigration policy-making is corrupted by information asymmetries which generate a 'temporal illusion' during the early stages of immigration: the general public believe that immigration will only be temporary (that migrants are 'guests', not permanent settlers). Opposition to migration in its early stages is stultified and slow to organise. In this respect, Freeman argues that publics have been 'sold a bill of goods ... which were elite driven and packaged with what turned out to be, in retrospect, seriously misleading promises'. At the same time, advocates of expansive immigration policies, particularly business interests, which can see the advantages of cheap sources of migrant labour, are well organised, have the ear of relevant government departments, and are able to ensure that policies remain expansive. Clientelist politics emerge because there is an incentive for the beneficiaries of policy to organise and, concomitantly, little incentive for the opponents of policy to do likewise, at least in migration's early stages. Over the course of the immigration cycle, it is predicted that clientelist arrangements will evolve into a relatively stable interest group politics founded on construction of a political consensus designed to minimise populist exploitation of anti-immigration sentiment.

These arguments about expansive policies are less developed in respect of tendencies towards inclusion. Freeman argues that there is a Tocquevillian sympathy for immigrants who are viewed as people like ourselves trying to make their way in the world (although it is also noted that the asylum crisis has prompted a partial policy reversal). In a more detailed analysis of trends towards social and political inclusion in Europe (although the analysis mainly looks at France), Hollifield, focuses on the opening of 'new political spaces' for migrants and their descendants.[13] Trends towards inclusiveness, Hollifield argues, are founded on the 'embedded liberalism' of the post-Second World War era and the consequent development of rights-based regimes which emphasise human rights and social justice from which immigrants and their children benefit. Not only this, but the deep-seated embeddedness of these liberal values means that the EU will open its free movement arrangements to third-country nationals. There are good reasons for doubting this optimistic vision of EU development, as even the most cursory glance at the Amsterdam Treaty shows that member states are determined to keep a tight grip on policy development and have not, so far, been particularly keen on the extension of free movement rights to third-country nationals. It has also been argued that trends towards inclusion have also been extended to post-national level as a consequence of international legal standards which contribute to deterritorialisation of rights.

Contrasting perspectives on national immigration regimes (understood in a very broad sense as including both immigration restriction and immigrant incorporation policies) have important implications for discussion of EU immigration policy. For instance, the post-national dimension appears to qualify Weberian zero-sum perspectives on state sovereignty as measured by a state's ability to control its borders and its people irrespective of intervening factors, such as pressure from the international environment. In contrast, state power has been construed as the ability to achieve desired outcomes. Thus, heightened interdependence implies that desired outcomes may be more readily attainable through cooperation or integration in key policy sectors with other states. Consequently, in this non-zero-sum context the ability to attain preferred outcomes is reflective of relations with other social actors and other states, rather than just a state's power over its people and its borders. This means that a government that holds and achieves restrictive immigration policy objectives in an integrated European policy framework, within which Weberian state sovereignty is compromised, can be judged as more successful than a state that fails to attain restrictive immigration policy objectives by acting unilaterally and clinging to a zero-sum notion of state power. To use a term familiar to analysts of European integration: states may attain their objectives across a range of policy issues by 'pooling' their sovereignty.[14]

European integration may also have consequences that there were not envisaged when decisions to integrate were made. For instance, 'gaps' in member state control may open. Pierson argues that: actors [by which he means national governments] may be in a strong initial position, seek to maximise their interests, and nevertheless carry out institutional and policy reforms that fundamentally transform their own positions (or those of their successors) in ways that are unanticipated and/or undesired. The resultant gaps increase the autonomy and agenda-setting capabilities of supranational political actors. Once opened these gaps are difficult to close because of supranational resistance, institutional barriers to change which mean political institutions are 'sticky', and high sunk costs and barriers to exit which mean that even suboptimal decisions can become self-reinforcing over time. Analyses of these gaps have tended to focus on areas where supranational institutions have relatively clearly defined powers – such as for social policy where EU competence has increased significantly since the Single European Act (SEA).[15] The tight control by member states of immigration policy suggests that these gaps are, at best, very small and that, consequently, political opportunities for groups seeking to represent migrants are limited.[16]

EU Policy Responsibilities

The crowning achievement of the SEA was the plan for free movement for people, services, goods and capital. In fact, the attainment of many of the objectives outlined in the SEA has probably been the EU's most notable success. Free movement of people also raised the salience of immigration and asylum issues: if member states were to remove internal frontiers then cooperation on external frontier control seemed necessary.

The preference for intergovernmental cooperation on immigration and asylum policy rather than the creation of an integrated policy framework was in line with the neo-realist prediction that integration is less likely to occur in areas of 'high politics' that impinge more directly on state sovereignty. In the SEA's aftermath, between 1986 and 1991, cooperation occurred outside of the formal Treaty framework and beyond the remit of the Commission, European Parliament and European Court of Justice, as well as largely beyond the reach of structures of accountability at national level.

This form of informal intergovernmental cooperation was very limited in the objectives it could achieve. It relied on adoption of conventions in international law, as opposed to supranational law. International conventions are not directly enforceable at national level, unlike supranational EU law which can have direct effect and establish European Court of Justice jurisdiction. Conventions also need to be ratified at national level, which can be a very lengthy process. These informal intergovernmental procedures were also seen as widening the 'democratic deficit' by channelling discussion of immigration-related policy to secretive intergovernmental forums.

The Treaty of European Union (TEU) sought to counteract some of the weaknesses of informal intergovernmentalism by creating a Justice and Home Affairs (JHA) 'pillar' which recognised immigration and asylum as matters of common interest and introduced a Treaty obligation to cooperate within the EU's single institutional structure. A clear distinction was made between the supranational community 'pillar' and the new mode of intergovernmental cooperation established within the two flanking pillars (JHA and 'common foreign and security policy' (CFSP)).

Title VI of the TEU outlined JHA provisions. Articles K.1.1–3 delineated EU responsibilities for asylum policy, rules governing the crossing of external frontiers, and immigration policy and policy regarding nationals of third countries. The Council was to act by unanimity when deciding on 'conventions', 'joint actions' or 'joint positions'. A 'double lock ' mechanism was created whereby Council decision's to establish conventions in international law needed also to be ratified by national parliaments. It has been argued that the JHA pillar did little to reduce the democratic deficit, and may even have accentuated it, because the Councils' endemic secrecy meant that most immigration and asylum-related discussions were beyond the purview of national legislatures and the European Parliament (which had only the right to be informed about JHA decisions, Article K.6).

The draft Amsterdam Treaty (ToA), agreed by the heads of government on 18 June 1997, made further changes to the immigration and asylum related provision of the treaties. At the time of writing, the Treaty has been signed and awaits ratification. It is unlikely that the Treaty will come into effect until 1999 at the earliest. Indeed, the TEU's travails (the Danish rejection and France's *petit oui)* suggest that ratification should not be taken for granted. The draft ToA covers both the Treaty establishing the European Community (i.e. the community pillar) and the TEU (covering the 'second' and 'third' intergovernmental pillars). The ToA adds a new Title IV to the first pillar dealing with immigration, visas, asylum and other issues relating to free movement of persons. Title IV sets a five year target (from ratification) for: attainment of free movement of persons; measures on the crossing of external borders, including rules on visas; a common visa list; procedures for a uniform visa; and free movement within the EU for a period of up to three months for third-country nationals. A five year target is also set up for aspects of asylum policy, measures to combat illegal immigration and temporary protection of refugees. For these five years, unanimity is required in the Council of Ministers except for provisions on the common visa list and visa format which since the SEA have already been in the first pillar and determined by qualified majority vote.

The most significant development is the transfer of key aspects of the 'Schengen' arrangements into EU. They are attached to the JHA pillar and the member states will then decide what goes where, i.e. what issues move into the new Title IV in the main pillar and what go into what remains of the JHA pillar which mainly deals with policing and judicial cooperation. Provisions are also made for incorporation of the Schengen Secretariat into the General Secretariat of the Council of Ministers. The Schengen Agreement was signed in the eponymous town in Luxembourg in 1985 by Germany, France, Belgium, the Netherlands and Luxembourg. In 1990 a Convention implementing the Agreement was signed. Since this time, accession agreements have been reached with Italy (27 November 1990), Spain and Portugal (25 June 1991), Greece (6 November 1992), Austria (28 April 1995), and Denmark, Finland and Sweden (19 December 1996). Iceland and Norway – both members of the European Economic Area – are associated with the Schengen Agreement. By the summer of 1997, Italy, Greece, Finland and Sweden have not completed national ratification processes. This means that seven states had signed, ratified and implemented the Schengen Agreement (France, Germany, Belgium, the Netherlands, Luxembourg, Spain and Portugal) and six member states were not yet implementing it (Austria, Denmark, Sweden, Finland, Greece, and Italy). All Schengen signatories are committed to the removal of external frontiers. To complicate matters, Britain has not joined Schengen because British governments (both Labour and Conservative) have preferred to maintain national border controls. Because of its free movement arrangements with Britain, Ireland has also been prevented from participating. Their stances on Schengen meant that Britain and Ireland opted-out of the provisions of Title IV. This variable geometry implies that the single market – a defining principle of European integration – is compromised in what Curtin describes as 'a very serious [and] ... unprecedented, breach of the acquis communautaire'.[17] In a protocol attached to the Treaty, Ireland expresses a willingness to participate in the new arrangements so far as is compatible with maintenance of the Common Travel Area with Britain.

Title VI of the TEU – the 'old' JHA pillar which dealt with immigration and asylum issues before Amsterdam shifted them to the new Title IV – is left to focus on sensitive matters linked to police cooperation and judicial cooperation. The result of the separation of JHA matters is that the Council will deal with 'first' pillar questions under the free movement, asylum and immigration provisions, with police and criminal 'third' pillar issues raised within the revised Title VI, and with the further development of the Schengen protocol.

The ToA's Schengen protocol gives the Council of Ministers sole power to 'determine the legal basis for each of the provisions or decisions which constitute the Schengen *acquis*', i.e., to determine which bits of the Schengen agreement go where. As Curtin points out, this means that the bulk of the Schengen decisions, which were adopted in secret by civil servants, are translated straight from the Schengen *acquis* into the EU *acquis* without democratic scrutiny. Between 1990 and 1995 there were 173 of these decisions, but a list of them is not attached to the ToA (a list of the principal headings of the Schengen protocol is contained in Table 10.1, below). As Curtin notes:

> What this seemingly innocuous provision in effect does is to give the status of
> binding law to decisions adopted by civil servants more or less in total secrecy
> without any parliamentary or political control. Is the European Union which

has incorporated this acquis even in possession of an up-to-date list of all the decisions in question?[18]

It hardly needs to be added that this is unlikely to make too great a contribution to the decision-making transparency that the ToA also mentions.

Table 10.1   The Schengen Protocol (the possible future location, i.e., 'pillar', in which the policy issues will be placed is also indicated)

Title II: Articles 2–38
Abolition of checks at internal borders and the movement of persons (first pillar)
3 decisions on internal borders
22 decisions on external borders
4 decisions on readmission
23 decisions on visas
4 decisions on asylum

Title III: Articles 39–91
Police and Security (third pillar)
5 decisions on police cooperation
11 decisions on judicial cooperation
3 decisions on extradition
10 decisions on drugs

Title IV: Articles 92–119
The Schengen Information System (SIS) (first and third pillars)
31 decisions on the SIS
16 decisions on SIRENE
4 decisions on the joint supervisory body

Title V: Articles 120–125
Transport and movement of goods (first pillar)
2 decisions on this Title

Source: *Statewatch*, May–June 1997.

The European Court of Justice's powers of oversight in these areas are extremely limited. Article B of the Schengen protocol states that the Court 'shall have no jurisdiction on measures or decisions relating to the maintenance of public order or the safeguarding of internal security'. This catch-all provision could, if member states were so minded, lead to the exclusion of the Court of Justice from Schengen-related matters which are incorporated into the 'first pillar'.

Representation of Migrant Interests

The institutional structures created for management of immigration-related issues insulate decision-makers from public opinion. As well as being a symptom of the democratic deficit, this could be viewed as a European level replication of national patterns of immigration control. Clearly, neither of these explanations for insulation bode well for representation of migrant interests. The picture is complicated still further when it is borne in mind that aggregation and articulation of migrant interests is also likely to be hampered by the diverse backgrounds and formal status (some are citizens, some are not) of migrant and migrant-origin groups which renders effective organisation and articulation of interests problematic. Moreover, the fact that many people of migrant origin are, in fact, citizens of the member state in which they reside further complicates the picture. Finally, migrants tend to be concentrated – although, of course, not uniformly so – in lower socioeconomic groups which, research into political participation shows, are less likely to become active in the political process.[19]

It has been argued that in areas where interests are relatively diffuse and/ or poorly organised, supranational institutions, particularly the Commission, can protect interests that may be neglected by national governments. In such circumstances, 'policy entrepreneurship' can result.[20] The necessary starting point is, though, empowerment of supranational institutions as a precondition for innovation. Even though the Commission may have expressed willingness to promote the rights of third-country nationals, its legal remit is limited. Similarly, the European Parliament has voiced its concern about the civil liberties implications of immigration and asylum policy provisions and has paid particular attention to the resurgence of racism and xenophobia,[21] but the Parliament has little part to play in the decision-making processes. The Parliament tends to be informed about policy developments after they take place. Therefore, scope for effective alliance building at supranational level by groups seeking to represent the interests of migrants is limited. Even if the Commission and European Parliament were to be subjected to intensive lobbying, the effects on decision-making in the Council may well be marginal.

The firm intergovernmental grip on policy development for at least five years after ToA ratification implies that EU policy is likely to continue to emphasise control of numbers. Lowest common denominator policy-making makes it less likely that member states will be able to agree upon a common European paradigm for social integration of migrants and their descendants given the divergent patterns in operation at national level. The British Commission for Racial Equality may, for instance, like to see the development of a European 'race relations' policy combining the British emphasis on immigration control with anti-discrimination legislation that covers both direct and indirect discrimination. The adoption of such a framework is, though, likely to be rejected by France, which eschews policies formulated in 'race-related' terms.

Despite these differences there are areas of policy where EU initiatives could make a difference. A 'Resident's Charter' could extend the rights of free movement to currently excluded third-country nationals. A Resident's Charter is particularly relevant when it is remembered that many so-called third-country nationals were, in fact, born in an EU member state, but are not citizens of it. The position of many Turks in Germany is a good example of this. A second area where EU initiatives could make a difference is in respect of anti-discrimination measures. EU member states have been swift to denounce racism and xenophobia via grand declarations. These declarations, though, do not have legal effect. Where anti-discrimination provisions have been incorporated into the Treaty – via a new Article 6a – there are limitations. The new Treaty article empowers the Council, acting by unanimity, on the basis of a proposal from the Commission and after consulting the European Parliament, to take appropriate action to combat discrimination based on sex, racial or ethnic origin, religion or belief, age or sexual orientation. Article 6a does not prohibit discrimination in the way that Article 6 forbids discrimination on grounds of nationality. Rather, it enables the Council to adopt measures to deal with discrimination. Article 6a is, therefore, a power conferring rule that is unlikely to apply to third country nationals.

Problems with representation of migrant interests also arise as a result of the sheer diversity of migrant-origin communities across Europe. The Commission-sponsored European Community Migrants Forum (ECMF) was established in 1986 in a bid to co-opt migrant opinion and produce some input – albeit limited given the constrained role of the Commission itself – into decision-making processes. However, a problem for the ECMF is that its name renders it unacceptable to many people of migrant origin who are in fact citizens of the country in which they reside. The problems for citizens of immigrant origin are often associated with exercise of citizenship rights rather than with access to national citizenship, or the rights associated with long-term residence (known as 'denizenship').

Conclusion

The development of EU policy responsibilities for immigration related issues has not been accompanied by the opening of political opportunities for groups seeking to represent the interests of migrants and their descendants. The structure of political opportunity is closely related to the emergent institutional structures put in place to manage immigration-related issues. It is also framed by a broader social context which contributes to marginalisation of migrant interests by delegitimising migrant participation as a result of, for example, racist ideologies.

The immigration policy structures that have been put in place at supranational level emphasise control of numbers of immigrants and concentrate decision-making competence in the Council of Ministers with unanimity as the basis of decision-making. Supranational level allies for groups seeking to represent the interests of migrants are limited. Even though the Commission and European Parliament may express concern about the rights and social position of migrants and their descendants, their legal power in these areas is very limited. So, even though research has shown that the extension of EU regulatory capacities can prompt protection of interests that might be neglected by national governments, the characteristics of EU immigration policy suggest that scope for 'policy entrepreneurship' is limited.

Limitations on representation of migrant interests – the democratic deficit, the limited role of supranational institutions and the organisational weakness of migrant interest groups – suggests that pressure for a broader notion of EU immigration policy which combines measures to restrict immigration with steps to promote better integration of migrants and their descendants will be difficult to exert. A 'Resident's Charter' and anti-discrimination provisions with direct effect are areas where EU competence could improve the social position of migrants and their descendants. Interested observers would be well advised not to hold their breath while waiting for developments to occur. In the years to come, EU member states are more likely to be concerned with the migration implications of enlargement to central and eastern Europe than they are with measures to promote better integration of migrants and their descendants. The focus on restriction within existing institutional structures appears likely to crowd out a more broadly focused policy.

Notes

1   The recent politicisation of the asylum issue, particularly since the increase in east-west flows following the end of the Cold War, has meant that the 'immigration issue' has been broadened to include asylum-seekers. This is in the sense that many asylum-seekers are seen as being disguised economic migrants seeking to avoid the immigration legislation put in place since the mid-1970s. Asylum-seekers are, of course, not immigrants *strictu sensu*, because movement is not voluntary. The point is that they are widely perceived as part of the 'immigration problem' that EU policy seeks to address.

2   On this point see I. Katznelson, *Black Men, White Cities: Race, Politics and Migration in the United States 1900-30 and Britain 1948-68*, London, Oxford University Press, 1973.

3   For an elaboration see J. Crowley, 'Immigration and the politics of belonging: some theoretical considerations' in A. Favell and A. Geddes (eds), *The Politics of Belonging: Migrants and Minorities in Contemporary Europe*, Aldershot, Ashgate, 1998 forthcoming.

4   On the development of agenda-setting capabilities see G. Garrett and G. Tsebelis, 'An institutional critique of intergovernmentalism', *International Organization*, Vol. 50, 1996, pp. 269-99. On the opening of 'gaps' in member state control see P. Pierson, 'The path to European integration: an historical institutionalist analysis', *Comparative Political Studies*, Vol. 29, 1996, pp. 123-63.

5   On the EU's democratic deficit post-Maastricht and its relation to immigration policy see A. Geddes, 'Immigrant and ethnic minorities and the EU's democratic deficit', *Journal of Common Market Studies*, Vol. 32, 1995.

6   For a particularly strong statement of this perspective on fortress Europe see the special issue of *Race and Class* entitled *Europe: The Wages of Racism*, Vol. 39, 1997.

7   These perspectives are developed in W. Cornelius, P. Martin and J. Hollifield, *Controlling Immigration: A Global Perspective*, Stanford, Stanford University Press, 1994.

8   S. Castles, 'Migrants and minorities in Europe. Perspectives for the 1990s: eleven hypotheses' in J. Wrench and J. Solomos (eds), *Racism and Migration in Western Europe*, Oxford, Berg, 1993.

9   C. Joppke, 'Asylum and state sovereignty: A comparison of the United States, Germany and Britain', *Comparative Political Studies*, Vol. 30, 1997, pp. 259-98.

10 M. Baldwin-Edwards, 'The emerging southern European immigration regime: some reflections on implications for southern Europe', *Journal of Common Market Studies*, 1997 forthcoming.

11 There is quite an extensive literature in this vein going back for over 20 years. For particularly influential statements see S. Castles and G. Kosack, *Immigrant Workers and Class Structure in Western Europe*, London, Oxford University Press, 1985, 2nd edn; S. Castles, H. Booth and T. Wallace, *Here for Good. Western Europe's New Ethnic Minorities*, London, Pluto Press, 1984; M. Castells, 'Immigrant workers and class structure in advanced capitalism: the Western European experience', *Politics and Society*, Vol. 5, 1975, pp. 33-66; F. Bovenkerk, R. Miles and G. Verbunt, 'Comparative studies of migration and exclusion on the grounds of "race" and ethnic background in Western Europe: a critical appraisal', *International Migration Review*, Vol. 25, 1991, pp. 375-91.

12 G. Freeman, 'Modes of immigration politics in liberal democratic states', *International Migration Review*, Vol. 29, pp. 881-902.

13 J. Hollifield, *Immigrants, States and Markets*, Cambridge, Mass., Harvard University Press, 1992.

14 G. Marks, L. Hooghe and K. Blank, 'European integration in the 1980s: state centric v multi-level governance', *Journal of Common Market Studies*, Vol. 34, 1996.
15 Pierson, op. cit.
16 On the structure of political opportunity and its application to the EU see S. Tarrow, 'The Europeanisation of conflict: reflections from a social movement's perspective', *West European Politics*, Vol. 18, 1994.
17 D. Curtin, 'The Schengen protocol: attractive model or poisoned chalice?', *Statewatch*, May–June 1997, pp. 18–9.
18 Curtin, op. cit., p. 19.
19 S. Verba and J.-O. Kim, *Participation and Political Equality: A Seven Nation Comparison*, Cambridge, Cambridge University Press, 1978.
20 G. Majone, *Regulating Europe*, London: Routledge, 1996.
21 European Parliament, *Committee of Enquiry into Racism and Xenophobia. Report on the Findings of the Enquiry*, Luxembourg, Office for the Official Publications of the EC, 1991.

11 A Concept of European Union Citizenship: Problems and Possibilities[1]

JO SHAW

Introduction

The loyalty of citizens to a single political authority can no longer be taken for granted. In a world with high levels of migration, complex political and economic interdependencies, new political formations and structures of government at subnational, national and international level, global telecommunications and mass media, and an increasingly splintered notion of personhood which makes 'universal citizenship' difficult to envisage, this loyalty may need to be competed for by states, governments and other political authorities.[2] This contention is particularly strong if it is applied in the context of citizenship of the European Union, a legal concept introduced by the Treaty of Maastricht (or Treaty on European Union). This Treaty brought about crucial amendments to the Treaty of Rome establishing what is now known as the European Community, especially in the arena of 'political union', as well as the perhaps better known developments in relation to Economic and Monetary Union and the introduction of a single currency. Our focus of interest in this chapter is Union citizenship, which brings about a new level of complexity in relation to the constellation of identities within Europe, if only because at its most basic it decouples the link between nation and citizen and establishes an embryonic and as yet largely unexplored new relationship.

Citizenship of the Union has been established by constitutional *fiat*, through the medium of Treaty provisions signed, ratified and consequently formally accepted in full by all the member states of the EU (Part Two of the Treaty – Articles 8–8e EC). It will receive further constitutional affirmation when, as anticipated, the Treaty of Amsterdam, agreed in June 1997 and formally signed on 2 October 1997, is ratified and comes into force.[3] The new Treaty confirms the existence of the status of Union citizen, as *complementary* to national

230

citizenship. Notwithstanding this *complementarity*, important rights and duties are contained in these Treaty provisions – and in certain derivative legislative instruments adopted by Council of the EU – on matters such as free movement, voting in European parliamentary and local elections, consular and diplomatic protection and petitions to the European Parliament and applications to the European Ombudsman. Compliance with these principles – if only at the formal level – has largely been brought about through implementation of these legislative instruments at national level by the member states[4] or through necessary EU-level innovations such as the appointment of the Ombudsman. However, whatever the character of these rights in legal or constitutional terms, their very existence does not in itself establish any claim to citizens' loyalty on the part of the European Union or European Community. The legal structures do not bring about a *community* or *union*[5] of those persons covered by the legal definition of citizenship of the Union – namely nationals of the member states. In other words, while the legal structures certainly establish a formal *vertical* relationship between the EU structures of government (the EU 'polity-in-the-making') and the class of Union citizens, we can derive no assumptions from this about the nature or existence of the *horizontal* relationship (e.g. sense of cultural identity, of nationhood or of civic obligation) between those citizens which binds them together.[6]

It is entirely understandable (if not predictable) that a form of citizenship would take root in the EU legal order in the 1990s, both because of internal preoccupations with the affective and political dimensions of integration and because of external concerns with the continuing relevance of 'citizenship' in the (post)modern world against a paradoxical background of simultaneously increasing globalisation (including cultural globalisation) and sharpening senses of regional identity and ethno-nationalism. At the same time, it is equally clear that the EU's engagement with concepts of citizenship could never be a simple and straightforward adoption and application of existing concepts developed within the forum of the nation state and nation state-building, once the full historical legacy of citizenship is acknowledged. The recognition of that legacy demands, as we shall see, the acceptance of citizenship as a contested domain in both the political and the intellectual senses of the term.

Thus, attempts by the EU institutions, in particular the Commission, to 'compete' directly for the loyalty of citizens by seeking to construct some form of 'European identity' by the top-down imposition of symbols of statehood such as a 'European' anthem or flag have generally been doomed to failure or, worse, derision and the accusation that public money is being needlessly wasted. On the other hand, more sophisticated, and also successful, attempts to ginger up a sense of 'Europeanness' can be found especially in the domain of education, where funding programmes have proved exceptionally popular and have encouraged widespread mobility of students and staff in universities. Ultimately, however, European citizenship cannot offer a simple panacea for other inadequacies of the 'European project', such as the lack of democracy or a sense of remoteness from the European Union political institutions which have led to widespread discontent and alienation in many member states. This is because citizenship, while a popular concept in both political and intellectual discourse, is itself a multi-textured and intensely contested concept, offering a many-faceted set of lenses through which to observe aspects of the 'human condition'. As such, it offers one way of understanding or postulating, for example, the balance between wealth creation based on individualism and social protection based on social and economic solidarity, or the relationship between humankind and the environment.

The story of citizenship is intimately linked to the story of the emergence of the nation state as a dominant form of political organisation. A legal concept of 'nationality', more or less loosely connected to an ethnic sense of the 'nation', is frequently invoked to distinguish between the citizen insiders and the alien outsiders. But the formal legal concept is an inadequate description of the meaning of 'citizenship' as it is currently constituted. In the late twentieth century, the discourse of citizenship is used almost as often as a (sociological) framework for understanding and investigating the extent to which individuals can lay claim to full membership of an (economic) society, bearing in mind the increasing crisis of the modern welfare state, or as an (anthropological) framework for understanding psychosocial concepts of identity, as it is in relation to concepts of nationalism. Similarly, it is clear that concepts of 'social citizenship' are less obviously connected to the vocation of a particular nation state, but they too are highly controversial. In that context, in particular, the degree of contestation within citizenship has increased as it is used as a vehicle for argument both by those seeking the recognition of difference and by those whose primary reference point is a concept of equality. The plasticity of citizenship allows it to be reconceptualised to incorporate elements of both universalism ('we are all equal') and difference ('equality cannot be allowed to mask the fact that we are divided by race, gender, ethnicity, religion, etc. as well as unified by our personhood'). All of these insights reinforce the highly complex nature of citizenship as a prism or lens through which to examine aspects of the human condition and suggest that any given notion of citizenship cannot simply be transplanted from one economic or political location to another without full regard to context.

The objectives of this chapter are to present in brief terms the nature and scope of citizenship of the Union, as a legal construct (Section II), focusing upon its emergence in the Treaty of Maastricht and its implementation hitherto. Working outwards from this construct, I shall then present a critical account of both the problems and the possibilities which are associated with citizenship when applied in the EU context (Section III). The discussion of problems will concentrate upon the limitations inherent in discussing citizenship as an object of study, if no account is taken of the very specific conditions offered by the dynamic project of 'integration' within which Union citizenship has emerged and is now developing or of the essentially contested nature of citizenship which demands a critical approach. The discussion of possibilities concentrates on understanding citizenship as having a context-specific meaning, as a potential lens for aspects of the 'European condition' and indeed, as a useful vehicle for explicating certain fundamental problems of polity-formation in the EU context. In particular, its utility can be seen in relation to issues such as democracy, legitimacy and accountability, the status of individuals and individual rights, and the efficiency and efficacy of government. In that sense, citizenship is deployed less as an object of study in itself and more in view of the methodological richness and diverse theoretical heritage that citizenship studies in general can offer. The final section outlines in summary form an approach to citizenship of the Union which is sensitive to the rich heritage of both citizenship studies and integration studies. Space precludes both detailed discussion of the legal content of citizenship of the Union as it currently stands and detailed empirically based explication of how the model set out in Section IV might operate within the EU.[7]

The Nature and Scope of Citizenship of the Union

Citizenship of the European Union finds formal 'constitutional' expression in Part Two of the EC Treaty which sets out the two classic elements of citizenship, namely a definition of membership which allows the identification of the class of citizens and statements constituting the citizen as holder of rights and bearer of duties. Thus Article 8 EC provides:

1. Citizenship of the Union is hereby established. Every person holding the nationality of a Member State shall be a citizen of the Union.
2. Citizens of the Union shall enjoy the rights conferred by this Treaty and shall be subject to the duties imposed thereby.

Articles 8a–8e set out in more detail what are the principal rights associated with Union citizenship. There is in fact no further reference to duties and that aspect of citizenship – ordinarily understood in a broader citizenship theory context to be a key element of how individuals are constituted as sovereign within a given polity – remains wholly obscure as yet. Principal amongst these rights are freedom of movement and consequential rights of residence for EU citizens, rights to consular and diplomatic protection, voting and standing rights in local and European Parliament elections, and political rights of access to the EU institutions and the European Ombudsman. However, not all citizenship rights are clustered in the citizenship section of the Treaty; in addition, they are to be found in other provisions of the EU Treaties,[8] in the case law of the Court of Justice where rights – especially free movement and nondiscrimination rights – have been formulated, restated or reinforced, and in secondary legal instruments adopted by the EU institutions.

One reason for this complex legal structure is that citizenship was not in truth a policy innovation of the Treaty of Maastricht. The contribution of that Treaty was, of course, the introduction of the formal provisions presented here, which were included after extensive and important debate during the Intergovernmental Conference on political union which concluded in 1991, a debate which was initiated principally by a Spanish Memorandum on citizenship. Behind that Memorandum and that constitutional move, there lay, in truth, a developing 'practice' of citizenship policy, extending over a period of 20 years, which was to be found principally in the activities of the Court of Justice and the European Commission.[9] This has seen a gradual solidification of the resources of citizenship from 'mere' ideas into concrete policy outcomes with legal force. Hence the clustering of certain rights in Part Two of the EC Treaty lies over an existing framework of legal rules and policy-making activities deeply embedded in the day-to-day practices of the EU institutions.

One might usefully summarise the *status quo* of Union citizenship rights by reference to the tripartite grouping of citizenship rights suggested by T.H. Marshall[10] and adopted by many writers since then: civil rights, political rights and social rights. As will be apparent, in the EU domain these rights appear as something of a patchwork; moreover the pattern is so far incomplete and lacking in a certain degree of coherence. Although what follows is not a complete restatement, but merely highlights some key features of citizenship rights in the EU context, it is nonetheless an inclusive approach in its coverage of the varieties of source of citizenship rights. It has regard to the full range of EC law and policy, allowing us in turn to flesh out the 'thin' or 'minimal' statements in Part Two of the EC Treaty, employing a form of contextualisation within the framework of a 'thicker', 'maximal' vision of what it is to be a full 'member' of the EU under the legal, political and socioeconomic orders of the EU.[11] That contextualisation forms an important stepping stone towards the interpretation of Union citizenship suggested in Section IV.

Civil Rights

The civil rights of EU citizens are primarily constituted through the existence of the European Community as a 'community of law'. So, according to Deidre Curtin;[12] 'the unique sui generis nature of the Community, its true world-historical significance [is constituted by its character] as a cohesive legal unit which confers rights on individuals.'

It is customary to credit the European Court of Justice with the achievement of 'constitutionalising' the EC Treaties, principally by upholding the authority of EC law in relation to national law. Thus EC law is superior to national law, and takes effect within the national legal orders as a superior and autonomous source of law such that individuals can very often derive individual justiciable rights from provisions of EC law which national courts must uphold. This process of 'constitutionalisation' has assisted in the institution of a 'rule-of-law' ideology within the European Community, allowing partisans of the process of integration to point to the extent to which, and the length of time for which, the EC and now the EU has resembled a developed federal system, within which respect for the law and a settled hierarchy of norms with EC law at the apex of the pyramid is paramount. Other key elements have included the development of a jurisprudence of fundamental rights, and the elaboration of key principles such as that contained in Article 6 EC which prohibits (within the scope of competence covered by the EC Treaty) discrimination on grounds of nationality against nationals of member states. Furthermore, the underlying market principles of EC law, in particular the free movement of persons, have been elevated to the status of 'fundamental' right. Of course, the message that this delivers is a little mixed since it creates a confusion between the idea of the 'market citizen', the *Marktbürger*, who is a limited figure of the economic sphere, and the 'true' citizen who must be sovereign within a democratic political system.[13]

In other words, the question remains whether the extent of preoccupation with the civil rights of citizens of the Union has not been simply driven by the twin pillars of the logic of the rule-of-law and integration teleologies pursued by the Court of Justice and the logic of the market framework of the treaties.

A significant change may come about once the Treaty of Amsterdam is ratified and brought into force, because this will create the possibility for the Council of the EU to adopt – albeit in relation only to the spheres of competence covered by the EC Treaty itself – measures guaranteeing a comprehensive right to nondiscrimination on grounds of sex, racial or ethnic origin, religion or belief, disability, age or sexual orientation.[14]

Political Rights[15]

It is well known that many of the elements of 'political structure' in the EU lag way behind the relatively sophisticated edifice of the legal system. Both the practice of democracy, and the associated political rights for citizens, remain pale shadows of the national 'versions' of democracy. The EC Treaty itself concentrates upon limited electoral rights in local and European parliamentary elections, and upon forms of nonjudicial access to the political institutions through the medium of petitions and complaints. Democratic participation in the form of European Parliament input into legislative decision-making has been growing at a steady rate, but the absence of a cross-European culture of political parties maintains a dislocation between the laudable work of MEPs to ensure democratic accountability and the basis upon which people actually vote in European parliamentary elections.

A key area of development is that of transparency, especially the right of access to the documents of the EU institutions. Initiatives of a non-constitutional nature arising particularly out of the post-Maastricht malaise have created the opportunity for actions to be brought in the two EU courts by individuals, and indeed by one member state, with a strong culture of openness in government (the Netherlands).[16] Judicial developments have seen the Court declaring in Netherlands vs Council that:

> The domestic legislation of most Member States now enshrines in a general manner the public's right of access to documents held by public authorities as a constitutional or legislative principle.
>
> In addition, at Community level, the importance of that right has been reaffirmed on various occasions, in particular in the declaration on the right of access to information annexed (as Declaration 17) to the Final Act of the Treaty on European Union, which links that right with the democratic nature of the institutions. Moreover, (...) the European Council has called on the Council and the Commission to implement that right.[17]

To an extent, that concern will be mirrored in the new post-Amsterdam Treaties.

Article A TEU[18] will provide for decisions to be taken as 'openly as possible' and new provisions in the EC Treaty,[19] while avoiding taking the key step of announcing a constitutional 'citizens' right to freedom of information, provide for access to European Parliament, Council and Commission documents subject to general principles which will allow the Council to continue to protect the secrecy of much of its business by invoking the 'public interest'.

Social Rights

At first blush, in view of the rather fragmentary 'social dimension' of the EU, one might be tempted to conclude that the social rights of EU citizens are exceedingly sparse. However, if one reads social citizenship in the EU against a broader canvass of socioeconomic citizenship this allows a revisioning of social rights of citizenship in three parts: market citizenship, industrial citizenship and welfare citizenship. Perhaps the strongest message of a review of social citizenship rights in the EU is how the market order established by the framework of 'fundamental freedoms' to be found in the EC Treaty simultaneously both empowers and constrains the EU citizen. It offers new possibilities and rights in relation to the domains of employment, production and consumption, where the exercise of individual 'choice' can in some senses be seen as contributing to the process of building the EU as a political as well as economic entity. But it also constructs a limited market-oriented picture of the citizen in which welfarist principles find it hard to establish a foothold in hostile territory. For instance, in relation to sex discrimination law – long lauded as a 'success' of EU social policy – the Court of Justice draws a stark distinction between employment related discrimination, and issues which arise directly out of (traditional) divisions of labour within the domestic household or the family.[20]

At the same time, the rhetoric of social policy remains strong. The Commission is a forceful proponent of the idea of a 'European Social Model';[21] moreover, the 1996 report of the independent *Comité des Sages* on a 'Europe of civic and social rights' also contains a powerful defence not only of the need for such rights in a 'People's Europe' but also of the empowering nature of bottom-up processes of constitution-building in which individuals and social groups are involved in the formulation of key statements of citizens' rights.[22]

Problems and Possibilities of a Concept of Union Citizenship

This section presents some of the difficulties often encountered in studies of citizenship in the EU context, leading to a discussion of possible ways of overcoming the conceptual obstacles to a fuller account of Union citizenship.

The approach so far taken in this chapter has been essentially descriptive of the legal rights of EU citizens – with elements of normativity and prescription in circumstances where I have seen fit to suggest what EU citizens rights *should* be. In terms of approach, a contextualised perspective has been adopted, with legal rights placed in a broader context of the overall political and socioeconomic systems of the EU. However, it is difficult for any work on Union citizenship to go beyond the level of description or contextualised description without a critical reading of how Union citizenship should be conceptualised. This limitation is evident whether the descriptive focus is upon the implications of the nationality referent for Union citizenship in Article 8 EC which depends upon the legal and constitutional systems of the Member States, upon the centrality of the right of free movement and its market origins (Article 8a EC with links to provisions such as Articles 48 and 52 EC), or upon the detailed operationalisation of the political rights of petition or complaint or the electoral rights provided for elsewhere in Part Two of the Treaty.

Critical work on Union citizenship thus far has tended in two directions. It has offered either a critique of the narrow terms of the definition of 'who is an EU citizen' and in particular the exclusion of lawfully resident third country nationals from EU citizenship and consequently rights of free movement, or an analysis of the limited scope of citizenship rights such as to lead, for example, to the practical exclusion of certain groups such as non-workers, or gays and lesbians.[23] In truth, work which critically examines the limits of EU citizenship needs to go a step beyond this approach, and acknowledge that a critical concept of citizenship must be deployed from the outset, and not merely as a critical perspective on the scope of Union citizenship. Only then will it be possible to scratch below the surface veneer of discussions of nationality rules and positive legal rights which dominates much mainstream EU citizenship scholarship,[24] especially that appearing in the legal studies domain.[25]

So, for example, one might adopt a theory of constructive citizenship, against the background of the acknowledged indeterminacy in political and social relationships generated by the increasingly uncertain coupling of nation, state and nationalism. From within the domain of political philosophy, Theodora Kostakopoulou[26] suggests seven propositions which uphold her theory of constructive citizenship; of these, perhaps the most important is the one which rejects an essentialist concept of individual identity or foundational communities as the basis for citizenship but suggests instead that the European Union might evolve as a 'community of concern and engagement'.[27] Set alongside this underlying precept are propositions about the need for a problematised politics of 'belonging' or membership, a critical reinvention of the language of rights, the acceptance of a public domain for decision-making and participatory democracy, the upholding of values of social justice, and the awareness of multiple commitments and shifting identities which affect people's abilities to be 'full' and active citizens. Her paper concludes with a call for an open concept of political life which allows constant contestation to be a way of life rather than a deviant practice.[28]

Similarly, Antje Wiener examines the constructive potential of Union citizenship, but from a perspective which uses a socio-historical frame of analysis, drawn from critical social history and critical international relations scholarship, to set out the creeping development and concretisation of the 'resources' of citizenship from ideas into practical policies.[29] The detailed presentation of empirical evidence concerning these policies demonstrates the point at which this approach diverges from the more abstract approach of Kostakopoulou. Wiener's work is grounded in the process of interpreting and explaining the evolution of European integration, from a broad institutionalist perspective on how those policies are made and with a focus on the governmental processes and institutions of a polity-in-the-making.[30] Following closely this methodological and theoretical approach, I would argue that it is important to adopt an approach to interpreting and using a construct of Union citizenship which draws not only upon the critical theories of citizenship, but also upon the contribution of regional integration theory in order to a) understand how and why policies emerge in the EU context and b) to identify the crucial actors and interests within different policy fields and at different levels of policy-making. It is an approach which takes full advantage of the rich theoretical canvasses offered by both citizenship theory and integration theory at the present time.

Reinterpreting Union Citizenship

The first element of the approach centres on theoretical approaches to citizenship which focus on a dialectic of identity and rights, producing a space in which a 'practice' of citizenship is constantly negotiated and renegotiated.

An evocative statement of this position comes from Charles Tilly who identifies 'citizenship as a set of mutual, contested claims between agents of states and members of socially-constructed categories: genders, races, nationalities and others'.[31] This goes well beyond – but is not inconsistent with – the accepted political definition of citizenship as 'full membership of a community'.[32] Tilly's approach has to be read in the light of the overriding principle of equality, although it suggests that 'equality' in conditions of fractured and multiple identities is unlikely to be easy to 'fix' and may in fact be a dynamic rather than a static concept. In terms of the meaning of Union citizenship, it is not so dissimilar to the approach suggested by Michelle Everson who sees this form of citizenship, at this stage of its development, as concerning (equal) rights of participation in 'the institutionalisation of a nascent form of European civil society'.[33] However, it adds to that an additional dimension concerning the formation and negotiation of identity which can, as has been shown, for example, by Raymond Breton, contribute in crucial ways to the formation of transnational polities.[34] As will become apparent, it is assumed in this approach that the community of citizens or members may be 'beyond the nation-state', in other words, that it will be post-national in the sense of rejecting the definitive nature of the national tie. Thus the community in question could be either a 'supranational' or even 'subnational' community, equally as easily as it could be a 'national'. Such a postnational community – especially if it is a supranational community – cannot rely for its cohesiveness on the vocation of the modern nation state to provide for the security, economic well-being and cultural identity of its citizens,[35] or indeed its vocation to claim the loyalty of citizens, but must look elsewhere for such cohesiveness.[36]

Turning to the other side of the dualism of identity and rights, it is essential to take a broad 'access-oriented' concept of rights in order to bridge the gap between rights rhetoric and reality. 'Access' can provide the strategy to translate formal equality of rights into something approaching substantive equality of outcomes.[37] The importance of the concept of access is apparent whenever discussions arise not only of who has what rights 'in the name of citizenship', but of how and why those rights have come to be defined, and the (participatory or exclusionary) processes which have led to the 'giving' or 'taking' of rights. This suggests an approach to rights and rights discourses in the EU which goes well beyond the formal surface of rights claims before the Court of Justice, or national courts. Rights should not be seen passively, but should be part of the continual contestation or negotiation of identity which goes to the very root of the definition of citizenship applied here.

The second dimension is provided by theoretical approaches to European integration which invite discussion of much the same space, but viewed this time as the dialectic or tension between the grand history-making and constitution-building side of the rise of the European Union, dominated by the sweep of a rhetoric of an 'ever closer Union', and the day-to-day negotiation of policies through the interactions of the institutions, the member states, sub-state governmental actors and non-governmental actors. In focusing on the steady and constant conjunction of constitution-building and policy-making, I would also stress the need to take seriously the rule-of-law bargain which underlies the normative authority of the Union and its legal order.[38] However, this bargain has important institutional dimensions which stretch beyond the Court of Justice, which is so often picked out as the primary protagonist for a centralising concept of integration in law and legal norms; thus it is vital to include also the institutional roles of the other institutions (especially the Commission's policy entrepreneurship), as well as factors such as the routinised processes of policy-making and the learning-by-doing which has characterised the work of those institutions.[39] In sum, the approach to European integration which I have used to develop my understanding of citizenship derives most directly from the use of notions of institutionalism and governance in order to theorise the development of the Union polity.[40]

One insight to emerge from a citizenship thinking which offers an essential background frame for the specific Union context considered here is that many of the concepts of nationality, national identity and nation which underlie the classic 'statist' approaches to the notion of citizenship are in fact plastic in character. What this leaves is a fertile and relatively untouched terrain at the transnational level for institutional innovation, in accordance with a set of principles driven by values of equality, justice, democracy and legitimacy which I would argue must operate in a liberal and pluralistic community. But more fundamentally the analysis also reveals a level of indeterminacy and uncertainty about the precise *causal* relationship between citizenship as an institution and the very existence of stable, identified and cohesive communities. Is it citizenship which constitutes communities, or the reverse? There seems no conclusive position on this question. While it is not at all difficult to specify the significance of the decoupling of nationality and national identity which suggests the need for an emergent 'political' concept of citizenship which could attach to other aspects of identity formation, it is much more problematic to suggest effective and detailed alternatives to the traditional approaches based on nationalism and nationhood, precisely because the notion of a linear progress between institutions and communities has been fatally undermined.

One compromise position might be to suggest a virtuous circle of reciprocal reinforcement between 'postnational' communities and a conception of democratic citizenship incorporating both a sense of membership and a body of substantial rights (including political and socioeconomic rights). This has the advantage of including both a 'top-down' perspective of citizenship as a set of constitutionally given rights, and a 'bottom-up' perspective which acknowledges citizenship as one practical response to citizens' claims, incorporating also the imperative of identifying and understanding how these claims can be transformed into 'rights' in the EU context.[41] It can be shown that the formal institution of citizenship conceived in these terms can and does reinforce the sense of community, but also that other policy instruments which likewise feed into strengthening the community (for example – applying this insight to the Union policy on education and training for migrant workers and their families and the rights which thereby arise) can help to make the existence of any given form of membership more meaningful for that community of Union citizens. As I have already noted, there is a close parallel between the 'space' or 'tension' emerging from the juxtaposition of 'top-down' or 'bottom-up' approaches to constitutionalism and the role thereby envisaged for the citizen, and the 'space' between moments of 'constitution-building' (which occur spasmodically) and the 'day-to-day politics' which marks the characteristic mode of governance in the Union. The precise location of these 'spaces', and their articulation through a form of citizenship which is simultaneously both ideal-type and historically embedded material practice, represents the unique vocation of the citizenship figure in the Union.

It is easy to see how an agenda for further investigation can emerge from these ideas about citizenship and constitutions, and the juxtaposition of dual arenas of constitution-building and day-to-day politics. Let us take just two key areas of contestation for the Union citizenship: the issue of participation, and the issue of membership.

Turning first to participation in processes of constitution-building, we see that these processes are particularly important, for they embody also the symbolic dimension of the Union. They represent much of the substance of the Union's claim to legitimacy. In turn, they must, therefore, enshrine the recognition of the status and the claim of the citizen. Yet within the Union, participation in that form is formalised only in the context of ratification procedures for new Treaties (e.g. in referendums). Citizens are not directly included in the constitution-making forum itself, the Intergovernmental Conference, where they are represented instead by their governments who have not necessarily been elected upon a platform of articulated negotiating premises but by reference to national electoral preoccupations. As to participation in day-to-day policy-making in the Union, here it is the banalities of the well-known 'everyday' democratic deficit[42] which threaten constantly to disempower the citizen.[43]

A second area of contestation is the dilemma of membership in the Union citizenship context. On one hand, we have the constitutional formalism of Article 8, which restricts 'membership' to nationals of the member states. Is it this formalism which truly defines the scope of membership, or the deeply embedded market structures underpinning the practices of EC law which restrict unfettered access by non-workers and by certain categories of workers or their families (e.g. gay and lesbian partnerships) to 'full membership' of a EU (market) polity? Or perhaps, rather than in the arena of market citizenship, is it through the practice of 'claiming' openness in EU decision-making, especially that in the Council, that the constitution of the Union citizen will truly emerge?

Conclusions

My conclusion from this analysis is that citizenship of the Union – as a historically, geographically and culturally contingent institution, but one perhaps capable of offering a new postnational model for citizenship – can only be fully understood by reference to *both* the broader theory of citizenship, *and* situation-specific ideas about European integration (including the legal dimensions of integration) which stress the dynamic, open-ended nature of that process. It is the latter alone which allow us to see citizenship not only as a symbolic flag waved from time to time by actors such as the Commission, the European Parliament and even the member states, but also as one facet of the day-to-day policy-making activities of all those institutions in which 'rights' represent an important concrete output. This means that any attempt to draw up all or part of a balance sheet of citizenship rights drawn not only from Treaty provisions, but also from diverse 'hard' and 'soft' law instruments in the various fields of Union policy (including the Second and Third Pillars, as appropriate), is not just an exercise in codification or consolidation, but also a recognition of citizenship as an integral part of the Union polity understood as a dynamic governance structure. This includes understanding the political participation rights of individuals (and social groups) in Union policy-making – so far as they exist – as an aspect of the construction of citizenship in an active sense. However, the approach to rights must be critical, just as a critical concept of citizenship must be adopted. It must be sensitive to the context in which rights might operate, sensitive to the importance of access and, above all, hostile to formalism.

Notes

1　This article draws heavily upon a larger project entitled 'Citizenship of the Union: Towards Post-National membership', *Collected Courses of the Academy of European Law 1995*, Vol. VI, no. 1, The Hague, Kluwer Law International 1997/98 forthcoming; Harvard Jean Monnet Working Paper No. 6/97. Sections of the paper draw heavily upon an earlier manuscript: 'The Many Pasts and Futures of Citizenship in the European Union', *European Law Review*, 22 (December), 1997. Permission to republish material is acknowledged with thanks.

2　M. Hanagan, 'Recasting citizenship: Introduction', *Theory and Society*, 26, 397, 1997.

3　Rewording of Article 8 EC [Article 17 after the anticipated renumbering exercise has been completed].

4　'Real' implementation must, in many cases, be doubted: see Second Report of the European Commission on Citizenship of the Union: http://europa.eu.int/comm/dg15/citizen/citeng.htm.

5　Use of the lower case is intentional.

6　Note, 'The Functionality of Citizenship', *Harvard Law Review*, 110, 1814, 1997.

7　For further exposition see J. Shaw, 'Citizenship of the Union: Towards Post-National Membership', *Collected Courses of the Academy of European Law 1995*, Vol. VI, no. 1, The Hague, Kluwer Law International, 1997/8 forthcoming; also published as Harvard Jean Monnet Working Paper No. 6/97; ibid., 'European Citizenship: The IGC And Beyond', *European Integration On-line Papers*, Vol. 1, No. 004, 1997 (http://eiop.or.at/eiop/); ibid., 'European Union Citizenship: The IGC and Beyond', 3 *European Public Law*, 413, 1997; ibid., 'The Many Pasts and Futures of Citizenship in the European Union', 22 *European Law Review*, December, 1997; ibid., 'Interpreting European Union Citizenship: A Contribution to European Identity?', 61 *Modern Law Review* (1998, forthcoming).

8　Perhaps the most significant of these is Article 6 EC [Article 12 EC after renumbering] which provides for nondiscrimination on grounds of nationality, which likewise only protects EU citizens/nationals of the member states.

9　On the development of the practice of citizenship see A. Wiener, *Citizenship Practice: Building Institutions of a Non-State*, Boulder, Col., Westview, 1997; ibid., 'Assessing the Constructive Potential of Union Citizenship – A Socio-Historical Perspective', *European Integration Online Papers*, Vol. 1, No. 017, 1997 (http://eiop.or.at/eiop).

10　T.H. Marshall, *Citizenship and Social Class*, Cambridge, Cambridge University Press, 1950, esp. pp. 28–9. A point of interest is, however, that the development of citizenship rights has not followed the classic linear pattern of civil, followed by political, followed by social. For a fuller audit of EU citizenship rights see Shaw, 'Citizenship of the Union: Towards Post-National Membership', op. cit.

11　Terminology drawn from M. Walzer, *Thick and Thin: Moral Argument at Home and Abroad*, Notre Dame, University of Notre Dame Press, 1994.

12 'The Constitutional Structure of the Union: A Europe of Bits and Pieces', 30 *Common Market Law Review*, 17, 1993, p. 67.

13 See generally M. Everson, 'The Legacy of the Market Citizen' in J. Shaw and G. More (eds), *New Legal Dynamics of European Union*, Oxford, Oxford University Press, 1995.

14 New Article 6a EC [Article 13 EC after the anticipated renumbering exercise has been completed]. For more details see Shaw, 'European Union Citizenship: The IGC and Beyond', op. cit.; E. Szyszczak, 'Building a European Constitutional Order: Prospects for a General Non-discrimination Standard' in A. Dashwood and S. O'Leary (eds), *The Principle of Equal Treatment in EC Law*, London, Sweet and Maxwell, 1997.

15 See further Shaw, 'European Union Citizenship: The IGC and Beyond', op. cit.; H. Lardy, 'The Political Rights of Union Citizenship', 2 *European Public Law*, 611, 1996.

16 Case T–194/94 *Carvel and The Guardian* v. *Council of the EU* [1995] ECR II–2765; Case C–58/94 *Netherlands* v. *Council of the EU* [1996] ECR I–2169; Case T–105/95 *WWF (UK)* v. *Commission*, judgment of 5 March 1997.

17 Case C–58/94 *Netherlands* v. *Council* [1996] ECR I–2169, paras. 34 and 35.

18 Article 1 TEU, after renumbering.

19 Article 191a EC [Article 255 EC after renumbering].

20 E.g. Case 184/83 *Hofmann* v. *Barmer Ersatzkasse* [1984] ECR 3047; see generally T. Hervey and J. Shaw, 'Women, work and care: women's dual role and double burden in EC sex equality law', 8 *Journal of European Social Policy*, no. 1, 1998; G. More, 'Equality of Treatment in European Community Law: the Limits of Market Equality' in A. Bottomley (ed.), *Feminist Perspectives on the Foundational Subjects of Law*, London, Cavendish, 1996.

21 See generally Shaw, 'The Many Pasts and Futures', op. cit.

22 *For a Europe of civic and social rights*, Report by a Comité des Sages chaired by Maria de Lourdes Pintasilgo, Luxembourg: OOPEC, 1996.

23 E.g. C. Lyons, 'Citizenship in the Constitution of the European Union: rhetoric or reality?' in R. Bellamy (ed.), *Constitutionalism, Democracy and Sovereignty: American and European Perspectives*, Aldershot, Avebury, 1996; M. Feldblum, 'Reconfiguring Citizenship in Europe' in C. Joppke (ed.), *Challenge to the Nation-State: Immigraton in Western Europe and the United States*, New York and Oxford, Oxford University Press, 1998; R.A. Elman, 'European Union Citizenship: New Rights for Whom?' in P.-H. Laurent and M. Maresceau (eds), *The State of the Union*, Vol. 4, Boulder, Col., Lynne Rienner, 1997; A. Kiernan, 'Citizenship – the real democratic deficit of the European Union?', paper delivered to the European Community Studies Association Conference, Seattle, Washington, May/June 1997. Cf. R. de Lange, 'Paradoxes of European Citizenship' in P. Fitzpatrick (ed.), *Nationalism, Racism and the Rule of Law*, Aldershot, Dartmouth, 1995, whose critique extends also to a critique of the rule-of-law ideology of the Court of Justice which represents such a crucial driving force within the EU.

24 For a more extended critique of citizenship scholarship in the legal domain see Shaw, 'Interpreting European Union Citizenship: A Contribution to European Identity?', op. cit.

25 Examples of such scholarship include A. Rosas and E. Antola (eds), *A Citizens' Europe. In Search of a New Order*, London, Sage, 1995; C. Closa, 'The concept of citizenship in the Treaty on European Union', 29 *Common Market Law Review*, 1137, 1992; ibid., 'Citizenship of the Union and Nationality of Member States', 32 *Common Market Law Review* 487, 1995; D. O'Keeffe, 'Union Citizenship' in D. O'Keeffe and P. Twomey (eds), *Legal Issues of the Maastricht Treaty*, Chichester: Chancery/Wiley, 1994; S. O'Leary, *The Evolving*

Concept of Community Citizenship, The Hague, Kluwer International, 1996; E. Marias (ed.), *European Citizenship*, Maastricht, European Institute of Public Administration, 1994; S. Hall, *Nationality, Migration Rights and Citizenship of the Union*, London, Graham and Trotman, 1995.

26 D. Kostakopoulou, 'Towards a Theory of Constructive Citizenship in Europe', 4 *Journal of Political Philosophy*, 337, 1996.

27 Ibid., p. 346. Compare the different approaches of J. Habermas ('constitutional patriotism' in 'Citizenship and National Identity' in B. van Steenbergen (ed.), *The Condition of Citizenship*, London, Sage, 1994), J. Weiler ('supranationalism' in Weiler, 'Does Europe Need a Constitution? Reflections on Demos, Telos and the German Maastricht Decision', 1 *European Law Journal*, 219, 1995), and E. Tassin ('public spaces of fellow-citizenship' in 'Europe: A Political Community' in C. Mouffe (ed.), *Dimensions of Radical Democracy*, London, Verso, 1992) to non-ethnic notions of a 'community' of Europeans. So far as each of these (and indeed other) models lack empirical detail, the choice between them seems largely an abstract one at this stage.

28 Cf. Z. Bankowski and E. Christodoulidis, 'Citizenship Bound and Citizenship Unbound', ms. Edinburgh, June 1997: 'a community can only come about in contesting its very constituency and thus forever postponing its fixity'.

29 Wiener, 'Assessing the Constructive Potential of Union Citizenship – A Socio-Historical Perspective', op. cit.

30 See P. Schmitter, 'Is it Really Possible to Democratize the Euro-Polity? And if so, what role might Euro-Citizens play in it?', ms. Stanford, January 1996.

31 C. Tilly, 'Citizenship, Identity and Social History' in C. Tilly (ed.), *Citizenship, Identity and Social History*, Supplement 3, *International Review of Social History*, Cambridge: Cambridge University Press, 1996, pp. 4–6.

32 David Held offers the following definition: 'Citizenship has meant a reciprocity of rights against, and duties towards, the community. Citizenship has entailed membership, membership of the community in which one lives one's life. And membership has invariably involved degrees of participation in the community': D. Held, 'Between State and Civil Society: Citizenship' in G. Andrews (ed.), *Citizenship*, London, Lawrence and Wishart, 1991, p. 20.

33 M. Everson, 'Women and Citizenship of the European Union' in T. Hervey and D. O'Keeffe (eds), *Sex Equality Law in the European Union*, Chichester, Chancery Wiley, 1996, p. 205.

34 R. Breton, 'Identification in Transnational Political Communities' in K. Knop, S. Ostry, R. Simeon and K. Swinton (eds), *Rethinking Federalism: Citizens, Markets and Governments in a Changing World*, Vancouver, University of British Columbia Press, 1995.

35 R. Axtmann, *Liberal democracy into the twenty-first century. Globalization, integration and the nation-state*, Manchester, Manchester University Press, 1996, p. 2.

36 For uses of post-nationalism see D. Curtin, *Postnational Democracy. The European Union in search of a political philosophy*, Inaugural Lecture delivered at the University of Utrecht, April 1997; Y. Soysal, *Limits of Citizenship. Migrants and Postnational Membership in Europe*, Chicago/London, University of Chicago Press, 1994.

37 See generally D. Majury, 'Strategizing in Equality', 3 *Wisconsin Women's Law Journal* 169, 1987; H. Fenwick and T. Hervey, 'Sex Equality Law in the Single Market: New Directions for the European Court of Justice', 32 *Common Market Law Review*, 443, 1995.

38 C. Joerges, 'Taking the Law Seriously: On Political Science and the Role of Law in the Process of European Integration', 2 *European Law Journal*, 105, 1996.

39 L. Cram, 'The European Commission as a multi-organization: social policy and IT policy in the EU', 1 *Journal of European Public Policy*, 195, 1994.
40 See generally S. Bulmer, 'The Governance of the European Union: A New Institutionalist Approach', 13 *Journal of Public Policy*, 351, 1994; P. Pierson, 'The Path to European Integration. A Historical Institutionalist Analysis', 29 *Comparative Political Studies*, 123, 1996; G. Marks, F. Scharpf, P. Schmitter and W. Streeck, *Governance in the European Union*, London, Sage, 1996; M. Jachtenfuchs, 'Theoretical Perspectives on European Governance', 1 *European Law Journal*, 115, 1995; B. Kohler-Koch, 'Catching up with change: the transformation of governance in the European Union', 3 *Journal of European Public Policy*, 359, 1996. For a brief general review, written from the perspective of the relevance of these theories for lawyers, see K. Armstrong, 'Regulating the free movement of goods: institutions and institutional change' in Shaw and More, op. cit., pp. 165–73; for a more extended treatment of new institutionalism and the potential for applying the insights it offers into the integration process to the specific issue of law and legal studies see K. Armstrong, 'New Institutionalism and EU Legal Studies' in P. Craig and C. Harlow (eds.), *Law-Making in the European Union*, London, Sweet and Maxwell, 1997. The concept of socio-historical institutionalism suggested by Wiener (op. cit. may well offer a useful framework for analysis of the broad legal-institutionalist dimensions of Union citizenship.
41 See V. Della Sala and A. Wiener, 'Constitution-Making and Citizenship Practice – Bridging the Democratic Gap in the EU?', SEI Working Paper No. 18, Sussex European Institute, University of Sussex, 1997 (forthcoming in 1997 *Journal of Common Market Studies*).
42 See D. Wincott, 'Institutional Interaction and European Integration: Towards an Everyday Critique of Liberal Intergovernmentalism', 33 *Journal of Common Market Studies*, 597, 1995.
43 See J. Weiler, 'The European Union Belongs to its Citizens: Three Immodest Proposals', 22 *European Law Review*, 150, 1997.

12 Political Identities and Social Struggle in Africa

GRAHAM HARRISON

Introduction

It is the purpose of this chapter to analyse the concept of political identity within the context of the changing social space of the African city. This will be done firstly by considering the location of identity within a broader framework of political and economic change; secondly, by exploring the rise of a kind of 'identity politics' in contemporary African cities; and finally by relating the political phenomenon of ethnicity to identity.

Identity's main claim to distinction is its resonance within 'the personal'; it is affective, and as flexible and multifaceted as the human personality itself. Identity is generated through culture – especially language – and it can invest itself in various meanings: an individual can have an identity as a woman, a Briton, a Black, a Muslim. Herein lies the facility of identity politics: it is dynamic, contested, and complex. However, the value of identity as a flexible and affective unit of analysis is rendered hollow if one unties identity from broader social forces and relations. This dislocation partly explains how analyses of identity politics have gained their contemporary salience, not only with the impact of postmodernism, but also hand-in-hand with many recent 'post-Marxisms':[1] for example, David Bailey and Stuart Hall argue that 'identities are floating ... meaning is not fixed and universally true at all times for all people and ... the subject is constructed through the unconscious in desire, fantasy, and memory'.[2]

Identity politics can only be given its full meaning if it is understood within a broader political economy. In other words, one must start with a *problematic* of identity politics, which is the degree to which the latter reflects, enhances, embellishes, or reworks broader changes in state and class relations. Unless we embrace the postmodern idea that anything except what is apparent (the surface) is a mystification, or worse (an authoritarian attempt at metanarrative), we need to understand identity as a social construct, and as a

248

construct not innocent of class relations. Should we really satisfy ourselves with academic writing such as Thornton's postmodern account of the new South Africa?

> South African identities cross-cut each other in multiple ways and in multiple contexts. There is no fundamental identity that any South African clings to in common with all, or even most other South Africans. South Africans have multiple identities in multiple contexts, depending on factors of expedience, recruitment and mobilisation, and the company one keeps.[3]

The concern of this chapter is to examine identity *politics* in urban Africa. Rather than examine the psychological aspects of identity, or the legislative constructs within which civilian identities are formed, this chapter will understand identity as a social construct: a result of the shared social environment in which a group of people identifies itself as a form of commonality, and which produces this identity partly as a response to that broader social context, partly as an assertion against it. This reflects the basic semantic origins of the word identity: to identify with others, and to assert an identity against others.

This kind of understanding reminds us of debates about that potent and controversial form of identity – national identity – and the degree to which it is created from below or imposed from above. It is wise to be cognizant of both directions: states and broader forces of social and economic change create a terrain in which social groups, not without a degree of innovativeness and with their own cultural and social resources, create meaning and resist, promote, or modify forces of change over which they have, at best, partial control.

Having made these initial comments on the approach to identity taken here, there is a need briefly to explore the academic legitimacy of analysing *African* identities, in a continent which has over 750 million people and a huge diversity of cultures. The justification derives from the specific focus of this chapter: political identities which have emerged from the recent and drastic changes in African political economies. At this level of analysis, the following factors are extremely important:

- African states' origins lie in the colonial imposition of Jacobin nation-state forms;[4]
- post-colonial regimes, for all their significant variations, have pursued one form or other of nationalist modernisation;

- the vast majority of African states have economies based on primary commodity exports – whether oil, copper, cash crops, or fish.[5] Africa's position within the world economy has meant that the influences of global economic change have been similar for almost all African countries;[6]
- most recently, all African states have implemented a package of economic and political reforms, commonly known as Structural Adjustment Programmes (SAPs).

Most often sponsored by the World Bank and International Monetary Fund (IMF), but sometimes 'home-grown', these SAPs are clearly a response to the crisis of post-colonial regimes of accumulation and political rule. Whatever the origins of this crisis, the crisis itself has resulted in a drastic loss of sovereignty for African states, now at the behest of World Bank and IMF debt rescheduling. One can certainly agree that '[t]he extreme dependence of the continent as a whole on external forces has conditioned developments within specific countries and also given Africa a certain uniformity'.[7] It is substantially the case that the historic confluence of these broad social dynamics explains the unstable and impoverished nature of African society today: it is no statistical coincidence that African countries exclusively occupy the lowest 19 places on the United Nations Development Programme's ranking of the human development index in 1997.[8]

The Location of Identity

In African studies generally, there has been a recent shift in emphasis towards ideas such as 'identity', 'contingency', 'indeterminacy' and 'complexity'.[9] All political scientists will recognise these terms as part of the intellectual terrain of poststructuralism. To some degree (but we must be careful here not to construct straw men and women[10]) there is a growing affinity here to postmodernism in African studies which is explicit in the increasingly common usage of the term 'post-colonial': the *post* here is a clear attempt to locate post-colonial studies within the current and enduring declaration of a rejection of the certainties of enlightenment paradigms.

Not all writers explicitly define themselves as post-colonial writers, but one can see a growing area of academic work which can reasonably be defined as post-colonial. This work, as far as African studies is concerned, has emerged principally from anthropology. Two of the most important additions in this regard are an edited volume called *Postcolonial Identities in Africa*, and a special issue of the influential *Journal of Contemporary African Studies*, entitled 'The Politics of Identity'.[11] Whereas, more generally, post-colonial studies has emerged from within literary criticism,[12] the place of anthropology in post-colonial studies of Africa has been to highlight the importance of non-class factors in African societies. The symbolisms and practices of African ethnic societies are not artefacts of a pre-colonial age; nor are they the epiphenomenal manifestations of class struggle; rather, they are real and fundamental facets of the 'lived in world' of Africans.[13]

Furthermore, following from Jean-François Bayart's influential book *The State in Africa: the Politics of the Belly*,[14] the various localised ethnic practices and relations of African society provide a site in which the post-colonial state's authoritarianism is resisted. But this resistance is not 'struggle' in the conventional sense, with its evocations of the modern politics of classes, parties, unions, protests, boycotts and so on. Rather, the localised, ethnic challenge to the state involves a parody of state power, or the appropriation of the state for local ends. This focus opens up space for a more explicit ontology of postmodernism, into which 'games' and 'irony' enter. The irony, according to Werbner, is that Africans conspire in their own oppression; the game of post-colonial politics is that now the *leitmotif* is 'the wink', a less-than-serious expression of 'the baroque style of political improvisation in which everyone indulges'.[15]

The corollaries of post-colonial studies are quite clear: a rejection of the possibility of social struggle defined as organised resistance to oppression, the lack of utility of the concept of class within African societies, and a general hostility towards what the contributors to the *Journal of Contemporary African Studies* call 'exposé analysis': analysis based on the idea that all is not what it seems, that beneath the surface of appearance, there lie important relations and processes which profoundly define the conditions of social life. This (potential) shift in African studies is in fact quite problematic but not entirely unwelcome. Its actual academic purchase is yet to be discerned as it is still embryonic. Furthermore it contains within it two contradictions which thus question the extent to which it should be defined as a new paradigm at all.

Firstly, much writing within the post-colonial literature unequivocally locates itself within a more conventional political economy, very often with Marxist overtones.

Ahmad raises this point within post-colonial literature more generally, arguing that much post-colonial writing eclectically takes Marxist ideas, thus doing violence to the holistic nature of Marxism, but perhaps filling in certain 'gaps' in its own epistemology.[16] In regard to post-colonial studies on Africa, the realities of global capitalism are clearly 'signposted' in many cases. Thus, Werbner mentions, *in passing*, the following:

> With political independence in Africa has come no freedom from the imperial grip, through often, but importantly not always, a change in the alien hands in effective if mediated, command. The ever more pervasive condition is late capitalist domination by Western metropolitan powers, including the transnational corporations and global agencies which are metropolitan based.[17]

After this acknowledgment, two alternative paths are faced: to proceed to ignore the considerations of political economy; or to relate considerations of culture, identity, and even the politics of 'games' and 'irony' to the fact that however nebulous social relations and (self-) portrayals become, they do not exist in a vacuum or develop exclusively from their own dynamic. This chapter will argue for the second 'pathway' by looking at African urban identities. This approach is also of value if one re-reads some of the existing work on African politics.

Post-colonial studies sells itself as a libertarian paradigm in which there is ample scope for indeterminacy, individual agency, contradiction, and various forms of humorous escapism. The currency of these features is that they are supposedly an advance on the austere formulations of various kinds of Marxism in which classes and states are the final and absolute reductions of social reality. This is a most crude retrospective on Marxist political writings on (and in) Africa.

One can see this even in the first radical analyses of Africa in the postwar period: consider Fanon's descriptions of schizophrenia or even 'massive psychoexistential complex[es]'.[18] These socio-psychological terms have resonance in post-colonial studies generally, along with other emphases on existentialism and the individual which can be traced back to Sartre. In fact this continuity is acknowledged by post-colonial writers, many of whom put ideas of the self-reflection of the writer at centre stage: very much the concern of blacks born in the colonised world but living in the imperial realm (Fanon himself, or George Lamming for example).[19] But Fanon's legacy is not merely one of self-reflexivity and unstable psychological conditions. More importantly, it is one of class struggle and national self-determination. Fanon quite clearly privileges these analytical tools over and above the former: it is the arrogance, privilege, and brutality of the 'settler class' which creates the dehumanised (nervous) condition of the 'native' as a social identity. And who can forget Fanon's eloquent invective against the national middle class,[20] peppered with phrases describing the cultural weakness of this class and the way in which it was, in a sense, a parody? But again, it is a parody of the metropolitan bourgeoisie; the parody is one of an over acquisitive, but economically weak, class trying to reach *embourgeoisment* but only achieving a caricature of this position. Fanon was hardly the last radical political writer (academic and/or militant) effectively to use ideas of culture and identity within their expositions of class formation, accumulation, and statehood, as the next section will show.

Identities in Urban Africa

Culture, Identity, and Class

African workers have, in common with almost all workers, never defined themselves in any corporate social form which does not include, in some fashion, a cultural identity. In keeping with E.P. Thompson's emphasis on culture in the English working class or Burawoy's work on American workers and political organisations,[21] African workers' cultural identities are central to their 'classhood'. In this respect, most attention has been paid to the fact that African workers have either recently arrived at the workplace from rural areas, or that they may intend to return to the village after a delimited period of time. Thus, some have argued for the elaboration of a kind of hybrid class based on the 'dualistic' identity of the rural and urban: the worker-peasant, or even the peasantariat.[22] These definitions raise the question of how rural social relations affect social relations in the workplace and vice versa. Others have looked at the way in which rural *and* urban social structures infuse an individual's identity.[23] In urban areas, elations of ethnic affiliation and the use of common African languages are actively reconstructed within the factory as part of a construction of class identity and solidarity.[24] For example, Adesina, in examining the social community of the shop-floor in an oil plant in Nigeria, found 'lateral community work relations' which used cultural relations to galvanise worker solidarity, for example through the use (and transformation) of the yoruba credit system, *Esusu*, to establish a credit cooperative which allowed workers autonomy from state and employer patronage.[25] In another article, Adesina explicitly outlines 'the understanding of work collectivities – as 'cultural repositories of oppositional and protest activities'[26] as follows:

... to the extent that work and non-work relations are bound up in workers' self-awareness, their self-identity is defined by and within specific cultural and experiential contexts. Work relations therefore acquire specific meaning: agrarian idioms, and … allusion to chieftain relations are just two such cases. ….The important thing is that consciousness is a process of constitution within definite socio-cultural contexts.[27]

Thus, post-colonial innovations such as 'hybridity', often following the ideas of Homi Bhabha,[28] or the fanfaring of the salience of culture and ethnicity are themselves hardly removed from political economy. In many parts of Africa a recent proletarianisation (for example in Nigeria, Algeria, or Libya since the oil price hikes in 1973), or the creation of a system of migrant labour, principally to create a flexible and cheap workforce for mining capital (as in the case of southern Africa)[29] have reconfigured cultural identities and created a variety of intermixings of 'the new' and 'the old'. In other words, hybridisation is not so much suggestive of the indeterminacy of political identity and a sign of the 'floating' nature of personality and perceptions of life vis-à-vis 'the social'; rather it is a reflection of the 'hybridity' of African society itself. This process has its own repercussions, but the experience of labour migration, seasonal or permanent, reflects a recent and precarious rural urban migration.[30] The juxtaposition of rural and urban life, the experience of the city, and the possible subsequent return to the village, all provide the social conditions in which subjects (people) internalise a whole range of diverse social rules and relations. In this sense, there is a real *political economy of hybridisation*: the real import of culture within the workplace can only be understood within this defining context. This is the underlying argument of Berry's considerations of migration and class formation in Western Nigeria: both class formation and lineage-based patronage politics define and reinforce each other in a situation of constant mobility and low levels of productivity.[31]

The centrality of the state has been a defining feature of the 'formal' African economy. In all independent African economies, the state has constituted a major employer of wage labour, within the civil service, education, health, and nationalised industries. The public waged sector has predominantly been analysed using ideas of corporatism – i.e. the incorporation of potentially oppositional social groups within a broadly defined state-project in order to shore up state hegemony. With economic decline and World Bank and IMF-dictated structural adjustment programmes, the capacity of the state to maintain its corporatist framework has been reduced drastically, a concern that we will return to.[32]

Petras and Morley[33] identify the same change – a reduction in state corporatism – in Latin America during the 'age of cholera'.[34] They show how this has been related to a rise in interest in urban identity politics: the end of the certainty of state employment within a framework of state led development has created a large fluid and informal society in urban areas. This idea of increasing informalisation is also very prevalent in African studies. In both cases 'informalisation' connotes a whole range of contingent social processes and relations which replace more rigid ideas of corporatism: informal social networks based on common religious or ethnic identity are emphasised; people's strategies of livelihood are portrayed as flexible, dynamic, and interactive. But this rise in urban identities, situationally located in an infinitely complex web of ever-changing social relations, is itself only significant as a manifestation of state and economic restructuring. Petras and Morley argue that the replacement of 'working class' politics with 'identity' politics misses the substantial point that wage workers *as a class* are having their conditions of work restructured. Now families survive on a combination of waged income, petty commodity production, recycling and various forms of 'crime'.

The parallel with Africa is striking, as demonstrated in studies of informalisation in Nigeria. On this subject, Mustafa has developed the idea of multiple modes of livelihood, in which families typically undertake a whole range of activities in order to scrape a subsistence: state employees become taxi drivers in the night, women farm small gardens in urban areas, men and/ or women trade goods in informal markets.[35] Similar processes are at work in Mozambique and Zimbabwe.[36] In fact, wage employment is often central to these variegated survival strategies: state resources are used to support other 'private' activities, or connections with other state personnel business contacts. Thus, one can see the decline of corporatism and the increasing informalisation of the urban economy not as a sign of the decay of the urban working class, but rather of its *reformulation* into a realm of fiscal austerity and speculation. From this perspective, the rise of identity politics has less to do with the 'death of the subject' and more to do with the unceasing attempts of the World Bank and the IMF to squeeze interest payments on debt from debtor states.

Youth

The social category of 'youth' has become the focus of increasing attention recently. The term youth concerns itself with men who have left school but have not started families. Beneath this very broad socio-temporal categorisation, one finds various subsets of youth: the urban unemployed, university students, wage labourers, and peasants. Here we are concerned with the first two categories, manifestly urban forms of youth identity.[37] Growing academic attention given to youth politics in urban Africa is principally a result of the spectacular upheavals in African cities, driven by urban youth groups. It has been the youth who have been at the forefront of anti-dictator street protests throughout the 1980s, for example in Mali.[38] In other cases, youth have been responsible for less evidently political uprisings, involving looting and destruction of property. Each of these cases suggest an important part of youth identity in urban Africa: its association with – or even definition by – violence.

In his 1996 article on 'Youth and Violence' which appeared in *Africa Now*, El-Kenz begins with a greatly revealing and sympathetic case study, of Ibo, an 18-year-old who lives near Dakar, the capital of Senegal. Ibo leaves his village in order to establish his independence and to find a more rewarding way of survival than the austere conditions of agricultural production. In the city, he cannot find any stable employment. His only way of surviving is to take any kind of petty employment which is available. Criminality and violence become part of his life, as he subsidises his income through theft and as he joins one of the street gangs who protect their trading patch from other hawkers (informal traders). He joins an organised protest, not fully understanding the nature of the political grievance. The feeling of empowerment which he had never experienced before, along with the chance to destroy the wealth to which he had customarily to prostrate himself in order to earn a crust, brings him to the forefront of the protest and into direct conflict with the police: 'His eyes are burning from the tear gas, but he has never felt so dignified, or so much a man … Ibo finds himself with stones in his hands that he hurls with all his might at the cars … he has so often cleaned and guarded.'[39] Ibo is shot in the leg, which later has to be amputated. El-Kenz ends the short narrative thus: 'Ibo: a permanent victim of the violence in which he was an actor for one day.'

Youth has always been at the forefront of violent anti-state protest in Africa, and indeed elsewhere.[40] So, why has the youth's presence on the streets increased during the last 10 years? The answer to this question requires that we look at the broader social changes of Africa's cities and the specific impact of these changes on Africa's urban youth. In order to deal with the first concern, we can look to the states of the Mahgrib because they highlight particularly well a broader trend in African social change. The North African states have been through an extreme but not exceptional post-colonial history. In analysing democratisation in the Middle East, Bromley[41] notes the widespread revolutions which overthrew various forms of *ancien régime* and replaced them with secular republican regimes, whose central concern was nationalist modernisation. For Africa, we can easily see Tunisia, Algeria, Libya, and Egypt in these terms.[42] Secular modernisation, and especially the provision of wage employment and social welfare by the state, was the foundation of the legitimacy of the revolutionary regimes. The relative wealth of the North African economies has facilitated a more extensive state-led modernisation compared to sub-Saharan Africa, but the general social programme of modernisation has been a defining characteristic of the whole continent, despite quite limited advances south of the Sahara.[43]

Again, in common with Africa south of the Sahara, the Mahgribian states have undergone severe crisis since the early 1980s. The nature of this crisis is complex, and its interpretation still quite controversial,[44] but its repercussions, at least in one sense, are unequivocal: the crisis of the African state has manifest itself as a crisis in the whole modernising project upon which the state based its legitimacy, or minimally, its right to rule. The Mahgribian states can no longer afford preexisting levels of social provision and subsidy. Protests at the decline in standards of living which the collapse of modernisation has created provokes an increasing recourse to authoritarianism, an authoritarianism which had in any case always accompanied the modernising project.[45] This, then, is the context in which the youth have expressed growing violent opposition to the state in Africa: the increasingly difficult conditions of life and the patent lack of capacity for the regime to address the concerns that economic crisis creates; in a word, the failure of the modernising state. The repercussions of this on the urban youth are easily teased out of El-Kenz's narrative of Ibo, but consider the following passage on the roots of social protest in Algeria.

> From 1985–86, the social situation became explosive ... social inequalities were mounting ... The core problem, however, was that Algerian society has been split into two distinct halves. The haves included those more or less integrated into the ... system. The have-nots were the outsiders. These outsiders live ... on the fringes of the city. Among them, the younger generation live the tragedy of exclusion in a particularly straightforward, brutal fashion. The overwhelming majority are out of school ... Their chances of getting into the productive work chain are slim, because urbanisation no longer goes hand in hand with industrialisation. These people are in 'social quarantine'. Unemployment rates climbed from 16 per cent in 1983 to ... 23.6 per cent in 1989. And these young people make up the overwhelming majority of those counted in these statistics.[46]

This passage clearly argues the particular condition in which the youth find themselves during the crisis of the state. The social trajectory from school to wage employment, which was the cornerstone of social stability during modernisation, has been cut. Urban school leavers, and increasingly graduates, leave the academic institution to face unemployment. The incorporative facets of modernisation have been destroyed as industrialisation has come to a halt. It is the temporal manifestation of the rupture in this process which gives youth identity its contemporary salience. These themes emerge in journalistic reportage:

> They [young men in urban Algeria] speak about lying under *hongra*, a word always on the lips of the young; it implies being both excluded and held in contempt. It means being jobless for years, not having influential relations who can work the system and having abandoned all hope of marriage because there is nowhere to live at a price that can be afforded.[47]

Remaining with the example of Algeria, Salah Tahi[48] notes that the first 20 years of independence were dominated by the 'revolutionary generation', those whose political views were strongly influenced by the anti-colonial struggle and who were accustomed to the state-based modernisation paradigm which, fuelled by oil revenues, prevailed until the mid 1980s. The collapse in this social régime and the impact this has had on the young has given a strong generational edge to the ongoing contestation and conflict over Algeria's future.

Two other themes are worth teasing out of the quotation. Firstly, the economic crisis, and the way it has been dealt with has led to a marked process of social differentiation: an increasingly stark division between the haves and have-nots. This differentiation is reflected in the changing nature of work in urban areas. Recall Ibo's satisfaction in smashing the cars which he usually cleaned. In the absence of wage employment, young men often try to scrape a living by offering their services in some temporary casual way to the elites – as car washers, bag carriers, car guards, or ambient traders of cigarettes and newspapers. In Maputo, capital of Mozambique,[49] the social differentiation and changes in economic activity are clearly visible. There are increasing numbers of young men who spend their days holding up tourist gifts in front of cafés, and each morning in the luxury areas of the city young men walk the guard dogs of the rich (Mozambican and Western) so that the dogs don't foul their owners' garden lawns. These occupations constitute, psychosocially speaking, an extremely degrading way of life for young men whose ideal is to establish the independence and control which a full time waged job would provide. This relates back to the present failure of modernisation, as O'Brien notes: the 'independence generation' grew up in a period of (albeit slow and unstable) economic growth, but the present generation of youth have none of the prospects of economic security which their parents enjoyed. This moves O'Brien to talk of a 'lost generation ... [which] marks the rupture from the relatively comfortable socialisation procedures of the period from 1960 to the late 1970s'.[50]

The second point emerges from the intriguing phrase 'social quarantine'. Here we promptly arrive at the language of the post-colonial. What Chikhi is alluding to is the fact that the youth are in a kind of social limbo: brought into the urban sphere with ideas of education, employment and independence, the impossibility of this future life leads the youth to reject the order of urban life. But this is a highly ambivalent relation: it involves both an aspiration to integrate into the urban formal social system, and its patronage, and a violent attempt to destroy it. The same equivocation is evident in another category of urban youth: students. Student protests have grown alongside the more pedestrian protests of the underemployed youth. Like their unlettered cousins, students have been a strong force behind anti-government protests which have subsequently toppled dictatorships. But whilst challenging corrupt dictatorships, part of the politics of student protests has been to gain access to the very networks of patronage which dictatorships produce. Thus, in Mali, student protests were pivotal in the overthrow of the Traore regime, but in 1993, after multiparty elections, students rioted and sacked the now democratic Ministry of Education in pursuit of better scholarships.[51] Returning to the Algerian example, there is strong evidence that the Islamic militancy (*integralisme*) of the FIS (Islamic Salvation Front) – which had a social base within the university student body – was underpinned by an attempt to redefine access to existing forms of power, rather than overthrow the state form *tout court*.[52]

Broadly speaking, one can see that the collapse of authoritarian modernisation has set in train a whole series of equivocal relations between society and the state, which challenge both the rigid differentiations between state and civil society and ideas of secular change and progress which were the stock-in-trade of most political science on Africa until recently.[53] Young people, both unemployed and underemployed, and students are disillusioned by the apparent failure of modernisation. They find themselves temporally (and unfortunately) situated in a longer term process of economic decline and structural transformation. Their rejection of state politics is a result of their marginalisation within this project, rather than necessarily[54] a result of their disapproval *per se*: Mamdani's retrospective on the political role of the post-colonial African university eloquently outlines its usual uncritical alliance with the régime of the day.[55] To use a metaphor, the student is not pounding on the door of the Ministry of Education in order to destroy the building, he (politically active students are mainly men) is trying to open the door and negotiate a better deal.

Briefly to summarise, the salience of youth identities derives from a broader set of changes. Economic crisis has had a direct and negative impact on the post-colonial sociopolitical project of modernisation. The ensuing ruptures to social life have impacted on the whole of urban society. As outlined above, they are notably part of the context in which the working class has become fractured and informalised. But the particular situation of youth, either leaving school to find employment, dignity and independence, or leaving the university to join the middle classes, predominantly through linkages with the state, gives a peculiarly sharpened twist to the experience of Africa's recent economic decline. Without an understanding of these broader changes, identity politics – involving reference to the age-old conflict between young adults and their parents, or perhaps the rise of a Western consumer culture in African cities – remains an arena of description rather than analysis – that is, identity as a lowest common denominator.

Political Identity and Ethnicity

Ethnicity is a term whose definition is still rather vague and contested.[56] Succeeding the racist nomenclature of 'tribe', with its primordial connotations,[57] ethnicity refers to a social identity formed around shared language, beliefs, ideas of a common history (ancestry), or 'homeland'. This basic empirical categorisation is the lowest common denominator of ethnic identity. Real issues emerge when we take ethnic identity and engage with the events of contemporary African society.

The main application of ethnicity during the late 1960s and 1970s was used to reveal various forms of 'false consciousness'. People's ethnic identity was an expression of other more important social forces. The 'false consciousness' approach can be taken with varying degrees of sympathy,[58] but all approaches couch ethnic identity in negative terms, ultimately as a sign of a lack of 'true' consciousness. These analyses do provide considerable insight into the construction of contemporary ethnicity, but they also tend to reduce those who carry an ethnic identity to an unwitting dupe in the broader forces of class struggle.

For this reason, studies of ethnicity have increasingly looked at this identity in terms of its popularity and 'grassroots' construction, what one might call *l'étnie par le bas*.[59] This kind of rethinking can be found in the special issue of the *Journal of Contemporary African Studies* referred to above, which itself (as a collection of papers from a conference in South Africa in 1995) was born out of a particular set of circumstances. As Wilmsen et al. state, since the end of apartheid – which made 'ethnicity' a dirty word as part of the National Party's racist strategy of 'divide and rule' – academics' understanding of ethnicity (both within and outside of South Africa) has shifted from associations with conflict and oppression, towards potentially legitimate or popular forms of social identity.[60]

One result of the general move away from 'false consciousness' ethnicity is to see ethnicity as both progressive and regressive. Hussein Adam traces a 'plea for social justice' within the rise of 'clanism'[61] in Somalia; Ibrahim distinguishes between the 'ethnicity of oppression' and the 'ethnicity of expression' in Nigeria, something which Osaghae supports in his categorisation of Nigerian 'positive' and 'negative' ethnicities.[62] Importantly, this moves the concept of ethnicity out of the realm of the negative, or even pejorative in more crudely modernist formulations.

A productive approach is competently suggested by Ekeh's work on ethnicity.[63] Ethnic identities in Ekeh's article are fully integrated in the changing political economy of West Africa. Thus, 'tribes' expanded, militarised, collapsed, and reformed as the political economy of the region moved from slaving through to 'effective' colonial occupation, then to independence. But these changes in the political construction and representation of ethnicity interacted with village-level bonds of solidarity which provided a kind of 'social glue' to weather the storms of capitalist modernisation.[64] The importance of this article is that it locates ethnicity within broader forces of historical social change which give ethnic identity much of its content.

Once we understand ethnicity as a part of broader social formations in which states and classes also act, interact, and conflict, the concept is stripped of its peculiarity; rather, it is required that we deconstruct ethnicity itself, as much as one might use ethnicity to deconstruct classes. But this deconstruction does not bring us back to the false consciousness approach, for two main reasons. Firstly, one must recognise the fact that ethnicity can be *popularly* constructed; the point here is that this does not allow us to shy away from investigating it as a potentially contradictory construction. As Wilmsen et al. state:

by deconstructing or desegregating the concept [of ethnicity] we cannot wish it away or pretend to have solved the problem. Historical deconstruction certainly robs ethnicity of the mythic sense of timelessness on which it thrives, but *to say that ethnicity is artificially constructed does not enable us to dismiss it as illegitimate.*[65]

Secondly, we must recognise that the construction of ethnicity is immensely *political*. This might seem like a truism, but if one recalls the 'false consciousness' arguments, one is reminded that this perspective often attempts to reduce ethnicity to a basic economic contradiction, a mask which obscures a process of accumulation or competition. By 'bringing the politics back in',[66] we can evaluate a whole range of political agencies and individual actors whose strategies for aggrandisement (not necessarily concerned with exploitation in the Marxist sense, as much as with enrichment, pure and simple) create significant political forces of their own, often associated with the phenomenon of ethnicity.

We now have the coordinates for an analysis of ethnicity which contextualises ethnic identity within a broader political economy, but does not merely reduce the former into the latter. This is because ethnic *constructions* are undertaken by particular people, often, but not always, of elite social origins who might employ a wide gamut of discourses and political strategies as part of a plan to empower or defend themselves. It follows that the politics of ethnicity is crucial to its existence. This is especially so in two senses: a) the importance of 'ethnic entrepreneurs' within contemporary ethnicity; and b) the centrality of the state within the process of defining ethnic groups.

Mangosuthu Buthelezi, and the manoeuvres of his Inkatha Freedom Party (IFP) during the transition to democracy in South Africa from 1990, is an example of an ethnic entrepreneur *par excellence*. Gerard Maré has revealed how Buthelezi, once Prime Minister of the Kwa Zulu homeland[67] and therefore part and parcel of the apartheid system, revived an old Zulu cultural association (Inkatha) as a platform from which he could elbow himself a position of power within the post-apartheid dispensation.[68] His success in this regard is remarkable: from apartheid lackey, he was, briefly acting president for South Africa in Mandela's absence in late January–early February 1997! Buthelezi's success derived from the way he constructed a discourse of aggressive Zulu nationalism, making selective and distorted references to a grand militaristic Zulu history and mobilising a sense of chauvinistic ethnic pride around the institution of the king. The effect of this ethnic construction, defined and reinforced by violence, was to put Buthelezi in control of a potentially disruptive, perhaps explosive, social upheaval which forced both the ANC and the NP to ensure that Buthelezi was satisfactorily (that is, satisfactory for him) incorporated into the transition so that the threat of serious civil disorder would be avoided. The 'Zuluness' of Buthelezi was reinforced in rural areas through the system of headmen, installed by Buthelezi as part of his homeland administration; it also reproduced itself within the social antagonisms created by apartheid itself, notably in the use of migrant labour hostels near African townships as effective military barracks for young IFP militias.[69] Its other social base existed within the petty bourgeoisie which had consolidated itself within the Kwa Zulu homeland. Furthermore, the Inkatha gangs, whose violence underline the gravity of Buthelezi's bellicose words with blood, were supported by the shadowy apartheid security services.[70]

Even this greatly condensed outline of the emergence of Zulu ethnicity from the mid 1980s makes it clear that it is impossible to understand this phenomenon of Zulu identity without deconstructing it as part of the ongoing reconfiguration of South Africa away from apartheid towards some form of nonracial democracy. This example also shows the importance of ethnic entrepreneurialism – the evocation of a specific kind of ethnic identity as part of a strategy to accumulate political capital.

The second area in which politics is central to ethnicity rests in the way in which the state defines ethnic identity. This is one of the central themes to the history of South Africa since 1948[71] (and Buthelezi can, in this sense be seen as a legacy of this history), but there are many other examples. Mamdani, when analysing the origins of the Rwandan genocide, outlines a model of the 'conquest state',[72] created by German and Belgian colonialism, which, through a whole series of policies and strategies, set in train what Prunier calls 'demographic rule', that is, the rule of the majority Hutu over the minority Tutsi, a mode of rule defined precisely in terms of these ethnic identities.[73] Rwandese society before colonialism was a feudal kingdom in which Tutsi cattle owners extracted rent from Hutu agriculturalists. But there were Hutu chiefs as well as Tutsi chiefs; Tutsi 'Lords' were obliged to honour certain obligations to their 'subjects'; and a Hutu who managed to accumulate enough cattle could become a Tutsi. This shows us that Tutsi and Hutu ethnic identities were fluid, permeable, and interactive.

The stark, polarised logic of ethnic conflict can only be understood as part of the construction of indirect rule by the colonial state,[74] which froze (Prunier uses the phrase 'modernised, simplified and ossified' on page 36) ethnic identities in the institution of the state,[75] making one ethnic group part of the colonial state (Tutsi) and the other the victims of that ethnic group

(Hutu).[76] This ethnic polarisation gained popular resonance in a number of ways: for poor Tutsi during the colonial period, identification with their elites, now integrated into the Belgian colonial state, provided them with a psychological wage[77] which allowed them to consider themselves as existing on the rung above their equally poor Hutu neighbours. Furthermore, the insecurities created by the out-migration of Tutsis and their reinvasion from the eve of independence onwards provoked ethnic violence which contained within it the expanding logic of attack and counterattack. If polarised ethnicity in Rwanda was a result of the colonial conquest state and the internalisation of its polarised identities within Rwandese civilians, the practice of ethnic genocide was very much a state-orchestrated affair. The militias were armed and provided with hit lists by groups with the Army and the CDF (*Coalition pour la Défense de la République*) and MRND (*Mouvement Révolutionaire National pour le Développement*). But beyond the immediate and pre-planned massacre in Kigali, the wider rural genocide which ensued was a result of the constant state propaganda which did no less than invoke Hutu to kill Tutsi. Consider *African Rights'* account of the build-up to genocide:

> Hutu extremism was not a fringe phenomenon: it was cultivated by those holding high government office, to justify and entrench their position. Hence, the extremists had all the state-controlled organs of mass communication at their disposal... These were what made them so powerful. [...] Using a finely tuned propaganda machine, they worked towards a ferocious dream that was to reach its climax in the genocide unleashed in April 1994.[78]

The 'work' involved an entreaty to Hutu's to destroy 'the enemy' or 'the cockroaches' (*inyenzi*), that is, all Tutsi. The genocide was also propelled by a macabre form of patronage politics, in which all Tutsi property would be reallocated to those who participated in the ethnic cleansing. It was the transitional government, the central author of the genocide which allocated the property of the dead in order to establish networks of patronage.[79]

Conclusion: Re-evaluating Identity Politics in Africa

This chapter has related the phenomenon of identity politics in Africa to broader socioeconomic change. But this has not been done in order to explain away identity politics, but rather the reverse: to infuse identities with their full social import, as manifestations of the complex interaction between class struggle,

African cultures, history, and the nature of political competition and empowerment. If we accept these factors as the coordinates around which identities can be usefully investigated we will also avoid a potential pitfall of poststructuralist analysis which is a lack of a theory of agency, and relatedly little to offer for considerations of progressive change and social emancipation. Kwame Anthony Appaiah argues strongly that Africa's post-colonial literature should not become postmodernised precisely out of moral concerns of agency and progressive change, and for this reason he is worth quoting at length in order to end this chapter.

> Far from being a celebration of the [African] nation, then, the novels of the second stage – the postcolonial stage – are novels of delegitimation: rejecting the Western imperium, it is true; but also rejecting the nationalist project of the postcolonial national bourgeoisie. And, so it seems to me, the basis for that project of delegitimation is very much not the postmodernist one: rather, it is grounded in an appeal to an ethical universal; indeed it is based, as intellectual responses to oppression in Africa largely are based, in an appeal to a certain simple respect for human suffering, a fundamental revolt against the endless misery of the last thirty years. …[These writers] are hardly likely to make common cause with a relativism which might allow that the horrifyingly new-old Africa of exploitation is to be understood – legitimated – in its own local terms.[80]

Notes

1   I take this phrase from Norman Geras' meticulous critique of E. Laclau and C. Mouffe, *Hegemony and Socialist Strategy*, London, Verso, 1985 in *New Left Review*, 1987, p. 163.
2   Cited in K. Malik, 'Universalism and Difference: Race and the Postmodernists', *Race and Class*, 37, 3, 1996, pp. 4–5.
3   R. Thornton, 'The Potentials of Boundaries in South Africa: Steps Towards a Theory of the Social Edge' in R. Werbner and T. Ranger (eds), *Postcolonial Identities in Africa*, London, London, Zed Press, 1996. This work compares rather unfavourably with A. Norval, *Deconstructing Apartheid*, London, Verso, 1996, who also employs poststructural approaches, and Saul Dubow's analyses of apartheid, eugenics, and concepts of modernisation which were all generated and contested by academe before and during the apartheid era. See for example S. Dubow, 'Race civilisation and culture: the elaboration of segregationist discourse in the inter-war years' in S. Marks and S. Trapido (eds), *The Politics of Race, Class and Nationalism in Twentieth Century South Africa*, Essex, Longman, 1987; S. Dubow, 'The Elaboration of a Segregationist Ideology' in W. Beinart and S. Dubow, (eds), *Segregation and Apartheid in Twentieth-Century South Africa*, London, Routledge, 1995.

4   B. Davidson, *The Black Man's Burden: Africa and the Curse of the Nation-State*, Oxford, James Currey, 1992.

5   In 1992, the 12 African countries with the lowest GNP per capita relied on primary commodities for 89 per cent of their export revenue. See World Bank, *World Development Report*, Oxford, OUP, 1994, pp. 190–1, as well as B. Sutcliffe, 'Africa and the Economic Crisis' in P. Lawrence (ed.), *World Recession and the Food Crisis in Africa*, Oxford, James Currey, 1986; M. Barratt-Brown, *Africa's Choices: After Thirty Years of the World Bank*, London, Penguin, 1995.

6   There are two partial caveats: changes in the price of oil in 1973 and 1979 differentiated states such as Algeria, Nigeria and Angola from oil importing states; and some countries have achieved a small industrial base, for example Nigeria, Kenya and Zimbabwe. Nevertheless, all of these still rely substantially on primary commodity exports.

7   H. Goulbourne, 'The State, Development, and the Need for Participatory Development in Africa' in P. Anyang' Anyong'o (ed.), *Popular Struggles for Democracy in Africa*, London, Zed, 1987, p. 40.

8   United Nations Development Programme, *Annual Development Report*, New York, UNDP, 1997.

9   See for example, R. Werbner in Werbner and Ranger, op. cit.; A. Mbembe, 'Provisional Notes on the Postcolony', *Africa*, 1992, 62, 1. Compare also the work of McCaskie and Wilks on the pre-colonial Asante. McCaskie rejects Wilks' 'rationalist' use of class and notions of linear progress, embracing instead conceptual tools such as a 'mentalist framework' involving the development of Asante thinking and symbolism and its repercussions on Asante society. Compare T. McCaskie, 'Accumulation, Wealth and Belief in Asante History I. To the Close of the Nineteenth Century', *Africa*, 53, 1, 1983; T. McCaskie, 'Death and the Asantehene: A Historical Meditation', *Journal of African History*, 30, 1989; I. Wilks, *Asante in the Nineteenth Century: The Structure and Evolution of a Political Order*, Cambridge, Cambridge University Press, 1975. The same direction of change is suggested in the recent revisions of the history of the Mfecane (if one can still call it that), and the explicit critique of modernist assumptions by J. Ferguson in 'Mobile Workers, Modernist Narratives: A Critique of the Historiography of Transition on the Zambian Copperbelt', *Journal of Southern African Studies*, 16, 3 and 4, 1990, and reply by Macmillan in *Journal of Southern African Studies*, 19, 4, 1993, and finally Ferguson's last word in *Journal of Southern African Studies*, 20, 4, 1994. On the Mfecane, see the two articles by J.D. Omer-Cooper and J.B. Peires in *Journal of Southern African Studies*, 19, 2, 1993; and the two articles by E. Eldredge and C. Hamilton in *Journal of African History*, 33, 1992.

10 Some emphasise the importance of interaction and self-awareness in their explications of post-colonial, which are surely salutary. See for example S. Arnfred (ed.), *Issues of Methodology and Epistemology in Postcolonial Studies*, Sussex, IDS, 1995, or the editors' emphasis on the term 'post-colonial' as a way of stressing the fact that neo-colonialism is still an important global force, B. Ashcroft, G. Griffith and H. Tiffin (eds), *The Post-colonial Studies Reader*, London, Routledge, 1995, p. xv.

11 Ibid., and *Journal of Contemporary African Studies*, 15,1, 1997.

12 Ashcroft et al., ibid. See also A. Ahmad, 'The Politics of Literary Postcoloniality', *Race and Class*, 36, 3, 1995.

13 The term 'lived in world' is part of the anthropologists' lexicon, and is used for example in England's contribution to Werbner and Ranger, op. cit.

14 J.-F. Bayart, *The State in Africa: the Politics of the Belly*, London, Longman, 1993.
15 R. Werbner, 'Introduction' in Werbner and Ranger, op. cit.
16 A. Ahmad, *In Theory: Classes, Nations, Literature*, London, Verso, 1992.
17 Op. cit., p. 5. See also F. de Boeck, 'Postcolonialism, power, and identity: local and global perspectives from Zaire' in Werbner and Ranger, op. cit., pp. 76, 89, 98.
18 F. Fanon, *Black Skin, White Masks*, London, Penguin, 1993.
19 A thoughtful reflection on Afro-American visions of Africa is S. Lemelle, 'The Politics of Cultural Existence: Pan-Africanism, Historical Materialism and Afrocentricity' amongst other contributions in S. Lemelle and R. Kelley (eds), *Imagining Home: Class Culture and Nationalism in the African Diaspora*, London, Verso, 1994.
20 F. Fanon, *The Wretched of the Earth*, London, Penguin, 1990.
21 E.P. Thompson, *The Making of the English Working Class*, London, Penguin, 1980; M. Burawoy et al. *Ethnography Unbound: Power and Resistance in the Modern Metropolis*, Berkeley and Los Angeles, University of California Press, 1991. On the interaction of language and class, see D. McNally, 'Language History and Class Struggle', *Monthly Review*, 47, 3, 1995; A. Callinicos, 'Postmodernism, Post-Structuralism and Post-Marxism?', *Theory Culture and Society*, 2, 3, 1985.
22 For example, R. First, *Black Gold*, Sussex, Harvester, 1983.
23 An impressive and detailed treatment of this theme is P. Harries, *Work, Culture and Identity*, Oxford, James Currey, 1994.
24 J. Adesina, 'The Construction of Social Communities in Work: The Case of a Nigerian Factory', *Capital and Class*, 40, 1990; F. Barchiesi, 'The Social Construction of Labour in the Struggle for Democracy: the Case of Post-Independence Nigeria', *Review of African Political Economy*, 69, 23, 1996.
25 Adesina, op. cit., pp. 135–6.
26 J. Adesina, 'Worker Consciousness and Shopfloor Struggles: A Case Study of Nigerian Refinery Workers', *Labour, Capital and Society*, 22, 2, 1989, p. 318.
27 Ibid., p. 317.
28 H. Bhabha, 'Signs Taken for Wonders' in Ashcroft et al., op. cit., p. 34.
29 Amongst a voluminous literature, Cohen's overview is most useful. See R. Cohen, *The New Helots: Migrants in the International Division of Labour*, Aldershot, Avebury, 1987.
30 F. Cooper (ed.), *Struggle for the City: Migrant Labour, Capital, and the State in Africa*, Beverly Hills, Sage, 1983; J. Baker and T. Aina (eds), *The Migration Experience in Africa*, Uppsala, Nordiska Afrikainstitutet, 1995; J. Baker and P. Perderen (eds), *The Rural-Urban Interface in Africa: Expansion and Adaptation*, Uppsala, Nordiska Afrikainstitutet, 1992.
31 S. Berry, 'Work, Migration, and Class in Western Nigeria: A Reinterpretation' in Cooper (ed.), op. cit.
32 The effects of fiscal austerity and retrenchment in African societies undergoing structural adjustment are well-documented. See for example, B. Onimode (ed.), *The IMF, World Bank and African Debt*, Vols. 1 and 2, London, Zed Press, 1989; G. Dhai (ed.), *The IMF and the South*, London, Zed, 1991; J.Walton and D. Seddon, *Free Markets and Food Riots: The Politics of Global Adjustment*, Oxford, Basil Blackwell, 1994.
33 J. Petras and M. Morley, *US Hegemony Under Siege*, London, Verso, 1990.
34 J. Petras and M. Morley, *Latin America in the Time of Cholera: Electoral Politics, Market Economics and Permanent Crisis*, London, Routledge, 1992, after Gabriel Garcia Marquez, *Love in the Time of Cholera*.

35 A. Mustafa, 'Structural Adjustment and Multiple Modes of Livelihood in Nigeria' in P. Gibbon et al. (eds). *Authoritarianism, Democracy and Adjustment: The Politics of Economic Reform in Africa*, Uppsala, SIAS, 1992.

36 N. Kanji and N. Jazdowska, 'Structural Adjustment and the Implications for Low Income Urban Women in Zimbabwe', *Review of African Political Economy*, 56, 1993; J. Marshall, *War Debt and Structural Adjustment in Mozambique*, Ottawa, North-South Institute, 1992.

37 The importance of youth in rural conflict in Africa is important enough to merit a footnote referring to some of the literature on this topic. See A. Geffray, *Causa das Armas: Antropologia da Guerra em Moçambique*, Porto, Afrontamento, 1991; S. Ellis, 'Liberia 1989–1994: a Study of Ethnic and Spiritual Violence', *African Affairs*, 94, 375, 1995; P. Richards, *Fighting for the Rainforest: War, Youth and Resources in Sierra Leone*, Oxford, James Currey, 1996.

38 For details, see J. Turrittin, 'Mali: People Topple Traoré', *Review of African Political Economy*, 52, 1992. The relation between violence and student politics is also clearly brought out in Z. Kay Smith, 'From Demons to Democrats: Mali's Student Movement 1991–1996', *Review of African Political Economy*, 24, 72, 1997.

39 All subsequent quotations on Ibo from A. El-Kenz, 'Youth and Violence' in S. Ellis (ed.), *Africa Now: People, Policies, Institutions*, Oxford, James Currey, 1996, pp. 42–4.

40 Consider the inner city riots of the early and mid-1980s in Britain.

41 S. Bromley, 'The Prospects for Democracy in the Middle East' in D. Held (ed.), *Prospects for Democracy: North South East West*, Cambridge, Polity, 1993.

42 Morocco remains monarchical. Of course, the particular conditions which created national-modernising and secular states has to be understood in the context of the expansion and collapse of the Ottoman empire.

43 See M. Doornbos, 'The African State in Academic Debate: Retrospect and Prospect', *Journal of Modern African Studies*, 28, 2, 1991. On the repercussions of the collapse of the modernising state, see S. Ellis, 'Africa After the Cold War: New Patterns in Government and Politics', *Development and Change*, 27, 1, 1996.

44 Amongst the better interpretations in a voluminous literature are P. Lawrence (ed.), *World Recession and the Food Crisis in Africa*, Oxford, James Currey, 1986; M. Szeftel, 'The Crisis in the Third World' in R. Bush et al. (eds), *The World Order: Socialist Perspectives*, Cambridge, Polity, 1987; M. Barratt Brown and P. Tiffin, *Short Changed: Africa in World Trade*, London, Pluto, 1992.

45 See, for example, D. Seddon, 'Bread Riots in North Africa: Economic Policy and Social Unrest in Tunisia and Morocco' in Lawrence (ed.), op. cit.

46 S. Chikhi, 'The Working Class, The Social Nexus and Democracy in Algeria' in M. Mamdani and E. Wamba-dia-Wamba (eds), *African Studies in Social Movements and Democracy*, Dakar, CODESRIA, 1995, pp. 325–6.

47 In the *Economist*, 343, 8021, 1997.

48 M. Salah Tahi, 'Algeria's Democratisation Process: A Frustrated Hope', *Third World Quarterly*, 16, 2, 1995, p. 198.

49 The author researched in Mozambique in 1995 and 1997.

50 C.C. O'Brien, 'A Lost Generation? Youth Identity and State Decay in West Africa' in R. Werbner and T. Ranger (eds), *Postcolonial Identities in Africa*, London 2nd edn, 1996, p. 57.

51 Ibid., p. 65.

52 Salah Tahi, op. cit., p. 215.

53 Even when it became clear that the state-centred modernising project was crumbling, writers still assumed a dualised state-civil society perspective, arguing that society was 'disengaging' from the state. See D. Rothchild and N. Chazan (eds), *The Precarious Balance: State and Civil Society in Africa*, Boulder, Westview, 1988.

54 The qualification 'necessarily' is important here because some political parties and student organisations have opposed authoritarian governments since independence. *Review of African Political Economy* occasionally publishes manifestos and commentaries from these small radical organisations.

55 M. Mamdani, 'University Crisis and Reform', *Review of African Political Economy*, 58, 1993.

56 See e.g., M. Szeftel, 'Ethnicity and Democratisation in South Africa', *Review of African Political Economy*, 60, 21, 1994.

57 See M. Stephen, 'Rwanda: Ethnic Identities and Nationalist Constructions', paper, BISA, Reading University, 1996.

58 M. Shaw, 'Ethnicity as the Resilient Paradigm for Africa: from the 1960s to the 1980s', *Development and Change*, 17, 4, 1986 directly correlates ethnicity to the growth and decline of resource availability. C. Charney, 'Political Power and Social Class in the Neo-Colonial African State', *Review of African Political Economy*, 38, 1987 (the allusions to Poulantzas are purposeful) usefully highlights the vertical nature of ethnic social relations which reduces the possibility for horizontal social organisation with a more clearly redistributionist or egalitarian agenda. S. Amin, 'Democracy and National Strategy in the Periphery', *Third World Quarterly*, 9, 4, 1987 sees ethnic conflict as a result of the Machiavellian strategies of empowerment of the various factions of the comprador ruling class.

59 The use of French here reflects the fact that much of the writing in this vein has come from France.

60 E. Wilmsen with S. Dubow and J. Sharp, 'Introduction: Ethnicity, Identity and Nationalism in Southern Africa', *Journal of Southern African Studies*, 20, 3, 1994.

61 Somali society is divided into clan-families which acts as decentralised autochthonous groups within a broader Somali ethnicity which might be characterised by its pastoral way of life, its language, and its adherence to Islam.

62 H. Adam, 'Somalia: Militarism, Warlordism or Democracy?', *Review of African Political Economy*, 54, 1992; J. Ibrahim, 'Religion and Political Violence in Nigeria', *Journal of Modern African Studies*, 29, 1991, 1; E. Osaghae, *Structural Adjustment and Ethnicity in Nigeria*, Uppsala, SIAS, 1995.

63 P. Ekeh, 'Social Anthropology and Two Contrasting Uses of Tribalism in Africa', *Comparative Studies in Society and History*, 32, 4, 1990.

64 See also L. Vail, 'Ethnicity in Southern African History' in L. Vail (ed.), *The Creation of Tribalism in Southern Africa*, Oxford, James Currey, 1989.

65 Wilmsen, op. cit., p. 348, emphasis added.

66 All of the contributors to *Journal of Contemporary African Studies* explicitly reject poststructuralism because of its wilful rejection of political economy because of the importance of political struggle, elite accumulation, etc.

67 G. Maré, 'Inkatha and Regional Control: Policing Liberation Politics', *Review of African Political Economy*, 45/6, 1989. Buthelezi has always been something of a darling to the white Right. He admired the way Thatcher dealt with the miners during the strike in 1984, and was voted Man of the Year by the *Financial Mail* in 1985. See J. Saul and S. Gelb, *The Crisis in South Africa*, London, Zed, 1986, p. 41.

68 G. Maré, *Ethnicity and Politics in South Africa*, London, Zed, 1993.

69 See especially the special issue of *Journal of Southern African Studies*, 18, 3, 1992.

70 See, for example, J. Saul, 'South Africa: Between Barbarism and "Structural Reform"', *New Left Review*, 188, 1991; M. Murray, *The Revolution Deferred*, London, Verso, 1994.

71 For an eloquent overview of ethnic/racial apartheid discourse, see S. Dubow, 'Ethnic Euphemisms and Racial Echoes', *Journal of Southern African Studies*, 20, 3, 1994.

72 M. Mamdani, 'From Conquest to Consent as the Basis for State Formation: Reflections on Rwanda', *New Left Review*, 216, 1996.

73 G. Prunier, *The Rwanda Crisis: History of a Genocide*, London, Hurst, 1995, ch. 1.

74 Mamdani elaborates on the importance of this in more detail in his *Subject and Citizen*, Oxford, James Currey, 1996.

75 This process of 'freezing' was strongly symbolised in the issuing of all Africans with an ID card, stating their ethnic group. As a result, ethnic mobility was curtailed. The salience of this 'freezing' was more terribly revealed when, during the genocide, ID cards were used by the *Interahamwe* (Hutu militias) to locate Tutsis who would then be murdered.

76 For details of this ethnic polarisation, see Prunier, op. cit.; African Rights, *Rwanda: Death Despair and Defiance*, London, African Rights, 1994, ch.1; D. Waller, *Rwanda: Which Way Now?*, Oxford, Oxfam, 1993; G. Vassal-Adams, *Rwanda: An Agenda for International Action*, Oxford, Oxfam, 1994.

77 Prunier, op. cit., pp. 38–9. See also P. Uvin, 'Prejudice, Crisis, and Genocide in Rwanda', *African Studies Review*, 40, 2, 1997.

78 *African Rights*, op. cit., p. 35.

79 *African Rights, Rwanda: 'A Waste of Hope' The United Nations Human Rights Field Operation*, London, African Rights, 1995, p. 7.

80 K. Appiah, *In My Father's House: Africa in the Philosophy of Culture*, London, Oxford University Press, 1992, p. 152. Appiah is talking here about Yambo Ouologuem's *Le Devoir de la Violence* (*Bound to Violence*, London, Heinemann, 1968), which he sees as part of a 'second stage' in African literature.

13 Bilingualism and the Construction of a New 'American' Identity

CHRIS JULIOS

In the past 30 years, the transformation of Manhattan's immigrant population has led to the establishment of *El Barrio* (The Neighbourhood), an East Harlem enclave housing the largest concentration of Puerto Ricans in the city. This community of Spanish speakers is giving way to a new generation of coloured Catholic US-born Hispanics whose mother tongue is not English. As members of a pluralistic society, these young Puerto Ricans should be able to associate with the 'American' identity. However, changes taking place in their self-identification patterns point towards a very different picture of the reality of multiculturalism. While second generation immigrants may originally have seen themselves as American, their experience of poverty, illiteracy, social exclusion and racism now makes them perceive themselves as the marginalised, the 'other', the Puerto Rican. In addition to being defined as outsiders by the dominant group, American-born Hispanics are being rejected by their own ethnic cohort, for their inevitable assimilation into the dominant American culture. As a result, a new kind of 'transnational' identity surpassing racial, cultural and linguistic barriers is emerging. This notion of identity, which refers to a person's sense of uniqueness, is transforming the traditional concept of 'American' identity as a predominantly English-speaking white Anglo-Saxon ideal. The present chapter addresses the construction of such an identity.

The Traditional Notion of 'American' Identity

The social origins of the conventional notion of 'American' identity can be traced back to the eighteenth century and the period of Independence, where a single hegemonic 'American' ideal was created. Although, this model was

271

supposed to epitomise the 'melting pot' approach, in reality, such an identity was overtly white and dominated by the Anglo-Saxon culture, with strong connotations of social class, racial superiority and exclusiveness. Not surprisingly, the so-called WASPs (White Anglo-Saxon Protestants) would soon come to embody the meaning of 'Americaness'. The original English settlers in the United States created a New World society which was modelled on their national, cultural, religious, racial and linguistic heritage. In the *Declaration of Independence*, in the *Constitution*, in the process that transformed the Thirteen Colonies into a federal nation-state, the notion of 'We, the People' constituted an undisguised colonial presumption, an 'ethno-national putsch'.[1] For the 'the People' were none other than the 'English' settlers. The true 'first nations', the native inhabitants of the American continent were dispossessed of their land, exploited, and had their cultural heritage and language virtually destroyed. In their turn, the Africans were also to follow a similar fate.

Between 1820 and 1927, some 37 million immigrants entered the United States. Approximately 32 million having emigrated directly from Europe; predominantly from Great Britain, France, Germany, Russia, Austria-Hungary and Italy. These immigrants and their descendants rapidly built the American nation. In 1800, the population of the United States was 5.3 million; by 1905 it had grown to 105.7 million.[2] Regardless of the extent to which the newcomers were able, or willing, to give up their ethnic and linguistic heritage and assimilate into the new order, the ideology of 'Americanisation' was powerful enough for these immigrants to assert a collective citizenship. Once inside the United States, successive generations of immigrants were inevitably transformed into English-speaking American citizens. Such an identity was firmly embedded in the original sociopolitical and linguistic outlook of the first English settlers, whose unchallenged 'cultural colonisation' of the United States would continue long after their territorial domination had ended.[3]

One significant area of American life which has served as a flagship for Anglo-Saxon values, is the American educational system. This most basic institution has helped promote a stereotypical notion of 'American identity'. For the past 30 years, the US primary and secondary educational curricula have consistently placed an emphasis on 'unity in civic values', and 'the American way of life'. During the 1960s, when formal political indoctrination, despite the Vietnam War, was less severe, over 70 per cent of high school seniors believed that 'patriotism' and 'loyalty to the American ways' were the most important requirements of a 'good citizen'.[4] If we add the widespread practice of such nationalistic ceremonies as parades, flag salute rituals, the frequent singing of the national anthem, and other formal and informal means of glorification of the 'American way of life', the actual amount of patriotic rhetoric and indoctrination appears incalculable.

The public policy domain has also provided fertile ground for the development of stereotypical instances of 'Americaness'. We need only look at the prominence given in the 1988 presidential campaign to 'patriotism' and the debate over the validity of requiring students to recite the *Pledge of Allegiance* in schools. The 1992 and 1996 presidential election contests focused on the 'moral attributes' and 'sense of duty' pertinent to the American Presidency, with veterans of war George Bush and Bob Dole levying charges of draft dodging against their then opposing candidate Bill Clinton. Nowadays, mounting suggestions regarding President Clinton's extramarital affairs are not only threatening his tenure, they dwell on the same 'character issue', and the nature of 'American' values. After years of denial of past sexual misbehaviour, we are witnessing renewed allegations involving the president and a number of White House personnel. Under the headlines 'Clinton's Temptations' and 'If it's True, Go', the *Economist*[5] analyses the implications of Clinton's actions for the American government as well as the 'American' character. While the latter embodies the values of integrity, loyalty and trustworthiness, 'trust is not an ideal that will carry much weight for him [the president], until this latest scandal has gone away'.[6]

A contemporary phenomenon which has contributed decisively to further this idea of 'Americaness' is the globalisation of the English language. As the means of communicating within the North American culture, English has become inherent to the 'American' ideal. Whether American politics, religion, music, or sports, they are all being transmitted in English. Here, being 'American' implies speaking English. The most recent advent of the super-information highway and the US-led Internet has not only provided the English language with a universal dimension, it has given this 'Anglicised' American culture an unprecedented impetus of worldwide proportions. Ultimately, projecting the ideology of 'Americanisation' as the collective ethos of an English-speaking American society.

The socioeconomic gains of different ethnic minorities have progressively transformed the overtly racial connotations of the original WASPs' prototype into a multi-ethnic American ideal. Since the Civil Rights Movement struggles of the 1960s, prominent figures from marginalised groups have come to the forefront of American politics, media, sports and arts, serving as 'role models' for entire generations of Americans. As a result, the notion of 'American' identity has become divided-up into countless sub-categories such as; 'African-

American', 'Hispanic-American' and 'Asian-American' thus denoting ethnic origin. Notwithstanding, this growing fragmentation, a common shared ideology of 'American' citizenry has been maintained. Inherent in this universal ideal has been a combination of Anglo-Saxon values, and the English language in which these have been transmitted.

Changing Migration Patterns

With the end of Second World War and the subsequent macro-changes in the global geopolitical situation of the United States, it has become increasingly difficult to ascertain the exact nature of this 'American' identity. From the 1950s onwards there have been important developments in international migration trends affecting the composition and demographic distribution of the population in the United States. Continued migration has not only produced a fundamental shift in the ethnic and linguistic boundaries of the immigrant communities, but it has also transformed the composition of the indigenous American population. At the turn of the century, the bulk of immigrants entering the United States was of 'Anglo-Saxon' and 'northern European' stock, including waves of British, French, German, Polish and Russian immigrants. The first half of the century witnessed the arrival of 'southern Europeans' into the country, with Spanish, Italian and Greek migrants moving in. The second half gave way to successive cohorts of 'Asians' coming from Japan, China and Korea. This latter group was to be followed by the 'Latin Americans', particularly Mexicans, Cubans, Dominicans and Puerto Ricans. The unprecedented numbers of this final group have come to dominate the migration scene of the past thirty years. In the autumn of 1993, the US Bureau of Census reported that by the year 2010, Central and South Americans will eclipse African-Americans as the nation's largest minority group. The Bureau predicted that, by the year 2050, the US population will have increased by 52 per cent, to 392 million, of whom one half will be minorities (including those who identify themselves as 'Hispanics' with Central and South American lineage), and the other half will be whites of European descent. The latter group will have decreased proportionally from 76 per cent in 1993, to 68 per cent in 2010, and 53 per cent in 2050. By contrast, in the same year, the Census category of 'Hispanics' is predicted to constitute 23 per cent; African-Americans 16 per cent; Asian-Americans 10 per cent; and American Indians one per cent of the population.[7] This projected shift has already occurred in some urban areas, notably Los Angeles and Miami. In other metropolitan areas such as New York, Chicago, Houston and San Diego the transformation is well under way. According to these demographic projections, Americans of European descent will effectively have become a minority group in the United States, sometime during the next century.[8]

There is another key demographic factor to be considered, namely that nearly 40 per cent of new immigrants to the United States have the same mother tongue: Spanish. Although at the turn of the century, European immigrants were relatively large in number, they were scattered across a wide range of national origin groups and languages (i.e. German, Russian, Polish, Italian, Czech, and Greek). For these European immigrants the only *lingua franca* was English. In contrast, Spanish is spoken by immigrants from a dozen different countries, being the official language of Spain, Mexico, Puerto Rico, Dominican Republic, as well as the majority of Central and South American countries, with the exception of Portuguese-speaking Brazil. Although first generation immigrants come to understand English, and their offspring decisively embrace it while being brought up in the United States, the prospect of cultural and linguistic 'fragmentation' has been pointed out by some scholars.[9] The new ethnic Hispanic communities are not only concentrated linguistically, they are also clustered geographically, creating large enclaves in metropolitan areas.[10] This has led contingency theorists[11] to predict what looks like an inevitable outcome in the shape of 'two-way assimilation', with Euro-Americans learning Spanish and consuming Latin cultural products, as well as Hispanics learning English and consuming Anglo-American goods. In short, the prospect of bilingualism and biculturalism within the same national territory.

The combination of continuous influxes of immigrants of non-European lineage into the United States, with high regional and linguistic concentration, is changing the composition of the indigenous US population. It is also impacting upon the American nation's social, political and cultural outlook in totally unanticipated ways. These immigrants' overwhelming physical presence combined with their equally ubiquitous cultural and linguistic influence are producing further cracks in the already segmented 'American' ideal. First generation immigrants are giving way to a second cohort of younger, coloured American-born Hispanics whose mother tongue is not English. The self-identification patterns of the latter will provide essential clues as to the direction towards which this new migrant-led 'American' identity is moving.

Deconstructing Identity

The US Bureau of Census asks people to assign themselves to an ethnic group on the basis of questions combining colour and country of origin, therefore making it possible to record how many people perceive themselves to be members of each group. Although the analysis of such inquiry sheds considerable light on the 'American' identity question, it also brings about its intrinsically complex nature. For self-identification patterns of ethnic minorities seem to blur the boundaries between 'racial' and 'ethnic' categories. The former having phenotypical connotations, while the latter implies national origin and cultural values.

In 1995 the federal government re-evaluated the process by which it collects and publishes racial and ethnic data. The current statistical regime dates from 1978, when the OMB (Office of Management and Budget) issued *Statistical Policy Directive No. 15* ('Race and Ethnic Standards for Federal Statistics and Administrative Reporting') in an effort to standardise across departments and agencies the volumes of new data required by *Affirmative Action,* the *Voting Rights Act,* and other similar race conscious policies. Explicitly denying any scientific or anthropological authority for its determinations, *Directive No. 15* nevertheless established five basic racial categories to be used by federal agencies: 'White', 'Black', 'Hispanic', 'Asian' or 'Pacific Islander', and 'American Indian' or 'Alaskan Native'. The OMB went on to stipulate that these are racial categories, with the exception of the 'Hispanic' which was defined as an ethnic classification. Though all Hispanics share similar distinctive physical attributes which qualify them as a racial group, they are also part of a larger Latino ethos with its Spanish-speaking culture that singles them out as an ethnic community. In other words, as it is often stated in the fine print at the bottom of government documents, 'Hispanics can be of any race'.[12]

In the subsequent federal *Survey for Testing Methods of Counting by Race and Ethnicity,* 100,000 respondents were asked how they preferred their racial or ethnic group to be identified. Typically, this issue of self-identification progresses warily, mainly because the groups under discussion often remain unclear as to how they wish to be identified. Hence, the categories prescribed under *Directive No. 15* came under scrutiny with suggested denominations such as 'Latinos' for 'Hispanics' or 'African-Americans' for 'Blacks'. Similarly, groups not specifically designated under the official classifications, such as the Arab-Americans, lobbied for a separate categorisation, while the Hawaiians seemed to feel inadequately represented by the 'Asian' and 'Pacific

Islander' categories.[13] Nevertheless, the results of the survey clearly show that these groups' identities are hardly as fixed or rigid as it has been typically assumed. For instance, Americans who trace their ancestors back to Africa do not necessarily prefer to be called 'African-American'; only 28 per cent of them actually chose to be labelled as 'Afro-American', while 44 per cent preferred to be identified simply as 'black'. In the same way, 58 per cent of Americans tracing their lineage back to Latin American countries favoured the term 'Hispanic' as an identifier rather than the more voguish 'Latino' denomination which was only picked out by a mere 12 per cent of respondents.[14]

The self-identification of 'Hispanics' was a central concern of the federal survey. In the first instance, 'Hispanic' was not represented as a racial category. Instead, respondents were given the option of identifying themselves as; 'white', 'black' 'American Indian', 'Eskimo/Aleut', 'Asian/Pacific Islander', 'Something else' or 'Multiracial'. Only 1.7 per cent chose to be categorised as 'Multiracial'. However, when the questionnaire format was changed to include 'Hispanics' as a racial option, over 10 per cent of respondents self-ascribed themselves to this group.[15] While substantial numbers of Hispanics identified themselves as racially 'white' under the OMB's current approved categories, when given the option to identify themselves as a racial group, fewer Hispanics identify themselves as 'white'. Indeed, when 'Hispanic' was present as a racial choice, the overwhelming majority of Mexicans (85.2 per cent), and Puerto Ricans (71.5 per cent) identified themselves as racially 'Hispanic'.[16] This data, in conjunction with other findings from the same federal survey, confirms an inherent fluidity in the ethnic and racial categories under observation. The variety of classifications chosen by the ethnic groups appears as a reflection of the intricate, multifaceted and constantly evolving nature of ethnic identity. Moreover, the different ways in which minority members perceive themselves are far removed from the stereotypical racial perceptions long held by the dominant white majority. Professor Ana Celia Zentella, reflecting on such self-identification patterns of the Hispanic group, indicates how across the different ethnic groups and generations there exists an array of identity categories varying from a strong 'Latino' ascription, through the use of hyphenated intermediate classifications such as 'Puerto Rican-Americans' or 'Dominican-Americans'; to the totally 'American' identification.[17] The result is a complex puzzle of diverging, and at times overlapping, ethnic identities. Furthermore, Zentella hints that environmental factors play an important role in shaping such intricate identification tendencies. As she puts it: 'it all depends where they [Hispanic children] have been brought up. If they are raised in a neighbourhood with the dominant group, they consider themselves to be Americans. Otherwise, they consider themselves to be Hispanic'.[18] Clearly, group boundaries and identities are not as rigid as they have traditionally been assumed to be or as contingency theories would have us believe. Certainly not for the Hispanics, soon to became the largest ethnic and linguistic minority group in the United States.

This striking flexibility of ethnic identity patterns revealed at the macro-level federal survey is corroborated by a micro-level study recently completed by the author in New York City. In October 1997, fieldwork was carried out at Seward Park High School, a comprehensive school with a high proportion of students of Hispanic origin situated in the 'Latino' Lower East side of Manhattan. The study, which concentrates on second generation, Hispanic immigrants, not only explores the nature of their 'self-identification' patterns, but also specifically analyses the complexity of their 'dual identity', and the conflicts faced by these American-born Hispanics whose first language is not English. Above all, it reveals the existence of an ever increasing gap between bilingual/bicultural children's ethnic aspirations and the actual realisation of those desires. The main themes explored in the survey being the pupils' perceptions of 'identity' and 'language' as well as their aspirations and hopes for the future. In terms of the ethnic composition of the Hispanic students, an overwhelming majority in the school originate from the Dominican Republic,[19] their ages being in the 16–19 year old range. This older school leaving group represents the archetype of 'second generation' immigrants about to enter their adult life, while still facing inbred conflicting ethnic, linguistic and cultural loyalties. Their particular approaches to 'language' and 'identity' will shape the sociocultural outlook of successive generations.

The ethnic make-up of the survey's respondents at Seward Park High School is a mirror image of that prevailing in the Lower East Side of Manhattan where Hispanics of Dominican origin command a conformable majority. Ninety-six point four per cent of the school population are of Hispanic origin, with 84.2 per cent of those coming from the Dominican Republic, 5.2 per cent from Mexico, 3.5 per cent from Ecuador, and 1.7 per cent respectively from Venezuela and Panama. As far as the students' perceptions of 'identity' and 'self-ascription' to a particular ethnic group are concerned, the results of this local poll not only confirm the findings of the previous macro-level federal survey, they go much further. By framing the question in terms of 'nationality' rather than 'race', it is possible to ascertain the degree of assimilation of these ethnic minority children into the dominant 'American' culture. Hence, obtaining an insight into the emerging 'identity' patterns of the successive generations. After stating their country of origin, the children were asked to identify themselves with a particular 'nationality'. Unlike the federal survey, no particular *racial* or *otherwise* category was given. The specific question examined was: 'what is your nationality?'. Table 13.1 displays the pupils' chosen nationality in relation to their country of origin. Not surprisingly, an overwhelming majority (95.5 per cent) of those born in a Latin American country identified themselves as being 'Hispanic', however, a small but significant minority (4.2 per cent) already preferred to be considered 'American'. On the other hand, the response given by those born in the United States was slightly more even. With over half of them (66.6 per cent) indicating that their identity was 'American', and a high proportion (33.3 per cent) still choosing to identify themselves as being 'Hispanic'.

Table 13.1   Pupils' self-identification

Country of Birth	Total	Chosen Nationality			
		Hispanic	American	Both	Other
Latin America	49	47	2	0	0
USA	6	2	4	0	0
Other*	2	0	0	0	2
Total	57	49	6	0	2

*   The category 'Other' includes two respondents from China who self-identified as being Chinese. As far as the Hispanic children are concerned the overwhelming majority have both parents born in a Latin American country, in most cases the Dominican Republic.

This data is further evidence of the inherent fluidity of ethnic self-identification that includes both children born in Latin America thinking of themselves as American, and those born in the United States choosing a Hispanic identity. Most importantly, these results reflect the gradual but inevitable pace of integration into the dominant culture experienced by these ethnic minority children living in the United States. It is very significant that of those born in the United States, the majority already self-identify as 'American'. This clearly reveals that in one single generation the 'identity' patterns have already shifted in favour of the dominant culture. Even more significant is the fact that a small proportion of children born in a Latin American country, who in most cases have not spend more than two years in the United States, and whose mother tongue is Spanish, nevertheless consider themselves to be 'American'.

The comments of Yanilka Fernandez, a 17-year-old Dominican who has only spent 22 months in Manhattan are a crude reflection of the astonishing pace of change experienced by these new generation of immigrants. When asked whether she saw herself living in the United States in the future, she answered: 'Si. Yo me veo ya' (Yes. I see myself already).[20]

It is precisely in this choice of 'country of future residency' that we find more evidence of the degree of integration into the American culture and society experienced by such ethnic minority children. While many of their parents may have entered the United States on a temporary basis, with the purpose of returning to their place of origin, these children, regardless of their country of birth, have no intention of going back to their native homelands. On the contrary, they see themselves as future members of North American society. As they put it, they 'live here' and realistically it is in 'this country' (USA) where they will be 'settling down'. The vivid accounts of some of the children interviewed speak for themselves:

> What you must do is to adapt to the country where you are living. If you are here [USA], you cannot pretend that the entire way of living that you had there [Dominican Republic], your whole culture, you can bring it over here and do it all over. You have to adapt according to the environment in which you are. If your routine here is coming to school, then going to work, then going home. You do it. But may be in Santo Domingo you didn't do that. You came back from school and you could go for a walk, go playing and so on. Then if you go over there to visit, you can continue living in the same way you were living before, and enjoy that moment. And when you come here you must do what you do here. Adapting to the environment where you are.[21]

> It is very difficult when you have the desire to continue your studies and the situation does not allow you to. That is why even if you didn't want to get used to the country [USA], you must get used to it. My parents also came from the same reason. Because of the economic situation. Because in our countries such as the Dominican Republic, they are countries of scarce resources, economic growth is not very high. It is not the same than here, where you can obtain financial assistance or something like that through programs. This is the same reason why I am here: that my parents want a better future, for the development of their lives as well as mine.[22]

> I like [living in the USA] because unlike my country, here there are many opportunities available to the student, that unfortunately we don't have in our Latino countries. And that is the reason why I had to stay here, because I didn't like it so much. But I have got used to it.[23]

As Table 13.2 below indicates, the overwhelming majority of those surveyed chose the United States as their future country of residence. Eighty-nine point seven per cent of respondents who originated in Latin America selected the United States as their final destination, while a mere 6.1 per cent preferred returning to their original countries. On the other hand, five out of six children born in the United States chose to remain there. Although two thirds (63.6 per cent) of those who selected the United States as their final place of residency, chose to continue living in the impoverish Manhattan neighbourhoods of the Lower East Side and the Upper West Side, a significant one third expected to move to the more leafy Midtown and Downtown neighbourhoods. Signalling the intention of some to 'break away' from their enclosed and deprived 'Hispanic' surroundings towards more affluent white dominated 'American' residential areas. Undoubtedly, a further step in their inevitable process of acculturation.

Table 13.2 Pupils' preferred future country of residence

Future Country of Residence

Country of Birth	Total	(NYC) USA	Latin America	Other*
Latin America	49	44	3	2
USA	6	5	1	0
Other	2	2	0	0
Total	57	51	4	2

* a) In the category 'other' there was one respondent who would have preferred to live in Italy in the future while another one was undecided.
  b) For the majority who chose to stay in New York City, the preferred locations within Manhattan were: LES (Lower East Side) where they actually live (27), Midtown (13), Downtown (3), and Upper West side (1).
  c) Two respondents chose Brooklyn and one Queens.

The second topic considered in the survey is the children's perception of 'language' as part of their identity. Both English and Spanish were put to the test. The intention was to determine these pupils' preferences in the use of language and the value in terms of 'usefulness' that they attach to each of them. As the following figures confirm, English language was overwhelmingly chosen as the most useful Modern Language. Figure 13.1 shows the pupils' perceptions of Spanish language's usefulness. The question put to them was:

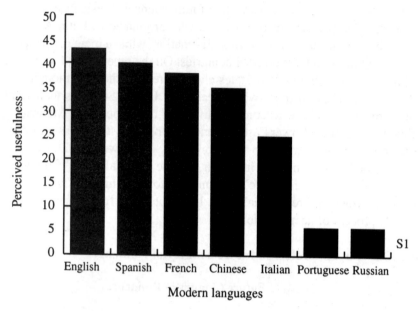

Figure 13.1 Pupils' perceptions of Spanish language's usefulness

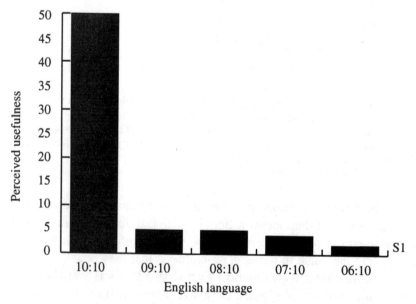

Figure 13.2 Pupils' perceptions of English language's usefulness

'name the three most useful Modern Languages taught in the School Curriculum'.

Out of 47 pupils surveyed, the top three Modern Languages selected were English (87.2 per cent), Spanish (78.7 per cent) and French (74.4 per cent). Although Spanish was voted the second most useful language, it is significant that Spanish-speaking children should choose 'English' as the most relevant language. Clearly signalling their belief in the undeniable worth of the English language as both the dominant language in the United States and an indispensable tool in their efforts to achieve academic progress and social mobility.

This belief is reinforced by their perception of the English language in its *economic* dimension. Three more questions were put to them, this time regarding the English language. Firstly, they were asked: ' in a scale of one to ten, how important is learning English to getting a job?'. Here, the intention was to ascertain their understanding of the English language as an indispensable means towards educational attainment and as the key to improving their prospects in the labour market. Their answers reflect their full awareness of these facts. Figure 13.2 indicates that 48 (84.2 per cent) out of 57 students gave English top marks (10:10). A mere two (3.5 per cent) respondents awarded the lowest score (6:10). Secondly, they were asked: 'should non-English speaking pupils be taught in their mother tongue?'. Most students (82.4 per cent) expressed the belief that native languages should be used in the classroom only to help students temporarily in their transition to English. As they put it themselves, non-English speaking pupils should use mother tongue in the classroom 'at the beginning, yes. But after they learn English, no'. Lastly, they were asked: 'should all immigrants coming to the USA learn English?'. Fifty-two out of 57 respondents answered 'yes' to this question.

Most students thought it important to master both English and Spanish. Comments such as: 'being bilingual is very important', 'both languages are important' or 'a bilingual person has more opportunities than a person that only speaks one language' cropped up constantly. However, the socioeconomic supremacy of the English language over Spanish (or otherwise) remains undisputed in these children's minds. Thus, their unanimous assertions:

English is the vehicle for communicating in the United States.[24]

English is the main language here in the United States. It has to be learned in order to achieve development.[25]

English is the basis. Because if you don't know the language you are not going to have the ability to study and progress in this world over here.[26]

This clarity of purpose regarding English is brought into full perspective by the last topic addressed in the survey. Namely, the question of pupils' aspirations and hopes for the future. It was important to determine which role these children see themselves performing in American society during their adult lives. They were asked: 'what occupation would you like to have in the future?'. From a total of 57 students surveyed a staggering 56 (98.2 per cent) indicated a professional occupation. These ranged from medicine, education, and law to computing and psychology. Clearly, these children were only too aware of the actual role that the English language plays in the realisation of their future desires.

The above data, and the accompanying opinions expressed by the children, confirm two realities. Firstly, that there is an inherent fluidity in the identity patterns of ethnic minorities. Particularly, the second generation Hispanic cohort seems to fluctuate between a strongly ethnic 'Latino' identity, through intermediate hyphenated 'Hispanic-American' perceptions, to the ultimate assimilationist 'American' ideal. Moreover, the evidence suggests an increasing trend towards acculturation into the dominant American culture. Among others, this fact is becoming clear by the self-identification of Latin American children as 'Americans' and their overwhelming choice of the United States as their future country of residence. Secondly, there is no doubt about the predominance of English language in the lives of these Spanish-speaking second generation immigrants. Thus, their unreserved acceptance of this fact as well as their decisive embracing of English as an integral part of their existence. For these students, English language is not only an inherent element of their everyday lives but, most importantly, it is the key to their academic performance. Ultimately, becoming instrumental in their gaining access to the labour market in their chosen career paths.

The Globalisation of English Language

Societies usually experience a correlation between language use and ethnic identification.[27] One of the most important aspects of any society is its language structure which can be said to be entwined with the ethnic order. Since different social groups may vary by economic status, class, customs, race or religion, language may be the strongest factor determining ethnicity.[28] Here, the sharper the language divide, the clearer are the ethnic lines of division. While language is widely regarded as a central element of 'peoplehood', it is important to understand the impact that the predominance of English language may have in these Hispanic children's self-identification patterns, and how it will ultimately shape their emerging notions of 'American' identity.

Zentella explains how a progressive erosion of community languages at the hands of English is taking place in New York City. The gap seems to be widening between aspirations to know one's mother tongue and the implementation of those desires. As the level of knowledge is not maintained across generations, there is the danger of losing those native languages. Many young Hispanics admittedly cannot read or write Spanish, and the spoken use of their community language is increasingly restricted to home and family. Although members of this youthful cohort consider it important to hand down the Spanish language to the next generation, in reality they are unable to carry out this task. In the words of Zentella, second generation Hispanics 'are losing Spanish at a faster pace than the rest of the groups in this country'.[29] All available evidence suggests that within 10 years of living in the United States a language shift occurs among Hispanic immigrants, with their offspring moving decisively into English at the expense of Spanish. Moreover, children who attend bilingual programmes in American schools start discontinuing the use of their native language within six months. It is only those pupils who go back to their countries of origin on vacation, or on exchange programmes, that manage to maintain some fluency in their mother tongue.[30] The Director of the Centre for Puerto Rican Studies at City University of New York, Pedro Pedraza, explains how, among different generations of Hispanics, a language displacement from Spanish into English progressively occurs:

> In our investigations in the Hispanic community we have seen that bilingualism is being maintained, but that does not mean that Spanish has not changed its role in the community. The first generation come with a dominant Spanish and learn English ... The second generation are bilingual, although their dominant language shifts from Spanish into English, because of their education and many other factors. Then, the third generation is clearly dominant in English, but with a residue of Spanish.[31]

The acquisition of English and the simultaneous erosion of the native language is a process that takes place in most migrant ethnic communities. As their time in the receiving countries increases their offspring inevitably become acclimatised to their new surroundings and, among other cultural traits, they embrace the dominant language. The latter eventually becoming their main means of communication with the outside world. Pedraza's conclusions point to the progressive replacement of mother tongue as vehicle of communication by an altogether more powerful tool: the English language. New cohorts of young parents, already accustomed to speaking English to their siblings, are handing this practice down to the next generation. The case of Daniel Davis, a 17-year-old Dominican reflects this trend. Having spent only 16 months in Manhattan, he is already experiencing a language shift from Spanish into English: 'sometimes one forgets Spanish ... if one is only speaking in English'.[32]

The fact remains that there is a general decline in the use of community languages, mainly because they are not practical languages of everyday life. Even at the private level, these ethnic tongues are not essential for communication within families beyond a limited period of time. In contrast, the English language with its 'universal' appeal, continues to increase its number of speakers. Nowadays, the 'globalisation' of the English language is undisputed, it is the most widely spoken language in the world, having become a well-established international vehicle of communication both at private and public levels. This is particularly so in the present age of mass media, telecommunications and digital information technology. No other language can claim such predominance. Even Spanish, which is spoken in over a dozen countries, and which is effectively the second language in the United States, cannot compete at this level. As Zentella indicates, the main reason why the latter still continues to exert an important influence in the United States is to be found in *migration* patterns of the Hispanic community: 'The continuous migration of Latinos helps to strengthen the Spanish language as well as the culture in other ways. If that ceased to exist, then the Latino group would not even survive another generation. But because it has always existed, and increased, the number of people that continue to contribute keeps growing.'[33]

It is this continuous influx of Hispanic immigrants into the United States that keeps the Spanish language and Latino cultural traditions alive, and creates a 'market' in American society for the delivery of these goods. With increasing numbers of first generation Hispanics entering the country with little or no English skills at all, there is a constant demand for Spanish-speaking services and products. Hence, the array of ubiquitous Hispanic radio stations, television channels, newspapers, advertising, businesses, organisations and institutions catering for these particular needs. In the words of Pedraza: 'there are [Hispanic] television stations, radio, music, theatre, everything. There is a nucleus here in New York that can maintain Spanish commercially, because there is an economic benefit.'[34]

As long as the Hispanic community comprises a large stake of the country's population, companies tapping into the 'Spanish' market are poised to make substantial profits. The future of the Spanish language in the United States appears inevitably linked to the development of Hispanic migration trends. With the number of Latin American countries from which migrants originate on the rise, the use of such language is expected to be maintained well into the next century. On the other hand, the younger Hispanics already in the United States are experiencing an accelerated rate of acculturation, with the progressive loss of mother tongue skills. Continuation of this trend in successive generations can be anticipated. The testimony of Awilda Davis, a 17-year-old from the Dominican Republic, who has spent the last 16 months in Manhattan, points in this direction. Asked in which language she would communicate with her children, Awilda replied: 'I think that you should speak to them in English first. Then, when they are fluent, at about five years of age, you can start teaching them Spanish. Because they already master English.'[35]

Constructing the 'New' American Identity

A number of factors determine the ethnicity and identity of human groups, these include phenotype, language, common ancestry, culture, religion, and group symbolism. All of these elements are relevant in shaping the way in which individuals perceive and classify a member of another group. Some of these indicators are self-evident, and play an important role in establishing certain images and stereotypes. For instance, one's phenotype or observable appearance cannot be readily altered, being the first evidence upon which a judgment of a person is based.[36] From the outset, this single element determines the fact that one's self-identity often differs radically from the category in which one might be placed by others.[37] A Mexican-American child born and raised in the United States may consider him/herself to be a US citizen, however it will hardly be regarded in the same fashion by members of the dominant white American citizenry. Similarly, a Bangladeshi child brought up in the East End of London may see him/herself as being wholesomely English, however it is unlikely that the rest of the indigenous white English population truly considers him/her as being one of them. Racial discrimination, prejudice, and stereotyping of the Hispanic community have clearly been a constant in their relationship with the dominant English speaking culture. As Angelo Falcon, the President of the Institute for Puerto Rican Policy, argues, 'negative images' in the media, the 'stereotypical' and 'pejorative representation' of

Hispanics, and the existing 'lack of positive role models' have shaped the self-identification patterns of members of this ethnic minority.[38] On the one hand, these ethnic minorities' cultural patterns have adapted to their English-speaking environment, and as a result members of the Hispanic community have become more 'Americanised'. It is also the case that their experience of discrimination, harassment and rejection have left them feeling isolated and ostracised, giving way, within the second generation to an 'ethnic backlash'. Zentella explains how the 'racial' way in which the dominant group defines ethnic minorities determines the mode in which they, in turn, perceive themselves. She recalls the case of an American-born Puerto Rican girl, who at the age of eight identified herself as being 'American'. Ten years latter, her self-ascription has shifted to the 'Puerto Rican' group. The reason being her experience with the dominant group that defines her as being 'not American'.[39] These emotions were shared by most children interviewed at Seward Park High School. They not only felt discriminated against by the dominant white American group, but ironically they were also rejected by their own ethnic communities, which resented them having 'changed' and having become 'Americanised'. In the words of Daniel Davis, a 17-year-old Dominican: 'if somebody is born here and go to Santo Domingo, they say he is a "Dominicanyork". Because his parents are Hispanics, Dominicans, but he was born here in New York.'[40]

Tensions created by the inherently multi-ethnic nature of American society pose major challenges to these bicultural individuals who must affirm their unique identity within a diverse pluralistic framework. For members of minority groups, such struggles begin earlier in life. Consider the Hispanic child who discovers that the language of his/her parents is not understood by his/her classmates, while at the same time being bombarded by television, books, and magazines with the message that all successful, powerful or beautiful people are white. From these children's perspectives, becoming adults in a society that devalues their minority status increasingly makes them question who they are, and forces them to embrace attitudes and ideas that are alien to them.[41] As a result, there are inherent contradictions in the attitudes of second generation American-born Hispanics. On the one hand, few seem to be happy to see their native Spanish language disappear, because they consider it an important part of their cultural heritage and ethnic identity. Their own ability in such language, however, is rather limited. With most remaining unable to hand down their linguistic tradition to the next generation. The gap between their own cultural and ethnic expectations and the reality of implementing those desires, thus continues to widen. The feelings of Yanilka

Fernandez sum up such predicament:

> One must never loose one's roots. Because you can be living here, but you must also know where you come from, which is your identity. Being sure of what you want. Just because you are here, [USA] it doesn't mean that you are going to stop being yourself or lose your nationality. However, in certain ways life changes, it changes a great deal. Because you don't do the same things you did in your country, you don't speak the same language you spoke in your country, and the customs change completely. Everything changes. So, somehow you adapt to the American life.[42]

These contradictions are the reflection of the clashing loyalties to which these second generation ethnic individuals are exposed. By being brought up in a bicultural and bilingual environment, they are torn apart between simultaneous but incompatible desires, realities and drives. Such forces are further compounded by the rapidly changing demographics that separate them from their roots and take away those certitudes of identity that once were passed from generation to generation.

As the frontiers of colour, ethnicity, culture and language are being expanded within the American national territory, the notion of 'identity' is also being stretched well beyond those limits, becoming something altogether different. In the words of Pedraza, we are witnessing the emergence of a 'transnational ethnic identity'. An identity that surpasses conventional notions of race, ethnicity and language. A notion ultimately based on a very personal belief, and a rather abstract ideal of national identity. He exemplifies his argument with the case of a Puerto Rican community in Hawaii. Established at the turn of the century, this Hispanic group has maintained an existence detached from both Puerto Rico and the United States. These people firmly self-identify with a Puerto Rican identity. In their present form, however, they do not speak Spanish, they do not consume Puerto Rican goods, their customs and habits are not typical of mainland Puerto Ricans. Their community networks do not resemble those of their forebears, they have intermarried with Hawaiians, Filipinos and Japanese, and even the music they listen to is not strictly Hispanic. 'How can these people claim to be Puerto Ricans?', 'how can they maintain a Puerto Rican ideal?', and more importantly, what does it mean for them?', he ponders.[43] Let us consider the opposite case. Yoko is a 17-year-old Chinese-born girl, who spent the first seven years of her life in China, after which she moved to Mexico for a further six years. Presently, she lives in the Lower East Side of Manhattan, and considers herself to be 'American'.

Psychological studies have demonstrated that there is no simple link between ethnic minority behaviour and identity.[44] In other words, 'self-identification' and 'cultural practice' are two different things. For instance, young British-Bengalis who may think of themselves as Bengali, may well be found to be British in their cultural outlook as opposed to Bengali. Conversely, British-Bengalis who may speak Bengali and culturally behave like Bengalis, may not consider themselves to be Bengali, but rather British. Similarly, second generation Hispanic-Americans who may think of themselves as Hispanics, may conduct themselves as English-speaking white Anglo-Saxon Americans. On the other hand, members of the Hispanic-American ethnic minority embracing the Spanish-speaking tradition may consider themselves to be Americans rather than Hispanics. These peoples' identities which have moved beyond traditional notions of ethnicity and language, clearly belong in the realm of the personal belief, or what Stephen Thermstrom has called a 'state of mind'. They are neither defined by the ethnic origin of those who profess them, nor by their relationship with the dominant group, or by the language spoken, or the culture they embrace. They are simply the result of an externalisation of very individual and personal ideals of the self. Viewed in this light, ethnic identity turns into a 'state of mind'. Where, as Stephen Thermstrom puts it: 'it doesn't matter if you don't think I look Chinese. I feel Chinese; ergo I am Chinese.'[45]

Conclusion

The overwhelming presence of non-European immigrants in the United States, for the first time, has signified a turning point in the composition of the US population of white European stock, as well as in the development of the traditional notion of Anglo-Saxon based 'American identity'. The latest mass influxes of Spanish-speaking Hispanic immigrants directly challenge such conventional notions of 'Americaness'. Giving a new meaning to the prospects of 'cultural' and 'linguistic fragmentation' in the United States. Their continuing expansion has not only tipped the ethnic and linguistic balance, it has already started redressing the 'identity' status quo.

The evidence presented in this chapter demonstrates that the Hispanic community's patterns of self-identification are constantly evolving. As time elapses, the forces of assimilation and the global predominance of the English language greatly accelerate this process. American-born Hispanics find themselves torn between conflicting loyalties and desires. They value the maintenance of their Latino culture and Spanish language. While succumbing to the inexorable influence of the all-powerful American culture and the English language. The reality of multiculturalism has meant being defined as outsiders by the dominant white American group, as well as being rejected by their own ethnic community for their inevitable acculturation. In the short-term, the younger cohort's reaction to such dilemma has been an ethnic backlash. In the long-term, it has generated a completely new identity: a 'transnational ethnic identity' surpassing racial, cultural and linguistic barriers. Becoming altogether something completely different: a 'state of mind'. An individual sense of identity which simply refers to a person's sense of uniqueness, of knowing who one is, and who one is not.

From a sociological point of view, the development of a stable sense of identity is one of the central processes of childhood and adolescence. Maintaining the integrity of one's identity is an ongoing struggle through adulthood. Within the framework of a pluralistic multicultural society, the relationship between notions of 'identity' and 'ethnicity' is an extremely complex one. The role played by 'language' as a vehicle of self-definition, and affinity to a particular group is even more obscure. Particularly so, when considering the experiences of native-born second generation immigrants. Having been brought up in a bicultural and bilingual environment, their problems of self-identification are monumental. Their particular predicament clearly calls for a redefinition of the notions of 'nationality' and 'citizenship'. The strength of prejudice and conservative nationalism in contemporary America, however, indicates that the issue of national identity and the political socialisation of ethnic minorities remains largely unresolved. It may well be seen as a reflection of deep-seated fears in the American psyche concerning their identity as a country and, ultimately their own future as one American nation.

Notes

1 R. Cohen, *Frontiers of Identity. The British and Others*, London, Longman, 1994, p. 26.
2 L. Potts, *The World Labour Market: A History of Migration*, London, Sez Books, 1990, p. 131.
3 See Cohen, op. cit.
4 R. Clearly, *Political Education in the American Democracy*, Scanton, Pennsylvania, Intext Educational Publishers, 1971, p. 52.
5 *Economist*, 24 January 1998, pp. 15–21 and 47; and 31 January 1998, pp. 23–5 and 53–5.
6 Ibid., 24 January 1998, p. 15.

7   D.S. Massey, 'The New Immigration and Ethnicity in the United States', *Population and Development Review*, Volume 21, No. 3, September 1995, p. 631.

8   See US Bureau of Census, *Statistical Abstract of the United States 1995, The National Data Book, and Country and City Data Book 1994. A Statistical Abstract Supplement*, Washington, DC, US Bureau of Census 1994 and 1995.

9   Massey, op. cit.

10 See *US Bureau of Census 1913*, Tables 15 and 16, and *US INS Immigration and Naturalisation Service 1991*, Tables 2, 17 and 18, Washington DC, US Bureau of Census 1913 and 1991.

11 See Cohen, op. cit., and Massey, op. cit., pp. 631–52.

12 P. Skerry, 'Many American Dilemmas. The Statistical Politics of Counting by Race and Ethnicity', *The Brookings Review. Education in America*, Summer 1996, Washington, DC, The Brookings Institution Press, 1996, p. 36.

13 It must be taken into account that the Americans' present emphasis on subjective self-identification can be explained, in part, as a reaction to their own past, when they did not afford individuals any such choices about the ethnic and racial groups to which they deemed to belong. It would seem that they are now swinging too far in the opposite direction. The possibilities and permutations for racial and ethnic identification are infinite; in reality they are as numerous as the actual numbers of persons to be counted, labelled and categorised. However, the fact remains that, in reality, the materialisation of subjectivity and individual choice is indeed limited.

14 See Skerry, op. cit.

15 Ibid., Table 1, p. 38.

16 Ibid.

17 Interview with Prof. Ana Celia Zentella, Director, Black and Puerto Rican Studies, Hunter College, City University of New York, Manhattan: Hunter College, 9 October 1997. The original interview with the author conducted in Spanish has been translated into English by the author.

18 Ibid.

19 Until recently, the Puerto Ricans have enjoyed a 'majority' status among the Hispanic groups based in New York city. Hence, the establishment and development of 'El Barrio' (The Neighbourhood) in East Harlem comprising the biggest concentration of Hispanics from Puerto Rico in the city. Current changing migration patterns, however, have resulted in the largest waves of Latin American immigrants originating in the Dominican Republic. As a result, Dominicans are rapidly becoming the dominant Hispanic cohort in New York city. Thus, the recent establishment and development of 'El Barrio Dominicano' (The Dominican Neighbourhood) in the Upper West side of Manhattan.

20 Interview with Yanilka Fernandez, 17-year-old from the Dominican Republic, 12th Grade, 22 months living in New York, Seward Park High School: Lower East Side of Manhattan, 15 October 1997. The original interview with the author conducted in Spanish has been translated into English by the author.

21 Interview with Awilda Davis, 20-year-old from the Dominican Republic, 12th Grade, 16 months living in New York, Seward Park High School: Lower East Side of Manhattan, 15 October 1997. The original interview with the author conducted in Spanish has been translated into English by the author.

22 Interview with Fernandez, op. cit.

23 Giselles Acevedo, 17-year-old from the Dominican Republic, 11th Grade, 2 years living in New York, Seward Park High School: Lower East Side of Manhattan, 15 October 1997. The original interview with the author conducted in Spanish has been translated into English by the author.

24 Interview with Fernandez, op. cit.

25 Interview with Daniel Davis, 17-year-old from the Dominican Republic, 10th Grade, 16 months living in New York, Seward Park High School: Lower East Side of Manhattan, 15 October 1997. The original interview with the author conducted in Spanish has been translated into English by the author.

26 Interview with Giselles Acevedo, op. cit.

27 See J.M. Yinger, *Ethnicity. Source of Strength, Source of Conflict?*, Albany, USA, State University of New York Press, 1994.

28 Ibid., p. 302.

29 Interview with Prof. Zentella, op. cit.

30 Ibid.

31 Interview with Pedro Pedraza, Director, Education and Linguistic Policy, El Centro, Centre for Puerto Rican Studies, Hunter College, City University of New York, Manhattan: City University of New York, 10 October 1997. The original interview with the author conducted in Spanish has been translated into English by the author.

32 Interview with D. Davis, op. cit.

33 Interview with Prof. Zentella, op. cit.

34 Interview with Pedraza, op. cit.

35 Interview with A. Davis, op. cit.

36 T.M. Stephens, 'The Language of Ethnicity and Self-identity in American Spanish and Brazilian Portuguese', *Ethnic and Racial Studies*, London, Routledge, 1989, p. 138.

37 Ibid.

38 Interview with Angelo Falcon, President, Institute of Puerto Rican Policy, Manhattan: IPP, 9 October 1997. The original interview with the author conducted in Spanish has been translated into English by the author.

39 See Prof. A. C. Zentella, *Growing Up Bilingual*, New York, Blackwell, 1997.

40 Interview with D. Davis, op. cit.

41 H.W. Harris et al., *Racial and Ethnic Identity: Psychological Development and Creative Expression*, London, Routledge, 1995, p. 1.

42 Interview with Fernandez, op. cit.

43 Interview with Pedraza, op. cit.

44 See H. Nimmi, *Ethnic Minority Identity, A Social Psychological Perspective*, Oxford, Clarendon Press, 1991.

45 Cited in Skerry, op. cit., p. 39.

Index